CALIFORNIA'S

LEGISLATURE

Published April 1998

By

E. Dotson Wilson
Chief Clerk of the Assembly

and

Brian S. Ebbert
Chief Editor

Preface

California's Legislature is regarded as one of the most authoritative and detailed sources on our state's legislative branch of government. It has long been utilized as a resource by scholars, citizens, elected officials, legislative staff and other students of the governmental process. This publication was last updated in June of 1994. Since then the make up of California government has experienced a wide array of changes that are incorporated into this edition.

A publication of this magnitude could not have been completed without the tireless dedication of several individuals on my staff, including Larry Murman, Assistant Chief Clerk; Brian S. Ebbert, chief editor and Principal Clerk; Melissa Swart-Weikel, Assistant Clerk II; Stephen J. Greene, former Assistant Clerk. I also wish to thank my colleague Greg Schmidt, Secretary of the Senate, and his staff as well as Celeste Cron, the State Printer, for their assistance.

This year's edition contains over thirty newly added pages of text, charts and historical photographs. In addition, over one thousand footnotes as well as hundreds of code citations and court cases were updated.

We hope you find this edition of *California's Legislature* to be a useful tool in helping you better understand state government and in particular the legislative process.

E. Dotson Wilson
Chief Clerk of the Assembly

vas first published as an insert in
article had expanded extensively
parate pamphlet in 1958 (*HR 45*,
n its original format, and the new
ximately every 2 years, with the

GALLERY OF PRESIDENTS PRO TEMPORE
1957–1998*

Hugh Burns (D)
Jan. 1957–May 1969

Howard Way (R)
May 1969–Feb. 1970

Jack Schrade (R)
Feb. 1970–Jan. 1971

James R. Mills (D)
Jan. 1971–Nov. 1980

David Roberti (D)
Dec. 1980–Jan. 1994

Bill Lockyer (D)
Jan. 1994–Feb. 1998

John Burton (D)
Feb. 1998–

* Presidents pro Tempore that have served since the Legislature became a "full-time, professional" body, upon the adoption of Proposition 1-a, November 8, 1966.

GALLERY OF SPEAKERS
1961–1998*

Jesse M. Unruh (D)
Sept. 1961–Jan. 1969

Bob Monagan (R)
Jan. 1969–Jan. 1971

Bob Moretti (D)
Jan. 1971–June 1974

Leo T. McCarthy (D)
June 1974–Nov. 1980

Willie L. Brown, Jr. (D)
Dec. 1980–June 1995

Doris Allen (R)
June 1995–Sept. 1995

Brian Setencich (R)
Sept. 1995–Jan. 1996

Curt Pringle (R)
Jan. 1996–Nov. 1996

Cruz M. Bustamante (D)
Dec. 1996–Feb. 1998

Antonio R. Villaraigosa (D)
Feb. 1998–

* Assembly Speakers that have served since the Legislature became a "full-time, professional" body, upon the adoption of Proposition 1-a, November 8, 1966.

ACKNOWLEDGMENTS

Contributing Editors

Lawrence A. Murman, Assistant Chief Clerk
Brian S. Ebbert, Principal Clerk
Melissa Swart-Weikel, Assistant Clerk

Leadership

Hon. Antonio Villaraigosa, Speaker of the Assembly (Feb. 1998–   )
Hon. Cruz M. Bustamante, Speaker of the Assembly (Dec. 1996–Feb. 1998)
Hon. Sheila James Kuehl, Speaker pro Tempore
Hon. Joe Baca, Assistant Speaker pro Tempore
Hon. Bill Leonard, Minority Leader
Hon. Robert Hertzberg, Chair, Assembly Rules Committee
Hon. Fred Aguiar, Vice Chair, Assembly Rules Committee
Hon. Curt Pringle, Assembly Member (Speaker of the Assembly, Jan. 1996–Nov. 1996)

Offices and Agencies

Administrative Office of the Courts
California Citizens Compensation Commission
California Constitution Revision Commission
California Research Bureau
California Secretary of State, Elections Division
California State Library
California Supreme Court
Center for California Studies
Legislative Counsel Bureau
Legislative Analyst Office
National Conference of State Legislatures
Office of the Governor
Senate Rules Committee
State Capitol Museum
State Treasurer's Office

Individuals

Stephen J. Greene, Esq., Assistant General Counsel, California Resources Agency
Akiba Howard, former Assistant Clerk
Linda Adams, Office of State Publishing
Dave Combies, Department of Personnel Administration
Pam Christopherson, Principal Clerk
Celeste Cron, California State Printer
Arvetta Downs, Chief Clerk's Office
Michelle Edwards, State Capitol Museum
Jerry Gillam, Capitol Press Corps
Tony Gonzalez, formerly of Assembly Republican Caucus
Shannon Hood, Chief of Staff, Senator James L. Brulte
Lily Hitomi, Legislative Bill Room
Gary Huckaby, Fair Political Practices Commission
Mike Kelley, former Legislative Intern
Lynn Johnson, State Capitol Museum
Charlotte Luallin, Legislative Data Center
Rich Milner, Speaker's Office
Michael Kilbane, Veterans Memorial Commission

Lynne Mayo, Judicial Council
Gary Mendez, former Legislative Intern
Joe Mette, Department of Parks and Recreation
Judy Morrison, State Capitol Museum
Sue Parker, Reading Clerk
Cyndy Perkut-Kelly, Assembly Engrossing and Enrolling Clerk
Jim Richardson, C.A.O., Assembly Rules (1996)
Ralph Romo, Chief Assistant Clerk
John Rovane, Assistant Secretary of the Senate
Greg Schmidt, Secretary of the Senate
V. Joseph Sgromo, State Capitol Museum
Hugh Slayden, former Legislative Intern
Doug Spitler, Treasurer's Office
LaDonna Stewart, Office of State Publishing
Russell Collins Stiger, Speaker's Office
Mike Taylor, Office of State Publishing
Jean Torcom, CSU Sacramento
Jonathon Waldie, C.A.O., Assembly Rules Committee

See page xi for photograph and illustration credits.

Table of Contents

List of Photographs and Illustrations
(credits in parentheses)

List of Tables and Charts

The full text of this publication is available to the public via the internet at: **"www.leginfo.ca.gov"**. Other useful legislative information, including bill text, California Codes, bill analyses, and bill histories are also available at this site.

CALIFORNIA: THE GOLDEN STATE
A Quick Information Guide

GENERAL INFORMATION

State Capitol..	Sacramento
Date California Admitted as a State	September 9, 1850
State Motto..	"Eureka" (Greek: "I have found it ! ")
Population [1]...	32,268,301
Number of Registered Voters [2]...................................	14,029,408
Population Density [3]...	188 people/sq. mi.
Land Area (includes 2,674 sq. mi. of inland water)	158,648 sq. mi.
Highest Elevation (feet above sea-level)....................	14,495 ft. (Mount Whitney)
Lowest Elevation (feet below sea-level).....................	282 ft. (Death Valley)
Total Number of Counties	58
Five Largest Cities (by population) [4]	
Los Angeles...	3,553,638
San Diego	1,171,121
San Jose	838,744
San Francisco	735,315
Long Beach	421,904
Five Largest Counties (by population) [5]	
Los Angeles	9,127,751
San Diego	2,655,463
Orange	2,636,888
Santa Clara	1,599,604
San Bernardino	1,598,358
Five Largest Counties (by square miles)	
San Bernardino	20,061
Inyo	10,192
Kern	8,141
Siskiyou	6,287
Fresno	5,963

GOVERNMENTAL/POLITICAL INFORMATION
FEDERAL LEGISLATORS

Members of Congress Representing California [6]	54
U.S. Senators Representing California........................	2
People Represented in Each Congressional District	574,000

GOVERNMENTAL/POLITICAL INFORMATION—continued
STATE EXECUTIVE OFFICERS

Number of Statewide Elective Officers	13 (Governor, Lt. Governor, Secretary of State, Attorney General, Treasurer, Controller, Superintendent of Public Instruction, Board of Equalization (4), Insurance Commissioner)
Term Limits for Statewide Officers.............................	2 four-year terms

STATE JUDICIARY

Number of Justices on State Supreme Court	7

STATE LEGISLATURE

Number of Members, California Legislature	120 (80 Assembly/40 Senate)
Length of Assembly Term	2 years
Length of Senate Term	4 years
Term Limits on State Legislators [7].............................	Assembly: 3 two-year terms Senate: 2 four-year terms
People Represented in Each Assembly District	373,000
People Represented in Each Senate District	746,000

LEGISLATIVE VOTING REQUIREMENTS

Vote Requirement to Pass Statutes	Majority (41 Assembly/21 Senate)
Vote Requirement to Pass Appropriations, Budget, Constitutional Amendments, and Urgency Bills	Two-thirds in each House (54 Assembly/27 Senate)
Veto Override Vote Requirement................................	Two-thirds in each House (54 Assembly/27 Senate)
Ratification of Amendment to U.S. Constitution..	Majority vote of each House (by Joint Resolution)

GOVERNMENTAL/POLITICAL INFORMATION—continued

MISCELLANEOUS LEGISLATIVE INFORMATION

Impeachment Power	Assembly indicts, drafts "articles of impeachment," and elects "managers" to prosecute; Senate tries and votes on impeachment.
Legislative Publications	Daily File Weekly History Daily Journal
Non-Member Officers of Legislature	Chief Clerk of Assembly Secretary of Senate Sergeant-at-Arms (in each House) Chaplain (in each House)
Motto of State Assembly	Legislatorum Est Justas Leges Condere (Latin: "It is the duty of Legislators to make just laws.")
Motto of State Senate	Senatoris Est Civitatis Libertatem Tueri (Latin: "It is the duty of a Senator to guard the liberty of the Commonwealth.")

ELECTED OFFICIALS' SALARIES

ANNUAL SALARIES OF ELECTED STATEWIDE OFFICERS [8]

Governor	$165,000
Lt. Governor	$123,750
Attorney General	$140,250
Secretary of State	$123,750
Controller	$132,000
Treasurer	$132,000
Superintendent of Public Instruction	$140,250
Insurance Commissioner	$132,000
Members, Board of Equalization	$123,750

[1] California has the largest population of any state. U.S. Census Bureau estimate, released 12-31-97.
[2] Secretary of State, February 1995.
[3] U.S. average population density is 69 people/square mile.
[4] U.S. Census Bureau, Nov. 18, 1997 estimate.
[5] U.S. Census Bureau, Mar. 20, 1997 estimate.
[6] U.S. Representatives serve 2-year terms; U.S. Senators serve 6-year terms.
[7] Although term limits for Members of Congress were approved by California voters in 1992 (Proposition 164), the U.S. Supreme Court in 1995 invalidated state-imposed term limits on Congressional representatives.
[8] Salaries effective December 1, 1998. See page 84 for legislators' salaries. See page 75 for Congressional salaries.

Capitol grounds, circa 1890.
(photo taken from hot air balloon)

California's

Legislature

The footnotes in this work contain the following abbreviations to legal reference materials:

U.S.—United States Reports (published opinions of the United States Supreme Court)
F. 2d—Federal Reporter, Second Series (published opinions of U.S. Circuit Courts of Appeal)
U.S.C.A.—United States Code Annotated
Fed. Reg.—Federal Register
Cal.—California Reports (published opinions of the California Supreme Court; inclusion of a number denotes subsequent series, i.e., **Cal. 2d** denotes California Reports, Second Series)
Cal. App. 2d—California Appellate Reports, Second Series (published reports of California Courts of Appeal; also, **Cal. App. 3d**)
Op. Att'y Gen.—California Attorney General Opinions
P.—Pacific Reporter (published opinions from courts of the pacific region; also, **P. 2d**)
A. 2d—Atlantic Reporter, Second Series (published opinions from atlantic region courts)
Pa., Okl.—Pennsylvania and Oklahoma Reports, respectively (court opinions from Pennsylvania and Oklahoma state courts)

For convenience, references to the California Constitution of 1879 are cited *"Constitution,"* while the federal document is identified as *"United States Constitution."*

Please note that the code citations contained herein represent the law of the State of California as it existed January 1, 1997. They do not, in many instances, reflect changes made during the 1997–98 session or later. Recent pertinent court decisions (e.g., term limits) have been included as late as Jan. 6, 1998.

Mission San Diego de Alcalá

California's first mission, founded in 1769 by Father Junípero Serra.

Chapter I

California's Historical Background

Exploration and Colonization

The discovery of the New World by Columbus ignited the aspirations of European powers and rekindled their efforts to find a westerly route to the "spice islands" of the Orient. Amerigo Vespucci and Magellan described the immense continent of South America, while John Cabot and others returned from North America without having found a northwest passage to the Indies. Enormous wealth, wrested from Mexico by Cortés and from Peru by Pizarro, called forth yet more exploration by land and sea for new riches as well as for the "Strait of Anian," fabled waterway to the treasures of the Orient.

One expedition after another crept up the west coast of Mexico and around the peninsula of Baja California. On September 28, 1542, a half-century after the discovery of America, a Portuguese navigator sailing under the Spanish flag set foot on the most southerly part of what is now the State of California. Juan Rodríguez Cabrillo had discovered San Diego Bay, which he named San Miguel.[1] This expedition of two small ships proceeded up the coast as far north as Point Reyes, claiming the land for Spain, but returned with neither stories of wealth nor clues to a western passage.

On June 17, 1579, the *Golden Hind,* laden with booty taken from the Spanish, anchored at an inlet north of San Francisco. Sir Francis Drake took possession of this land in the name of the English Queen, Elizabeth, and called the country Nova Albion, Albion being an archaic and poetic name for England.

In 1595, seeking ports of refuge and resupply for the Manila galleons, Sebastián Rodríquez Cermeno sighted what he called Cape Mendocino and later anchored the *San Agustin* in a bay somewhat north of San Francisco. On November 30, a storm dashed the ship against the shore, and Cermeno and his men set out in an open launch for Acapulco, charting the California coastline as they went.

In 1602, Sebastián Vizcaíno, a merchant rather than a mariner, set sail with specific instructions to explore the Pacific coastline as far north as Cape Mendocino. In November, Vizcaíno entered the bay previously discovered by Cabrillo, and renamed it San Diego. He then proceeded north and, one month later, anchored in the Bay of Monterey, which he named after the Viceroy of New Spain, the Count de Monterey. His description of the Port of Monterey as one of the finest along the coast encouraged continued Spanish interest in California. Contemporary names of many coastal features are attributed to this voyage.

Colonization and development of the northwestern provinces of New Spain (Northwest Mexico) eclipsed further interest in California. Serious attention was not given the area by the Spanish until the 1760's, when British and Russian interests began explorations into the North Pacific. "An order

---

[1] To commemorate this event, September 28 has been designated as "Cabrillo Day" in California. *Government Code,* Section 6708.

was sent the Viceroy of New Spain to investigate the Russian danger, but he was not told to colonize California. He transmitted this order to the visitador-general, José de Gálvez, and it was this officer who really determined that Alta California should be settled."[2]

Under the direction of Gálvez, a venture combining land and sea expeditions undertook to establish a base at San Diego with the further intent of securing the Port of Monterey as a presidio. In July, 1769, Gaspar de Portolá and Father Junípero Serra, leaders of the second of Gálvez's land expeditions, established a presidio and the mission of San Diego de Alcalá. The following year, Portolá founded the presidio of Monterey and the mission of San Carlos.

The Spanish approach to colonial development consisted of the creation of missions, for the Christianization and "civilization" of the Native American inhabitants; presidios, primarily to protect the missions and to guard against foreign aggression; and pueblos, established as an inducement for citizens to settle in the new country.

Twenty missions [3] were founded, extending in a chain along the California coastline northward from San Diego to San Raphael. The presidios were situated at strategic points along the coast, generally at the entrances to ports, and the pueblos were located adjacent to the missions and presidios.

Spanish rule continued until 1822, when Mexico won her independence from Spain, and California became a province of Mexico. The remote and fragile Mexican government, beset with internal problems, displayed little interest in and even less understanding of the problems of this distant region.

Ineffective political control of the province led to the disruption of already attenuated institutions. Many of the missions were separated from their agricultural holdings; the military shuffled loosely under northern and southern commands, and civil and military authorities clashed over jurisdiction. Into this troubled atmosphere came foreign settlers, such as the Swiss, John Sutter, and the pioneers from the United States who traversed the Sierra seeking land in the valleys. Throughout this period, coastal trade with British and Russian fur traders and merchants steadily increased.

With its crumbling internal order and concomitant vulnerability to foreign interests, California rapidly drew the attention of the United States government. In 1835, President Andrew Jackson tried unsuccessfully to purchase part of California from Mexico. The following year, California's Governor Alvarado issued a pronouncement regarding the province's independence. This proclamation raised the possibility of Russian or British intervention on California's behalf. Under President James K. Polk, America's westward expansion—"Manifest Destiny"—now faced the possibility of British control of the Pacific Coast. "Government explorers" were dispatched to California, and the United States Pacific Fleet kept close watch.

---

[2] John Walton Caughey, *California,* Second Edition, Prentice-Hall, Inc., 1953, p. 100.
[3] Under Mexican rule, the 21st, and last, of the missions was established at Sonoma on July 4, 1823.

Rumors of war, fears of American domination by native Californians, and the dissatisfaction of immigrant settlers with Mexican rule finally exploded into open hostility, culminating in the Bear Flag Revolution.[4]

The Bear Flag Revolution

On the morning of June 14, 1846, a group of American settlers, numbering from 32 to 35, unaware that a state of war existed between the United States and Mexico, captured General Mariano G. Vallejo, Mexican Comandante for Northern California, and took possession of the Pueblo of Sonoma.

William B. Ide, with the approval of the group, issued what has come to be known as Ide's Proclamation, the substance of which was to proclaim California independent of Mexico, under the title "California Republic."

The United States and Mexico had been at war since May of 1846, but the news did not reach California until several weeks later. On July 7, 1846, American marines and seamen under the command of Commodore John D. Sloat raised the American Flag over the Port of Monterey, and a courier was dispatched to San Francisco where, two days later, Commander John B. Montgomery took possession of San Francisco for the United States.

On the same day (July 9), the Bear Flag was lowered at Sonoma by Lieutenant Joseph Warren Revere, the grandson of the revolutionary patriot Paul Revere, and the Stars and Stripes unfurled in its stead. Thus ended the Bear Flag Revolution—less than four weeks after its beginning.[5]

The Admission of California

California[6] was admitted into the Union on September 9, 1850, as a free state,[7] and without ever having been a territory.

This great national and historical event was the result of a peculiar situation, due, partly, to the tremendous increase in population in California within a year's time (caused by the Gold Rush of 1848–1849) and to a compromise made by Congress in the Clay Omnibus Bill[8] which, among other items, included the admission of California as a state.

The debates in Congress on the admission of California were serious and prolonged. The first compromise resolution by Henry Clay was introduced in the United States Senate on January 29, 1850, and President Zachary Taylor presented copies of California's Constitution to Congress on February 13.[9] Many amendments, motions, proposals, and compromise offers were submitted and rejected.

The principal objections raised by opponents to the admission of California were to its acceptance as a free state, the extensiveness of its boundaries, the irregularity of the manner in which its Constitution was

---

[4] For a short history of the Bear Flag Revolution, *see California Blue Book 1954*, pp. 9–10.

[5] For brief descriptions of the Bear Flag, *see California Blue Book 1958*, p. 78; Joseph Warren Revere, *Naval Duty in California*, Bio Books, Oakland, California (1947 Centennial Edition); and, *Appendix F, infra*, p. 209.

[6] For origin of the name California, *see Appendix H, infra*, p. 223.

[7] The balance of power between North and South made the status of California as a slave or free state a paramount issue in Congress. At the time, the Union was composed of 15 free and 15 slave states.

[8] An omnibus bill is a legislative bill which makes a number of miscellaneous appropriations or contains several unrelated but distinct provisions.

[9] *Journals of the Senate and of the House*, 1st Session, 31st Congress, pp. 148, 529.

framed, its failure to have served a probationary period as a territory, and the fact that many of its residents were not citizens of the United States.

On March 11, 1850, President Zachary Taylor's message transmitting the Constitution of California was before the United States Senate for consideration. During the heated debate on the question, William H. Seward, then a Senator from New York, speaking in favor of the admission of California to the sisterhood of states, used these poetic and descriptive words:

> "California, that comes from the clime where the West dies away into the rising East—California, which bounds at once the empire and the continent—California, the youthful Queen of the Pacific, in her robes of freedom, gorgeously inlaid with gold—is doubly welcome."[10]

In this same eloquent speech, the distinguished Senator uttered these prophetic words: "The unity of our Empire hangs on the decision of this day."

After weeks of tiresome deadlock and caustic debate, the bill admitting California into the Union was passed by the Senate on August 13, 1850,[11] and by the House of Representatives on September 7.[12] Two days later, on September 9, 1850, President Millard Fillmore, who had succeeded to the presidency upon the death of President Taylor, signed the bill, and California became the thirty-first state in the Union.[13]

The following is a facsimile of the act providing for the admission of California into the Union:

---

[10] *Appendix to the Congressional Globe*, March 11, 1850, p. 261. (Special Order: Consideration of the President's Message transmitting the Constitution of the State of California.)

[11] *Journal of the Senate*, 1st Session, 31st Congress, p. 557.

[12] *Journal of the House*, 1st Session, 31st Congress, pp. 1423–24.

[13] By coincidence, California, the 31st state, was admitted to the Union by the 31st Congress.

Thirty-first Congress of the United States of America:

At the First Session,

AN ACT

For the admission of the State of California into the Union

Whereas the people of California have presented a constitution and asked admission into the Union, which constitution, was submitted to Congress by the President of the United States by message, dated February thirteenth, eighteen hundred and fifty, and which, on due examination is found to be republican in its form of government: Be it enacted by the Senate and House of Representatives of the United States of America in Congress assembled, That the State of California shall be one, and is hereby declared to be one, of the United States of America, and admitted into the Union on an equal footing with the original states in all respects whatever. Section 2 And be it further enacted, That until the representatives in Congress shall be apportioned according to an actual enumeration of the inhabitants of the United States, the State of California shall be entitled to two representatives in Congress. Section 3 And be it further enacted, That the said State of California is admitted into the Union upon the express condition that the people of said State, through their legislature or otherwise, shall never interfere with the primary disposal of the public land within its limits, and shall pass no law and do no act whereby the title of the United States to and right to dispose of, the same shall be impaired or questioned; and that they shall never lay any tax or assessment of any description whatever upon the public domain of the United States, and in no case shall non resident proprietors, who are citizens of the United States, be taxed higher than residents and that all the navigable waters within the said State shall be common highways, and forever free, as well to the inhabitants of said State as to the citizens of the United States, without any tax, impost or duty therefor. Provided, That nothing herein contained shall be construed as recognizing or rejecting the proposition tendered by the people of California as articles of compact in the ordinance adopted by the convention which formed the constitution of that State—

Approved September 9° 1850.

Millard Fillmore

Howell Cobb
Speaker of the House of Representatives
William R King
President of the Senate pro tempore.

Act for Admission of California

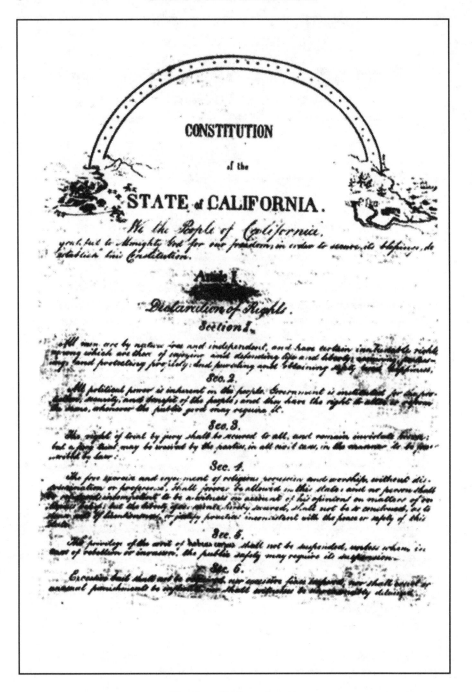

The Constitution of 1849

Chapter II

California's Constitution

Law and Order

In 1837, Mexico adopted a new constitution which created executive, legislative and judicial branches of government for the provinces. In California, considerable power was vested in the governor who, among other duties, appointed regional officers (prefects) and local magistrates (alcaldes), the latter acting in the capacities of mayor, judge and representative of the governor.

This system had little opportunity to take root before Commodore Sloat raised the American Flag at Monterey in 1846, proclaiming California a permanent possession of the United States, establishing military authority and promising constitutional rights, privileges and law. Many Californians objected to military rule and insisted upon immediate provisions for civil government.

"With the establishment of the American military government, the alcalde system was restored. On every bar, and in every gulch, and ravine, where an American crowd was collected, there an American alcalde was elected. And there were strange and often conflicting laws in adjoining neighborhoods, depending on the settlers or on the alcaldes, who made the laws, as the occasion required." [1]

After the treaty of peace with Mexico was signed in 1848, California was left with practically no government other than that provided by the local alcaldes, since the effect of peace was merely to take away the authority of the military government.

The American alcaldes were generally ignorant of the Spanish language and Spanish-Mexican law upon which the alcalde system was founded. The Americans were unwilling to abide by and unable to transact their business under the provisions of such an unfamiliar system. The inevitable result was that little law, other than that upheld by custom or tradition, existed.

The discovery of gold by James Marshall at Coloma, on January 24, 1848, brought to California, within a two-year period, an increase in population never before equaled in the history of this Nation. The influx of new people completely changed local conditions. Settlements devoid of any law or law enforcement sprang up overnight. Many of the newcomers were lawless persons who caused conditions to become so bad in some mining camps that, in aggravated cases, "miners' courts" were convened to mete out swift justice.

The combination of a bourgeoning population and an unfamiliar legal system resulted in chaos and stimulated the clamor for the establishment of a civil government based upon the concepts of the more familiar common law.

---

[1] 1 Cal. 577 (Appendix: The Alcalde System of California).

The question of providing a temporary government for California had been pending in Congress for several sessions, but Congress had failed to take any action. All of the other states, prior to their admission into the Union, had an established government on which to base their state organizations. This was not true of California, since its people were forced to form their own state government because of the political and legal tumult in which they found themselves while waiting upon Congress to act.

The Constitutional Convention of 1849

In December of 1848, a citizens' meeting was held in San Jose to consider the "propriety of establishing a provincial territorial government for the better protection of life and property." Resolutions were adopted recommending that a general convention meet in San Jose. Similar meetings were held early the next year in Sacramento, San Francisco, and Sonoma.

In late May of 1849, word reached the acting Governor, General Bennett Riley, that Congress had again adjourned without having provided a government for California. Upon receiving this information, Governor Riley, on June 3, 1849, issued a proclamation calling for the election of delegates to a constitutional convention.

Thus, California's first Constitution was drafted by citizens who met in convention at Colton Hall in Monterey on September 1, 1849—at a meeting which took place a year before California was admitted into the Union.

The Constitution, copies of which were printed in English and in Spanish,[2] was adopted by the convention on October 10, and ratified by the people on November 13, 1849.

The delegates chose an eclectic approach in drafting our first Constitution. The convention appears to have reviewed the constitutions of all of the states in drafting the California Constitution, which provided for a system very much like our present state government.

"In arrangement, the Constitution follows generally the Constitution of Iowa. Sixty-six of the 137 sections of the original Constitution of California appear to have been taken from the Constitution of Iowa, and 19 from the Constitution of New York. It is clear also that sections from the Constitutions of the States of Louisiana, Wisconsin, Michigan, Texas and Mississippi, and of the United States, were adopted. The sources of the other sections of the Constitution are not clear. Some sections appear to be modifications of sections from other constitutions, and some sections appear to be original." [3]

---

[2] *Resolved,* That certified copies of the Constitution in English and Spanish, be presented to the present Executive of California, and that 8,000 copies in English and 2,000 copies in Spanish, be ordered to be printed and circulated. *Journal of the Convention, Assembled to Frame a Constitution, for the State of California, Sept. 1st, 1849,* p. 156. All laws, decrees, regulations and provisions which from their nature require publication shall be published in English and Spanish. *Constitution of 1849,* Article XI, Section 21.

[3] Paul Mason, "Constitutional History of California," *Constitution of the United States—Constitution of the State of California,* California Legislature, Assembly, Sacramento, 1973, p. 91. *See also,* Cardinal Goodwin, *The Establishment of State Government in California,* McMillan Company, New York, pp. 230–243; *and,* J. Ross Browne, *Report of the Debates in the Convention of California, on the Formation of the State Constitution in September and October, 1849,* J. T. Towers, Washington, 1850, pp. 37, 56, 69, 70, 77, 110, 132, 165, 235, 248, 250, 292, 371, 380, and 385.

The Constitution of 1849

The Constitution as framed by the Convention of 1849 provided that upon the day of its submission for ratification the people should also, at the same time, vote for a Governor; a Lieutenant Governor; two Representatives in Congress; 16 State Senators and 36 Members of the Assembly, who were to compose the First State Legislature.[4] All of the above officers were elected for two-year terms, with the exception of the Assembly Members, who were elected annually. Within four days after its organization, the Legislature was to elect two United States Senators.

At that time, Article I, Section 3 of the Constitution of the United States provided that United States Senators be elected by their respective state's legislature. It was not until after the Seventeenth Amendment to the Federal Constitution was ratified on April 8, 1913, that United States Senators were elected by a popular vote of the people in their respective states.[5]

The election was held on the 13th day of November, 1849, and the people adopted the Constitution by a vote of 12,061 to 811.[6]

On the 15th of December, the Legislature met and organized. Governor Peter H. Burnett and Lieutenant Governor John McDougal were inaugurated on the 20th of December, and United States Senators John C. Fremont and William M. Gwin were elected by the Legislature on the same day. A Treasurer, Comptroller, Attorney General, Surveyor General, and three Justices of the Supreme Court were elected by the Legislature on December 22. The first Secretary of State was appointed by the Governor, and a complete working state government was established.

The Constitution of 1849 provided that the Comptroller, Treasurer, Attorney General, and Surveyor General were to be chosen by a joint vote of the two houses of the Legislature at its first session; but thereafter they were to be elected at the same time and places, and in the same manner as the Governor.[7]

The first Secretary of State was appointed by the Governor, by and with the advice and consent of the Senate, and continued to be an appointive office until 1862 when, by constitutional amendment, the office was made elective.[8]

Into the preamble of the Constitution of 1849 the delegates who made California a state wrote these words: "We, the people of [9] California, grateful to Almighty God for our freedom; in order to secure [10] its blessings, do establish this Constitution." Freedom and independence were guaranteed. It was further provided that "All political power is inherent in the people.

---

[4] Article IV, Section 6 of the *Constitution of 1849* did not specify membership of the Legislature, stating only that the number of Senators should be not less than one-third and not more than one-half the number of Members of the Assembly.

[5] *The Constitution of the United States—Analysis and Interpretations*—(Edwin S. Corwin, Editor) U.S. Government Printing Office, 1953, p. 48. *See also Dillon v. Gloss*, 256 U.S. 368 (1921).

[6] *Aggregate of the Votes for Governor, Lieutenant Governor, and Members of Congress (1849)*. State Archives, Sacramento, California.

[7] *Constitution of 1849*, Article V, Section 20.

[8] *Constitution of 1849*, Article V, Section 19.

[9] The words "the State of" were added in the *Constitution of 1879*.

[10] The words "and perpetuate" were added in the *Constitution of 1879*.

Government is instituted for the protection, security, and benefit of the people; and they have the right to alter or reform the same, whenever the public good may require it." [11]

The Constitution of 1849 contained only 12 articles and a schedule. Although in operation for 30 years, it was amended only three times—in 1856, 1862, and 1871.

The paucity of amendments to the original Constitution can be attributed, at least in part, to the amendment procedure which required that proposed amendments to the Constitution must first be "agreed to" by a majority vote of both houses of the Legislature proposing the amendment or amendments; published for three months next preceding the election of the next Legislature; "agreed to" by a majority vote of the newly elected Legislature; and then approved by a majority vote of the electors qualified to vote for Members of the Legislature. [12]

The Constitutional Convention of 1878

The Constitution of 1849 was a response to existing conditions in California and was framed to service those needs. With the swift and drastic changes California was to undergo after its adoption, it soon became apparent that it was an inadequate solution to the state's new and pressing problems of taxation, the banks, big business, land monopolization and particularly the railroads.

The social unrest and frustration resulting from the failure to cope with these troubles and the building resentment against the continuing influx of cheap Chinese labor motivated the Legislature to pass a bill in 1876 which submitted to the voters the proposition of whether or not to call a convention to frame a new constitution. [13] The proposition was subsequently approved by the voters at the general election of September 5, 1877. [14]

In accordance with the provisions of the Constitution of 1849 the Legislature at its next session in 1878 passed an enabling act calling for the election of delegates to the convention. [15] The bill provided for the selection of 152 delegates to be chosen at a special election on Wednesday, June 19, 1878. The elected delegates were to meet in the Assembly Chamber in the State Capitol on September 28, 1878, to draft a new Constitution for the State of California.

Of the 152 delegates elected, 145 were in attendance on the first day of the convention, four were absent, while one had resigned, and two others had died prior to convening. [16] The Convention adjourned *sine die* ("without day," meaning final adjournment) on March 3, 1879, 157 days after first being called to order.

---

[11] *Constitution of 1849*, Article I, Section 2.

[12] *Constitution of 1849*, Article X, Section 1.

[13] *Statutes of 1875–76*, Chapter 516, p. 791.

[14] *"A Complete Abstract of the whole number of Votes cast in the several Counties of the State (at the General Election for members of the Legislature, held on Wednesday, September 5th, 1877) 'For' and 'Against' a Convention to revise and change the Constitution of the State of California,"* State Archives, Sacramento, California. *See also Journal of the Assembly*, January 22, 1878, p. 240.

[15] *Statutes of 1877–78*, Chapter 490, p. 759.

[16] *Debates and Proceedings of the Constitutional Convention of the State of California, 1878–79*, Vol. I, E. B. Willis and P. K. Stockton—Editors, State Printing Plant, Sacramento, California, 1880, p. 13.

While the delegates attempted to deal with California's vexing problems, most commentators agree that they accomplished little more than creating a document that was the perfect example of what a constitution ought *not* to be.

The Constitution of 1879

The Constitution of 1879 was adopted at a convention at Sacramento on March 3 of that year, by a vote of 120 to 15.[17] The draft of the proposed Constitution was submitted to the electors on May 7, 1879, at which time the voters ratified the convention's action, adopting the new Constitution by a vote of 78,406 to 67,492.[18]

The new document fixed the membership of the Legislature at the current 80 Assembly Members and 40 Senators. Insofar as it related to the election of officers, the commencement of their terms in office, and the meeting of the Legislature, the new Constitution became effective at 12 m. on July 4, 1879. In all other respects, the effective date of the Constitution was 12 m., January 1, 1880.

A Declaration of Rights, not unlike the Federal Bill of Rights, is set forth in the State Constitution, in which the principle embodied in the Constitution of 1849 is reaffirmed: "All political power is inherent in the people. Government is instituted for their protection, security, and benefit, and they have the right to alter or reform it when the public good may require." [19]

California's historical position with regard to the federal government is stated as follows: "The State of California is an inseparable part of the United States of America, and the United States Constitution is the supreme law of the land." [20]

By reason of subsequent amendments, this Constitution has been altered considerably from the original document of 1879. A total of 583 amendments had been proposed by the Legislature and by the people through the initiative from 1880 through 1962. Of these, 334 were adopted by the voters.[21]

This haphazard and unbridled growth led the Legislature in 1963 to the conclusion that our Constitution had to be revamped. The Legislature felt that it was replete with unnecessary detail, inconsistent provisions and material that could more properly be contained in the statutes.[22] To remedy this situation they created the Constitution Revision Commission and directed it to make recommendations to the Legislature. While the ensuing acceptance of many of the commission's recommendations by the Legislature and the people significantly reduced the size of the Constitution, it remains a lengthy and detailed body of law.

---

[17] *Id.*, Volume III, p. 1521.

[18] The figures usually cited are taken from the *Canvass of Votes For and Against the New Constitution*. The figures in this document show a total of 145,212 votes cast: 77,959 for; 67,134 against; and 119 rejected. The *Canvass*, however, did not include the votes cast in Mariposa County. The June 7, 1879, edition of the *Sacramento Bee* also makes mention of this fact. A search of the State Archives by Dr. William N. Davis, Jr., California State Historian, produced a *Duplicate of the Elections For the New Constitution and Against the New Constitution* showing that 805 votes were cast in Mariposa County, making the total vote 146,017. Four hundred forty-seven of these votes were cast in favor of adopting the new Constitution, bringing that total to 78,406; the remaining 358 votes were cast against the new Constitution, making that total 67,492; none were rejected, leaving that figure at 119. The *Duplicate* was not received until June 26, 1879, and for that reason was not included in the *Canvass* which was completed on June 6, 1879.

[19] *Constitution*, Article II, Section 1.

[20] *Constitution*, Article III, Section 1.

[21] Compiled from Mason's *Constitution of California, Annotated, 1933*, California State Legislature, State Printing Plant, 1933, pp. 1769–1846; and *Statement of Vote, 1935–1962*, Secretary of State, Sacramento, California. *See also, Amendments to the Constitution of 1879, infra*, p. 13. Considering the *Constitution of 1879* originally contained 22 articles and totaled approximately 16,000 words, the numerous amendments from 1880 to 1962 left California with the most lengthy constitution of all the states.

[22] *Statutes of 1963*, Resolution Chapter 181.

Amendments to the Constitution of 1879,
Proposed and Adopted, 1880–1996

Year*	Proposed	Adopted	Year*	Proposed	Adopted
1884	3	3	1950 †	3	2
1886	1	0	1950	9	5
1887 †	3	1	1952	19	15
1890	1	1	1954	18	11
1892	5	2	1956	16	12
1894	9 [23]	7	1958	15	6
1896	6	3	1960 †	3	3
1898	7 [24]	1	1960	13	8
1900	8 [25]	5	1962	23	10
1902	9	7	1964	12	10
1904	6	3	1966	14	9
1906	14	8	1968	9	5
1908	14	11	1970	23	13
1910	8	8	1972	21	17
1911 †	23	22	1973 †	1	0
1912	4	2	1974	20	15
1914	30 [26]	18	1976 †	10	8
1915 †	9	0	1976	9	6
1916	4	1	1978 †	11	6
1918	19	9	1978	3	2
1919 †	1	1	1979 †	4	4
1920	12	5	1980 †	9	5
1922	22	9	1980	7	4
1924	16	10	1982 †	4	3
1926	23	15	1982	5	1
1928	17	14	1984 †	4	3
1930	21	10	1984	7	4
1932	17	10	1986 †	6	6
1933 †	8	6	1986	6	5
1934	18 [27]	11	1988 †	3	1
1935 †	3	0	1988	10	10
1936	20 [28]	4	1990 †	7	5
1938	19	6	1990	12	4
1939 †	1	0	1992 †	1	0
1940	16	8	1992	7	3
1942	15	6	1993 †	6	2
1944 †	1	1	1994 †	4	2
1944	11	7	1994	5	4
1946	14	11	1996 †	1	1
1948	15	6	1996	2	2
1949 †	11	10		820 [29]	494

* Refers to the year that the amendment appeared on the ballot and was voted upon by the electors.
† Special or statewide primary election.

[23] A proposed amendment to the Constitution, *Statutes of 1893*, Chapter 34, p. 657, was declared invalid by the Supreme Court (*Livermore v. Waite*, 102 Cal. 113) and was not placed on the ballot; therefore, it is not included in the proposed total for 1894.

[24] In 1897, the Legislature adopted Senate Concurrent Resolution 4, *Statutes of 1897*, Chapter 35, p. 650, calling for a convention to revise the Constitution. The proposal appeared on the 1898 ballot, but as it did not propose to amend any specific article of the Constitution, it is not included in the proposed total for 1898.

[25] Two proposed amendments to the Constitution, *Statutes of the Extraordinary Session of 1900*, Chapters 6, 10, pp. 26, 29, were declared invalid by the Supreme Court (*People ex rel Attorney General v. Curry*, 130 Cal. 82) and were not included in the proposed total for 1900.

[26] In 1913, the Legislature adopted Assembly Concurrent Resolution 17, *Statutes of 1913*, Chapter 75, p. 1714, calling for a convention to revise the Constitution. The proposal appeared on the 1914 ballot, but as it did not propose to amend any specific article of the Constitution, it is not included in the proposed total for 1914.

[27] In 1933, the Legislature adopted Assembly Concurrent Resolution 17, *Statutes of 1933*, Chapter 45, p. 3002, calling for a convention to revise the Constitution. The proposal appeared on the 1934 ballot, but as it did not propose to amend any specific article of the Constitution, it is not included in the proposed total for 1934.

[28] In 1936, an initiative constitutional amendment was invalidated by the Supreme Court (*Clark v. Jordan*, 7 Cal. 2d 248) and it did not appear on the ballot; therefore, it is not included in the proposed total for 1936.

[29] Two amendments, one each in 1920 and 1930, were adopted by the Legislature, calling for constitutional conventions by amending Article XVIII of the Constitution. Neither of these amendments were adopted by the people, but as they did appear on the ballot and proposed the amendment of an article of the Constitution, they are included in the proposed totals for the respective years. An initiative constitutional amendment, adding Section 26 to Article I, was approved by the electorate at the Nov. 3, 1964 general election, but was subsequently declared unconstitutional both by the California Supreme Court and the United States Supreme Court (*Mulkey v. Reitman*, 64 Cal. 2d 529; *Reitman v. Mulkey*, 387 U.S. 369). This amendment appears in both the proposed and adopted totals for 1964.

Constitution Revision Commission

Until 1962, California's Constitution could be revised extensively only by means of a constitutional convention. Article XVIII, Section 1, made provision for amendment, but that provision apparently indicated something less than a comprehensive constitutional revision.[30]

In 1960, the Legislature, acting upon the recommendation of an interim committee,[31] adopted a constitutional amendment providing for revision of the Constitution, i.e., by complete or partial changes. Previously, amendments could provide only specific or limited changes in the Constitution. This amendment was approved by the people in 1962 by more than a two-to-one vote.[32]

The Legislature, in the 1963 First Extraordinary Session, adopted a concurrent resolution establishing the Constitution Revision Commission under the Joint Committee on Legislative Organization. By the terms of the resolution,[33] the commission was to consist of not more than 50 citizen members appointed by the Joint Committee on Legislative Organization, three Members of the Senate appointed by the Senate Committee on Rules, three Members of the Assembly appointed by the Speaker, and the members of the Joint Committee on Legislative Organization, who were to serve as ex officio members.

In February 1966, the commission made its initial report to the Legislature.[34] Revisions of Articles III, IV, V, VI, VII, and XXIV of the Constitution, dealing with the legislative, executive, and judicial branches of government and the civil service system, were recommended.

Constitutional revision was placed on "special call" during the 1966 First Extraordinary Session and the commission's proposals, with the exception of those affecting Article XXIV, were introduced in the form of Assembly Constitutional Amendment 13 [35] and subsequently passed by the Assembly and Senate. Placed on the November 8, 1966, ballot as Proposition 1-a, it was approved by the people by a vote of 4,156,416 to 1,499,675.[36]

The revised Article IV effected a number of important substantive changes relative to the legislative branch of government.

Under former constitutional provisions, the Legislature met in general session during odd-numbered years and in budget session during even-numbered years. The amendment eliminated the budget session and provided for regular annual sessions of unspecified duration.[37]

Prior to this time, the Legislature could meet for a period not to exceed 120 days, excluding Saturdays and Sundays, during the odd-numbered years; nor for more than 30 days, exclusive of a recess no longer than 30 days, during the even-numbered years. The adoption of Proposition 1-a in 1966 removed these limitations.

---

[30] *McFadden v. Jordan* (1948) 32 Cal. 2d 330, cert. denied; 336 U.S. 918; *Livermore v. Waite* (1894) 102 Cal. 113.

[31] *Report of the Assembly Interim Committee on Constitutional Amendments to the California Legislature,* November 15, 1960, pp. 25–34.

[32] 2,901,537 to 1,428,034, Secretary of State, *Statement of the Vote, General Election, 1962,* Sacramento.

[33] *Statutes of 1963 First Extraordinary Session,* Resolution Chapter 7.

[34] *Proposed Revision of the California Constitution,* February 1966, California Constitution Revision Commission, San Francisco.

[35] *Statutes of 1966 First Extraordinary Session,* Resolution Chapter 139.

[36] Secretary of State, *California Statement of Vote and Supplement, November 8, 1966 General Election,* p. 27.

[37] *Constitution,* Article IV, Section 3(a). [1967]

Compensation for Members of the Legislature had been set at $500 per month since 1954 and could not be altered except by constitutional amendment. Pursuant to additional provisions of Proposition 1-a, a 1966 statute initially set the Members' salaries at $16,000 per year. The Legislature further was permitted to set its own compensation by a two-thirds vote of each house. Increases of more than 5 percent per year could not be passed for each calendar year following the operative date of the last adjustment, and such increase was subject to the Governor's veto and the initiative and referendum processes. No salary adjustment was operative until the beginning of the regular session commencing *after* the next general election following the enactment of the statute making the adjustment.[38] In this manner, all Members of the Assembly and at least one-half of the Senators who voted for an increase in compensation could not benefit from it unless they were reelected after they had voted for or against such increase.

Related to the commission's recommendation was the passage of Assembly Bill 173 of the 1966 First Extraordinary Session. The provisions of this bill, contingent on the adoption of Proposition 1-a, established a legislative conflict-of-interest law and enacted provisions governing travel expenses and retirement benefits for legislators.[39] This bill also provided that Members of the Legislature are entitled to living expenses at the same rate established for other elected state officers by the State Board of Control.[40]

The amendment reduced the signature requirement for initiative statute petitions from 8 to 5 percent of registered voters but retained the 8-percent requirement for constitutional amendments.[41]

Changes in the executive article included, among others, authority for the Governor to reorganize the executive branch of government[42] and permission for the Legislature to provide for gubernatorial succession by statute.[43]

Article VI, relating to the judicial branch, also underwent revision. Retaining the requirement of a superior court in each county, the revision permitted the Legislature to provide, with the concurrence of the board of supervisors of the affected county, that one or more superior court judges be selected to serve in more than one county.[44]

Municipal court judges are required to have been members of the California State Bar for at least five years immediately preceding their appointment. The other state court judges (superior, appellate and Supreme Court judges) require membership in the California State Bar for 10 years immediately preceding their appointment.[45] Incumbent judges of trial courts

---

[38] *Constitution,* Article IV, Section 4; *Government Code,* Section 8901. For current legislative compensation provisions, see Chapter VII, *infra,* p. 71.

[39] *Government Code,* Sections 8903, 8920–8926, 9359.11, 9359.12, and 9360.10. For current legislative retirement provisions, see Section 9350, et seq.

[40] *Government Code,* Section 8902. 1987 amendments to this section provide for reimbursement at the same rate provided to federal employees traveling to Sacramento. *See also, Constitution,* Article IV, Section 4(b).

[41] *Constitution,* Article IV, Section 22(b) [1967]. *See now, Constitution,* Article II, Section 8 (section renumbered in 1976).

[42] *Constitution,* Article V, Section 6.

[43] *Constitution,* Article V, Section 10; *Government Code,* Sections 12058, 12058.5, 12059.

[44] *Constitution,* Article VI, Section 4.

[45] *Constitution,* Article VI, Section 15. Prior service as a judge of a court of record (municipal court) is an alternative qualification for selection to the superior, appellate and Supreme courts.

(superior, municipal and justice) in the state need not have their names printed on the ballot if they were unopposed.[46]

In 1968 the Constitution Revision Commission submitted a proposal affecting Articles IX, X, XI, XII, XVII and XVIII. Many of the provisions of the commission's proposal were incorporated in Assembly Constitutional Amendment 30, which was adopted by the Legislature. This measure was defeated by the voters in the 1968 general election.

A review of this public rejection of the commission's proposal resulted in the submission of separate and more succinct propositions to the electorate.

The June 1970 ballot contained four of the commission's suggestions, of which only Proposition 2 was adopted.[47] This amendment made extensive revisions in Article XI relating to local government. Among the major changes made by this amendment are those requiring voter approval for county consolidation, formation of new counties, and annexation or consolidation of cities; those permitting all cities to be charter cities regardless of population; those requiring the election rather than the appointment of boards of supervisors; and those permitting counties complete jurisdiction over certain matters previously requiring legislative approval.

Subsequent elections in 1970, 1972 and 1974 saw the adoption of several propositions recommended by the commission. In the main, these changes deleted obsolete provisions, altered and clarified language in numerous sections, and brought others into conformity with Supreme Court decisions and provisions of the U.S. Constitution.

After studying and reporting on every article of the Constitution, the commission's existence was terminated by the Legislature in 1974.[48] Interest in the revision of the State Constitution was renewed, however, in the 1993–94 Regular Session. The Legislature and Governor approved Senate Bill 16 in 1993, creating a new Constitution Revision Commission, which operated from 1994 to 1996.[49] This 23 member body was charged with examining the state budget process, the relations between state and local government, and considered suggestions as to how to improve on these areas. To gain input from the public, as well as from local government officials and organizations, the commission held public hearings throughout the state focusing on various issues.

On September 15, 1995, the Commission reported its preliminary findings and recommendations to the Legislature.[50] In a sweeping series of proposals, the Commission suggested several reforms, among which included the following: the Governor and Lieutenant Governor should be elected on the same "ticket"; reduce the number of elective statewide officers by giving the Governor the power to appoint the State Treasurer, Insurance Commissioner, and Superintendent of Public Instruction; overhaul the state civil service

[46] *Constitution*, Article VI, Section 16(b); *Elections Code*, Section 25304.
[47] *Statutes of 1969*, Resolution Chapter 331.
[48] *Joint Rules Committee Resolution 57*, March 4, 1974. For a comprehensive summary of the commission's activities and recommendations, see Jay Gould, *Report on Materials of Constitution Revision Commission Relating to Provisions in California's Constitution Recommended or Endorsed by Commission*, December 10, 1974, pp. 1–147.
[49] *Statutes of 1993*, Chapter 1243.
[50] *Assembly Daily Journal*, September 15, 1995, p. 3934.

system; replace the two-house Legislature with a unicameral body of 121 members, serving no more than three four-year terms; prohibit legislators from fundraising while the Legislature is in session; replace the state's annual budget process with a two-year budget cycle; reduce the vote threshold for legislative passage of the state budget bill from a two-thirds vote to a majority vote; shorten the time period during which bills must be "in-print" prior to being considered from 30 days to 10 days; restructure the public school system to provide more accountability and flexibility; and realignment of state and local government responsibilities and financing.[51]

After further hearings and testimony, a final report and recommendation was published and presented to the Legislature on August 6, 1996. The final report included most of the original recommendations, but some changes were made to reduce initial legislative opposition to specific proposals, such as the unicameral legislature proposal. The bulk of the recommendations were drafted into Senate Constitutional Amendment 39 and Assembly Constitutional Amendment 49, both of which failed to pass the 1995–96 Legislature. As a result, no revision of the Constitution was offered to the voters for consideration.

Differences Between the Federal and the State Constitutions

Article VI of the Constitution of the United States declares that: "This Constitution, and the Laws of the United States which shall be made * * * under the authority of the United States, shall be the Supreme Law of the Land; and the Judges in every State shall be bound thereby, anything in the Constitution or Laws of any State to the contrary notwithstanding."

The fundamental difference between the California Constitution and the Constitution of the United States is that the Federal Constitution is a grant of power to Congress and is also a limitation upon its powers, whereas the State Constitution is a limitation upon the power of the State Legislature. The powers of the Legislature are inherent and are only restricted by the State Constitution and the Constitution of the United States. The sphere of state activity is more extensive than that of the federal government since its powers are original and inherent, not derived or delegated, as are the powers of the federal government.

Perhaps the best description of this concept was set forth by Chief Justice John Marshall, discussing the Federal Constitution in the early and famous case of *McCulloch v. The State of Maryland*,[52] when he stated:

> "The Government of the Union, * * * is, emphatically, and truly, a government of the people. In form and in substance it emanated from them. Its powers are granted by them, and are to be exercised directly on them, and for their benefit.

---

[51] *"Summary of Preliminary Recommendations,"* California Constitution Revision Commission, September 1995.
[52] 17 U.S. (4 Wheat.) 316 (1819).

"This government is * * * one of enumerated powers. The principle, that it can exercise only the powers granted to it, would seem too apparent to have required * * * argument * * * .

"It is the government of all; its powers are delegated by all; it represents all, and acts for all.

"The Government of the United States, then, though limited in its powers, is Supreme; and its laws, when made in pursuance of the Constitution, form the Supreme law of the land."

Other significant differences between the United States Constitution and the Constitution of California include the fact that under the Federal Constitution, revenue bills originate only in the House of Representatives.[53] In California, revenue bills may originate in either house.

Among the contrasting powers of the executive, the Federal Constitution gives the President the power to call both houses of Congress or either of them into extraordinary session. The Governor of California has no power to call only one of the houses into extraordinary session; the Governor must call into session the entire Legislature.[54]

The U.S. Congress, when so convened, may legislate on subjects which are not specified in the President's proclamation. In an extraordinary session of the California Legislature, however, the houses may legislate only on those matters itemized in the Governor's proclamation.

In the arena of foreign relations, the President of the United States, by and with the advice and consent of the U.S. Senate, provided two-thirds of the senators present concur, is empowered to make treaties with foreign governments.[55] Further, the U.S. Constitution prohibits states from entering into any treaty with a foreign government.[56]

The California Constitution explicitly recognizes the U.S. Constitution as the supreme law of the land,[57] and consequently, no provision for "treaty making" is vested in the Governor.[58] With the increasing importance of the global economy, however, the Governor, through the Trade and Commerce Agency, does maintain California Overseas Trade and Investment Offices in Frankfurt, Hong Kong, Jerusalem, Johannesburg, London, Mexico City, Taipei, and Tokyo.[59] Additionally, the California World Trade Commission biennially conducts a "California Pacific Rim Conference" to advance awareness, knowledge, and commitment to economic development with Pacific Rim nations.[60] As this book went to print, more California trade offices were planned for Shanghai, Seoul, and Sao Paulo.

---

[53] *United States Constitution,* Article I, Section 7.

[54] *United States Constitution,* Article II, Section 3; *Constitution,* Article IV, Section 3(b).

[55] *United States Constitution,* Article II, Section 2(2).

[56] *United States Constitution,* Article I, Section 10.

[57] *Constitution,* Article III, Section 1.

[58] The Supreme Court of California has ruled that treaties entered into by the President are also the supreme law of the land, and that the states are bound thereby, notwithstanding anything in their laws or constitutions to the contrary. *See Fujii v. State of California,* 38 Cal. 2d 718.

[59] *Government Code,* Section 15310, et seq., Section 15363 et. seq.

[60] *Government Code,* Section 15364.6.1.

Constitutional Amendments

California Constitutional Amendments

The people of California have a direct and final say in the amending of their state's constitution. Article II, Section 8 and Article XVIII of the California Constitution give the voters authority to approve or reject amendments to the State Constitution. Private citizens or groups may propose an amendment, or the Legislature may place an amendment on the ballot, if the proposal passes each House by a two-thirds vote. In either case, all proposed constitutional amendments must eventually be approved by a majority vote of the people in order to be adopted.[61]

The Legislature proposes amendments by passing a Senate Constitutional Amendment (S.C.A.) or an Assembly Constitutional Amendment (A.C.A.); neither require approval of the Governor. When the Legislature approves an A.C.A. or S.C.A., it is assigned a "proposition number" and placed on a statewide ballot, giving the electorate the power to ratify or reject such a change.

Citizens also have the power to propose their own amendments via the initiative process. A citizen, or group of citizens, may draft an amendment to the California Constitution and have it placed on a statewide ballot for approval by the voters. Strict constitutional and statutory guidelines and deadlines must be followed in order to have an initiative placed on the ballot, yet California citizens have successfully amended their Constitution numerous times this century.

Article XVIII gives the California Legislature the power to place on the ballot a call for a constitutional convention, provided such a call passes each House by two-thirds vote. Once the convention delegates agree to language for amendment(s), the proposition(s) would be placed on the ballot via the initiative process. The Legislature has not called for a convention since 1879, and has instead created Constitution Revision Commissions to study and recommend constitutional changes.

United States Constitutional Amendments

The process governing amendments to our nation's constitution is outlined in Article V of the *U.S. Constitution*. It should be noted that the method of amending *California's* Constitution differs greatly from amending the *federal* document. As mentioned above, all amendments proposed to the State Constitution must eventually be approved by a popular vote of the California electorate, whereas amendments to the *U.S. Constitution* do *not* go to a direct vote of U.S. voters; state legislatures *or* conventions are given the sole power of amendment ratification. Like California's amendment procedure, the chief executive (the President) plays no formal role in the federal constitutional amendment process.

---

[61] For more information on initiatives and how the California Constitution is amended, see Chapter 3. Note: If the provisions of two or more measures approved at the same election conflict, those provisions of the measure receiving the highest affirmative vote shall prevail. *Constitution, Article XVIII, Section 4.*

An amendment to the *U.S. Constitution* may be submitted to the states for ratification in two manners: two-thirds of state legislatures (34 out of 50) may call for a constitutional convention to formulate a proposed amendment; or, by two-thirds vote of each House, Congress may propose an amendment. The requisite number of states have never called for the assembling of a national constitutional convention. Congress, however, has proposed a total of 31 constitutional amendments since 1787.

Once an amendment has been officially proposed to the states, the ratification process may begin. Three-fourths of the states (38 out of 50) must ratify, or approve, the proposed change. The Constitution allows Congress to determine the method of ratification: an amendment may be ratified by three-fourths of all state legislatures, or by three-fourths of conventions held in each state. Interestingly, Congress has only submitted a proposed amendment to *state conventions* once (for the 21st amendment); all other constitutional amendments have been subjected to ratification by state legislatures.

How state legislatures actually ratify an amendment varies from state to state. Most states require a simple majority vote in each House, while others require an absolute or supermajority vote in one or both chambers.[62] In California, a U.S. Constitutional amendment is ratified by joint resolution, passed by an absolute majority vote of each House (41 Assembly Members, 21 Senators). The resolution may originate in either House (i.e., A.J.R. or S.J.R.).

The most recent movement to change the U.S. Constitution has been the "Balanced Budget Amendment," which has yet to pass the Congress for submission to the states. In total, 27 amendments have been added to the U.S. Constitution from 1787 to present, the most recent was ratified in 1992.[63]

Distribution of Powers of Government

The powers of the government of the United States and the powers of the government of the State of California are divided into three separate departments—the Legislative, the Executive and the Judicial. While the Constitution of the United States does not expressly provide for this division, the Supreme Court of the United States has stated that "the rule established by the American Constitutions, both State and Federal, divides the government into three separate departments—the legislative, executive and judicial." [64]

The California Constitution, however, does specifically provide that the powers of government be divided into these three separate departments; and that no person charged with the exercise of powers properly belonging to one of these departments shall exercise any functions appertaining to either of the others except as the Constitution expressly directs or permits.[65]

---

[62] See *"State Ratification of Amendments to the U.S. Constitution"*, by Christopher Zimmerman, National Conference of State Legislatures, as appeared in *"Legisbrief,"* May 1995.

[63] The 27th Amendment was proposed in 1789, yet was not fully ratified until 1992 (203 years later). The amendment prohibits Congress from increasing salaries of its own Members during the same legislative session; however, Congress may still approve salary increases to take effect after the Congressional elections. Note: The California Legislature ratified the 27th Amendment over two months after it had already been fully ratified by the necessary 38 states.

[64] *Springer v. Philippine Islands*, 277 U.S. 189.

[65] *Constitution*, Article III, Section 3.

One of the exceptions to the constitutional provision providing for three separate and distinct coordinating branches of government occurs when the Senate sits as a court of impeachment, thereby serving in a judicial capacity. As long as the constitutional guarantees have been complied with, the courts have no jurisdiction or power of review in impeachment proceedings or their results.[66]

Confirmation of Appointments

Many of the appointments made by the President of the United States must be confirmed by the United States Senate before the appointees may hold office.[67]

Similarly, most appointments made by the Governor must be confirmed by a majority vote of the State Senate before the appointment becomes effective. The appointees to the State Board of Education,[68] the Public Utilities Commission,[69] the South Coast Air Quality Management District Board,[70] and the State Adjutant General [71] are but a few examples of the offices over which the Governor has appointment power and for which State Senate confirmation is required.

The California State Assembly shares the confirmation power with the State Senate in only two instances: gubernatorial appointments to fill a vacancy in a statewide office, and approval of actuarial appointments. In each instance, an affirmative vote of both the Assembly and the Senate is required for the appointment to take effect, and if either house fails to confirm the appointment, it is considered denied. When a vacancy occurs in specified statewide offices (i.e., Lt. Governor, Atty. General, etc.), the Governor's nomination of a replacement is subject to confirmation by a majority vote of the membership of the Assembly and Senate.[72] In the event the nominee is neither confirmed nor denied within 90 days of the appointment, he or she shall take office as if having been confirmed. Likewise, when the Governor wishes to appoint an actuary for the Board of the Public Employees Retirement System, the nominee is submitted to each house of the Legislature. Thereafter, the Legislature has 60 calendar days within which to confirm or deny the nomination; a majority vote in each house is required for approval. If the nominee is neither confirmed nor denied during this period, the appointment shall become effective on the 61st calendar day after the date of the nomination.[73]

Impeachment

The Legislature may be considered the most important of the three branches of government, for, while it is in session, the Legislature not only

---

[66] See, e.g., *Nixon v. U.S.,*—U.S.—, 113 S. Ct. 732 (1993). *See also, State (Oklahoma) v. Chambers,* 220 P. 890, 96 Okl. 78 and *In re Dauphin County Grand Jury, September, 1938 (Pennsylvania),* 2 A.2d 802, 332 Pa. 342.

[67] *United States Constitution,* Article II, Section 2(2).

[68] *Education Code,* Section 33000.

[69] *Government Code,* Section 14502.

[70] *Health and Safety Code,* Section 40420.

[71] *Military and Veterans Code,* Section 162.

[72] *Constitution,* Article V, Section 5. If the 90-day period ends during a period of joint recess, the confirmation period is extended to the sixth day following the reconvening of the Legislature.

[73] *Government Code,* Section 20006(b). If the 60-day period ends during a period of joint recess, the confirmation period is extended to the sixth day following the reconvening of the Legislature.

has the last word in the enactment of laws through its power to override the Governor's veto, but the Assembly has the sole power of impeachment, and the Senate is designated as the tribunal for trying such impeachments.[74]

All impeachments must be by resolution originating in the Assembly and adopted by a majority vote of that house. If the resolution of impeachment is adopted, the Assembly then elects managers who prepare the articles of impeachment, present them at the bar of the Senate, and prosecute them.[75]

The trial must be before the Senate sitting as a court of impeachment.[76] When sitting for that purpose, the Senators are upon oath or affirmation. No Member of the Senate can act or vote upon the impeachment without having taken such oath, and no person shall be convicted without the concurrence of two-thirds of the members elected.[77]

State officers elected on a statewide basis, members of the State Board of Equalization, and judges of state courts are subject to impeachment for misconduct in office;[78] but judgment in such cases may result only in the removal or suspension from office and the disqualification to hold any office of honor, trust, or profit under the state.[79] The person impeached, whether convicted or acquitted, is also subject to criminal punishment according to law.[80]

The Constitution of the United States has similar provisions relative to impeachment. Should the President of the United States be tried, the Chief Justice of the Supreme Court would preside.[81] In California, the Lieutenant Governor, by virtue of his or her office as President of the Senate, presides over all impeachment proceedings except when the Lieutenant Governor is impeached.[82]

Local officials are not impeached but may be removed by other means. Any county, city or district officer, whether elected or appointed may be removed for willful or corrupt misconduct in office. Removal requires that an accusation, in writing, be presented to the grand jury. If at least 12 of the grandjurors concur, the accusation is presented to the district attorney by the foreman of the grand jury. The officer accused may then answer by denying the sufficiency of the accusation in writing or deny its truthfulness at a jury trial. If the defendant officer pleads guilty or refuses to answer the accusation or if the officer is convicted by the jury, he or she may be removed from office.[83]

---

[74] *Constitution*, Article IV, Section 18; *Government Code*, Sections 3020–3040.

[75] *Government Code*, Sections 3021, 3022.

[76] *Government Code*, Section 3022.

[77] *Constitution*, Article IV, Section 18; *Government Code*, Sections 3031, 3032.

[78] *Constitution*, Article IV, Section 18(b); *Government Code*, Section 3020. For trial proceedings, *see Judge Levi Parsons*, Proceedings in the House of Assembly of California in 1851, 1 Cal. 539; *Trial of the Impeachment of Judge Carlos S. Hardy*, Senate of the State of California (Editor, Joseph A. Beek, Secretary of the Senate), California State Printing Office, Sacramento, California, 1930. Impeachment proceedings have been held only four times in California's history: State Treasurer Henry Bates (1857); State Controller G.W. Whitman (1857); Judge James H. Hardy (1862); and Judge Carlos S. Hardy (1929). *The California Legislature*, Joseph A. Beek (1980), pp. 209–215.

Alternative procedure for the removal of justices and judges may be found in *Constitution*, Article VI, Section 18. Recall provisions for elected state and local officers are contained in *Constitution*, Article II, Sections 13–19.

[79] *Government Code*, Section 3035.

[80] *Constitution*, Article IV, Section 18(b); *Government Code*, Section 3040.

[81] *United States Constitution*, Article I, Section 3(6), (7).

[82] *Government Code*, Section 3039.

[83] *Government Code*, Sections 3060–3074.

Governor James Rolph, Jr. delivers his inaugural address on the
west steps of the State Capitol, January 6, 1931.

Chapter III

Elections

Right of Suffrage

In 1972, the people adopted a constitutional amendment substantially revising California's voting qualifications. The new Article II reflected changes brought about by federal legislation and court decisions. The provisions of this article regulate the right of the people of this state to vote in federal, state, and local elections.[1]

It provides that any citizen who is 18 years of age and a resident of California is entitled to vote.[2] The power to define residence and to provide for registration and free elections resides in the Legislature.[3]

Furthermore, the Constitution provides that no person who is mentally incompetent or imprisoned or on parole for the conviction of a felony is qualified to vote in California.[4] The voter's right to cast his or her vote in secrecy is also guaranteed by the California Constitution.[5]

The language formerly contained in the Constitution and the statutes pertaining to suffrage was, perhaps, the most misleading and confusing area in California law as many of the requirements contained therein had been stricken by the courts as being unconstitutional.

For example, the prerequisite that a person be able to read the Constitution in the English language was declared to be a violation of the equal protection clause of *Amendment XIV, U.S. Constitution,* and the voter, if otherwise eligible, need only be literate in another language and have access to sources of political information published in that language.[6] The *Federal Voting Rights Act of 1970* also declared that literacy tests required before voting were unconstitutional.[7]

Likewise, the residency requirements for state elections of one year in the state, 90 days in the county, and 54 days in the precinct prior to the election, and the 54-day residency requirement in the state for presidential and vice presidential elections have also been declared unconstitutional as being in violation of the equal protection clause and as an infringement on a person's constitutional right to travel.[8]

However, until the adoption of the current Article II and the enactment of conforming statutes these provisions remained in the text of our Constitution and statutory law.

In summation, the courts have concluded that any durational residency requirement exceeding 30 days is unconstitutional unless the state can show that such an imposition is not merely an administrative convenience but an

---

[1] *Constitution,* Article II, Sections 2–4.
[2] *Constitution,* Article II, Section 2. Eighteen years of age is also the federal requirement, *United States Constitution,* Amendment XXVI.
[3] *Constitution,* Article II, Section 3.
[4] *Constitution,* Article II, Section 4. In California a "felony" is a crime which is punishable with death or by imprisonment in a state prison. *Penal Code,* Section 17.
[5] *Constitution,* Article II, Section 7.
[6] *Castro v. State of California,* 2 Cal. 3d 223.
[7] 42 U.S.C.A. 1973aa. This section was held to be constitutional by the United States Supreme Court, *Oregon v. Mitchell,* 400 U.S. 112.
[8] 42 U.S.C.A. 1973aa-1; *Dunn v. Blumstein,* 405 U.S. 330; *Keene v. Mihaly,* 11 Cal. App. 3d 1037; *Young v. Gnoss,* 7 Cal. 3d 18.

administrative necessity which promotes a compelling state interest. The courts have consistently stricken residency requirements exceeding 30 days.

The California statutory provisions are now in conformity with these decisions. A person may be registered at any time up to and including the 29th day prior to the election.[9] A new resident who meets the requirements of Article II, Section 2 of the California Constitution, except the residency requirements, may vote for the president and vice president if he or she registers to vote up to and including the eighth day prior to the election.[10]

The Legislature has also made provision for the casting of absentee ballots by registered voters who do not wish to cast their ballots at the polling place or who expect to be absent from their precincts or who are unable to vote because of disability on the day on which the election is held.[11] Any registered voter may choose to cast an absentee ballot.[12] Additionally, an absentee voter who, because of illness or disability, is unable to return his or her ballot by mail or in person may designate an immediate relative to deliver the ballot to an elections official.[13]

The voter must apply to the county clerk or other proper official for an absentee ballot. The application must be made not more than 28 nor less than eight days prior to the election. However, any ballots received prior to the 29th day shall be kept and processed during the application period. Ballots must be received by the clerk from whom they were obtained by the time the polls close on election day.[14]

On election day after the polls are closed, the number of ballots cast are counted and compared with the total number of voters who have signed the precinct roster. The number of votes for and against each candidate and proposition are then tabulated or they are forwarded to a central counting center for tabulation. The count is open to the public and when once begun must be carried on continuously until its completion. The results of the count are posted outside the polling place or counting center. No information regarding the results of the election may be disclosed until after the polls have closed. When the count has been completed the ballots and copies of the tally sheets are forwarded to the county clerk.[15]

The Legislature has provided for different methods of voting and tabulating the results including the use of voting machines, punch cards and computers.[16] The most notable use of the mechanical voting machine has occurred in the City and County of San Francisco which has utilized this method of voting since the early part of this century.

---

[9] *Elections Code,* Section 2107.

[10] *Elections Code,* Sections 332, 3400.

[11] *Elections Code,* Sections 3000–3023. *Elections Code,* Section 3005 permits voters living in a precinct which contains 250 or less registered voters and which contains no polling place to cast their votes by absentee ballot.

[12] *Elections Code,* Section 3003.

[13] *Elections Code,* Section 3017.

[14] *Elections Code,* Sections 3001, 3020.

[15] *Elections Code,* Sections 15050–15202. *See also* 47 *Op. Att'y Gen.* 167.

[16] *Elections Code,* Sections 315, 344, 345, 358, 19004–19213.

Primary and General Elections

California holds primary and general elections to choose most of its state officeholders. The law regulates the direct nomination of candidates for public office by electors, political parties, or organizations of electors without conventions at the primary election and prescribes the conditions to be complied with by electors, political parties, or organizations of electors in order to participate in any such primary.[17]

Only officially qualified political parties may participate in primary and general elections. There are two ways a proposed political party may qualify as an official party in the state: by registering voters in the new party's name, or by gathering signatures via petition. The law prescribes that if a proposed party chooses the first option, it must achieve a statewide registration with that party's name equaling at least 1% of the total votes cast at the preceding gubernatorial election (e.g., 89,006 registrations for the 1998 general election). Qualifying by petition, on the other hand, requires signatures by voters equal in number to at least 10% of the total votes cast in the preceding gubernatorial election (e.g., 890,064 signatures for the 1998 general election).[18]

At present, there are eight officially qualified political parties in California: the American Independent; the Democratic; the Green; the Libertarian; the Natural Law; the Peace and Freedom; the Reform; and the Republican. Of these eight parties, two (Natural Law Party and Reform Party) gained qualified status in late 1995. The Green Party qualified in 1992, whereas the Libertarian Party achieved qualified status in 1980.[19]

Closed Primaries (1960–1996)

The purpose of the direct primary is to nominate party candidates who will run for office at the ensuing general election. Until Proposition 198 was adopted by the voters in March 1996, California held "closed" primaries. In these elections, only party members could participate in the election of their own party's candidates in the primary (e.g., only registered Democrats could vote for Democratic candidates running in a primary election). Separate ballots were printed for each party so as to facilitate the closed primary process. Once a primary election had determined which candidates would run in the general election, voters from all parties could "cross party lines" to vote for any candidate appearing on the general election ballot.

Open Primaries (1996–present)

California now has an open primary system wherein all voters, regardless of political affiliation, can vote for any candidate running in the primary.[20] For example, a Green Party member could vote for the Democratic candidate if the voter wished to, or for any other candidate listed on the ballot. Unlike

---

[17] *See generally, Elections Code.*

[18] For more specific information on political party qualification process, see *Elections Code,* Sections 5000–5200.

[19] Sixteen parties have qualified for primaries since the beginning of the modern primary election process in 1910. The Democratic and Republican Parties have participated in state primary elections since 1910, whereas the American Independent and Peace and Freedom Parties qualified in 1968. *"1996 Elections Calendar,"* Secretary of State, Sacramento, p. 2.

[20] Proposition 198 (open primary law) was upheld in federal court on November 17, 1997 (*California Democratic Party v. Jones,* 1997 WL 725980 (E.D. Cal. 1997)).

the previous years of closed primaries, when multiple ballots were printed (one for each party), the open primary ballot now shows all the candidates' names. The ballots contain a random listing of the candidates; they are not grouped by party affiliation. The candidate from each party who receives the most votes becomes that party's nominee at the upcoming general election. However, the election of political party officers, such as a member of a party's central committee, is still only open to members of that political party.

Crossfiling System (1910–1960)

It should be noted that from 1910 to 1960, the primary system allowed candidates to "crossfile." This process gave a person the opportunity to file for candidacy in their own party's primary as well as filing in another party's primary. For example, a Republican's name could appear on both Democratic and Republican primary ballots and therefore secure both party's nominations for the general election. In the upcoming election, this crossfiled candidate who had won both party's primaries would therefore run unopposed, virtually guaranteeing his or her election. Candidates with high name recognition, particularly incumbents, had substantial advantages under the crossfiling system. Since the candidates' true political party affiliation was not indicated on the primary ballot, a voter could easily vote for the opposite party's candidate (based on name recognition) without realizing it. However, a candidate could not appear on the general election ballot if he or she won the other party's primary, but failed to win his or her own party's nomination.[21]

Presidential Primaries

Like the direct open primary, a presidential primary is also held to nominate candidates who will run for office in the general election. In a presidential primary, the voters decide the number of votes their party's nominee or nominees receive from California at the national convention which selects the party's candidate for the office of the President of the United States. The presidential primary is also an "open" system in California. The direct primary and presidential primaries are consolidated to maximize voter turnout and provide for a more efficient electoral system. Initiatives also often appear on primary ballots, therefore making primary elections more than just a simple party nomination process but, instead, substantial policy-oriented elections.

Historically, the direct primary election in California has been held on the first Tuesday after the first Monday in June (e.g., June 2, 1998).[22] However, in an effort to increase California's influence in presidential politics and to increase voter participation, legislation was enacted in 1993 to move California's presidential primary from June to March 26, 1996. Interestingly, many other states soon followed suit and moved-up their primaries as well, thereby diminishing the impact of California's earlier election. Since new

---

[21] *See also* p. 28, footnote 31.
[22] *Elections Code*, Sections 316, 1001, 1201.

legislation has not been enacted to make this earlier election time permanent, the California primary will return to the original June date after the 1996 primary.[23] The general election is held in the even-numbered year on the first Tuesday after the first Monday in November (e.g., November 3, 1998).[24]

Special Elections

The Constitution gives the Governor the authority to call a special statewide election for initiative and referendum measures.[25] The Governor must call a special election if a vacancy should occur in the office of either Assembly Member, State Senator or in California's delegation in the House of Representatives or the United States Senate.[26] A special primary election follows the Governor's proclamation and all of the candidates, regardless of political affiliation, are listed on a single ballot. If any one candidate receives a majority of all the votes cast at this special primary election, he or she shall be elected and no additional special election shall be called. In the event that no one receives a majority of all votes cast, the candidate of each qualified political party who receives the most votes cast for the candidates of that party is placed on the ballot as the candidate of that party at the ensuing special general election.[27]

Partisan and Nonpartisan Offices

In California there are two classes of offices to which candidates are elected—partisan and nonpartisan. Partisan offices are offices for which a political party may nominate a candidate. Nonpartisan offices are offices for which no political party may nominate a candidate.[28] A constitutional amendment was adopted by the people in 1986 which prohibits any political party or party central committee from endorsing, supporting, or opposing a candidate for a nonpartisan office (Article 2, Section 6(b)). This provision, however, was recently declared to be in violation of the federal constitution and was permanently prohibited from being enforced.[29] The Governor, Lieutenant Governor, Secretary of State, State Treasurer, Attorney General, Controller, Insurance Commissioner, and United States Senators are partisan officers elected by a vote of the electors of the entire state. Assembly Members, State Senators, Representatives in the United States Congress, and Members of the State Board of Equalization are also partisan officers, but they are elected by the voters in the districts they represent.

Candidates for partisan offices are nominated by the voters at the open primary election in June and elected or defeated by all the qualified voters at the general election in November.

---

[23] *Statutes of 1993*, Chapter 828.
[24] *Elections Code*, Sections 324, 1200.
[25] *Constitution*, Article II, Section 8(c), 9(c).
[26] *United States Constitution*, Article I, Section 4; *Constitution*, Article IV, Section 2(d); *Elections Code*, Sections 2650, 2651. For filling a vacancy by appointment for the office of U.S. Senator from California, *see Elections Code*, Section 25001 and 44 *Op. Att'y Gen. 30*.
[27] *Elections Code*, Sections 10702–10706.
[28] *Elections Code*, Sections 334, 337, 338.
[29] *California Democratic Party v. Lungren*, 919 F.Supp. 1397 (N.D. Cal. 1996).

As previously stated, for many years, California allowed a candidate for public office to seek the nomination of another party or parties in addition to his or her own party nomination at the primary election.[30] This procedure was known as "crossfiling." A candidate who won both major party nominations was practically assured of being elected at the general election in November as his or her name would be the only one to appear on the general election ballot.

The candidate who won his or her own party's nomination, but failed to win the nomination of the other party, had a runoff with the other party's nominee at the general election. However, a candidate who failed to win his or her own party's nomination could not be the nominee of any other party in the November election, even though he or she may have received the most votes for the other party's nomination.[31]

The 1959 session of the Legislature enacted a new section which precluded a candidate for partisan office from crossfiling. Though a candidate for partisan office may no longer crossfile, there is nothing in the law which precludes the candidate who receives the nomination of his or her declared party and the nomination of another political party by write-in votes from being the candidate of both parties, provided that his or her write-in votes are also equal to 1 percent of all votes cast for that office at the last preceding general election.[32]

The Justices of the Supreme Court and the Superintendent of Public Instruction are nonpartisan officers elected by the voters of the entire state. Justices of the appellate courts and judges of the superior courts are nonpartisan officers elected by the voters of the districts in which they serve.

Any candidate for a judicial, school, county, municipal, or other nonpartisan office, who at a primary election receives a majority of all votes cast for candidates for the office, shall be elected to that office [33] and that office does not appear on the general election ballot.[34]

If no candidate receives a majority of the total votes cast for a nonpartisan office in the primary election, the names of the two candidates receiving the highest number of votes will appear on the general election ballot.[35]

In the event two or more candidates are to be elected to a given nonpartisan office, and a greater number of candidates receive a majority than the number to be elected, the candidates, equal in number to the offices to be filled, who have received the highest votes of those securing a majority, shall be elected.[36]

---

[30] *Statutes of 1913*, Chapter 690. *See also Statutes of 1939*, Chapter 26. "The primary election of 1913 (*Stats. 1913*, pp. 1379, 1389) specifically provided that a person could become the candidate of more than one political party for the same office. This provision was held constitutional (*Hart v. Jordan*, 168 Cal. 32). Although this provision was not retained when the *Elections Code* was adopted, it remains the rule (*Shaffer v. Jordan*, 213 F. 2d 393)." *Jones v. McCollister*, 159 Cal. App. 2d 708.

[31] *Elections Code*, Section 2742, repealed by *Statutes of 1959*, Chapter 284; reenacted by Chapter 31 of the *Statutes of the First Extraordinary Session of 1960*; and renumbered and reenacted as *Elections Code*, Section 6611 by *Statutes of 1961*, Chapter 23; repealed. *Statutes of 1976*, Chapter 1191. In the direct primary election of August 1918, James Rolph, Jr., a Republican lost his own party's nomination but won the Democratic Party nomination, defeating Democrat Francis J. Heney by more than 14,000 votes. However, because he had not won his own party nomination, he was not permitted to run as the Democratic candidate at the general election in 1918. *See Heney v. Jordan*, 179 Cal. 24, 27–29.

[32] *Elections Code*, Section 8605. *See also* 35 *Op. Att'y Gen.* 206; 59 *Op. Att'y Gen.* 414.

[33] *Elections Code*, Sections 334, 8140.

[34] *Elections Code*, Section 8140.

[35] *Elections Code*, Sections 8141, 8142. *See also* 20 *Op. Att'y. Gen.* 53.

[36] *Elections Code*, Section 8140.

The Elections Code also provides for situations where numerous candidates are running for numerous nonpartisan offices in a primary (e.g., five persons running for three school board seats), which may cause some of the offices to be filled immediately, and others to be filled at the general election ("runoff"):

> "If no candidate has been elected to a nonpartisan office . . . or if the number of candidates elected at the primary election is less than the total number to be elected to that office, then candidates for that office at the ensuing election shall be those candidates not elected at the primary who received the next higher number of votes cast for nomination to that office, equal in number to twice the number remaining to be elected to that office, or less, if the total number of candidates not elected is less."[37]

For example, if there were three nonpartisan offices to be filled and there were six candidates for these offices, and if only one of the candidates received a majority of the votes cast at the primary election, the other two offices would remain vacant and the four candidates who received the next highest vote but did not attain a majority would become candidates at the ensuing election. On the other hand, if there were only four candidates running for three nonpartisan offices and only one candidate received a majority of the votes cast, the other three would become candidates for the remaining two offices at the ensuing election.

Campaign Financing and the Fair Political Practices Commission

The Political Reform Act of 1974, an initiative measure known as Proposition 9, established the Fair Political Practices Commission (FPPC) and empowered it to oversee particular relationships between public officeholders and seekers and financial influence. Prime attention was directed toward the disclosure of campaign contributions and expenditures through the use of mandatory reports.

The FPPC administers regulations required under the Political Reform Act and specified campaign laws, and imposes fines and penalties when the regulations have been violated. Public officials must comply with wide-ranging reporting requirements, ranging from gift limits to disclosure of personal financial interests. With thousands of registered lobbyists, candidates, public officials, and "designated employees," the commission must monitor volumes of financial and campaign information.

The aim is to make obligatory public disclosure of the sources and expenditures made in support of the candidate and to inhibit any improper election practices; the means is a vast network of information continuously being funneled into the commission where it is reviewed and made available to the public.

---

[37] *Elections Code,* Sections 8141, 8142.

The Secretary of State is also responsible for receiving reports from lobbyists and their employers regarding expenditures, such as lunch or a football ticket, resulting from their association with state officeholders. Statements of economic interest are annually filed by public officials, their staffs, and anyone in governmental employ whose position might allow some proximity to the decisionmaking process of state and local officials.[38]

State voters passed a campaign finance reform initiative in November 1996. Proposition 208 placed new limitations on lobbyist contributions and candidate fundraising, but was ruled unconstitutional by a federal judge on January 6, 1998.[39]

The Electoral College and Choosing the President

The United States employs a presidential election procedure known as the Electoral College. This body consists of 538 persons,[40] appointed by various methods in each state. These individual electors, grouped by state, meet in their respective state capitols after the general election to vote for a presidential and vice presidential candidate. A candidate for the presidency must receive the majority of electoral votes (270) to become President of the United States. Currently, most states follow a "winner takes all" process whereby the winner of the state's popular vote is entitled to receive all the state's electoral votes (e.g., the popular vote winner in California receives 54 electoral votes).

The number of electors each state is entitled to is determined by the number of representatives the state has in the U.S. Congress. Since California has 52 members in the House of Representatives and two U.S. Senators, the state has 54 electoral votes. No state may have less than three electoral votes because each state is entitled to at least one Member of Congress and two U.S. Senators. (Each state has its own system of appointing presidential electors; California's process is outlined at the end of this section).

This process of choosing the chief executive has existed since the adoption of the U.S. Constitution in 1787. Although the Electoral College has usually served as a "ceremonial" function in the 20th century, this somewhat convoluted system has actually impacted elections in the past.

History of the Electoral College

A brief description of how the electoral college came into existence and the manner of selecting the President may provide the reader a cursory view of the procedure followed in electing the chief executive.

The Constitutional Convention of 1787, after prolonged debate, finally reached a compromise in the method to be used in selecting the President of the United States. The manner of this selection has not been materially changed since the adoption of the original proposal by the convention.

---

[38] *Government Code*, Sections 86107–86111, 87200 et seq.

[39] *California Prolife Council Political Action Committee v. Scully* (E.D. Cal. 1998).

[40] The total number of electors in the Electoral College is determined by the total number of federal legislators. Although there are 435 Members of Congress and 100 U.S. Senators (for a total of 535 presidential electors) the 23rd Amendment to the U.S. Constitution grants the District of Columbia 3 presidential electors, therefore bringing the total to 538 electors.

It was generally agreed that the President should be elected rather than appointed. The dispute at the convention arose whether the President should be elected by a vote of the people, the Congress, by the state legislatures, or be chosen by electors. The resolution of this problem found its way into Article II of the Federal Constitution which provides that each state shall appoint, in such manner as the Legislature may direct, a number of electors, equal to the whole number of Senators and Representatives to which the state may be entitled in the Congress;[41] but no Senator or Representative, or person holding an office of trust or profit under the United States, shall be appointed an elector. These electors would then meet and vote for "two persons." This ambiguous language resulted in the famous tie vote for the presidency between Thomas Jefferson and Aaron Burr (each received 73 votes), and Jefferson was subsequently elected by the House of Representatives. As a result, the 12th Amendment to the United States Constitution was ratified in 1804. This amendment reads in part as follows:

"The electors shall meet in their respective States and vote by ballot for President and Vice President, one of whom, at least, shall not be an inhabitant of the same State with themselves; *they shall name in their ballots the person voted for as President, and in distinct ballots the person voted for as Vice President,* and they shall make distinct lists of all persons voted for as President, and of all persons voted for as Vice President, and of the number of votes for each, which lists they shall sign and certify, and transmit sealed to the seat of the government of the United States, directed to the President of the Senate;—The President of the Senate shall, in the presence of the Senate and House of Representatives, open all the certificates and the votes shall then be counted;—The person having the greatest number of votes for President, shall be the President, if such number be a majority of the whole number of electors appointed; and if no person have such majority, then from the persons having the highest numbers not exceeding three on the list of those voted for as President, the House of Representatives shall choose immediately, by ballot, the President. But in choosing the President, the votes shall be taken by States, the representation from each State having one vote; a quorum for this purpose shall consist of a member or members from two-thirds of the States, and a majority of all the States shall be necessary to a choice * * * ".

This method of electing the President and Vice President has been highly controversial over the years and more than 100 attempts have been made in Congress to alter or abolish the system. The major complaint is that it is possible for a candidate to receive a greater number of votes than his or her opponent, but fail to win the requisite number of electoral votes. Thus, it is possible for the candidate receiving a lesser number of popular votes to be elected President or Vice President.

For example, in 1876, Samuel J. Tilden received 4,284,757 votes and 184 electoral votes, as opposed to Rutherford B. Hayes, who received 4,033,950 votes but 185 electoral votes. Mr. Hayes was elected President. In 1888,

---

[41] *United States Constitution,* Amendment XXIII. This amendment provides Washington, D.C., with presidential and vice presidential electors equal to what they would be entitled to if they were a state, but in no event shall they have more than the least populous state.

Benjamin Harrison received 5,444,337 votes and 233 electoral votes; Grover Cleveland received 5,540,050 votes, but only 168 electoral votes. Harrison was elected President. This problem can be compounded if the House of Representatives elects the President. In the presidential election of 1824, Andrew Jackson received a plurality of the popular and electoral votes, but in neither case did he receive an absolute majority. At that time there were 24 states represented in the Congress and, therefore, 13 votes were required to elect the President. If the Congressional delegations followed the choice of the electors in their states, Jackson would have received 11 votes; John Quincy Adams, 7; William H. Crawford, 3; and Henry Clay, 3. However, Mr. Adams received 13 votes, and was elected President of the United States. It is evident that several delegations had not followed the wishes of their constituents. Mr. Clay was shortly thereafter appointed the Secretary of State.[42]

Despite all of the objections that have been raised to this system, it is still the method we use to elect our President and Vice President.

California's Electoral College Process

The selection process for presidential electors varies from state to state, and from party to party. In California, the electors are chosen by each political party to form a "slate" of presidential electors. The designation of each party's slate of electors must be filed with the Secretary of State prior to October 1 preceding the election.[43]

Each political party has its own method for selecting its electors. The Democratic Party allows each Democratic Congressional nominee and each U.S. Senatorial nominee to appoint a person as a Democratic elector. If there is no party nominee for a particular district, the State Party designates a presidential elector for that respective district.[44]

The Republican Party appoints its slate of electors in a different manner. Each Republican Party nominee for statewide office (i.e., Governor, Attorney General, etc.) serves as a presidential elector. Also, the most recent Republican nominees for the U.S. Senate, the two Republican state legislative leaders, and other designated Republican Party leaders also serve as electors. The Chair of the Republican Central Committee fills any vacancies.[45]

The Electoral College never meets as a whole body *per se*. However, the electors of individual states do meet in their respective state capitols a few weeks after the popular general election to cast their votes for President and Vice President. The general election determines which party's slate of electors will travel to Sacramento to exercise their lawful duties. The presidential candidate receiving the most popular votes on election day is entitled to all 54 of California's electoral votes. In effect, when citizens cast their votes on election day, they are actually voting for the candidate's slate

[42] *Register of Debates in Congress*, Vol. I, February 9, 1825, pp. 526–527. *See also* Augustus C. Buell, *History of Andrew Jackson*, Vol. II, Charles Scribner's Son, New York, 1904, pp. 172–175.
[43] *Elections Code*, Sections 7100, 7300.
[44] *Elections Code*, Sections 7050, 7100.
[45] *Elections Code*, Sections 7250, 7300.

of presidential electors. Subsequently, on the first Monday after the second Wednesday in December, the winning slate of electors convene at 2 p.m. in the State Capitol to cast votes for President and Vice President. The result of the vote is then transmitted to the President of the U.S. Senate.[46]

In January, the President of the Senate (the Vice President of the United States) presides over a joint session of Congress to tally the sealed electoral college votes of all 50 states and the District of Columbia. The candidates receiving the requisite 270 electoral votes are then announced as the President-elect and Vice President-elect.[47]

As mentioned previously, if no candidate receives a majority of electoral votes, it is the duty of the House of Representatives to elect the President and Vice President. Each state's congressional delegation is entitled to only one vote, and the candidates receiving a majority (26 out of 50 states) become the next President and Vice President.[48]

Recall Elections [49]

The Constitution provides that every elective public officer of the State of California may be removed from office at any time, even immediately upon assuming such office, by the electors entitled to vote for a successor of such incumbent. This procedure is known as the recall.[50]

To recall an incumbent state officer elected at a statewide election (e.g., Governor, Lieutenant Governor, Controller, Treasurer, Secretary of State, Attorney General, Superintendent of Public Instruction, Insurance Commissioner, and Supreme Court Justices) a petition signed by qualified voters equal to at least 12 percent of the entire vote cast at the last election for all candidates for the office in question is required. The petition must be circulated in not less than five counties and must be signed by qualified electors in each of these counties equal in number to not less than 1 percent of the votes cast in each of the counties for that office at the last election.[51]

To recall an incumbent state officer elected in a political subdivision of the state (e.g., Assembly Members, State Senators, justices of the appellate courts, and members of the State Board of Equalization) a petition signed by qualified voters entitled to vote for a successor to the incumbent equal in number to at least 20 percent of the entire vote cast at the last election for all candidates for that office is required.[52]

Prior to initiating a recall petition against a state officer, the proponents of the recall must publish a notice of intention to circulate such petition; serve

---

[46] *Elections Code,* Sections 6900–6909.

[47] *United States Constitution,* Article II, Section 1.

[48] *United States Constitution,* Article II, Section 1.

[49] *Constitution,* Article II, Sections 13–19. These sections provide the basis for the procedure to recall elective state officials. The provisions for the recall of county and city officials differ slightly from the provisions governing the recall of state officials. *See Elections Code,* Division 16, Ch. 1–4.

[50] Members of the Congress of the United States from California are not subject to the recall provisions of Article II. "The courts have on many occasions held that a member of the Congress of the United States is a 'Federal Officer' rather than a 'State Officer.' The conclusion is inescapable that a California Member of the Congress is not an elective public officer of the State of California as those words are used in Article II, Sections 13, 14 and that therefore he is not subject to the recall provisions of the California Constitution." 11 *Op. Att'y Gen.* 14.

[51] *Constitution,* Article II, Section 14(b).

[52] *Id.*

the notice upon the officer sought to be recalled; and, file a copy of the notice and proof of service on the officer to be recalled with the Secretary of State.[53]

The notice of intention must include a statement of the grounds upon which the recall is being sought.[54] This statement, along with a rejoinder filed by the officer against whom the recall is being sought, appears on the petition for the information of the voters. Should the officer fail to answer, a statement to that effect shall appear on the petition.[55]

When the petitions have been circulated they are filed with the county clerk who verifies that the signatories are qualified electors. Upon each submission of petitions or sections thereof, if less than 500 signatures are included, the elections official must count the number of signatures, and forward the results to the Secretary of State. If more than 500 signatures are submitted, the official may verify a random sampling of 3 percent of the signatures, or 500, whichever is less.[56]

When the Secretary of State determines and certifies that the requisite number of signatures have been obtained, the Secretary notifies the Governor, who then calls for an election on the question of recall not less than 60, nor more than 80 days, from the date of certification. The recall may be consolidated with another election in that jurisdiction if the regularly scheduled election occurs within 180 days of the recall certification. Prior to 1994, the State Constitution did not give the Governor the flexibility to consolidate a recall with another election. The increased time frame (180 days, instead of the strict 60 to 80 day window) now gives the Governor the opportunity to consolidate recall elections with other regularly scheduled elections in that jurisdiction, thereby reducing costs and perhaps increasing voter turnout.[57]

Accompanying, or as part of, the sample ballot are copies of the statement of the proponents' reasons desiring the officer's removal and the officer's answer (if any) defending his or her conduct in office.[58]

On the election ballot the following question is posed:

"Shall [name of officer sought to be recalled] be recalled (removed) from the office of [title of office]?"

Following the question are the words "Yes" and "No" on separate lines, with a blank space at the right of each, in which the voter indicates his or her vote for or against recall.[59]

If a majority or exactly half of those voting on the recall of the incumbent state officer vote "No," the incumbent shall continue in office, and be repaid from the State Treasury any amount legally expended as expenses of such

---

[53] *Elections Code*, Sections 11020, 11021, 11022.
[54] *Elections Code*, Section 11020.
[55] *Elections Code*, Section 11041.
[56] *Elections Code*, Sections 11101, 11102.
[57] *Constitution*, Article II, Section 15; *Elections Code*, Sections 11103, 11104. *Constitution*, Article II, Section 15, as amended by Proposition 183, November 8, 1994. It should be noted that if a recall election cannot be consolidated with another election being held within 180 days, then the recall must still be held within the 60 to 80 day time limit prescribed by the *Constitution*.
[58] *Elections Code*, Sections 11320, 11325.
[59] *Elections Code*, Sections 11320, 11322, 11323.

election. No proceedings for another recall election shall be initiated against a successful incumbent within six months after such a recall election.[60]

If the majority voting at a recall election vote "Yes" the incumbent shall be deemed removed from office, upon the qualification of a successor.[61]

Candidates may be nominated for an office to be filled at a recall election in the same manner prescribed for nominating such candidates for that office at a regular election. The nominating petition must be filed with the Secretary of State not less than 68 days preceding the recall election.[62]

The names of any candidates so nominated shall appear on the recall ballot below the question of recall. No vote cast for a candidate is counted unless the voter also voted on the question of recall. The name of the person against whom the recall petition is filed cannot appear on the ballot as a candidate to succeed himself. If the officer is recalled, the candidate who receives the highest number of votes at the election recalling such officer is elected for the remainder of the term of the recalled officer. If the person securing the highest number of votes fails to qualify within 10 days after receiving the certificate of election, the office is deemed vacant and must be filled according to law.[63]

There have been seven state recall elections held in California since 1913 (one in 1913, two in 1914, one in 1994, and three in 1995). In four of these elections, incumbents were successfully recalled.[64] 1995 saw a record three recall elections of state officers; all three recalls targeted Members of the State Assembly.

Similar statutory provisions govern the recall of elected local officers, the major difference being that these local officers are provided a "grace" period after assuming office before recall proceedings may be commenced against them.[65]

Measures on the Ballot

The electoral process in California is not limited to the election of candidates for statewide or local offices, but for the passage of laws as well. The California Constitution has given the people the power to "legislate" on any given subject matter vis-a-vis statewide ballot initiatives. Measures are placed on the ballot in various ways: the Legislature may propose laws, bond measures, or constitutional amendments; or citizens may propose (via the initiative and referendum) their own laws, constitutional amendments, or the

---

[60] *Constitution*, Article II, Section 18; *Elections Code*, Section 11383.

[61] *Constitution*, Article II, Section 15; *Elections Code*, Section 11384.

[62] *Elections Code*, Section 11381.

[63] *Constitution*, Article II, Section 15; *Elections Code*, Sections 11381, 11382, 11385, 11386.

[64] The four state officers that have been recalled in California are as follows: Senator Marshall Black, recalled January 2, 1913; Senator Edwin E. Grant, recalled October 8, 1914; Assembly Member Paul V. Horcher, recalled May 11, 1995; and Assembly Member Doris Allen, recalled November 27, 1995. The three officers who survived recall attempts are as follows: Senator James C. Owens, survived recall held March 31, 1914; Senator David Roberti, survived recall held April 12, 1994; and Assembly Member Mike Machado, survived recall held August 22, 1995.

[65] *Constitution*, Article II, Section 19; *Elections Code*, Sections 11007, 11200–11242. Recall proceedings may not be commenced against officers of a city, county, special district, school district, community college district or a member of the board of education until he or she has been in office for at least 90 days. If a recall election has been held and is determined in favor of the incumbent, no new recall may be commenced for six months. Also, a recall may not be commenced against a local official within the final six months of his or her term.

repeal of laws the Legislature has enacted. In any case, an amendment to or a revision of the Constitution, bond issues, and acts amending or repealing initiative acts (proposed by the Legislature)[66] and initiative and referendum measures (proposed by the people)[67] must be approved by the electorate before they become effective.[68]

Qualified measures are assigned a "Proposition Number," and placed on the ballot in a specific order, as follows: (1) Bond measures in the order in which they qualify; (2) Constitutional amendments in the order in which they qualify; (3) Other legislative measures in the order in which they are approved by the Legislature; (4) Initiative measures in the order in which they qualify; and (5) Referendum measures in the order in which they qualify.[69]

Prior to the election, a ballot pamphlet prepared and published by the Secretary of State is mailed to the address of each registered voter.[70] The pamphlet contains the text of the measures to appear on the ballot, an official summary prepared by the Attorney General, an analysis of each proposition, prepared by the Legislative Analyst; and arguments for and against each measure, written by the proponents and opponents of the measures, a concise summary of the general meaning and effect of "yes" and "no" votes on each measure, and the total number of votes cast "for" and "against" the measure in the Senate and the Assembly if it is a measure passed by the Legislature.[71] Additionally, at each statewide election where state bond measures are on the ballot, the pamphlet must include a statement, prepared by the Legislative Analyst, discussing California's current bonded indebtedness situation.[72]

If any provision or provisions of two or more measures, approved by the electors at the same election, conflict, the provisions of the measure receiving the highest affirmative vote prevails.[73] Any amendment to the Constitution, proposed by the Legislature, and submitted to the people for ratification, takes effect the day after its adoption by a majority vote of the people at the election.[74] Any act, law, or amendment to the Constitution submitted to the people by either initiative or referendum petition and approved by a majority of the votes cast thereon, at any election, shall take effect the day after the election.[75]

---

[66] *Constitution*, Article XVIII, Sections 1–4; Article XVI, Section 1; Article II, Section 10(c).

[67] *Constitution*, Article II, Sections 8, 9.

[68] These measures may be voted upon at the general election, the direct primary election, or at a special election called by the Governor. For further information on ballot propositions, see Initiatives and Referendums, next page.

[69] *Elections Code*, Section 13115. Note, however, that in 1966 the Legislature enacted, and the Governor signed, Chapter 105, *Statutes of 1966*, which provided that notwithstanding these provisions of the *Elections Code*, Assembly Constitutional Amendment No. 13 would appear first, and be numbered 1-a on the ballot for the 1966 general election.

[70] *Elections Code*, Sections 9081, 9082, and 9094.

[71] *Elections Code*, Sections 9084–9087; *Government Code*, Sections 88001–88003; *Statutes of 1993*, Chapter 156.

[72] *Elections Code*, Section 9088.

[73] *Constitution*, Article II, Section 10(b); Article XVIII, Section 4.

[74] *Constitution*, Article XVIII, Section 4.

[75] *Constitution*, Article II, Section 10(a).

To prevent individuals or corporations from achieving unjust power or financial gain from the passage of a ballot measure, no proposed statute or amendment to the Constitution may be placed on the ballot that would name any individual to hold any office or identify or name any private corporation to perform any function or to have any power or duty.[76]

The Initiative and the Referendum

In California the Constitution provides the people with the power to propose statutes and amendments to the Constitution, and to approve or reject statutes or parts of statutes enacted by the Legislature. These powers which the people have reserved to themselves are called the "initiative" and "referendum," respectively.[77]

The Initiative

By use of the initiative, the people have a direct means of enacting laws and adopting amendments to the Constitution, independent of the Legislature and the Governor. This is accomplished by submitting the initiative measure directly to the electors.

Prior to the circulation of an initiative petition, a draft of the proposal must be submitted to the Attorney General, who must prepare a title and a summary of the main purposes and provisions of the proposed measure.[78] In the event the Attorney General is a proponent of a proposed measure, the Legislative Counsel shall perform this function.

The initiative petition must set forth in full the proposed law or amendment to the Constitution. No initiative measure may relate to more than one subject.[79]

Initiative petitions are presented to the Secretary of State after certification that they have been signed by qualified electors equal in number to at least 8 percent (if they are to amend the Constitution) or 5 percent (if it is a statute) of all the votes cast for all candidates for Governor at the last preceding general election at which a Governor was elected.[80] The total number of signatures required for initiative statutes which qualify before the November 1998 gubernatorial election is 433,269. Initiatives amending the Constitution currently require 693,230 signatures.[81]

The Secretary of State must place the measure on the ballot at the next succeeding general election which is held at least 131 days after the qualification of the measure, or on the ballot at any statewide special election which is held prior to the general election.[82]

---

[76] *Constitution,* Article II, Section 12. In 1947 an initiative amendment to the Constitution was adopted naming Mrs. Myrtle Williams to serve as the Director of the Department of Social Welfare and Assemblyman Gordon R. Hahn to serve in the event she declined to act; and if Mr. Hahn declined to act, Assemblyman John W. Evans was to act as director. Article XXV, Section 4, *Constitution of 1947,* repealed November 8, 1949.

[77] *Constitution,* Article II, Sections 8(a), 9(a); Article XVIII, Section 3.

[78] *Constitution,* Article II, Section 10(d); *Elections Code,* Sections 9001–9003, 9050, 9051.

[79] *Constitution,* Article II, Section 8(b), 8(d).

[80] *Constitution,* Article II, Section 8(b).

[81] *California Ballot Initiatives,* revised 1995 booklet, p. 4. Secretary of State, Sacramento.

[82] *Constitution,* Article II, Section 8(c).

Initiative measures adopted by the people are not subject to the Governor's veto, nor can they be amended or repealed except by a vote of the electors, unless otherwise provided in the initiative measure. The Legislature may enact a proposal to amend or repeal an initiative act. However, the amendment or repeal will not become effective until submitted to and approved by the electors.[83]

The Referendum

The second power reserved to the people is known as the referendum. The referendum provides a means whereby the people can approve or reject laws or sections of laws passed by the Legislature and signed by the Governor from going into effect.

Prior to the circulation of any referendum petition for signature, a draft of the proposition must be submitted to the Attorney General, who prepares a title and a summary of the measure.[84] The referendum measure may be placed on the ballot by presenting the Secretary of State with a petition certified to have been signed by electors equal in number to 5 percent of the total number of votes cast for all candidates for Governor at the last preceding gubernatorial election.[85] Currently, 433,269 signatures are required to qualify a referendum measure for the statewide ballot. The petition must be presented within 90 days after the enactment of the statute in question.[86]

The referendum may ask that any statute or section or part of any statute passed by the Legislature be submitted to the electors for their approval or rejection. The Secretary of State shall then submit to the electors, for their approval or rejection, such act, or such statute, section or part of such statute, at the next succeeding general election occurring at least 31 days after the referendum has qualified or at any special election which may be called by the Governor for the purpose of voting on the measure.[87]

Any act that is the subject of a referendum on the ballot is automatically considered inactive until the referendum is decided at the polls. If a referendum petition is filed against a portion of a section or statute, the remainder of the act is not affected by the referendum petition or election.[88] A majority vote of the electors is required to approve a referendum measure.[89] If the referendum is approved, the statute in question (or section thereof) is nullified the day after the election, unless the measure provides otherwise. If the referendum fails, the statute that was in question goes into effect in accordance with the law.

---

[83] *Constitution,* Article II, Section 10(c).
[84] *Constitution,* Article II, Section 10(d).
[85] *Constitution,* Article II, Section 9(b).
[86] *Id.*
[87] *Constitution,* Article II, Section 9.
[88] *Constitution,* Article II, Section 10(a).
[89] *Id.*

However, not all acts of the legislature are subject to referendum. Statutes containing urgency clauses, appropriations for the usual current expenses of the state, tax levies, or those calling for special elections are not subject to the referendum power.[90] The fact that these measures go into immediate effect logically exempts them from this process. This exception does not necessarily place a great hindrance on the referendum, since most bills passed by the Legislature and signed into law do not contain such urgency provisions, and therefore do not take immediate effect.

Referendum statutes approved by the people under the referendum provisions may be amended or repealed by the Legislature subsequent to their adoption.[91]

---

[90] *Constitution*, Article II, Section 9(a).
[91] *Constitution*, Article II, Section 10(c).

Governor Pete Wilson signs a bill into law in 1992.
Accompanying the Governor are former Assembly Speaker Willie L. Brown, Jr. (r.)
and former Assembly Republican Leader James L. Brulte (l.).

Chapter IV

The Executive Department

The Governor

The supreme executive power of the State of California is vested in the Governor, whose duty it is to see that the law is faithfully executed.[1] The Governor is elected by the people for up to two terms of four years, [2] and receives an annual salary of $165,000.[3]

No person is eligible for the office of Governor who is not 18 years of age, and who has not been a citizen of the United States and a resident of this state for five years immediately preceding his election.[4]

The present Governor of California is former U.S. Senator and Mayor of San Diego, the Honorable Pete Wilson. Governor Wilson is the 36th person to serve as Chief Executive of the State.

The Governor is Commander in Chief of the militia of this state.[5] He is the sole official organ of communication between the government of this state and the federal government and the other states of the United States.[6] He must supervise the official conduct of all executive and ministerial officers, and he must see that all offices are filled and their duties performed.[7]

The Governor may appoint and fix the salaries of such assistants and other personnel as he deems necessary for the proper conduct of his office. The salaries of these staff assistants may not exceed the salaries paid to certain statutorily appointed state officers.[8] The Governor normally appoints a member of his staff to serve as his legislative secretary whose primary function is to maintain liaison between the executive office and the Legislature.

In the event of a vacancy occurring in the office of Lieutenant Governor, Secretary of State, Attorney General, Treasurer, Controller, Superintendent of Public Instruction, or on the State Board of Equalization, the Governor nominates a person to fill the vacancy subject to confirmation by the majority of the Senate and a majority of the Assembly. A successful nominee would hold office for the balance of the unexpired term.[9]

---

[1] *Constitution,* Article V, Section 1.

[2] *Constitution,* Article V, Section 2. "In case any two or more persons have an equal and highest number of votes for either Governor or Lieutenant Governor, the Legislature shall, by a joint vote of both houses, choose one of the persons to fill the office." *Elections Code,* Section 20503.

[3] *Constitution,* Article V, Section 12. *Government Code,* Section 12000. This section set the Governor's salary at $85,000 as of January 1987. On June 5, 1990, the voters adopted Proposition 112, which added Article III, Section 8 to the Constitution, creating the California Citizens Compensation Commission. The commission has the authority to review and increase the salary levels of the Governor, Lt. Governor, Atty. General, Controller, Treasurer, Sec. of State, Sup. of Public Instruction, Insurance Commissioner, Board of Equalization Members and Members of the State Legislature, and has set the Governor's salary at its current level. *See,* "California Citizens Compensation Commission Salary and Benefit Resolution, March 26, 1998." Salaries take effect Dec. 1, 1998.

[4] *Constitution,* Article V, Section 2. This section requires that the Governor be an elector. An elector is described as a person of the age of 18 years. *United States Constitution,* Amendment XXVI; *Constitution,* Article II, Section 2. The President of the United States must be a natural born citizen, 35 years of age and a resident of the United States for 14 years. *United States Constitution,* Article II, Section 1(5).

[5] *Constitution,* Article V, Section 7.

[6] *Government Code,* Section 12012.

[7] *Government Code,* Sections 12010, 12011.

[8] *Government Code,* Sections 11550, 11552, and 12001.

[9] *Government Code,* Section 1775.

When any office becomes vacant and no method is provided by law for filling such vacancy, the Governor may, by appointment, fill the vacancy until a successor qualifies.[10]

The Governor's appointment power also extends over two significant areas of state government. First, the Governor has authority to fill vacancies in the judiciary (municipal, superior, appeals and Supreme courts) and to fill newly created judgeships.[11] Second, the Governor has power to appoint a large number of positions throughout the executive department, subject to confirmation by the State Senate.[12]

The Governor may offer rewards, not exceeding $50,000, for information leading to the arrest and conviction for certain crimes.[13]

When a fugitive from justice under the laws of another state is found in this state and a written demand for his or her extradition has been received, it is the duty of the Governor to have him or her arrested and delivered up to the executive officer of the demanding state.[14]

The Governor is required to report to the Legislature each reprieve, pardon and commutation granted, stating the pertinent facts in each case and his reasons for granting it. The Governor may not, however, grant a pardon or a commutation in a case of impeachment or to a person who was twice convicted of a felony unless a majority of the Supreme Court (four justices) concurs.[15]

The Governor must communicate with the Legislature, during each calendar year, regarding the condition of the state and may make recommendations.[16] The Governor must also submit an itemized budget to the Legislature within the first 10 days of each year.[17] He may, on extraordinary occasions, convene the Legislature by proclamation, stating the purposes for which he has convened it; and, when so convened, the Legislature has no power to legislate on any subject other than those specified in the proclamation.[18] The call for a special session of the Legislature may be expanded by the Governor adding additional items after the Legislature has convened and prior to adjournment.[19]

The Governor may veto any bill passed by the Legislature and return it with his objections to the house of origin. He may also reduce or eliminate one or more items of appropriation while approving other portions of the bill.[20]

---

[10] *Constitution*, Article V, Section 5.

[11] *Constitution*, Article VI, Section 16; *Government Code*, Section 71180.

[12] See Chapter II, *supra*, page 20.

[13] For a listing of the crimes for which the Governor may offer this reward, *see Penal Code*, Section 1547.

[14] *Penal Code*, Sections 1548.1, 1548.2; *United States Constitution*, Article IV, Section 2; 18 U.S.C.A. 3182.

[15] *Constitution*, Article V, Section 8; *Penal Code*, Section 4800. A pardon is usually understood to exempt an individual from his or her punishment for the crime of which he or she has been convicted, and additionally to remove any disqualification or disability that necessarily occurs as a result of the conviction. However, under the habitual criminal statute in California it has been held (*People v. Biggs*, 9 Cal. 2d 508) that it does not relieve the offender of the prior conviction within the meaning of that statute which prescribes increased punishment for habitual criminals or those previously convicted of a crime. *See also* 8 *Op. Att'y Gen.* 87.

[16] *Constitution*, Article V, Section 3. This is commonly referred to as the Governor's "state of the State message".

[17] *Constitution*, Article IV, Section 12(a); *Government Code*, Section 13337.

[18] *Constitution*, Article IV, Section 3(b). *See also, Martin v. Riley* (1942), 20 Cal. 2d 28 and *Legislative Counsel Opinion No. 2105, Journal of the Assembly, 1960 Second Extraordinary Session*, p. 13.

[19] 4 *Op. Att'y. Gen.* 53. "* * * while some doubt may exist as to the authority of the Governor, the applicable decisions in other jurisdictions and the practice in this State are such that the courts would hold that the Governor may supplement or amend his call to the Legislature after the session has been convened and prior to adjournment."

[20] *Constitution*, Article IV, Section 10(e). The power of item veto is not given to the President of the United States, who must approve or veto the bill in its entirety. *United States Constitution*, Article I, Section 7.

Prior to 1972, when legislative sessions were of an indeterminate duration, the Governor had the power to adjourn the Legislature if the two houses disagreed as to the time of adjournment.[21]

The Governor's Legislative Role

While the trichotomy of the separation of powers among the executive, legislative and judicial branches is quite convenient and useful, it can, like many other academic divisions, be misleading.

The Governor operates, out of necessity, as a "legislator" to accomplish and put into execution the policies of his administration. He initiates and influences legislation. He submits his views on the problems confronting the state and details policy proposals before the Legislature.

The exercise of his veto must be viewed as a quasi-legislative power. The Governor's Budget is replete with policy as well as fiscal implications. In addition, the Governor may call the Legislature into extraordinary session to consider specific issues identified, defined and limited by him.

Through the combination of these and other powers, and with the assistance of his staff, the Governor has considerable impact upon and involvement with the legislative process.

The Governor's Cabinet

In addition to his immediate staff, the Governor utilizes a cabinet, composed of the secretaries of the ten major state agencies (State and Consumer Services; Business, Transportation and Housing; Environmental Protection; Child Development and Education; Food and Agriculture; Health and Welfare; Resources; Trade and Commerce; Veterans Affairs; and the Youth and Adult Correctional Agency), plus the Director of Finance, the Director of Industrial Relations, and the Director of Information Technology.

This cadre serves as the Governor's chief policy advisory body and, in their individual capacities, implement and coordinate the Governor's policies throughout the state. Most agencies employ legislative liaisons who work directly with the Legislature on issues falling under the purview of their particular agency.

The cabinet supplies the Governor with a comprehensive view and current résumé of state operations and serves as a source for long-range planning.

Succession to Office of Governor

The Constitution provides that in the event of a vacancy in the office of Governor, the Lieutenant Governor shall succeed to that office. Upon succeeding to the office of Governor, the former Lieutenant Governor could then nominate a successor to the Lieutenant Governorship. He also serves as *acting* Governor during the impeachment, absence from the state, or other temporary disability of the Governor.[22]

---

[21] Acting Governor Hugh M. Burns did utilize this power to bring the 1968 Regular Session of the Legislature to a close. *See Journal of the Assembly, 1968 Session,* p. 7256 and 7311. See also *Journal of the Senate, 1968 Session,* p. 4907 and 4931. The regular sessions of the Legislature are now adjourned by operation of law. *See Constitution,* Article IV, Section 3(a).

[22] *Constitution,* Article V, Section 10.

In the event both the offices of Governor and Lieutenant Governor become vacant, the President pro Tempore of the Senate would then succeed to the office of Governor; if there is no President pro Tempore of the Senate, then the Speaker of the Assembly would become Governor; if there is no Speaker of the Assembly, then the Secretary of State; if there is no Secretary of State, then the Attorney General; if there is no Attorney General, then the Treasurer; or if none of them, then the Controller. If none of the above officers were available because of a war or an enemy-caused disaster, a person designated by law would become Governor.[23] The authority to raise the question concerning a vacancy in the office of Governor, or the existence of a temporary disability, is vested in a Commission on the Governorship. This commission is composed of the President pro Tempore of the Senate, the Speaker of the Assembly, President of the University of California, Chancellor of the State Colleges, and the Director of Finance. If such a question is raised, the Supreme Court of the State of California is vested with exclusive jurisdiction over the matter.[24]

In case of impeachment of the Governor or officer acting as Governor, his absence from the state, or his other temporary disability to discharge the powers and duties of office, then the powers and duties of the office of Governor devolve upon the same officer as in the case of vacancy in the office of Governor, but only until the disability shall cease.[25]

Two of California's Governors have died in office, and five have resigned. Thus, seven Lieutenant Governors have succeeded to the office of Governor since 1849.[26] No officer other than the Lieutenant Governor has ever succeeded to the Governorship.

The Lieutenant Governor

The Lieutenant Governor is elected at the same time and places and in the same manner as the Governor. Also similar to the Governor are his qualifications, term of office, and limit to two terms.[27] In case of a vacancy in the office of Governor he shall become Governor. In the event of impeachment, absence from the state or temporary disability of the Governor, he shall serve as acting Governor.[28] The salary of the Lieutenant Governor is $123,750 per annum.[29]

The Constitution provides that the Lieutenant Governor shall be President of the Senate, but that he shall have only a casting vote.[30] The purpose of a casting vote is to break a tie. As a tie vote, in effect, defeats a proposition, the

---

[23] *Constitution*, Article V, Section 10; Article IV, Section 21; *Government Code*, Sections 12058, 12061. There are similar statutory provisions governing the succession to the office of Governor-elect and Lieutenant Governor-elect in the event of their death or disability or other failure to take office. *See Government Code*, Sections 12058.5, 12059.

[24] *Constitution*, Article V, Section 10; *Government Code*, Sections 12070–12076. *See also, In re Petition of Commission on Governorship* (1979), 26 Cal. 3d 110.

[25] *Constitution*, Article V, Section 10; *Government Code*, Section 12058.

[26] Lieutenant Governors who have succeeded to the office of Governor are: John McDougal, 1851, on resignation of Governor Peter H. Burnett; John G. Downey, 1860, on resignation of Governor Milton S. Latham; Romualdo Pacheco, 1875, on resignation of Governor Newton Booth; Robert W. Waterman, 1887, on death of Governor Washington Bartlett; Wm. D. Stephens, 1917, on resignation of Governor Hiram W. Johnson; Frank F. Merriam, 1934, on death of Governor James Rolph, Jr.; and Goodwin J. Knight, 1953, on resignation of Governor Earl Warren.

[27] *Constitution*, Article V, Sections 9, 11.

[28] *Constitution*, Article V, Section 10.

[29] *Government Code*, Section 11552.5. *See also Constitution*, Article III, Section 8 and footnote 3, *supra*, p. 41.

[30] *Constitution*, Article V, Section 9.

casting vote may be used only if it will provide the necessary majority required. For example, a bill in the California Senate requires 21 votes for passage and if the vote is 20 to 20, the Lieutenant Governor has a casting vote, but he does not have a casting vote if the vote is 19 to 19, because even if he would cast an "Aye" vote, there would only be 20 affirmative votes on the bill.

Until 1915, the duties of the Lieutenant Governor were to preside over the Senate and, under certain conditions, to act in place of the Governor. Since 1915, however, additional duties have been imposed upon him as a member of various boards and commissions. He is ex officio one of the Regents of the University of California; [31] Chairman of the Commission for Economic Development; [32] Vice Chairman of the Commission for the Californias; [33] and, a member of the State Lands Commission; [34] California Emergency Council; [35] the Reciprocity Commission; [36] World Trade Commission; [37] and, a Trustee of the California State University.[38]

The present Lieutenant Governor is former State Controller, the Honorable Gray Davis.

Other State Officers

The Secretary of State, Attorney General, Treasurer, Controller, and Superintendent of Public Instruction, are elected at the same time and places, and in the same manner as the Governor and Lieutenant Governor, to hold office for a maximum of two four-year terms.[39] The four elected members of the Board of Equalization are elected at the same time as the Governor to four-year terms and are also subject to a two-term limit.[40] Finally, there is the Insurance Commissioner who is elected to no more than two four-year terms, also at the same time and place, and in the same manner as the Governor.[41]

The Secretary of State

The Government Code provides that the Secretary of State shall keep a correct record of the official acts of the Legislative and Executive Departments of the government and perform such other duties as may be assigned by law.[42] The present Secretary of State is former Assembly Member, the Honorable Bill Jones. The Secretary's salary is $123,750 per annum.[43]

---

[31] *Constitution*, Article IX, Section 9.
[32] *Government Code*, Section 14999.1.
[33] *Government Code*, Section 8704.
[34] *Public Resources Code*, Section 6101.
[35] *Government Code*, Section 8575.
[36] *Vehicle Code*, Section 2600.
[37] *Government Code*, Section 15364.2.
[38] *Education Code*, Section 66602.
[39] *Constitution*, Article V, Section 11; *Constitution*, Article IX, Section 2.
[40] *Constitution*, Article XIII, Section 17.
[41] *Insurance Code*, Section 12900, as amended by *Statutes of 1993*, Chapter 1227.
[42] *Government Code*, Section 12159.
[43] *Government Code*, Section 11552.5. *See also Constitution*, Article III, Section 8 and footnote 3, *supra*, p. 41.

In case of vacancies in the offices of Governor and Lieutenant Governor, the Secretary of State becomes the third officer next in line of succession to the office of Governor.[44]

The Secretary of State is charged with the custody of the enrolled copy of the Constitution, all acts and resolutions passed by the Legislature, the Journals of each house, the Great Seal, and all books, records, deeds, parchments, maps, and papers, kept or deposited in the office pursuant to law.[45]

"Public documents must remain at the place designated by law, and can only be removed where authorized by law. The place for deposit of the enrolled copy of the Constitution and the original laws is the office of the Secretary of State and no authority is granted expressly or by implication to exhibit them elsewhere." [46]

The Secretary of State is the custodian of the public archives and must maintain and properly equip safe and secure vaults for the preservation of the documents placed in his charge.[47] Any item that is required by law to be delivered to or filed with the Secretary shall be placed in the archives. [48] The Secretary, on his own initiative, may also place any item that he deems to be of historical value in the archives.[49] In addition, the Department of General Services may direct the Secretary to store items from state agencies. These materials may be returned to the agency, with the Department of General Services' approval, should the Secretary deem them to be without historical value.[50]

The Secretary of State is the chief elections officer of the state and has the responsibility for administering the provisions of the Elections Code.[51] Foremost among these duties is preparing and ordering the printing of the ballot pamphlet. This pamphlet contains a complete copy of the text of all the measures submitted to the voters; a summary of the measure prepared by the Attorney General; an analysis of the measure prepared by the Legislative Analyst; arguments in support of the measure and rebuttals thereto; and, the total vote on the measure in the Senate and the Assembly if the proposition was passed by the Legislature.[52] Pamphlet text is available online via the Secretary of State's internet website (http://www.ss.ca.gov).

A total of approximately 14 million election pamphlets were printed and distributed for the 1996 general election. Of this total, approximately 13.8 million pamphlets were printed in English, 129,000 in Spanish, 60,000 in Chinese, 26,000 in Vietnamese, 12,000 in Japanese, and 11,000 in Tagalog.

---

[44] *Government Code*, Section 12058. The Secretary of State succeeds after the President pro Tempore of the Senate and the Speaker of the Assembly.
[45] *Government Code*, Section 12160.
[46] 12 *Op. Att'y Gen.* 147. *See also*, 52 *Op. Att'y Gen.* 83.
[47] *Government Code*, Section 12222.
[48] *Government Code*, Section 12223.
[49] *Government Code*, Section 12224.
[50] *Government Code*, Sections 12224, 12225.
[51] *Government Code*, Section 12172.5.
[52] *Elections Code*, Sections 3569–3572; *Government Code*, Sections 88000–88003.

The Secretary must compile the election returns and issue certificates of election to successful candidates; [53] compile the returns and certify the results of initiative and referendum elections; [54] certify acts delayed by referendum and prepare and file a statement of the vote.[55]

He shall record all official acts of the Legislature; [56] conveyances made to the state; [57] all articles of incorporation filed in his office; [58] and the receipt of bonds for all officers required by law to be filed with the Secretary.[59] He compiles, publishes and distributes a roster of state and local public officials of California [60] and a directory of registered lobbyists.[61]

The Secretary's office also serves as a repository for the various registration forms, financial statements and expenditure reports which are required to be filed in accordance with the provisions of the *Political Reform Act of 1974.*[62] These documents which are submitted by candidates, elected officials, campaign organizations, political organizations and by lobbyists and their employers are available and open to public inspection in the Secretary's office.[63]

He must affix the Great Seal, with his attestation, to commissions, pardons and other public documents which require the Governor's signature.[64]

The Attorney General

The Attorney General is the chief law enforcement officer of the state and is elected at the same time and places as the Governor for a maximum of two four-year terms.[65] He receives a salary of $140,250 per year.[66]

In case of vacancies in the offices of Governor and Lieutenant Governor, the Attorney General becomes the fourth officer next in line of succession to the office of Governor.[67]

To be eligible for the office of Attorney General it is necessary to have been admitted to practice before the California Supreme Court for a period of at least five years immediately preceding election or appointment. While holding office, the Attorney General is prohibited from engaging in the private practice of law and is required to devote his entire time to the service of the state.[68]

Former U.S. Congressman, the Honorable Dan Lungren is the present Attorney General. It is his duty to see that the laws of the state are uniformly and adequately enforced in every county. He has direct supervision over

---

[53] *Elections Code,* Sections 6056, 17121, 17123, 25050. The candidates include those for statewide office, Assembly, Senate, Congress, Board of Equalization, and the Supreme, appellate, and superior courts.
[54] *Government Code,* Sections 12165; *Elections Code,* Section 17121.
[55] *Government Code,* Sections 12165, 12166.
[56] *Government Code,* Section 12159.
[57] *Government Code,* Section 12164.
[58] *Corporations Code,* Section 169.
[59] *Government Code,* Section 12163.
[60] *Government Code,* Sections 12240, 12241.
[61] *Government Code,* Section 86109.
[62] *Government Code,* Section 81000, et seq.
[63] *Government Code,* Section 81008.
[64] *Government Code,* Section 12162.
[65] *Constitution,* Article V, Section 11.
[66] *Government Code,* Section 11551.5. *See also Constitution,* Article III, Section 8 and footnote 3, *supra,* p. 41.
[67] *Constitution,* Article V, Section 10; *Government Code,* Section 12058. The Attorney General succeeds after the Secretary of State.
[68] *Government Code,* Sections 12503, 12504.

every district attorney, sheriff, and such other law enforcement officers as may be designated by law, in all matters pertaining to the duties of their respective offices.[69]

Whenever, in the opinion of the Attorney General, any law of the state is not being adequately enforced in any county, it is his duty to prosecute such violations of law over which the superior court has jurisdiction, and in such cases he has the powers of the district attorney.

When required by the public interest, or directed by the Governor, he assists any district attorney in the discharge of his duties.[70]

The Attorney General is the head of the Department of Justice, and, as such, he is the attorney in charge of all legal matters in which the state is interested, except the business of the Regents of the University of California or such other boards or officers as are authorized to employ their own attorneys. He is required to attend the Supreme Court and prosecute or defend all causes to which the state, any state officer, or county (unless the county's interest is adverse to the state) is a party.[71]

He may make such investigations as are necessary to determine whether or not there has been compliance with the provisions of the Education Code relative to the issuance of degrees or diplomas by private educational institutions and corporations.[72]

The law provides that, prior to circulation of any initiative or referendum petition for signatures, a draft of the petition must be submitted to the Attorney General with a written request that he prepare a title and summary of the chief purpose and points of the proposed measure.[73]

He must institute investigations for the discovery of all real and personal property to which the state may be entitled by escheat and is designated by statute to represent Native Americans in California before the U.S. Indian Claims Commission.[74]

It is also the duty of the Attorney General to give his opinion on questions of law, in writing, to the Legislature, to the Governor, the Secretary of State, Controller, Treasurer, State Lands Commission, Superintendent of Public Instruction, any state agency prohibited by law from employing legal counsel other than the Attorney General, and any district attorney, when required by their respective offices.[75] He serves as legal adviser to all the state departments, as well as other important state boards and commissions.[76]

In the absence of the Chief Clerk and the inability of the senior members-elect present to agree upon one of their number to preside on the opening day of a legislative session, the Attorney General or one of his deputies shall call the Assembly to order.[77]

---

[69] *Government Code*, Sections 12550, 12560.

[70] *Constitution*, Article V, Section 13.

[71] *Government Code*, Sections 12510–12512.

[72] *Education Code*, Section 94339. (Currently has sunset date of 6/30/96)

[73] *Constitution*, Article II, Section 10(d); *Elections Code*, Section 3502.

[74] *Government Code*, Sections 12523 and 12540. "In American Law 'escheat' signifies a reversion of property to the State in consequence of a want of any individual competent to inherit. The State is deemed to occupy the place and hold the rights of the feudal lord." —*Black's Law Dictionary*, Third Edition.

[75] *Government Code*, Section 12519. These opinions, while not controlling as a matter of law, have been accorded great deference by the courts.

[76] *Government Code*, Section 11157; and, e.g., *Business and Professions Code*, Sections 2020, 2317, 3027, 4804.

[77] *Government Code*, Section 9023.

The State Treasurer

The State Treasurer is elected at the same time and places and in the same manner as the Governor for a maximum of two four-year terms[78] and receives a salary of $132,000 per annum.[79]

The present treasurer is former Board of Equalization Member, the Honorable Matt Fong, the 30th person to serve in this office.

In case of vacancies in the offices of Governor and Lieutenant Governor, the State Treasurer becomes the fifth officer next in line of succession to the office of Governor.[80]

The Treasurer serves as the state's banker. It is his duty to receive and keep in the vaults of the State Treasury or on deposit in banks, all moneys belonging to the state not required to be received and kept by some other person, and he must receive and keep in the vaults of the State Treasury or on deposit with any Federal Reserve bank, or with certain designated banks or trust companies, bonds and other securities or investments belonging to the state.[81] The Treasurer must pay warrants drawn by the Controller and keep an account of all money received and disbursed.[82] A daily report must be filed with the Controller, indicating the amounts disbursed during the preceding day and the funds out of which they were paid.[83]

The State Treasurer is the Chairperson of the Pooled Money Investment Board which is charged with investing idle state moneys.[84] Earnings for the board's program for the fiscal year ending June 30, 1996 totaled $1.519 billion, representing an overall earning rate of 5.71%. He is the chairperson or a member of the California Housing Finance Agency,[85] the California Pollution Control Finance Authority,[86] the Chairperson of the California Educational Facilities Authority [87] and a variety of finance committees which approve the sale of bonds.

The State Treasurer is responsible for selling all state bonds. During the 1995–96 fiscal year, the Treasurer's office sold bonds totaling $3.3 billion. The various types of bonds sold during this time period and their subtotals were general obligation bonds (over $620 million); lease/purchase debt bonds ($635 million); and revenue anticipation (short-term) notes ($2 billion).

At the request of either house of the Legislature, or of any committee thereof, the Treasurer must give written information as to the condition of the Treasury, or upon any subject relating to the duties of the office.[88]

The State Treasurer's accountability for cash in securities as of June 30, 1996 was in excess of $45 billion.

---

[78] *Constitution*, Article V, Section 11.
[79] *Government Code*, Section 11552.5. See also *Constitution*, Article III, Section 8 and footnote 3, *supra*, p. 41.
[80] *Constitution*, Article V, Section 10; *Government Code*, Section 12058. The Treasurer succeeds after the Attorney General.
[81] *Government Code*, Section 12320.
[82] *Government Code*, Sections 12324, 12326.
[83] *Government Code*, Section 12328.
[84] *Government Code*, Sections 16480.1, 16480.2.
[85] *Health and Safety Code*, Section 50901.
[86] *Health and Safety Code*, Section 44515.
[87] *Education Code*, Section 94120.
[88] *Government Code*, Section 12330.

On or before the 15th day of September in each even-numbered year, the Treasurer must report to the Governor the exact balance in the Treasury to the credit of the state, and a summary of the receipts and payments of the Treasury during the two preceding fiscal years.[89]

The State Controller

The State Controller is the chief fiscal officer of the state and is elected at the same time and places and in the same manner as the Governor, for a maximum of two four-year terms.[90] She has a wide variety of duties which have been established both by the Constitution and by statute. Her salary is $132,000 per annum.[91]

In case of vacancies in the offices of Governor and Lieutenant Governor, the State Controller becomes the sixth officer next in line of succession to the office of Governor.[92]

No money can be drawn from the Treasury unless it is against an appropriation made by law, and upon warrants duly drawn by the Controller.[93]

Upon request, the Controller is required to provide the Legislature, or either house thereof, with written information relative to the fiscal affairs of the state or the duties of her office.[94]

Among other duties provided by law, the Controller must superintend the fiscal affairs of the state and suggest plans for the improvement and management of public revenues; [95] keep all accounts in which the state is interested, and keep a separate account of each specific appropriation, showing at all times the balance of the appropriation.[96]

The Controller supervises the state's fiscal concerns and audits all claims against it.[97] She directs the collections of all moneys due the state, and if necessary, she is authorized to go to court to recover the property or money owed.[98]

Claims for refunds under the Vehicle Fuel License Tax Law must be presented to and paid by her.[99] She has general supervision over the general procedure for tax sales, tax deeds, and redemptions and to this end may make any rules and regulations she deems advisable.[100]

In addition to the duties of her office, the State Controller is an ex officio member of the State Board of Equalization, [101] and serves on the Franchise Tax Board,[102] the State Lands Commission,[103] the State Board of Control,[104]

---

[89] *Government Code*, Section 12329.
[90] *Constitution*, Article V, Section 11.
[91] *Government Code*, Section 11552.5. *See also Constitution*, Article III, Section 8 and footnote 3, *supra*, p. 41.
[92] *Constitution*, Article V, Section 10; *Government Code*, Section 12058. The Controller succeeds after the Treasurer.
[93] *Government Code*, Section 12440.
[94] *Government Code*, Section 12462.
[95] *Government Code*, Section 12411.
[96] *Government Code*, Section 12412.
[97] *Government Code*, Section 12410.
[98] *Government Code*, Section 12418.
[99] *Revenue and Taxation Code*, Sections 8101–8103.
[100] *Revenue and Taxation Code*, Section 158.
[101] *Constitution*, Article XIII, Section 17.
[102] *Government Code*, Section 15700.
[103] *Public Resources Code*, Section 6101.
[104] *Government Code*, Section 13901.

the Pooled Money Investment Board,[105] the State School Building Finance Committee,[106] the California Water Resources Development Finance Committee,[107] and other important state boards and committees.

The present Controller is the Honorable Kathleen Connell, the 28th person to serve in this office.

The Superintendent of Public Instruction

The Superintendent of Public Instruction is a nonpartisan officer, elected to four-year terms at the same time and place as the Governor, and is subject to a similar limit of two terms.[108] The annual salary for this statewide officer is $140,250.[109]

Currently, the position is held by former Member of the Assembly, the Honorable Delaine Eastin.

The Superintendent is ex officio Director of Education [110] and a member of the Board of Regents of the University of California.[111] She is Secretary and Executive Officer of the State Board of Education,[112] and, under its direction, she executes the policies which have been decided upon by the board, and directs the work of all appointees and employees of the board.[113]

She must superintend the schools of this state and prepare, have printed, and furnish to teachers and officers charged with the administration of laws relating to public schools, such blank forms and books as may be necessary in the discharge of their duties. She shall cause to have bound all valuable school reports, journals, and documents in her office, or received by her.[114]

The California Schools for the Deaf and for the Blind are also under her supervision and administration.[115] She also administers three diagnostic schools for neurologically handicapped children.[116] She must prescribe rules for their government, appoint the superintendents and other officers and employees, fix the compensation of teachers, and contract with the University of California, or with other public or private hospitals or schools of medicine, for the establishment and maintenance of diagnostic service and treatment centers for neurologically handicapped children.[117] She may also authorize the schools to establish and maintain teacher training courses to prepare teachers to instruct neurologically handicapped children in special classes in the public school system; and she must prescribe the standards for admission to these courses and for the contents of the courses.[118]

---

[105] *Government Code*, Section 16480.1.
[106] *Education Code*, Section 15909.
[107] *Water Code*, Section 12933.
[108] *Constitution*, Article IX, Section 2.
[109] *Education Code*, Section 33101; *Government Code*, Section 11552.5. *See also Constitution*, Article III, Section 8 and footnote 3, *supra*, p. 41.
[110] *Education Code*, Section 33303.
[111] *Constitution*, Article IX, Section 9.
[112] *Education Code*, Section 33004.
[113] *Education Code*, Section 33111.
[114] *Education Code*, Section 33112. *See also* Sections 33113–33124.
[115] *Education Code*, Sections 59002, 59102.
[116] *Education Code*, Sections 59200–59204.5.
[117] *Education Code*, Section 59203.
[118] *Education Code*, Section 59211.

Not later than the 25th day of July of each year, she prepares an estimate of the amount of state school money that will be apportioned to each county or city and county for the current school year.[119]

The Board of Equalization

The Board of Equalization was created by the State Constitution of 1879. The board consists of five voting members: four members elected for four-year terms at gubernatorial elections and the State Controller, who serves ex officio. The state is divided into four Board of Equalization districts with the voters of each district electing one member to no more than two terms.[120] A member of the board must be an inhabitant of the district for which he is chosen for the one year preceding his election or appointment.[121] Each member of the board receives $123,750 per annum.[122]

The present Board members are the Honorable Johan Klehs (First District); the Honorable Dean Andal (Second District); the Honorable Ernest Dronenburg Jr. (Third District); the Honorable John Chiang, acting Member (Fourth District); and the Honorable Kathleen Connell (State Controller).

The board has a wide variety of duties established by the Constitution and by statute. The California Constitution directs the board to ensure equity and uniformity relative to the assessment of all properties assessed by the 58 county assessors,[123] annually assess pipelines, flumes, canals, ditches, and aqueducts lying within two or more counties and property, except franchises, owned or used by regulated railway, telegraph, or telephone companies, car companies operating on railways in the state, and companies transmitting or selling gas or electricity;[124] assess taxes on insurance companies;[125] and assess and collect the excise taxes on the manufacture, importation and sale of alcoholic beverages.[126]

The board performs quasi-judicial, quasi-legislative, and administrative functions.

In its quasi-judicial role, the board serves as the appellate body in hearing and adjudicating appeals on final actions of the Franchise Tax Board under the state's Bank and Corporation Tax, Personal Income Tax, and the Senior Citizens Property Tax Assistance Laws.

In its quasi-legislative capacity, the board adopts rules and regulations and issues directives for the guidance of taxpayers, county assessors, and county assessment appeals boards.

In its administrative role, the board determines the values of companies assessed by the state for local property taxation and is the sole administrative agency for the following taxes: sales and use,[127] Bradley-Burns uniform local

---

[119] *Education Code*, Section 33118.

[120] *Constitution*, Article XIII, Section 17. The districts are reapportioned by the Legislature after each decennial census. *Constitution*, Article XXI, Section 1; *Elections Code*, Sections 30040 et seq.

[121] *Government Code*, Section 15601.

[122] *Government Code*, Section 11552. *See also Constitution*, Article III, Section 8 and footnote 3, *supra*, p. 41.

[123] *Constitution*, Article XIII, Section 18.

[124] *Constitution*, Article XIII, Section 19.

[125] *Constitution*, Article XIII, Section 28(h).

[126] *Constitution*, Article XX, Section 22.

[127] *Revenue and Taxation Code*, Sections 6001–7176.

sales and use,[128] district transactions and use,[129] use fuel,[130] private railroad cars,[131] cigarettes and tobacco products,[132] alcoholic beverages,[133] timber yield,[134] energy resources surcharge,[135] 911 emergency telephone users surcharge,[136] and hazardous substances.[137]

The board assists in the administration of the motor vehicle fuel license tax (gasoline and aircraft fuel),[138] and the insurance tax.[139]

The Insurance Commissioner

The California Insurance Code establishes the office of Insurance Commissioner who is elected in the same place and manner as the Governor and serves a maximum of two four-year terms.[140] The Insurance Commissioner receives an annual salary of $132,000.[141]

The Insurance Commissioner determines the sufficiency of securities to be given by those engaged in the insurance business [142] and no person may transact any class of insurance business without first being certified by the commissioner.[143] Beyond these provisions, the Commissioner is given broad powers to directly supervise the Department of Insurance [144] and to perform all duties under law in regulating the business of insurance in the state.[145]

The Commissioner's powers to certify compliance with applicable state law extend to approval of insurance forms,[146] approval of an insurance company's corporate name (as a prerequisite to the Secretary of State's filing of the articles of incorporation),[147] and, upon request of the State Treasurer, certification of qualifications of surety insurers for state demand or timed deposits or state investments in federal bonds.[148] The Commissioner also is designated to receive and administer a $100,000 deposit from each title insurance company doing business in the state as a guarantee fund for the security and protection of title insurance policyholders.[149]

The current Insurance Commissioner is the Honorable Charles Quackenbush, former Assembly Member.

---

[128] *Revenue and Taxation Code*, Sections 7200–7212.
[129] *Revenue and Taxation Code*, Sections 7251–7273.
[130] *Revenue and Taxation Code*, Sections 8601–9355.
[131] *Revenue and Taxation Code*, Sections 11201–11702.
[132] *Revenue and Taxation Code*, Sections 30001–30479.
[133] *Revenue and Taxation Code*, Sections 32001–32556.
[134] *Revenue and Taxation Code*, Sections 38101–38908.
[135] *Revenue and Taxation Code*, Sections 40001–40191.
[136] *Revenue and Taxation Code*, Sections 41001–41150.
[137] *Revenue and Taxation Code*, Sections 43001–43651.
[138] *Revenue and Taxation Code*, Sections 7301–8404.
[139] *Revenue and Taxation Code*, Sections 12001–12170.
[140] *Insurance Code*, Section 12900. A term limit for the Insurance Commissioner was added by *Statutes of 1993*, Chapter 1227.
[141] *Government Code*, Section 11552. *See also*, footnote 3, *supra*, p. 41.
[142] *Insurance Code*, Section 12920.
[143] *Insurance Code*, Section 700.
[144] *Insurance Code*, Section 12906.
[145] *Insurance Code*, Section 12921.
[146] See, e.g., *Finance Code*, Sections 22505, 24458.1, 24505.
[147] *Corporations Code*, Section 201.5.
[148] *Government Code*, Sections 16527, 16616.
[149] *Insurance Code*, Section 12350.

HENRY A. LYONS,
Associate Justice,
Dec. 26, 1849 to Jan. 1, 1852.

S. C. HASTINGS,
Chief Justice,
Dec. 22, 1849 to Dec. 31, 1851.

NATHANIEL BENNETT,
Associate Justice,
Dec. 26, 1849 to Oct. 3, 1851.

The first Supreme Court of California, 1849.

The 1997 California Supreme Court.
From Left to Right: Associate Justices Ming W. Chin, Marvin R. Baxter, Stanley Mosk,
Chief Justice Ronald M. George, Associate Justices Joyce L. Kennard,
Kathryn M. Werdegar, and Janice R. Brown.

Chapter V

The Judicial Department

The Courts

The Constitution provides that the judicial power of the State of California is vested in its Supreme, appellate, superior, municipal, and justice courts, and that all these courts are courts of record. A court of record is one wherein its proceedings are taken down and kept as a permanent official record.[1]

The function of the courts of the State of California is to provide for the orderly settlement of disputes between parties in controversy, whether they be individuals or private or governmental entities; they determine the guilt or innocence of those who are accused of violating the laws; they are the instrumentality for settling the estates of deceased persons; they serve to preserve the distinction between the branches of government, as provided by the Constitution, and they protect the rights of individuals from encroachment by state or local government.

With 174 courts and 1,554 authorized judgeships (7 Supreme Court; 88 courts of appeal; 789 superior court; and 670 municipal court), the California judicial system is one of the largest in the world.[2]

The Supreme Court

The highest court in the state is the Supreme Court. The Supreme Court is the final interpreter of the laws of the State of California (both statutory and common law) and its decisions may only be reversed by the U.S. Supreme Court in instances where it is determined that California law conflicts with the U.S. Constitution. The decisions of this court are binding on all the other courts of California.

The court is composed of a Chief Justice and six Associate Justices.[3] The Justices of the Supreme Court are elected at statewide elections and serve for a term of 12 years.[4] No person is eligible for appointment or election as a Justice of the Supreme Court unless he or she shall have been a member of the California State Bar or has served as a judge of a court of record of the State of California for 10 years immediately preceding his or her appointment or election.[5]

The work of the Supreme Court is primarily confined to hearing and deciding appeals brought from the lower courts. In some special instances, such as habeas corpus petitions, proceedings may be initiated in the Supreme Court. In these instances, the court is said to be exercising original jurisdiction. In all cases where a judgment of death has been pronounced, an

---

[1] *Constitution*, Article VI, Section 1.
[2] Figures supplied by the Administrative Office of Courts. Of the 1,554 authorized judgeships, 1,523 were filled as of December 1996.
[3] *Constitution*, Article VI, Section 2.
[4] *Constitution*, Article VI, Section 16(a).
[5] *Constitution*, Article VI, Section 15.

appeal is automatically taken directly to the Supreme Court.[6] Overall, approximately 6,817 matters were filed in the Supreme Court during fiscal year 1993–94.

In addition to court cases, the Supreme Court is charged with reviewing reports of the Commission on Judicial Performance and the State Bar of California regarding investigations of misconduct and recommendations for discipline of judges and attorneys, respectively. The Supreme Court also hears appeals from decisions of the Public Utilities Commission.

Regular sessions of the court are held in San Francisco, Los Angeles and Sacramento. All the decisions of the court are published in the official case reporting volumes, California Official Reports,[7] as well as in a privately published series, West's California Reporter.

Courts of Appeal

The justices of the courts of appeal are elected by the voters within their respective districts for terms of 12 years.[8] The qualifications for appellate court justices are the same as those for Justices of the Supreme Court.[9]

It is interesting to note that neither the Constitution of 1849 nor the Constitution of 1879 made provisions for courts of appeal. At that time appeals from trial courts were made directly to the Supreme Court. By 1904, however, the volume of appellate litigation had increased to such an extent that a constitutional amendment was adopted authorizing the creation of three district courts of appeal to relieve the workload of the Supreme Court.

The 1904 constitutional amendments gave the legislature the power to divide the state into more than the three original appellate districts, each district containing a court of appeal with one or more divisions.[10] Since 1904, the legislature has exercised this power three times: in 1929 to create the Fourth District Court of Appeal;[11] in 1961 to create the Fifth District Court of Appeal;[12] and in 1981 to create the Sixth District Court of Appeal.[13] Should any new district or division be created, the Governor must appoint not less than three judges to service that district or division.[14]

At the present time, the Court of Appeal for the First District, consists of four divisions of four judges each and one division of three judges; in the Second District there are five divisions of four judges each and two divisions of three judges each; the Third District has one division of ten judges; the Fourth District consists of one division of eight judges and two divisions of five judges; the Fifth District has one division of nine judges; and the Sixth District is made up of one division with six judges.[15]

---

[6] *Constitution*, Article VI, Section 11.
[7] *Constitution*, Article VI, Section 14; *Government Code*, Section 68902; *California Rules of Court*, Rule 976.
[8] *Constitution*, Article VI, Section 16(a).
[9] *Constitution*, Article VI, Section 15.
[10] *Constitution*, Article VI, Section 3.
[11] *Statutes of 1929*, Chapter 691; *Government Code*, Section 69104.
[12] *Statutes of 1961*, Chapter 845; *Government Code*, Section 69105.
[13] *Statutes of 1981*, Chapter 959; *Government Code*, Section 69106.
[14] *Constitution*, Article VI, Section 3; *Government Code*, Section 69107.
[15] *Government Code*, Sections 69101–69106.

Counties embraced in the various district courts of appeal are as follows:

First Appellate District: Alameda, Contra Costa, Del Norte, Humboldt, Lake, Marin, Mendocino, Napa, San Francisco, San Mateo, Solano, and Sonoma.

Second Appellate District: Los Angeles, San Luis Obispo, Santa Barbara, and Ventura.

Third Appellate District: Alpine, Amador, Butte, Calaveras, Colusa, El Dorado, Glenn, Lassen, Modoc, Mono, Nevada, Placer, Plumas, Sacramento, San Joaquin, Shasta, Sierra, Siskiyou, Sutter, Tehama, Trinity, Yolo, and Yuba.

Fourth Appellate District: Imperial, Inyo, Orange, Riverside, San Bernardino, and San Diego.

Fifth Appellate District: Fresno, Kern, Kings, Madera, Mariposa, Merced, Stanislaus, Tulare, and Tuolumne.

Sixth Appellate District: Monterey, San Benito, Santa Clara, and Santa Cruz.[16]

The courts of appeal exercise appellate jurisdiction over the cases in which a superior court exercises original jurisdiction, except when the judgment of death has been pronounced.[17] Additionally, the courts of appeal, like the Supreme Court, exercise original jurisdiction in certain types of proceedings.[18] In the 1993–94 fiscal year, more than 24,000 appeals and original proceedings were filed in the Courts of Appeals.

Superior Courts

The Constitution provides that there shall be a superior court in each county of the state. The Legislature designates the number of judges for the superior court in each county, and may provide that one or more of these judges serve on more than one superior court.[19]

The number of superior court judges is usually dependent upon the population of the county involved. For example, Los Angeles County is entitled to over 200 judges of the superior court, while Lake County has but two.[20]

Judges of the superior court are elected by the voters of their respective counties for terms of six years.[21]

The qualifications for the office of superior court judge are the same as those for the Justices of the Supreme Court.[22]

The superior courts are commonly referred to as trial courts. They are the courts of general jurisdiction in our judicial system.

The superior court has original jurisdiction in all cases except those given to the other trial courts by statute. They are empowered to hear appeals from

---

[16] *Government Code,* Section 69100.
[17] *Constitution,* Article VI, Section 11.
[18] *Constitution,* Article VI, Section 10.
[19] *Constitution,* Article VI, Section 4; *Government Code,* Sections 69580–69615.
[20] *Government Code,* Sections 69586, 69585.7.
[21] *Constitution,* Article VI, Section 16(c).
[22] *Constitution,* Article VI, Section 15.

the decisions of the municipal and justice courts.[23] During the 1993–94 fiscal year, more than 1 million cases of all types were filed in the superior courts of California.

Municipal Courts

An amendment to Article VI of the Constitution, adopted in 1950, and subsequent legislation have given California a simple and uniform inferior court system. At one time, the lower court system included municipal courts and justice courts. A judicial district created within a county would contain a municipal court if its population exceeded 40,000; it would contain a justice court if there were less than 40,000 residents.

Proposition 191, adopted at the November 8, 1994 general election, eliminated the prior distinction between municipal and justice courts, by providing that all justice courts would henceforth be municipal courts.[24] Each county of the state is now divided into municipal court districts by that county's board of supervisors. In each district containing more than 40,000 residents, a municipal court with at least one judge is mandated.[25]

Judges of municipal courts are elected by the voters of their respective districts for terms of six years.[26]

To be eligible for election or appointment as a municipal court judge, the candidate must be eligible to vote in the judicial district in which he or she is appointed or seeking election for 54 days prior to his or her appointment or election.[27]

Municipal court judges must be admitted to practice before the Supreme Court of California for at least five years immediately preceding their appointment or election.[28]

Municipal courts exercise original jurisdiction in most civil cases where the amount in controversy is $25,000 or less, and in criminal misdemeanor and infraction cases (such as typical traffic violations).[29] Small claims courts are also a part of municipal courts.[30] In the 1993–94 fiscal year (when there were still municipal and justice courts), approximately 8 million nonparking cases were filed in these lower courts.

Terms of Office and Salaries of Judges

The following table shows the order in which different courts of this state are set up, and the terms of office and salaries of the judges:[31]

Court	Term (years)	Annual salary
Supreme Court............................	12	Chief Justice—$137,463
		Associate Justices—$131,085
Courts of appeal	12	Appellate Ct. Justices—$122,893
Superior court	6	Superior Ct. Judges—$107,390
Municipal court	6	Municipal Ct. Judges—$98,070

[23] Constitution, Article VI, Sections 10, 11.
[24] Constitution, Article VI, Section 5. If the county population is less than 40,000, the county must have at least one municipal court district.
[25] Proposition 191 passed by a 61.05% to 38.95% margin. Statement of Vote for November 1994 General Election, Secretary of State's Office.
[26] Government Code, Section 71145.
[27] Government Code, Section 71140.
[28] Constitution, Article VI, Section 15.
[29] Code of Civil Procedure, Section 86; Penal Code, Section 1462.
[30] Code of Civil Procedure, Section 116.220.
[31] Constitution, Article VI, Section 16(a), (c); Government Code, Sections 68200–68203, 71145. Salaries listed are effective through 12/97.

Judges—Disqualification and Suspension

The Constitution provides several methods for the removal of justices and judges in California. Procedures for their removal by impeachment and recall election have been discussed previously.

A judge is automatically disqualified from acting as a judge, without loss of salary, if there is pending: (1) an indictment or information charging him or her in the United States with a crime punishable as a felony under either California or federal law; or (2) a petition to the Supreme Court to review a determination by the Commission on Judicial Performance to remove or retire a judge.[32] A judge may be disqualified from acting as a judge by the Commission on Judicial Performance if the commission gives notice of formal proceedings charging the judge with judicial midconduct or disability.[33]

A suspension of a judge, without salary, is mandatory when in the United States he or she pleads guilty or no contest or is found guilty of a crime punishable as a felony under California or federal law, or of any other crime that involves moral turpitude.[34] If the conviction is reversed, suspension terminates and the judge is paid the salary for the period of suspension. If, however, the conviction becomes final, the judge is removed from office by the Commission on Judicial Performance. Any judge so removed is thereafter ineligible for judicial office and, unless otherwise ordered by the Supreme Court, is suspended from the practice of law in the state.

Judicial Administration

To assist the courts in their task, the Constitution provides for certain agencies to deal with judicial administration: the Judicial Council, whose principal function is to improve and expedite the administration of justice; the Commission on Judicial Appointments, which confirms all gubernatorial appointees to the Supreme Court and the courts of appeal; the Commission on Judicial Performance, which treats the censure, removal or retirement of judges for misconduct or disability.

The Judicial Council

The Constitution provides for a Judicial Council, consisting of 21 members: the Chief Justice (Chairperson), one additional Justice of the Supreme Court, three justices of the courts of appeal, five superior court judges, five municipal court judges (each judge member is appointed by the chairperson for a two-year term), four members of the State Bar (appointed by the State Bar Board of Governors), and a Member of each house of the Legislature (the Assembly Member appointed by the Speaker, the Senate Member appointed by the Rules Committee of the Senate).[35]

An executive officer, the Administrative Director of Courts, is appointed by the council and serves at its pleasure. He or she performs such functions

---

[32] *Constitution,* Article VI, Section 18(a).
[33] *Constitution,* Article VI, Section 18(b).
[34] *Constitution,* Article VI, Section 18(c).
[35] *Constitution,* Article VI, Section 6; *Assembly Rule* 26(b)(10); *Senate Rule* 13.

as delegated by the council or by its chairperson.[36] The salary and qualifications of the director are identical to those of a judge of a court of appeal.[37]

Members of the Judicial Council receive no compensation for their services, but are allowed their necessary expenses for travel, board and lodging incurred in the performance of their duties as members.[38]

The primary duty of the council is to improve the administration of justice. It is required to make a survey of judicial business and make recommendations to the courts and report annually to the Governor and the Legislature.

The council also adopts court rules of administration, practice, and procedure, which are not inconsistent with statutes, in the interests of uniformity and for expediting the business of the courts.

The Constitution requires the Chief Justice of the California Supreme Court to expedite the judicial business of the state, and to equalize the work of the various judges. To do this, it is necessary to bring the judges where the work is, that is, to assign judges from an area with a light caseload to those areas that have heavy calendars. To accommodate the Chief Justice in this task, the Constitution authorizes him or her to assign a judge from one court to another. Such assignment by the Chief Justice is mandatory, and the assigned judge may not refuse to accept, except that a judge of a higher court may only be assigned to a lower court with his or her consent. To assist the Chief Justice in making these assignments, judges are required to report to him or her concerning the condition of the business in their courts.[39]

In addition, the council has performed such other duties as requested by the Legislature. For example, a study of the procedure of administrative agencies and the judicial review of their decisions was provided to the Legislature, and as a result the Administrative Procedure Act, requiring uniform rules in issuing, suspending and revoking professional and business licenses was passed in 1945.[40] In response to another legislative request, the council recommended a plan for reorganization of the lower court system in California, which culminated in the reduction in the number and kinds of lower courts. Pursuant to statutory authority, the council also conducts orientation seminars for judges, the primary purpose being to keep them informed of new developments in the law and to promote uniformity in judicial procedure.[41]

Commission on Judicial Performance

In November 1960, the people approved a constitutional amendment authorizing the establishment of a Commission on Judicial Performance with power to recommend to the Supreme Court the removal, censure, or retirement of any judge. In November 1994, Proposition 190 was adopted by

---

[36] *Constitution*, Article VI, Section 6.
[37] *Government Code*, Section 68500.5.
[38] *Government Code*, Section 68510.
[39] *Constitution*, Article VI, Section 6; *Government Code*, Section 68548.
[40] *Statutes of 1945*, Chapter 111; *see Government Code*, Section 11370 *et seq.*
[41] *Government Code*, Section 68551. For the statutory duties and provisions governing the Judicial Council, *see Government Code*, Sections 68500–68554.

the voters which expanded the powers of the Commission and made a variety of procedural changes with regard to investigations into conduct of judges.[42]

In its current configuration, the Commission is authorized to conduct proceedings against any state judge if its investigation reveals willful misconduct in office, persistent failure or inability to perform the duties of the office, habitual intemperance, conduct prejudicial to the administration of justice, or a disability of a permanent character that seriously interferes with the performance of the judge's duties.[43] Based on these findings the Commission is then authorized to remove, retire or censure a judge (unlike the Commission prior to Proposition 190, which could only recommend such action to the California Supreme Court).

In order to conduct any investigation into the fitness of state court judges, the Commission may hire such employees as it deems necessary and is authorized to require state and local agencies to cooperate and provide information in connection with its investigation. It may administer oaths and issue subpoenas requiring the attendance of witnesses or the production of records relevant to its proceedings.[44]

All proceedings of the Commission are required to be public after formal charges are filed and the Commission is empowered to write its own rules.[45] Any judge removed, retired, or censured by the Commission may appeal that decision to the Supreme Court, which has the discretion to review the case, provided it does so within 120 days.

The Commission on Judicial Performance consists of eleven members: three judges appointed by the Supreme Court; four members appointed by the Governor (two attorneys and two non-attorney public members); and two public members each appointed by the Speaker of the Assembly and the Senate Rules Committee.[46] All appointees serve for a term of four years.

Commission on Judicial Appointments

The Commission on Judicial Appointments has the obligation of confirming or rejecting nominees or appointees of the Governor to vacancies on the courts of appeal or the Supreme Court of the State of California. The commission holds a veto power over the prospective nominees and appointees to these courts since no appointment is effective until the commission confirms the appointment.[47]

The commission consists of the Chief Justice of the Supreme Court, the Attorney General, and the presiding justice of the district court affected (or if there be more than one presiding justice in the district, the one who has presided the longest). In the event the vacancy occurs on the Supreme Court, the senior presiding justice of the courts of appeal shall serve in addition to the Chief Justice and the Attorney General.[48]

---

[42] *Constitution*, Article VI, Sections 8 and 18. The original name of the commission was the Commission on Judicial Qualifications. The name was changed to its current designation by constitutional amendment in 1976.

[43] *Constitution*, Article VI, Section 18.

[44] *Government Code*, Sections 68702, 68725, 68750.

[45] *Constitution*, Article VI, Section 18(j).

[46] *Constitution*, Article VI, Section 8.

[47] *Constitution*, Article VI, Section 16(d).

[48] *Constitution*, Article VI, Section 7.

The California State Assembly in Session, April 26, 1927.

Chapter VI

Legislative Sessions

The First Legislature [1]

The Members

The First California Constitutional Legislature, consisting of 16 Senators and 36 Assemblymen, proposed to meet in San Jose on December 15, 1849. The winter, however, had been unusually inclement, with a rainfall of nearly 36 inches for the season. The rains began on the night of October 28th, and by the 15th of December, the roads were so muddy that only six Senators and 14 Members of the Assembly were present for the opening day of session.[2] By the following Monday, December 17th, a quorum had arrived, and the Legislature began its deliberations.

The records of the First Legislature reveal that much difficulty was encountered in securing quorums. The Speaker of the Assembly resigned during his term, as did two Senators and three Assemblymen; the records indicate that one Assemblyman never officially attended the session. Many members were absent most of the time, indicating that there was no great importance placed upon political positions or politics.

The great gold rush of 1849 lured fortune seekers from all over the globe and from all walks of life to the gold fields. The composition of the First Legislature reflects this immigration, as many of the members had recently arrived in California and, so far as is known, not a single member of the first Assembly was a native-born Californian. The first Assembly was comprised of 19 members from northern states, 10 members from southern states, five members whose birthplace is unknown, and two members who were of foreign birth. The first Senate was composed of nine members from northern states, five members from southern states, and but two members who were native Californians.

Another indication of the gold rush influx upon the composition of the First Legislature is the fact that exactly one-half of the Members of the Senate (eight Senators) and one-half of the Members of the Assembly (18 Assemblymen) represented the mining areas of the Sacramento and San Joaquin Districts.

The First Laws

The First Legislature adopted 19 joint resolutions, and of the bills passed at the first session, 146 were approved by the Governor.

Hon. Peter H. Burnett, the newly elected Governor who was inaugurated on December 20, 1849, sent a message to the Legislature raising the question of the advisability of enacting laws before Congress had passed the bill

---

[1] For a more complete discussion of California's First Legislature *see* Bancroft's *History of California, VI;* Cardinal Goodwin, *The Establishment of State Government in California; California's State Capital*—2d Edition—Issued by State Department of Finance, 1956; and *The First Legislature of California* by Senator Herbert C. Jones before the California Historical Society, San Jose, December 10, 1949.

[2] *Journals of the Senate and Assembly,* December 15, 1849, pp. 3, 575.

making California a state.[3] Apparently precedent for the commencement of governmental operations before the admission of a state existed, for the Legislature proceeded with the enactment of the necessary laws.

One of the problems of the First Legislature was the division of California into counties. The Senate Committee on County Boundaries was assigned this task, and recommended that California be divided into 18 counties. Many areas, however, objected to being included in the counties proposed by the committee, and desired to establish counties of their own. The Legislature, on February 18, 1850, passed a bill subdividing California into 27 counties.[4] As set forth in the bill, the counties were:

1. San Diego	10. Marin	19. Yuba
2. Los Angeles	11. Sonoma	20. Butte
3. Santa Barbara	12. Solano	21. Colusi [sic]
4. San Luis Obispo	13. Yolo	22. Shasta
5. Monterey	14. Napa	23. Trinity
6. Branciforte [5]	15. Mendocino	24. Calaveras
7. San Francisco	16. Sacramento	25. San Joaquin
8. Santa Clara	17. El Dorado	26. Tuolumne
9. Contra Costa	18. Sutter	27. Mariposa

Other legislation of historical significance passed by the First Legislature included: an act creating the office of State Translator, whose duty was to translate laws and documents into Spanish;[6] an act setting the annual salaries of the Governor ($10,000), Secretary of State ($7,000), Comptroller ($8,000), Treasurer ($9,000), Attorney General ($7,000), Surveyor General ($7,500), Justices of the Supreme Court ($10,000), State Translator ($8,000), District Attorneys ($2,000), and Governor's Private Secretary ($2,000);[7] an act providing for the incorporation of cities;[8] acts providing for property taxes (levied at the rate of 50 cents on each $100 of taxable property) and poll taxes (levied at the rate of $5 per person on every male inhabitant over 21 and under 50 years of age);[9] an act adopting the English Common Law, so far as it was not inconsistent with the United States Constitution or the Constitution and laws of California, as the rule of decision in California courts;[10] an act providing that the acts of the Legislature would go into immediate effect unless another time was expressly stated in the bill;[11] and an act abolishing all laws then in force in California except those passed by the First Legislature.[12]

The tempers of many of the Members of the First Legislature were roused over the delay in Congress to accept the admission of California. Before adjourning, a committee of three members of each house drew up a terse "address by the people of California to the citizens of the United States on

---

[3] *Message of Governor Peter H. Burnett to the Legislature, Journal of the Senate* for December 21, 1849, pp. 31–32.

[4] *Statutes of 1850*, Chapter 15. Some of the county names proposed in the original Report of the Senate Committee on County Boundaries were changed by the bill. For instance, Oro was changed to Tuolumne, Mount Diablo to Contra Costa, Benicia to Solano, Fremont to Yolo and Redding to Shasta. *See Journals of the Senate and Assembly, 1849–50, Appendices E and F,* and *Journal of the Assembly,* February 12, 1850, p. 839. There are now 58 counties in California.

[5] *Statutes of 1850*, Chapter 61, changed the name of Branciforte County to Santa Cruz County.

[6] *Statutes of 1850*, Chapter 8.

[7] *Statutes of 1850*, Chapter 25.

[8] *Statutes of 1850*, Chapter 30.

[9] *Statutes of 1850*, Chapters 17, 52.

[10] *Statutes of 1850*, Chapter 95.

[11] *Statutes of 1850*, Chapter 7. The current provisions of the California Constitution are just the opposite—no act will go into immediate effect except acts calling elections, providing for tax levies or appropriations for the usual and current expenses of the state, unless the act itself states that it is to go into immediate effect.

[12] *Statutes of 1850*, Chapter 125.

the application of California for admission into the Union." Although this address was refused acceptance by the Assembly, the following quotation therefrom may be of interest:

"Yet, whatever be the fate of our prayer, we will not despair, nor will the continued neglect of Congress shake our attachment to our country or love for our countrymen. . . . we will not attempt any supplication—we need not—we would not. But we have one request which, we beg, will be deliberately and patriotically considered, that is to say, should Congress refuse to admit California as a state into the Union, we pray that their action will cease with the refusal, and that, as heretofore, they will neglect to pass any law for the benefit of California. Upon the happening of this event, we will not further ask the attention of Congress to our interests, and beg that our wishes will be considered as embodied in a simple request contained in three words, 'Let us alone.' " [13]

News of the admission of California into the Union reached San Francisco on October 18, 1850, months after the adjournment of the First Legislature, which adjourned on April 22, 1850, having been in session a little more than four months.

Sessions of the Legislature

Sessions—1849–1946

From 1849 until 1862, the Constitution provided that the Legislature meet annually on the first Monday of January. Terms of office for members were set at one year for Assemblymen and at two years for Senators, with one-half of the membership of the Senate being elected each year.

In 1862, the Constitution was amended to provide for biennial sessions, the Legislature meeting on the first Monday in December following the election of its members. No session was to continue longer than 120 days, and the terms of office for members were extended to two years for Assemblymen, and to four years for Senators. The Senators were again divided so that one-half would be elected each two years.

The Constitution of 1879 continued the biennial sessions, but changed the meeting date to the first Monday after the first day of January in the odd-numbered years, and removed the 120-day limitation on the length of the session.

An amendment to the Constitution, adopted on October 10, 1911, provided that the biennial sessions commence at 12 m., on the first Monday after the first day of January in the odd-numbered years, and continue for a period of not to exceed 30 calendar days; whereupon a recess of both houses for not less than 30 calendar days was required to be taken.

This session was known as a bifurcated session, so-called because there was an interim between the first and second parts of the session. The interim was known as the constitutional recess.

---

[13] *Journal of the Assembly,* April 22, 1850, p. 1283

Upon the reassembling of the Legislature after the recess, no bill could be introduced in either house without the consent of three-fourths of the members thereof, nor could more than two bills be introduced by any one member after such reassembling.

The January session was devoted almost exclusively to the introduction of bills, upon which there was no limit; and few measures, except those of an urgent nature, were passed. When the Legislature reconvened after the constitutional recess, it immediately proceeded to consider the bills which were introduced before the recess.

Sessions—1947–1966 (General and Budget)

On November 5, 1946, the people adopted an amendment to Article IV, Section 2, of the Constitution which again provided for annual sessions, instead of biennial sessions. Annual sessions in the odd-numbered years were to be known as general sessions, and annual sessions in the even-numbered years were to be known as budget sessions.

The 1946 amendment provided that the general sessions, held in the odd-numbered years, be the same as the biennial sessions previously held in the odd-numbered years, that is, they were bifurcated, with a 30-day period for bill introduction, followed by a 30-day recess before reconvening to consider the legislation previously introduced.

There was no limitation on the length of the general session after the constitutional recess until 1949, when the Constitution was amended to restrict the length of general sessions to 120 calendar days, exclusive of the constitutional recess.

At the 1958 general election, the people adopted another amendment to Article IV, Section 2, of the Constitution. This amendment abolished the constitutional recess and permitted a general session of not more than 120 calendar days in duration, not including Saturdays and Sundays. This, in effect, meant that the session could last as long as 166 days, as there are 46 intervening Saturdays and Sundays. It might be interesting to note that every general session held under this provision, though not required to continue for 166 days, never adjourned before the 166th day.[14]

This amendment also provided that at the general session no bill other than the Budget Bill could be heard by any committee or acted upon by the house until 30 calendar days had elapsed following the date the bill was first introduced, unless three-fourths of the members of the house authorized dispensing with this provision.

The 1946 amendment to the Constitution provided that the regular budget sessions should convene at 12 m. on the first Monday in March of the even-numbered years. In 1949, the budget sessions were restricted to a length of 30 calendar days, and to consideration of the Budget Bill for the succeeding fiscal year, revenue acts necessary therefor, the approval or rejection of charters and charter amendments of cities, counties, and cities and counties, and acts necessary to provide for the expenses of the session.

---

[14] See final day's Journal of the Assembly for the sessions of 1959, 1961, 1963, 1965.

On November 6, 1956, subdivision (c) was added to Section 2 of Article IV of the Constitution, changing the meeting date of the budget session to 12 m. on the first Monday in February, and providing that, after the Budget Bill had been introduced at a budget session, a recess of both houses could be taken for a period of not to exceed 30 calendar days. The length of the session, exclusive of such recess, was still restricted to 30 calendar days.

The 1958 Budget Session was the first to operate under the provisions of the 1956 amendment. The Legislature met on February 3, 1958; recessed the next day, February 4, reconvened on March 3, and adjourned *sine die* March 30, 1958. The Legislature was in session for a total of 30 calendar days, the maximum number of days allowed by the Constitution.

Operating under this provision of the Constitution, the Legislature succeeded on only one occasion, in 1960, in passing the Budget Bill during the allotted time. In 1958, 1962, 1964, and 1966, the Legislature was required to adjourn on the completion of the 30-day period provided by the Constitution, having failed to enact the Budget Bill. In each instance, the Governor was required to call a special session to enable the Legislature to enact a Budget Bill.[15]

Sessions 1967–1972 (Annual)

In 1966 the people of the State of California adopted a constitutional amendment revising the legislative article of the Constitution (Article IV) in its entirety. This amendment required the Legislature to meet each year in regular session, convening at 12 m. on the first Monday after January 1. The sessions were of unlimited length, and there was no restriction on the type of bills that could be introduced. In addition, the amendment provided that upon the completion of its work, the Legislature would recess for at least 30 days, then reconvene and reconsider any bills vetoed by the Governor. In effect this amendment abolished the budget session and eliminated the time restriction (120 days exclusive of Saturdays and Sundays), which formerly governed legislative sessions in California.

In 1971 the Legislature met on January 4, the first Monday after January 1, and did not adjourn until 364 days later, on January 3, 1972.

The 1972 Regular Session convened January 3, 1972, and adjourned January 5, 1973, a total of 369 calendar days.[16]

Sessions 1973–Present—(Biennial)

The Legislature currently meets in a two-year session as a result of a constitutional amendment (Proposition 4) adopted in 1972. The Legislature convenes on the first Monday in December of the even-numbered years (e.g., December 2, 1996) and must adjourn by midnight November 30 of the following even-numbered year (e.g., November 30, 1998).[17] The first

---

[15] When the Legislature failed to enact the Budget Bill during the 1958 Budget Session, there was some question as to whether or not the Governor could call the Legislature into special session to consider the budget. However, an opinion of the Legislative Counsel indicated that it would be proper to consider the Budget Bill in a special session if the Legislature failed to enact a budget during the regular budget session. *Opinions of the Legislative Counsel* (No. 2315), *Journal of the Assembly*, 1958, *Regular Budget Session*, March 27, 1958, pp. 454–495.

[16] *Journals of the Assembly and Senate*, 1972 Regular Session.

[17] *Constitution*, Article IV, Section 3.

biennial session (1973–1974) saw the Legislature adjourn on September 1, 1974, well in advance of the constitutional deadline. This practice has been followed in each successive biennium and is likely to continue because another section of the Constitution limits the Legislature to the consideration of Governor's vetoes and urgency statutes, statutes calling elections, appropriations for the usual and current expenses of the state and statutes levying taxes after August 31st of the even-numbered year.[18]

This type of session is similar to the one employed by the United States Congress which also meets in a two-year session.

Extraordinary Sessions

The Constitution provides that the Governor may call the Legislature into special session by proclamation. The proclamation contains certain subjects, and the Legislature's consideration is limited to the subjects specified, but it may provide for the expenses and other matters incidental to the session.[19]

With respect to the question of what measures may be considered under an item of the Governor's Proclamation convening the Legislature in extraordinary session, the California Supreme Court has stated as follows:[20]

". . . The duty of the Legislature in special session to confine itself to the subject matter of the call is of course mandatory. It has no power to legislate on any subject not specified in the proclamation. . . . But when the Governor has submitted a subject to the Legislature, the designation of that subject opens for legislative consideration matters relating to, germane to and having a natural connection with the subject proper. . . . Any matter of restriction or limitation becomes advisory or recommendatory only and not binding on the Legislature. . . ."

While the Governor controls the subject matter of legislation which may be considered during an extraordinary session, what is embraced in the subject as designated by the Governor is to be given a broad interpretation. The Legislature may consider matters germane or relating to or those having a natural connection with the subject contained in the proclamation.[21]

Extraordinary sessions were formerly called to enact legislation to meet unusual conditions which had arisen since the adjournment of the last regular session. The possibility of an extraordinary session was increased during the even-numbered budget session year as the Constitution restricted the Legislature to consideration of the Budget Bill, revenue bills, city and county charters, and acts providing for the expenses of the session. In order to enact legislation on any other subject during the budget year, the Legislature had to be called into extraordinary session. With the adoption of the constitutional amendment in 1966 abolishing the budget session, it was felt that there would

---

[18] *Constitution*, Article IV, Section 10(c). A separate section required the Legislature to convene its first biennial session (i.e., 1973–74 Regular Session) on January 8, 1973. All succeeding sessions, however, are convened in December of the even-numbered year, e.g., December 1994, December 1996, etc.

[19] *Constitution*, Article IV, Section 3(b). Note: In California the Governor must convene both houses of the Legislature; however, the President of the United States may convene either or both houses of Congress. *United States Constitution*, Article II, Section 3.

[20] *Martin v. Riley*, 20 Cal. 2d 28.

[21] *Opinion of Legislative Counsel* (No. 2105), *Journal of the Assembly, 1960 (Second Extraordinary Session)*, March 2, 1960, p. 13; *see also Opinion of Legislative Counsel* at p. 124, and *Opinion of the Attorney General* at p. 125, *Journal of the Assembly, 52d Session (1st Extraordinary Session)*, March 11, 1938.

be a reduction in the number of extraordinary sessions, as the Legislature could act on any type of legislation each year. However, the short experience under this provision indicates that this hope failed to materialize as in 1967, 1968, and 1971 the Governor called the Legislature into extraordinary sessions.

Now that the Legislature meets almost continuously it would seem that the only need for a special session would be to enact legislation which may not be enacted by urgency legislation during the regular session, e.g., change salaries, change the term of or create a new office, etc.[22] In these cases the extraordinary session could be advantageous as the bills become effective the 91st day after the adjournment of the extraordinary session as opposed to January 1 following the enactment of the bill as is the case in the regular session.[23]

The hope that the biennial session would reduce the use of the extraordinary session device has not been realized. The Legislature has met in extraordinary session on 20 occasions since 1973. Of these 20 separate extraordinary sessions, several were convened during a single legislative session (e.g., in the 1995–96 session, four separate special sessions were convened). In fact, since 1973, the only time the Legislature has not met in special session was the 1979–80 session.[24]

The current Joint Rules identify the regular session with the odd-numbered year following the general election followed by a hyphen and the last two digits of the next even-numbered year. For example, the current session of the Legislature convened on December 2, 1996, and will adjourn *sine die* at midnight, November 30, 1998, and is designated the 1997–98 Regular Session. It is likely that the next session of the Legislature, however, will be designated the 1999–2000 Regular Session, in order to accommodate references to the new century. Special sessions are similarly identified, i.e., 1997–98 First Extraordinary Session.[25]

Length of Extraordinary Sessions

Since the First Regular Session of the Legislature in 1849, California's various Governors have called the Legislature into extraordinary session on 78 different occasions—60 of which have been called since 1940. In the first half century of California's legislative history, there were but three special sessions called, but since the beginning of this century, 75 such sessions have been called.

From 1914 to 1918, during World War I, only one extraordinary session of the Legislature was called. In sharp contrast, World War II, with its tremendous problems, both immediate and future, caused the Legislature to be called into six extra sessions between December 8, 1941, when the United States entered the war, and "V-J Day" in 1945.

---

[22] *Constitution*, Article IV, Section 8(d).
[23] *Constitution*, Article IV, Section 8(c).
[24] *See Appendix A, infra*, p. 207.
[25] *Joint Rules 39, 50.*

The first time California's Legislature met in extraordinary session was on April 4, 1881, when Governor George C. Perkins issued a call to the 24th Legislature. The session lasted for 40 calendar days.

The longest special session was the First Extraordinary Session of the 53rd Legislature held in 1940, which met on January 29 and adjourned *sine die* on December 5 of that year, making a total of 312 calendar days. However, this session was at recess three times—from February 25 to May 13; from May 24 to September 21; and from September 22 to December 2, for a total of 266 calendar days—so it was in actual session only 46 calendar days.

The greatest number of extraordinary sessions ever held during one year was in 1940, when the 53rd Legislature met five times in special session. The 55th Legislature was called into special session four times, twice in 1943, and twice in 1944, while the 1995–96 Legislature convened four special sessions. The Legislature was also called into special session three times in 1950, 1962 and 1975.

When two or more sessions run concurrently, as, for instance, a regular session and an extraordinary session or two or more special sessions, each is separate and distinct from the other, requiring its own organization and election of officers.[26]

The five special sessions of 1940, some of which for a time ran concurrently, necessitated a division of the legislative day. During this period, at the time appointed, each of the sessions was called to order, the roll was called, the prayer was offered by the Chaplain, and all organizational matters were performed. At the conclusion of its "Order of Business," the daily session was adjourned, and the next extraordinary session was immediately called to order. This procedure, requiring as it did, five separate publications of the Journal, History, and File (which, in order to properly identify the sessions, were printed in different colors of ink for each session: black, brown, blue, green, and purple) was found to be so expensive and confusing that a policy was adopted under which the Governor, instead of issuing a new call for each new item, could add items to the original call.[27] Despite the ability of the Governor to add subject matters to special session proclamations, numerous concurrent special sessions have still been called at times. To increase publishing efficiency, the Office of State Printing now uses black ink for all sessions, but utilizes different colored paper to differentiate among special sessions (e.g., green paper for Second Extraordinary Session).

The right of the Governor to supplement, augment, or amend his proclamation convening the Legislature in extraordinary session has been discussed at length by both the Attorney General and the Legislative Counsel.[28]

However, the custom of adding to the Governor's agenda after the Legislature has been convened in extraordinary session has been in existence

---

[26] See Chapter VIII, *infra*, p. 83.
[27] For a listing of the regular and extraordinary sessions of the California Legislature, *see Appendix A, infra*, p. 183.
[28] 4 *Op. Att'y Gen.* 58 and *Opinion of Legislative Counsel, Journal of the Assembly, 52d Session (1st Extraordinary Session)*, March 11, 1938, pp. 126–129.

for many years. This practice has never been challenged and has been accepted as part of the legislative process.

At the First Extraordinary Session of 1958, which ran concurrently with the budget session, the Governor originally requested legislation on 28 items. The Governor on several occasions added to this call until the Legislature was requested to enact legislation on 51 different subjects.

At midnight on March 30, 1958, the 30 calendar days allowed by the Constitution for the budget session expired before an agreement between the two houses was reached on the Budget Bill. The Governor immediately called the Legislature into the Second Extraordinary Session for the purpose of considering and acting upon the budget. As previously discussed, this device has been used on numerous occasions to enact a budget when the Legislature failed to adopt one during a regular session.[29]

In 1960, the proclamation convening the First Extraordinary Session contained only one item to be legislated upon. Six subsequent amendments and supplements by the Governor brought the total of subject matter items upon which the Legislature could enact legislation to 40. This session ran concurrently with the budget session. Since then, as many as 68 different subject matters have been included in the Governor's proclamation calling for an extraordinary session (1966 First Extraordinary Session).[30]

Designation of Sessions

From 1849 until 1947, legislative sessions were designated by number, as, for instance, the 1849 session of the Legislature was designated as the First Session and the First Legislature, and the 1945 session was the 56th Session and the 56th Legislature.

Until 1948, the number of regular sessions and the number of Legislatures were the same. This was due to the fact that, when the early day annual sessions were held (1849–1863), the Members of the Assembly were elected for one-year terms and the Senators for two-year terms; and, when the Constitution was amended to provide for biennial sessions, the terms of the Assembly Members and Senators were changed to two and four years, respectively. Thus, there was a new Legislature at each regular session.

From 1947 through 1972, regular sessions were held annually, thus there were two legislative sessions held before the election of the next Legislature. The result, of course, was that the number of sessions began to exceed the number of Legislatures. In 1973, California reverted to the biennial session, restoring the one session to one legislature ratio.

In order to avoid some of the confusion resulting from the various types of sessions used in California, the sessions held from 1849 to 1947 are referred to by the *number* of the session, e.g., 56th Session (1945); those held from 1947 through 1972 are identified by the *year* in which they were held, e.g., 1947 Regular Session; while the present session is designated by the *years* in which it is held, e.g., 1997–98 Regular Session.

---

[29] *Journal of the Assembly,* 1966 Regular Session, p. 272.
[30] *Journal of the Assembly,* 1966 First Extraordinary Session, p. 1445.

War- or Enemy-caused Disaster Sessions

The Constitution provides that in the event of an enemy- or war-caused disaster the Legislature is authorized to convene itself in session. It may also provide for elections to fill vacancies occurring in the office of Governor or any other elective office provided for under the Constitution. Should one-fifth of the members of either house be killed, missing or disabled, the remaining Members of the Legislature are authorized to fill these vacancies. In addition, they may also provide for a temporary seat of government. While in session, the Legislature may act upon any subject that is designed to relieve or alleviate the consequences of the disaster or enact any measures to continue and restore a stable government.[31]

---

[31] *Constitution*, Article IV, Section 21; *Government Code*, Section 9036.

Assembly District Maps — 1992 Reapportionment

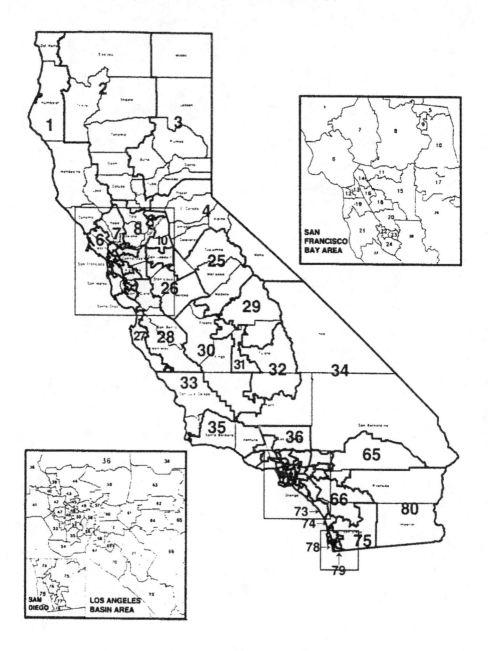

Current Reapportionment Map
1992 Court-Ordered
Assembly Districts

Chapter VII

Legislators' Districts, Qualifications, Terms, and Compensation

United States Senators

The Constitution of the United States provides that "The Senate of the United States shall be composed of two Senators from each State, elected by the people thereof, for six years . . ." [1] and that "No person shall be a Senator who shall not have attained to the age of 30 years, and been nine years a citizen of the United States, and who shall not, when elected, be an inhabitant of that State for which he shall be chosen." [2] The salary received by United States Senators is $136,673 per year.[3]

If a vacancy occurs in the representation of this state in the Senate of the United States, the Governor must issue a writ of election to fill the vacancy. However, the Governor may appoint and commission an elector of this state, who possesses the qualifications for the office, to fill the vacancy until his or her successor is elected and qualifies and is admitted to his or her seat by the United States Senate.[4]

Because the Federal Constitution provides that the two United States Senators from California are to be elected from the state at large, there is no apportionment of these districts by the Legislature.

House of Representatives

The United States Constitution provides that Representatives in Congress shall be apportioned among the several states according to their population.[5] In accordance with the 1990 federal census, California is entitled to 52 Representatives in Congress, more than any other state in the Union.

The California Constitution sets forth guidelines which the State Legislature must follow in the formation of the districts from which these Representatives are to be elected.[6]

The Federal Constitution provides that Representatives in Congress must be at least 25 years of age, they must have been citizens of the United States for seven years, and they must be inhabitants of the state from which they are chosen. Their terms of office are two years,[7] and their salaries are set at $136,673 a year.[8]

---

[1] *United States Constitution*, Amendment XVII.

[2] *United States Constitution*, Article I, Section 3(3). The Attorney General has opined that the language in the *Elections Code*, Section 10720, requiring the appointee to be a California elector enlarges upon the qualifications for the office of United States Senator as contained in the United States Constitution and is therefore invalid. 44 *Op. Att'y Gen.* 30.

[3] Effective January 1, 1998, the President pro Tempore, the Majority Leader, and Minority Leader of the U.S. Senate each receives $151,800 per year. The President of the U.S. Senate (the Vice President of the United States) receives $175,400 per year.

[4] *United States Constitution*, Amendment XVII; *Elections Code*, Section 25001.

[5] *United States Constitution*, Amendment XIV, Section 2.

[6] *Constitution*, Article XXI, Section 1.

[7] *United States Constitution*, Article I, Sections 1, 2.

[8] The Speaker of the House receives $175,400 and the House Majority and Minority Leaders each receives $151,800 per year as of January 1, 1998.

Congressional Term Limits (Declared Unconstitutional)

In May 1995, the U.S. Supreme Court struck-down the term limits on federal legislators recently added to the Arkansas Constitution. The court held that the individual states do not have the authority "to change, add to, or diminish" the age, citizenship, and residency requirements for congressional service as set forth in Article I of the U.S. Constitution.[9] This action by the court also nullified the similar Congressional term limit provisions adopted by California voters only three years earlier.

In November 1992, California voters had passed Proposition 164, which enacted a limitation on the number of terms a U.S. Senator or Representative from California may serve. This represented an expansion of the scope of term limits from Proposition 140, passed two years earlier, which only acted to limit the terms of elected *state government* representatives.

Under the provisions of Proposition 164 a candidate for the office of U.S. Senator or Member of the House of Representatives was denied access to appear on the ballot if he or she had served either (1) 12 or more of the previous 17 years as a U.S. Senator; or (2) six or more of the previous 11 years as a Representative.[10] All other qualifications for these two elected offices were unaffected by this now-defunct provision.

Senate and Assembly Districts

The Legislature of California is composed of a Senate consisting of 40 Senators who are elected for a maximum of two four-year terms and an Assembly of 80 members, each elected for no more than three two-year terms (see page 82).[11] Such a legislature, composed of two houses, is called bicameral, while a legislature with only one house is known as unicameral. California employs the bicameral system as do 48 other states. Nebraska is the only state in the Union with a unicameral legislature.

Reapportionment of Districts

Since 1880, the federal census, taken every 10 years, has been the basis upon which the Assembly, senatorial, and congressional districts have been apportioned.[12]

Prior to the adoption of the 1965 Reapportionment Plan, Senate districts could not be composed of more than three counties, and Assembly districts were based upon population. No county lines could be crossed in the formation of either Senate or Assembly districts, and, in the case of Senate districts, no county, or city and county could be divided, nor could any county, or city and county, contain more than one district.

---

[9] *U.S. Term Limits v. Thornton, 115 S.Ct. 1842 (1995).*

[10] *Elections Code,* Section 8700.

[11] *Constitution,* Article IV, Sections 1, 1.5 and 2(a). *See also* p. 82.

[12] *Constitution,* Article XXI, Sec. 1. Provision was made in the *1849 Constitution* that an enumeration of the inhabitants of this state should be taken, under the direction of the Legislature, in 1852 and 1855, and at the end of every 10 years thereafter. These enumerations, together with the federal census taken in 1850, and every 10 years thereafter, were to serve as the basis of representation for both houses of the Legislature.

The *Constitution of 1879,* Article IV, Section 6, provided that the federal census of 1880 and every 10 years thereafter be the sole basis for representation, and only those persons excluded from citizenship by the naturalization laws were to be omitted when making such readjustment. This section was amended November 2, 1926, to read "the Census taken under the direction of the Congress of the United States in the year 1920, and every 10 years thereafter, shall be the basis of fixing and adjusting the legislative districts."

1965 Reapportionment

In 1965, the California Supreme Court, prompted by a series of United States Supreme Court decisions espousing the "one man, one vote" principle,[13] and particularly a federal district court ruling holding that California's State Senate was unconstitutionally apportioned,[14] assumed jurisdiction and decided that both the Assembly and the Senate had to be reapportioned on the basis of population.[15] The court established certain criteria to govern the new reapportionment, and also presented an alternative plan, should the Legislature fail to reapportion itself. In compliance with this ruling, the Legislature passed Assembly Bill No. 1 in October 1965, in special session, drawing new Assembly and Senate districts.[16]

While greatly affecting the Senate, this measure called for relatively modest changes in the lower house. For instance, San Francisco's five Assembly districts were reduced to four, and a new one, the 35th Assembly District, comprising parts of Orange and San Bernardino Counties, was created.

Following the reapportionment of the Senate and Assembly, the California Supreme Court in its application of the "one-man, one-vote" principle, held that the 1961 apportionment of the congressional districts was repugnant to the provisions of the United States Constitution.[17] Prompted by this decision, the California Legislature in 1967 reapportioned California's congressional districts in accordance with the guidelines set forth by the United States Supreme Court.[18]

1971 Reapportionment

As required by the Constitution, in 1971 the Legislature passed bills providing for the reapportionment of congressional, Senate and Assembly districts, which were presented to the Governor.[19] These bills were subsequently vetoed by the Governor,[20] and as a result of this impasse, the issues were placed before the California Supreme Court.

The court held that the Governor had the authority to veto the reapportionment bills. However, the court, in the case of the congressional plan, was presented with the practical problem of deciding how to provide for the election of the five additional congressional seats to which California was entitled on the basis of the 1970 federal decennial census. In this case, the court held that Assembly Bill No. 16 would serve as the basis for electing California's Congressmen for the 1972 elections, as to hold otherwise would have required an extremely costly statewide election to fill the five additional

---

[13] The court initiated this series of cases with its decision in *Reynolds v. Sims,* 377 U.S. 533 (1964).

[14] *Silver v. Jordan,* 241, F. Supp. 576 (S.D. Cal. 1964), *aff'd,* 381 U.S. 415 (1964).

[15] *Silver v. Brown,* 63 Cal. 2d 270.

[16] Formerly *Elections Code,* Sections 30100, 30201 (repealed 1975). For current Assembly and Senate districts, *see Wilson v. Eu,* 1 Cal. 4th 707, 741 (Appendix: Report and Recommendation of Special Masters on Reapportionment).

[17] *Silver v. Reagan,* 67 Cal. 2d 452.

[18] *Elections Code,* Section 30000 (repealed 1975). For present congressional districts, *see Wilson v. Eu,* 1 Cal. 4th 707, 741 (Appendix: Report and Recommendation of Special Masters on Reapportionment).

[19] 1971 First Extraordinary Session: AB No. 16—congressional reapportionment; SB No. 2—Senate reapportionment; AB No. 12—Assembly reapportionment.

[20] *Journal of the Assembly, 1971 1st Extraordinary Session,* January 3, 1972, pp. 513–519; *Journal of the Senate, 1971 1st Extraordinary Session,* January 3, 1972, pp. 336–337.

seats and because the U.S. Congress had specifically mandated that the Members of Congress be elected from single member districts.[21]

However, in the case of the Assembly and senatorial districts, the court found no compelling reason to disregard the veto of the Governor, and held that unless the Legislature enacted valid legislative reapportionment statutes in time for the 1972 elections (i.e., that the Governor does not veto the bills, and that the veto was not subsequently overridden by the Legislature) that the Members of the California State Legislature would be elected from the existing districts.

In addition, the court retained jurisdiction to draft new reapportionment plans (for congressional, Senate and Assembly districts), governing the elections of 1974 through 1980, if valid legislation was not passed by the Legislature by the end of the 1972 Regular Session.[22]

By the end of the 1972 session, the issue of reapportionment had still not been resolved. In 1973 the court indicated that, while it retained and was exercising jurisdiction, it would entertain an application to dismiss the proceedings if valid congressional and legislative plans were enacted.

Accordingly, the Legislature, pursuing a different tack, presented to the Governor a single bill containing proposed California congressional, senatorial and Assembly districts.[23] Again, however, the Governor vetoed the bill.[24]

The Supreme Court, having anticipated an impasse similar to the one with which it was confronted in 1972, had early in 1973 appointed Special Masters and a staff to prepare reapportionment plans for the various districts involved. The plan, with minor variations, was adopted by the Supreme Court as the basis for the new districts for the 1974 elections.[25]

1981 Reapportionment

In 1981, the legislation was enacted creating new congressional, Assembly and senatorial districts.[26] The plans adopted were not acceptable to most of the Republican members and a referendum drive was launched almost immediately after the bills were signed by the Governor.

On December 15, the Secretary of State announced that the referendum petitions contained the requisite number of signatures (five percent out of all the votes cast for Governor at the last gubernatorial election) to place them on the ballot.

In the meantime, four separate suits had been brought against the chairmen of the California Republican Party and the Republican National Committee attacking the referendum petitions and asking the Supreme Court of

---

[21] 2 U.S.C.A. 2(c).

[22] *Legislature v. Reinecke*, 6 Cal. 3d 595. The court also held that the Reapportionment Commission, as constituted by Article IV, Section 6, of the California Constitution, has no jurisdiction to reapportion the Legislature.

[23] Senate Bill No. 195, *1973–74 Regular Session*.

[24] *Journal of the Senate, 1973–74 Regular Session*, June 27, 1973, pp. 3866–70.

[25] This ultimate "plan" took shape through a series of four Supreme Court decisions: *Legislature v. Reineke*, 6 Cal. 3d 595; *Brown v. Reagan*, 7 Cal. 3d 166; *Legislature v. Reineke*, 9 Cal. 3d 166; and *Legislature v. Reineke*, 10 Cal. 3d 396.

[26] *Elections Code*, Sections 30030–30032 (repealed 1994) and *Statutes of 1981*, Chapter 590 (Congress); *Elections Code*, Sections 30010–30012 (repealed 1994) (Assembly); *Elections Code*, Sections 30020–30023 (repealed 1994) (Senate).

California to use the newly formed districts in the 1982 elections.[27] The Supreme Court consolidated the proceedings and rendered its decision on January 28, 1982.

The court found merit in the petitioners' contention that the referenda contained substantive violations of statutory law, but held that the court's policy of liberally construing the power of referendum should be continued. The court decided that, although the referenda did not strictly comply with the legal requirements,[28] these defects were not sufficient to overcome the court's predilection to preserve the constitutional power of referendum and, therefore held the referendum valid. The Secretary of State was directed to place it on the June 1982 primary ballot.

On the question of which districts were to be used for nominating Assembly, Senate and congressional candidates for the June primary and the members-elect in November; the court was presented with a dilemma. The court found it necessary to weigh one constitutional provision against another, i.e. the peoples' referendum power in the California Constitution[29] versus the "equal protection" clause of the Federal and State Constitutions and the California Constitutional directive that the *Legislature* establish Assembly, Senate and congressional district boundaries.[30]

In reaching its decision, the court rejected the solution of conducting the elections in the *old* Assembly and Senate districts; which a previous court had reached. The court felt that the existing districts were too malapportioned as a result of population shifts occurring in the seventies to serve as the basis for 1982 elections and concluded that the equal protection (one man, one vote) considerations were the more compelling of the competing constitutional imperatives and concluded (four to three) that the 1981 legislation would be the basis for electing Assembly Members, Senators and California's Representatives in Congress in the 1982 primary and general elections.

The referendum was successful, and as a result the 1981 reapportionment plans were rejected and inoperable for elections after 1982.[31] When the 1983–84 Legislature reconvened for the regular session, the Governor issued a proclamation convening the 1983–84 First Extraordinary Session to consider again the questions of reapportioning Assembly, Senate and congressional seats.[32]

The Legislature responded by enacting new reapportionment plans for Assembly, Senate and congressional districts.[33] The bill affecting Assembly and Senate districts contained an urgency clause causing the bill to take effect immediately, thereby forestalling any referendum attempt.

With the referendum alternative denied, the opponents instigated a successful initiative petition. The initiative redrew the district boundaries

---

[27] *Assembly of the State of California v. Deukmejian*, 30 Cal. 3d 638.

[28] *See Elections Code*, Section 9020.

[29] *Constitution*, Article II, Section 10(a).

[30] *United States Constitution*, Amendment XIV; *Constitution*, Article I, Section 7 and Article XXI, Section 1.

[31] *Propositions 10, 11 and 12*, June 8, 1982 direct primary election.

[32] *Journal of the Assembly, 1983–84 First Extraordinary Session*, December 6, 1982, p. 3; and *Journal of the Senate, 1983–84 First Extraordinary Session*, December 6, 1982, p. 2.

[33] *Statutes of 1983–84 First Extraordinary Session*, Chapters 6 and 8.

contained in the latest legislatively approved districts.[34] The Governor subsequently called a special election to present the initiative to the electorate.[35] However, the Legislature and 28 members of California's congressional delegation petitioned and attacked the constitutionality of the initiative in the Supreme Court. The Supreme Court agreed with the petitioners.[36] The court found that, under Article XXI of the California Constitution, redistricting could occur only once during the 10-year period following the decennial census and that the Legislature had accomplished such redistricting, and, therefore, a second redistricting plan, even though proposed by initiative, could not be submitted to the voters. As a result, the California Members of Congress and the Members of the State Legislature were elected from districts created by the legislation passed in the 1983–84 First Extraordinary Session.

1991 Reapportionment

The decennial federal census conducted in 1990 began a familiar series of events on the road to redrawing district lines in California for Assembly, Senate, Board of Equalization and congressional districts.

In the closing months of 1991, the Legislature finalized and passed three different plans to redraw Assembly, Senate and Board of Equalization districts, and to provide for the seven new congressional seats to which California was entitled as a result of population growth.[37] All three of the bills were passed on partisan lines; all three were vetoed by the Governor.[38] Despite there being just seven months until the primary elections scheduled for June 1992, California was once again without a constitutionally valid set of districts.

As in previous years, the issue was brought before the State Supreme Court. On September 25, just two days after the Governor's veto of the three reapportionment bills, the Supreme Court announced its intent to appoint a panel of Special Masters to take on the task of redrawing district lines.[39] In making its decree, the court recalled its similar actions in 1973 and cited as justification its responsibility for ensuring that the protections of the federal Voting Rights Act and principles of equal protection were extended to all Californians.

Though the court noted the similarities between its actions here and the events of 1973, one fact in this case stood in contrast to that previous year. Where the court had given the 1973 Special Masters five months to prepare their report, the 1991 panel would have only two. This compressed time period, the court noted, was necessitated by a key statutory deadline before which the new district information for the June primary had to be in place.[40]

---

[34] The initiative was dubbed the "Sebastiani Plan" after its main proponent, Assemblyman Don Sebastiani.

[35] Governor's Proclamation, issued pursuant to *Constitution*, Article II, Section 8(c); *Elections Code*, Sections 12000, 10700, filed July 17, 1983. The election was set for December 13, 1983.

[36] *Legislature of the State of California v. Deukmejian*, 34 Cal. 3d 658.

[37] 1991–92 Regular Session, AB No. 2239, SB Nos. 287 and 587. Each individual bill contained a complete set of district lines for Assembly, Senate, Congress and Board of Equalization districts.

[38] *Journal of the Assembly, 1991–92 Regular Session*, September 23, 1991, p. 4845; *Journal of the Senate, 1991–92 Regular Session*, September 23, 1991, pp. 4456–4459.

[39] *Wilson v. Eu*, 54 Cal. 3d 471.

[40] *Elections Code*, Section 12101. Requires the Secretary of State to notify each county clerk of all offices in each district to which candidates may be nominated.

Over the next two months, the Special Masters studied the issue, taking public testimony at hearings in Sacramento, San Francisco, San Diego, and Los Angeles. Aided by the considerable advances in computer technology since 1973, the Special Masters were able to redraw all the district lines and complete their assignment on time by submitting their report to the Supreme Court on November 29, 1991. On January 27, 1992, with just 22 days remaining until the deadline, the Supreme Court formally adopted, with minor modifications, the plans submitted by the Special Masters.[41]

The lines adopted by the Supreme Court will remain in place until the next federal census takes place in the year 2000. The completion of that census and release of new population data will set the reapportionment process in motion once again.

Qualifications of Members of the Legislature

Members of the Senate and Assembly must be over 18 years of age, citizens of the United States, and inhabitants of the state for three years, and of the district each represents for one year immediately preceding their election.[42]

The Constitution provides that each house shall judge the qualifications and elections of its members.[43]

In 1911, women were granted the right to vote in California,[44] although women's suffrage was not included in the Federal Constitution until 1920, when the 19th Amendment was ratified by the states. This amendment provides that "the right of the citizens of the United States to vote shall not be denied or abridged by the United States or by any State on account of sex." The 19th Amendment did not confer upon women the right to vote, but it did prohibit the various states from discriminating against them in suffrage qualifications.

In 1918, four women (Esto Broughton, Grace Dorris, Elizabeth Hughes, and Anna Saylor) became the first women to serve in the California State Legislature, after they were successfully elected to the Assembly. When Senator Rose Ann Vuich was elected in 1976, she became the first woman ever to serve in the California State Senate.

Since 1918, a total of 61 women have served in the Assembly and 11 in the Senate. Of this total, 20 women currently serve in the Assembly and 7 serve in the Senate.

---

[41] *Wilson v. Eu*, 1 Cal. 4th 707.

[42] *Constitution*, Article IV, Section 2(c). The *Constitution of 1849*, Article IV, Section 5, provided that a Member of the Legislature was required to be a citizen and inhabitant of the state for one year and of the county or district from which he was chosen for six months preceding his election. An amendment in 1862 upped the residence requirement to one year in the county or district from which he was to be chosen.

[43] *Constitution*, Article IV, Section 5.

[44] *Constitution*, Article II, Section 1 (Amendment of 1911). *See now Constitution*, Article II, Section 2. Statewide suffrage was first granted to women in 1869 in Wyoming.

California Term Limits

In November 1990, California voters narrowly passed Proposition 140, an amendment to the California Constitution limiting the terms of state constitutional officers and Members of the Legislature.[45] Proponents of the measure argued that term limits would end the "unfair incumbent advantage" that discourages qualified candidates from seeking public office. Those in opposition responded, in part, that Proposition 140 would take away a voter's right to elect the public official of his or her choice.

Under Proposition 140, Senators are restricted to two four-year terms and Members of the Assembly to three two-year terms.[46] The limitation is a lifetime ban and applies to any member elected after November 1990. If a candidate is elected to fill more than half the remaining term of a previously elected member, that entire term will be counted toward the candidate's total allowable number of terms.[47]

In April 1997, a federal district court ruled that the term limits imposed by Proposition 140 were in violation of the United States Constitution. This decision was later upheld by a three-judge panel of the Ninth Circuit Court of Appeals, which agreed that Proposition 140 should not be enforced, but for entirely different reasons. The district court had ruled that the "lifetime ban" on legislative service violated incumbents' federal rights, whereas the appellate panel found that the proposition did not provide California voters with sufficient notice that the measure imposed lifetime (rather than consecutive) term limits, and therefore the law was invalid. Term limits had now been declared void by two separate courts, but one more court ruling would actually determine the fate of Proposition 140.[48]

In November 1997, the Ninth Circuit commenced an *en banc* review of the entire case. In December, the *en banc* panel reversed the two prior court decisions, declaring that "Proposition 140 makes no distinction on the basis of the content of protected expression, party affiliation, or inherently arbitrary factors such as race, religion, or gender," and therefore does not impinge on the federal rights of incumbents. The judges opined that "entrenched legislators may obtain excessive power," which justified the imposition of term limits as adopted by the voters. Term limits thus remain in force.

Other provisions of Proposition 140 (not addressed in above court cases) limit the state in paying the employer's share for any legislator to participate in a retirement system. With the exception of "vested" retirement benefits, the measure prohibits the accrual of any additional pension or retirement

---

[45] Secretary of State, *Statement of Vote and Supplement, November 6, 1990, General Election*, p. 14. There were 3,744,447 votes for (52.2%) and 3,432,666 votes against (47.8%) the measure. The constitutionality of Proposition 140, with the exception of limits on vested legislative retirement benefits, was upheld by the California Supreme Court. *Legislature v. Eu*, 54 Cal. 3d 492. On March 9, 1992, the U.S. Supreme Court refused to review the California Supreme Court's decision. *Legislature v. Eu*,—U.S.—, 112 S. Ct. 1292 (certiorari denied).

[46] *Constitution*, Article IV, Section 2.

[47] *Constitution*, Article XX, Section 7.

[48] The suit was filed by former Assembly Members Tom Bates and Barbara Friedman, incumbent Assembly Member Martha Escutia, and several of their constituents. The district judge ruled that the lifetime term limits "impose a severe burden on Plaintiff's First and Fourteenth Amendment rights of voting and association." *Bates v. Jones*, 958 F.Supp.1446 (N.D. Cal. 1997). After a three-judge appellate panel affirmed the district court decision (*Jones v. Bates*, 127 F.3d 839 (9th Cir. 1997)), a majority of the active judges of the full appellate court then voted to rehear the case by an 11-judge "en banc" panel. This en banc panel reversed the previous district and appellate decisions, declaring term limits to be constitutional (*Bates v. Jones*, 1997 WL 799079,—F.3d.—(9th Cir. 1997).

benefits. Alternatively, members are allowed to participate in the federal Social Security program.[49]

Proposition 140 also has had a dramatic impact on the Legislature by drastically reducing the legislative operating budget by approximately 40 percent. The Legislative Analyst's Office had estimated that legislative expenditures for the fiscal year following passage of the initiative would be reduced $77.7 million. After the passage of the measure, this 40% reduction was implemented, resulting in massive layoffs in both houses of the Legislature and the premature retirement of many experienced and talented professional staff.[50]

The term limit provisions additionally preclude the Governor, Lieutenant Governor, Attorney General, Controller, Secretary of State, Treasurer, Superintendent of Public Instruction, and members of the Board of Equalization from serving more than two four-year terms in office.[51] Comparable restrictions, however, on retirement benefits and operating budgets are not applicable to these constitutional officers.

Prior to the 1993–94 session, the Insurance Commissioner was not subject to term limits, that office not having been included within the scope of Proposition 140. The Legislature passed a law in 1993, however, to subject the Insurance Commissioner to a limit of two four-year terms.[52]

Term limits have already dramatically impacted California politics. Since the adoption of term limits in 1990, almost 30 new members have been elected to the State Assembly every two years, and several new legislators have joined the Senate as well. Numerous special elections have been held, as incumbents leave their current positions to pursue openings in the other House, in Congress, or in local government. For example, 30-year legislative veteran Willie L. Brown, Jr., who served as Assembly Speaker for a record 15 years, left the Assembly one year before being "termed out," so that he could be elected as Mayor of San Francisco. The vacant Assembly seat was filled by special election a few months after he was sworn-in as Mayor.

The dramatic turnover rate has been applauded by some and frowned upon by others. Opponents of term limits argue that the "institutional memory" and effectiveness of the Legislature has been stripped away, leaving new legislators at risk of being excessively influenced by lobbyists and the executive branch. On the other hand, term limit supporters argue that having a high turnover rate provides the Legislature with "citizen politicians" who are more in touch with the issues of their district, and are less concerned with their own political careers. Regardless of these opinions, it is a fact that term limits have significantly impacted California's Legislature in the few years that they have been in place.

---

[49] *Constitution*, Article IV, Section 4.5.
[50] *Compiled from, After the Election: Analysis of Successful Propositions on the November 1990 Ballot*, California Senate Office of Research, pp. 14–15.
[51] *Constitution*, Article V, Sections 2 and 11; Article IX, Section 2; Article XII, Section 17.
[52] *Statutes of 1993*, Chapter 1227.

Compensation of Members

The Members of the First Legislature received $16 per diem and $16 mileage for every 20 miles traveled to and from the State Capitol, then located at San Jose.[53]

The Constitution of 1879 provided for per diems of not to exceed $8, mileage not to exceed 10 cents per mile, and contingent expenses not to exceed $25 for each session.

In 1908, the Constitution was amended to provide compensation of $1,000 each for each regular biennial session, and $10 per diem for extraordinary or special sessions (not to exceed 30 days), mileage not to exceed 10 cents per mile, and contingent expenses not to exceed $25 per member for each regular session.

The next change in legislators' compensation was made by a 1924 constitutional amendment which provided that they each receive $100 per month during the terms for which they were elected, and mileage of not to exceed 5 cents per mile. No allowance for contingent expenses was made.

In 1949, the Constitution was again amended, increasing the monthly salary to $300 during the term for which the members were elected.

In 1954, the Constitution was amended to provide that each Member of the Legislature receive for his or her services the sum of $500 for each month of the term for which he or she was elected.[54]

Legislative salaries on an annual basis were first enacted as a result of a constitutional amendment and passage of a statute by the Legislature in 1966, and were set at $16,000 per annum. From 1966 until 1988, this annual amount was increased by way of amendments to the statute that were passed by the Legislature, and the annual amount rose from $16,000 to $40,816.

In 1990, the voters passed Proposition 112 which amended the Constitution to establish and confer salary setting authority on the California Citizens Compensation Commission.[55] This seven-member commission was given the authority to set the salaries of legislators and elected statewide officers by way of a resolution adopted by a majority of the members at the end of each fiscal year.

In March 1998, the Compensation Commission established the current salaries for Members of the Legislature at $99,000 per year. [56]

Proposition 112 also amended the Constitution to require that no Member of the Legislature is to accept any honorarium, that the acceptance of gifts that might create a conflict of interest be strictly limited or banned altogether, and that the Legislature enact laws to implement these provisions.[57] Subsequent legislation codified the prohibition of acceptance of honoraria by elected state officers and limited acceptance of gifts in any year from a single source to no more than $250 in total value.[58]

---

[53] *Constitution of 1849*, Schedule, Section 15; *Statutes of 1850*, Chapter 16.
[54] Formerly, *Constitution*, Article IV, Section 4.
[55] *Constitution*, Article III, Section 8.
[56] *See*, "California Citizens Compensation Commission Salary and Benefit Resolution, March 26, 1998." These salaries take effect December 1, 1998.
[57] *Constitution*, Article IV, Sections 5(b) and 5(c).
[58] *Government Code*, Sections 89500–89505.

Each member is allowed and reimbursed for living expenses (per diem) incurred while attending regular and extraordinary sessions of the Legislature or attending committee meetings, legislative functions or to legislative responsibilities as authorized by the respective Rules Committees. Such per diem may equal, but not exceed, the rate provided to federal employees traveling to Sacramento. At the present time, the members are entitled to an allowance of $119 per day.[59]

The law also provides that Members of the Legislature, when traveling to and from sessions of the Legislature, committee meetings, legislative functions or responsibilities as authorized by the respective Rules Committees, are entitled to their actual travel expenses incurred when traveling by common carrier, or to $0.185 per mile if traveling by private conveyance. No travel expense is allowed when traveling in a conveyance owned or provided by a public agency.[60]

---

[59] *Government Code*, Section 8902; *Joint Rule 35. Constitution*, Article IV, Section 4(b).
[60] *Government Code*, Section 8903; *Joint Rule 35.*

Members-elect are sworn in as Senators during the organizational meeting
of the 1995–96 Regular Session, convened on December 5, 1994.

Chapter VIII

Organization of the Legislature

The New Member

During an election campaign, the attentions of the candidate are primarily focused on matters political, planning and building for the goal of gaining votes. When the excitement of election night has passed, the Member-elect begins a new journey, one which culminates in membership in the California Legislature.

After the election, the Secretary of State compares and estimates the vote cast and then delivers to the successful candidates a certificate of election which serves as *prima facie* evidence of the candidates' right to membership in the Legislature.[1]

As a first step to realization of this right, the new legislator appears in the Assembly Chamber, if he or she is an Assembly Member-elect, or in the Senate Chamber, if he or she is a Senator-elect, at 12 o'clock noon on the opening day of the session.[2] At that time the Chief Clerk of the last regular session calls the Assembly to order,[3] while the Lieutenant Governor performs the similar duty in the Senate.[4] A prayer is offered in each house by the respective Chaplain of the last regular session, after which the Reading Clerk (in the Assembly) and the Assistant Secretary (in the Senate) reads the certificate of duly elected members as certified by the office of the Secretary of State.

In the Assembly, the Reading Clerk then calls the roll of counties in alphabetical order. As the counties are called, the member-elect representing such county or counties takes the oath of office prescribed by the Constitution,[5] which is administered by a justice or judge of the California courts, or other appropriate official.[6] The procedure in the Senate is similar to that of the Assembly with the exception that only the newly elected half of the membership of the Senate takes office on the opening day of the general session, and the roll is called by district instead of by county.[7] Oaths of office in the Senate are also administered by a justice or judge of the California courts, or other appropriate official. The oath taken by each Member of the Legislature is reprinted in the journals of the respective houses.[8]

The Constitution provides that Members of the Legislature, before they enter upon the duties of their offices, must take and subscribe to the

---

[1] *Elections Code*, Section 15504; *Government Code*, Section 9021.

[2] *Constitution*, Article IV, Section 3(a); *Government Code*, Section 9020.

[3] *Government Code*, Section 9023. In case of the absence or inability of the Chief Clerk of the Assembly, the senior member-elect present shall take the chair. If there is more than one senior member-elect present and the senior members are unable to agree as to who shall call the session to order, the Attorney General or one of his deputies shall call the session to order.

[4] *Government Code*, Section 9022. In case of the absence or inability of the President of the Senate, the senior member present shall take the chair.

[5] *Constitution*, Article XX, Section 3; *Government Code*, Section 9023.

[6] See for example, *Journal of the Assembly, 1983–84 Session*, December 6, 1982, p. 5 (Members sworn in by the Governor); *Journal of the Assembly, 1979–80 Session*, December 4, 1978, p. 5 (sworn in by Legislative Counsel).

[7] *Government Code*, Section 9022.

[8] *Government Code*, Section 9025.

constitutional oath of office.[9] Members of the Legislature who do not take the oath of office on the opening day of the Legislature may take the oath at any time during the term for which they are elected.[10]

The President or President pro Tempore of the Senate may administer the oath of office to any Senator, and the Speaker or Speaker pro Tempore of the Assembly may administer the oath of office to any Assembly Member.[11] When this oath of office has been taken, the successful candidate has become a Member of the Legislature.

One of the first tasks confronting the new member, and it is an important one, is to meet and be met by other members. Nowhere is this activity more important than in the member's initial contact with his or her seatmate, whose company will be almost constant during floor sessions and upon whom the member will often rely for conversation and counsel.

Election of Assembly Officers

The first order of business after the new members have taken their oaths of office is the nomination and election of the officers of each house.[12] In the Assembly, a Speaker, a Chief Clerk, a Sergeant at Arms, and a Chaplain are nominated and elected by a majority vote of the duly elected and qualified members.[13] The Minute Clerk of the Assembly is appointed by the Chief Clerk, subject to approval by the Assembly Rules Committee. Each officer, upon his or her election, takes the constitutional oath of office.[14] The Speaker appoints a Speaker pro Tempore, and an Assistant Speaker pro Tempore whose duties are to preside over the sessions of the Assembly in the event of the absence of the Speaker;[15] a Majority Floor Leader is appointed by the Speaker; [16] and a Minority Floor Leader is selected by the minority caucus.[17] The Speaker, Speaker pro Tempore, Assistant Speaker pro Tempore, and the Majority and Minority Floor Leaders are chosen from the membership of the House, but the other elected officers are not Members of the Legislature.

The Speaker of the Assembly retains all of his or her rights as a member, and votes upon all measures that come before the Assembly. He or she does not, however, have tie-breaking vote capabilities and if there is a tie vote in the Assembly, the measure under consideration is defeated.[18]

During the 1961 Regular Session, the Assembly adopted new procedures to fill vacancies occurring in the elected officer positions while the Assembly

---

[9] *Constitution*, Article XX, Section 3. The second paragraph of the oath proscribing membership in organizations advocating overthrow of federal or state government was ruled unconstitutional (under the U.S. Constitution's freedom of speech protections) by the California Supreme Court in 1967. *Vogel v. Los Angeles County*, 68 Cal. 2d 18. This invalidation did not affect the first paragraph of the oath, however, which is still in use. *Smith v. County Engineer of San Diego County*, 266 Cal. App. 2d 645 (1968), and *Chilton v. Contra Costa Community College District*, 55 Cal. App. 3d 544 (1976).

[10] *Constitution*, Article XX, Section 3; *Government Code*, Section 9024.

[11] *Government Code*, Section 9190.

[12] *Constitution*, Article IV, Section 7(a); *Government Code*, Sections 9022, 9023.

[13] *Government Code*, Sections 9171, 9172. In effect this means that if all 80 Members of the Assembly have duly qualified (taken the oath of office), it would require 41 votes to elect a Speaker. However, the Legislative Counsel has indicated that if only 79 of the 80 members elected had taken the oath of office at the time the Speaker was to be elected, he or she could be elected by a 40 to 39 vote, as only 79 members would have been duly elected and qualified within the meaning of Government Code Section 9171. *See Journal of the Assembly, 1925 Session*, p. 4, where a Speaker was elected by a vote of 40 to 39. This same Journal (p. 1) indicates that 80 Members of the Assembly were elected, but only 79 had taken the oath of office prior to the election of the Speaker (p. 3).

[14] *Constitution*, Article XX, Section 3. *See also*, footnote 9, *supra*.

[15] *Assembly Rules 1, 3, 28, 29*.

[16] *Government Code*, Sections 9171, 9172; *Assembly Rules 1, 28*.

[17] *Government Code*, Sections 9171, 9172; *Assembly Rule 28*.

[18] *Assembly Rule 107*.

was not in session. One provided for the calling of a caucus to select a Speaker in the event of a vacancy in that office after *sine die* adjournment of the session. The requirement that a majority of the elected membership of the Assembly is necessary to select a Speaker was retained. The procedure at the caucus is the same as the procedure required for the election of a Speaker at the opening of a regular session.

The Legislative Counsel rendered his opinion that the Chief Clerk of the Assembly should preside over the caucus until the election of a Speaker.

When a vacancy occurred in the office of Speaker in 1961, a caucus of the Members of the Assembly was held on September 30, 1961, and the Honorable Jesse M. Unruh, was elected.[19] This was the first and only time in the history of the Assembly that this procedure was followed. Assemblyman Unruh continued to serve as Speaker of the Assembly until 1969.

The other change permitted the Rules Committee to fill any vacancy in any of the elected officer positions in the Assembly which occurred after adjournment of the session.[20]

The present Assembly Rules contain the same provisions but now provide for the filling of vacancies during joint recesses rather than after final adjournment. With the present biennial sessions, the period between adjournment and the convening of the next Legislature is only a few days while a joint recess may exceed three months.

1995–96 Organizational Session: An Assembly Stalemate

On December 5, 1994 the Assembly did not immediately organize and elect a Speaker due to an unprecedented set of circumstances. The simultaneous election of one person to both the Assembly and Senate, and the change in party registration of a Member-elect, led to a volatile political, parliamentary, and constitutional dilemma. In the ensuing events, the Assembly disqualified a Member, recessed several times for lack of a quorum, did not elect a Speaker for over one month, and the voters recalled two Members. A record number of Speakers (four) were also elected from January 1995 to January 1996. A brief description of the events will provide the reader with an overview of important elements of that historic situation.

The Democratic party had held the majority (at least 41 seats) in the Assembly for 25 years, but appeared to lose their majority status in the 1994 election, by winning only 39 seats to the Republicans' 41. However, of the 41 registered Republicans that were officially elected at the November 1994 general election, one Republican's name had appeared as a candidate for both the Assembly and Senate, and was therefore elected to both offices.[21] Assembly Member-elect/Senator-elect Richard Mountjoy indicated his intention to be sworn-in as an Assembly Member, participate in the election of Speaker, and then resign from the Assembly to take office as a Senator.

---

[19] On September 19, 1961, Speaker Ralph M. Brown resigned from the Assembly, and on September 30, 1961, Hon. Jesse M. Unruh was elected Speaker of the Assembly by the caucus. (*See Appendix to Journal of the Assembly*, 1961, p. 6210.)

[20] *Assembly Rule 34.*

[21] Normally, a candidate may not run for "incompatible offices." In this instance, a vacancy had occurred in the Senate after the Assembly candidate had already filed election papers to run for the Assembly in the general election. By coincidence (and by operation of law), the special election for the Senate vacancy and the general election for the Assembly seat were consolidated to occur on the same day.

Democratic legislators argued that Mr. Mountjoy could not serve in both Houses, and demanded that he take the oath of office for the Senate, thereby reducing the Republicans' Assembly membership to only 40 seats out of 80. Assembly Member-elect/Senator-elect Mountjoy argued that since he was duly elected and qualified to serve in each office, he could serve briefly in one House and subsequently serve in the other House, especially given the fact that there was no law prescribing any deadline for taking the oath of office once elected.[22]

Mr. Mountjoy's importance in the Speakership vote intensified when Republican Member-elect Paul Horcher changed party affiliation from Republican to Independent just prior to the organizational session. The House's partisan break-down thus became: 40 Republicans, 39 Democrats, and 1 newly registered Independent, Mr. Horcher. If Mr. Mountjoy were disqualified, and Mr. Horcher voted with the Democrats, then the Democrats would have a majority of the elected membership, and could therefore elect a Democratic Speaker.

To deny Mr. Mountjoy a seat in the Assembly, the House would have to disqualify Mr. Mountjoy by a majority vote, or expel him with a two-thirds vote. The Democrats pursued disqualification, based on Mr. Mountjoy's election to two incompatible offices.[23]

On December 5, 1994, Chief Clerk E. Dotson Wilson presided over the opening day of session pursuant to Government Code Section 9023. Democrat Members-elect moved that Member-elect Mountjoy should not be sworn-in or participate in the business of the Assembly until the body voted on his qualifications. However, the Governor had already sworn-in Mr. Mountjoy as a Member of the Assembly moments prior to the convening of the organizational session. Moreover, pursuant to Government Code Section 9023, the Chief Clerk ruled all motions out of order prior to the swearing-in of Members, since the body is not constituted until the oaths have been administered.

Further attempts to deny Mr. Mountjoy a seat in the Assembly were ruled out of order based upon the Government Code's language that "there shall be no other business, motion, or resolution considered before the election of Speaker, save and except a motion to adjourn or a motion for a call of the house."[24] Hours of parliamentary maneuvers followed, and finally the roll was opened for election of a Speaker, with Mr. Mountjoy being allowed to vote. A tie vote (40 votes for Democrat Willie L. Brown, Jr., and 40 votes for Republican James L. Brulte) brought the business of the House to a virtual

---

[22] According to case law and statutes cited by Legislative Counsel in an opinion issued on December 2, 1994 ("Legislators: Qualifications—#366) a member-elect must take the oath of office within a "reasonable time" after the election. However, neither the Senate nor the Assembly had rules that required members-elect to take the oath of office within a specified period of time after election. As a result, the Democrat-controlled Senate contemplated adopting a new rule to pressure Senator-elect Mountjoy to take the Senate oath, or risk forfeiture of his rights to serve as Senator.

[23] Election laws were vague enough on this issue so as to further fuel the debate. Since the Secretary of State's certificate of election clearly serves as *prima facie* evidence of the candidate's right to hold office, the fact that Mr. Mountjoy had received such certificates for both offices, as well as meeting the other requirements of election law (citizenship status, residency requirement, and age), it appeared as though he had a valid legal argument for serving in either house. However, there is clear case law that prohibits a citizen from serving in two incompatible offices (but not from actually being elected to two incompatible offices). The three crucial questions, in effect, became (1) should Mr. Mountjoy be allowed to take office in the Assembly?; (2) if he is seated, should he be allowed to vote on procedural motions leading up to a vote on his "duly elected and qualified" status?; and (3) is Mr. Mountjoy being "disqualified" (majority vote) or expelled (54 votes pursuant to the Constitution)?

[24] *Government Code*, Section 9023.

standstill.[25] Since no Speaker could be elected that day, the House adjourned until the following day. On December 6, 1994 senior Member Willie L. Brown, Jr. presided over session, but had to recess the House for lack of a quorum.[26] The Republican Members had refused to attend session, objecting to Assembly Member Brown presiding.[27]

On January 23, 1995, the Assembly finally resolved the crisis. The senior member, Willie L. Brown, Jr., was presiding and allowed Members to vote on Mr. Mountjoy's qualifications. On a 40 to 39 vote, the Assembly disqualified Assembly Member Mountjoy from serving as a Member of the Assembly (he was not allowed to cast a vote on the motion). Subsequently, on a 40 to 39 vote, the Assembly elected Willie L. Brown, Jr. as Speaker.[28]

In the 12 months that followed Speaker Brown's election, Republicans Doris Allen, Brian Setencich, and Curt Pringle were elected, respectively, as Speaker. Also, three recall elections were initiated against Assembly Members Paul Horcher, Doris Allen, and Mike Machado as a direct result of the Speakership fights of 1995. Assembly Members Horcher and Allen were recalled, while Assembly Member Machado's recall election failed.

Election of Senate Officers

The Constitution provides that the Lieutenant Governor shall be President and presiding officer of the Senate, therefore no election is required for that position.[29] The Senators do, however, elect a President pro Tempore from their membership to preside in the absence or disability of the Lieutenant Governor, and the Vice Chairperson of the Committee on Rules shall assume the duties and powers of the President pro Tempore in his or her absence.[30]

Members of the Committee on Rules, a Secretary and a Sergeant at Arms are also elected.[31] The Senate officers, upon their election, also take the constitutional oath of office. The Assistant Secretary, a Minute Clerk, and a Chaplain are appointed by the Senate Rules Committee.[32]

The Lieutenant Governor, even though he or she is the President of the Senate, does not have the right to introduce or debate a bill, nor can he or she vote upon a measure except when there is a tie vote in the Senate, at which time he or she may cast the deciding vote. When 21 votes are necessary to pass a bill,[33] the Lieutenant Governor would have a casting vote if the tie vote were 20 to 20, but he or she would not have a casting vote if the vote were 19 to 19, since his or her vote would not decide the question.[34] The Senator who has been elected President pro Tempore does not possess the tie-breaking vote capability, but retains all of his or her rights as a Senator.

---

[25] *Assembly Journal*, 1995–96 Regular Session, p. 11, December 5, 1994.

[26] *Assembly Journal*, 1995–96 Regular Session, p. 23, December 6, 1994.

[27] The Chief Clerk issued a statement on January 4, 1996, stating that the intent of Government Code Section 9023 is that "the Chief Clerk's role as presiding officer is limited to the day (December 5) and the hour (12 noon) as set forth in the Constitution . . . the selection of a Speaker is a matter to be determined by the Members (elected by the voters) in the course of governing its internal affairs . . . [therefore] the senior member present presides on January 4." *Assembly Journal*, 1995–96 Regular Session, p. 48–49.

[28] *Assembly Journal*, 1995–96 Regular Session, p. 133–137. January 23, 1995.

[29] *Constitution*, Article V, Section 9.

[30] *Senate Rule 7.*

[31] *Government Code*, Section 9170; *Senate Rule 10.5.*

[32] *Senate Rule 10.5.*

[33] *See Senate Rule 47* for actions which require 21 votes in the Senate; *also* for actions which require a greater or lesser number of votes.

[34] *Constitution*, Article V, Section 9; *Mason's Manual of Legislative Procedure* Section 513(2).

Inauguration of Governor and Lieutenant Governor

The members formerly had the opportunity of watching the Speaker of the Assembly open the sealed election returns for Governor and Lieutenant Governor,[35] and of then observing these newly elected officers take their oaths of office before the Legislature meeting in Joint Convention.[36] This was an impressive ceremony, but consumed a great amount of time, so the people, in 1940, amended the Constitution permitting the Legislature to regulate by law the manner of making election returns for Governor and Lieutenant Governor.[37] This provision was subsequently repealed as being unnecessary.[38]

The law now provides that when the Secretary of State has compared and estimated the vote cast, a certificate of election shall be made out and delivered, or transmitted by mail, to each person elected.[39]

In 1943, the law requiring that the Governor and the Lieutenant Governor take the official oath in the presence of both houses of the Legislature was repealed and a new law enacted which provided that each may take his or her oath at any time before taking office after receipt of his or her certificate of election and before any officer authorized to administer oaths.[40]

The Rules of the Legislature

The organization of the Legislature is completed with the adoption of Standing Rules which regulate the procedure of each house, and Joint Rules which govern procedure between the two houses.

The Constitution provides that each house shall adopt rules for its proceedings, and may, with the concurrence of two-thirds of all the members elected, expel a member.[41]

In essence, the Senate and Assembly Rules (the Standing Rules) prescribe the procedure of the houses as they relate to bills, amendments, committees, printing, expenses, parliamentary procedure, duties of the officers, and members' decorum and privileges.

---

[35] *Constitution*, Article V, Section 4 (repealed, November 5, 1940).

[36] *Political Code*, Section 905 (enacted 1872; repealed 1943).

[37] *Constitution*, Article V, Section 4.5 (enacted November 5, 1940; amended and renumbered Section 4, November 8, 1960; repealed, November 8, 1966).

[38] *Ballot Proposition 1-a, Assembly Constitutional Amendment No. 13*, 1966 First Extraordinary Session. *See Proposed Revision of the California Constitution*, February 1966, California Constitution Revision Commission, p. 74.

[39] *Elections Code*, Section 15504.

[40] *Government Code*, Sections 1360, 1362.

[41] *Constitution*, Article IV, Sections 5, 7.

Order of Business

Each house, by rule, provides and arranges its own order of business in such a manner that the routine work of the body is disposed of before debatable issues are considered.

The following orders of business have been adopted by the individual houses:

Senate [42]	*Assembly* [43]
1. Roll Call	1. Roll Call
2. Prayer by the Chaplain	2. Prayer by the Chaplain
3. Privileges of the Floor	3. Reading of the Previous Day's Journal
4. Communications and Petitions	4. Presentations of Petitions
5. Messages From the Governor	5. Introduction and Reference of Bills
6. Messages From the Assembly	6. Reports of Committees
7. Reports of Committees	7. Messages From the Governor
8. Motions, Resolutions, and Notices	8. Messages From the Senate
9. Introduction and First Reading of Bills	9. Motions and Resolutions
10. Consideration of Daily File	10. Business on the Daily File
(a) Second Reading	11. Announcements
(b) Special Orders	12. Adjournment
(c) Unfinished Business	
(d) Third Reading	
11. Announcement of Committee Meetings	
12. Continuation of Privileges of the Floor	
13. Leaves of Absence	
14. Adjournment	

Pledge of Allegiance to the Flag

Though not specifically listed in the order of business for the Assembly, the Rules of the Assembly provide that at each session, following the prayer by the Chaplain, the Members of the Assembly and its officers and employees shall pledge allegiance to the Flag of the United States of America.[44] The rule also directs the Speaker to invite guests present in the Assembly Chamber to join in the pledge.

---

[42] *Senate Rule 4.*
[43] *Assembly Rule 40.*
[44] *Assembly Rule 41.* This ceremony was first made a part of the Assembly Standing Rules on January 25, 1941, when House Resolution No. 39, offered by Assemblyman Thomas J. Doyle on January 17, 1941, was unanimously adopted by the Assembly. *Journal of the Assembly for the Fifty-fourth Session, 1941,* Volume 1, pp. 270, 574, 575. As a matter of practice the pledge of allegiance is recited at the beginning of each day's session in the Assembly.

THE LIFE CYCLE OF LEGISLATION—From Idea into Law

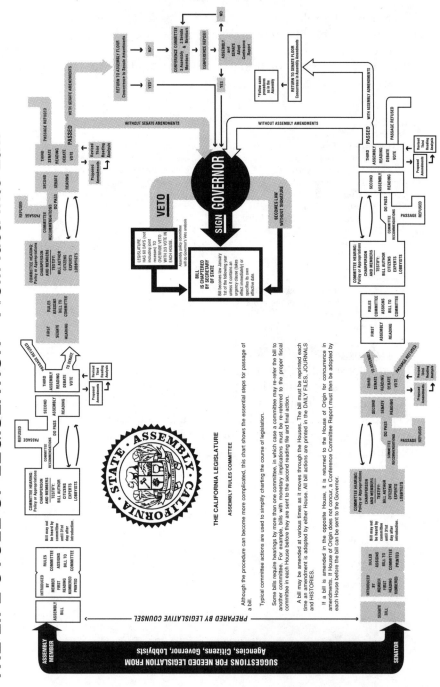

THE CALIFORNIA LEGISLATURE

Although the procedure can become more complicated, this chart shows the essential steps for passage of a bill.

Typical committee actions are used to simplify charting the course of legislation.

Some bills require hearings by more than one committee, in which case a committee may re-refer the bill to another committee. For example, bills with monetary implications must be re-referred to the proper fiscal committee in each House before they are sent to the second reading file and final action.

A bill may be amended at various times as it moves through the Houses. The bill must be reprinted each time an amendment is adopted by either House. All bill actions are printed in the DAILY FILES, JOURNALS and HISTORIES.

If a bill is amended in the opposite House, it is returned to the House of Origin for concurrence in amendments. If House of Origin does not concur, a Conference Committee Report must then be adopted by each House before the bill can be sent to the Governor.

Chapter IX

The Legislative Process

Bills and Bill Titles

In California, all laws are enacted by the passage of bills. A bill either proposes a new law or amends or repeals the existing law.

The Constitution provides that every act shall only embrace but one subject and that subject must be expressed in the title of the measure.[1]

The courts have been very liberal in their construction of what must be contained in the title of a bill.

"Where the body of the act embraces provisions germane to the general subject stated in the title, or when the title suggests the field of legislation which is included within the text of the act, the title will be held to be sufficient."

"The title should be liberally construed so as to uphold the statute if a reasonable reference to the subject matter included therein may be ascertained from the language employed."[2]

Every law must contain the enacting clause: "The people of the State of California do enact as follows:"[3]

A bill becomes a statute when it is signed by the Governor and given a final chapter number by the Secretary of State. The Governor's Office works in conjunction with the Secretary of State's Office to ensure that signed bills are enacted in the order intended by the Legislature and the Governor. Before a bill becomes law, it must be read by title on three different days in each house unless the house itself dispenses with this constitutional requirement by a two-thirds vote of the membership of the house. No bill may be considered for final passage by either house of the Legislature until the bill, with any amendments that may have been adopted, has been printed and distributed to the members. The vote on the passage of the bill must be entered in the Journals of the respective houses.

Non-urgency statutes enacted in the regular session before the Legislature adjourns for the "interim study recess" in the first year of the biennium shall go into effect on January 1 of the following year. For example, a non-urgency bill passed on September 12, 1997 would take effect on January 1, 1998. A non-urgency measure, however, that is enacted in the second year of the two-year session takes effect on January 1, following a 90-day period from the date of enactment.[4] For example, a bill that is enacted on or before October 2, 1998 would take effect on January 1, 1999. In contrast, a bill enacted on October 3, 1998 would not take effect until January 1, 2000. However, the likelihood of a regular statute (non-urgency, non-tax levy, etc.)

---

[1] *Constitution,* Article IV, Section 9.

[2] *People v. Oreck,* 74 Cal. App. 2d 215. Reaffirmed in *People v. Horner,* 137 Cal. App. 2d 615; *Orange County Water Dist. v. Farnsworth,* 138 Cal. App. 2d 518; *People v. Oosterveen,* 154 Cal. App. 2d 620.

[3] *Government Code,* Section 9501.5. The *Constitution of 1849,* Article IV, Section 1, provided that the enacting clause of every law be as follows: "The people of the State of California, represented in Senate and Assembly, do enact as follows:" a similar provision remained in the Constitution until the adoption of *Proposition 1-a* in 1966, which removed it from the Constitution. However, it was subsequently enacted as part of the Government Code.

[4] *Constitution,* Article IV, Section 8(c).

being enacted any time after August 31 in the second year is remote. In fact, the only regular (non-urgency, non-tax levy, etc.) legislation that can be enacted after August 31 in the second year would be a "regular" bill that was vetoed and then overridden by the Legislature during Final Recess. In other words, if the Governor vetoed a bill September 28, 1998, and the Legislature were to override the veto November 3, 1998, the bill would go into effect January 1, 2000. This 13-month delay is imposed by operation of the Constitutional requirement that dictates a statute's effective date as occurring on January 1 *next following a 90-day period from enactment.*

This provision does not apply to statutes calling elections, for tax levies or appropriations for the usual and current expenses of the state or if the bill itself contains an urgency section which consists of a statement of the facts constituting the necessity for its immediate effectiveness. The facts constituting an urgency in this instance require that they be related to and necessary for the immediate preservation of the public peace, health or safety. Such a statute may not have an immediate effect unless the urgency section and the bill each receive, upon a separate rollcall vote entered in the Journals, a two-thirds vote of the membership of both houses.[5]

In California the Budget Bill is introduced simultaneously in both houses. Unlike the Federal Constitution, the California Constitution does not require that appropriation measures be introduced only in the lower house; they may originate in either the Assembly or the Senate.

Bills in the Early Sessions

Many of the bills and amendments to bills in the early sessions of the Legislature were written in longhand. This did not present a difficult or serious problem as few bills were introduced in the First Legislature or during the early sessions.

Bills enacted into law were translated into Spanish by the State Translator, since the California Constitution of 1849 provided that "all bills, decrees, regulations and provisions which from their nature require publication shall be published in English and Spanish."[6]

In accordance with this constitutional provision, the First Legislature provided that 1,050 copies of each law be printed in English, and 350 copies be printed in Spanish.[7]

The new Constitution adopted in 1879 provided that all laws shall be published in the English language.[8] Notwithstanding this law, the publication of official proceedings in both English and Spanish continued to be a long standing practice into the early 1900's. As late as 1909, the Legislature provided that 240 copies of "laws, resolutions and memorials as may be designated by the Legislature" shall be printed in Spanish.

---

[5] *Constitution*, Article IV, Section 8(d).
[6] *Constitution of 1849*, Article XI, Section 21.
[7] *Statutes of 1850*, Chapter 24.
[8] *Constitution of 1879*, Article IV, Section 24. Repealed by Proposition 1-a 1966.

There has been a material change in legislative procedure and parliamentary practice over the years. One example is the following rule which was repealed more than 60 years ago:

"No amendment shall be received for discussion at the third reading of any bill, but it shall at all times be in order, before the final passage of such bill, to move its commitment to a Select Committee, under special instructions to amend."[9]

Conforming to this rule, the Speaker would appoint a member to act as a Select Committee of One, who would sit down at his desk in the Chamber, write the amendment, insert it in the bill, and report to the House according to its instructions. The House would then adopt or reject the amendment.

The current rules require that floor amendments be prepared and approved as to form by the Legislative Counsel. Additionally, all substantive floor amendments are analyzed by a Committee Consultant in conjunction with the Assembly Floor Analysis Unit in the Chief Clerk's Office. A copy of the amendments and analyses are distributed to each Member's desk and available on each Member's laptop computer prior to the commencement of floor debate.[10] There is, however, no requirement that the bill and the amendment be rereferred to committee. The amendments are presented, debated and adopted or defeated on the floor.

Governor's Message to the Legislature and the Budget

The Governor shall, on or before January 10 of each year, submit to each house, with an explanatory message, a budget containing a complete plan and itemized statement of all proposed expenditures of the state provided by existing law or recommended by him or her and of all estimated revenues, for the ensuing fiscal year. The budget shall also contain a statement of cash-flow for the preceding fiscal year and an estimate of the cash-flow for the current and the succeeding fiscal year and shall show for each month the income, expenditures and borrowing from individual funds.[11]

The Budget Bill

After the Governor has submitted his or her Budget, an appropriation bill, known as the Budget Bill, which reflects the Governor's proposed Budget, is introduced in each house of the Legislature and referred to the Assembly Budget Committee and the Senate Budget and Fiscal Review Committee, respectively. The Constitution requires that the Legislature pass the Budget Bill by midnight, June 15. Until the Budget Bill has been enacted, neither house shall send to the Governor any other appropriation bill, except emergency bills recommended by the Governor, or appropriations for the salaries, mileage and expenses of the Legislature. [12]

---

[9] *Assembly Rule 37,* 1925 Regular Session. Repealed in 1929. For example, *see Journal of the Assembly, 1925 Session,* March 30, 1925, p. 1373.

[10] *Assembly Rule 69.*

[11] *Constitution,* Article IV, Section 12(a); *Government Code,* Section 12021.

[12] *Constitution,* Article IV, Section 12(c).

All other bills may contain only one item of appropriation, and that expenditure must be for only one certain and expressed purpose. No bill that appropriates money from the General Fund, except appropriations for public school purposes, shall be operative unless passed by a two-thirds rollcall vote of the membership of each house.[13]

At regular sessions, no bill, other than the Budget Bill, may be heard by any committee or acted upon by either house until the 31st day after the bill is introduced, unless this provision is dispensed with by a three-fourths vote of the house.[14]

The 1996–97 fiscal year State Budget, as chaptered, totalled $47.2 billion. When all special and bond funds are included, the total Budget for 1996–97 exceeded $64.1 billion.

Of the $47.2 billion General Fund budget, approximately $12.2 billion was allocated to support the operation of state government, and $35 billion was allocated for assistance to local programs, government, and school districts. From the amount made available from the General Fund, about $14.5 billion was for health and public assistance programs, and $25.1 billion for education. The health, public assistance and educational expenditures comprised 83.7 percent of the General Fund budget.[15]

The Budget Bill and any other appropriation measures which come before the Legislature are considered by the fiscal committees of the respective houses, the Budget and Fiscal Review or Appropriations Committees in the Senate and the Budget or Appropriations Committees in the Assembly.

The items eliminated or reduced (item vetoed) by the Governor in the Budget Bill are reconsidered separately and this "item veto" may be overridden in the same manner as bills.[16]

Constitutional Amendments [17]

Constitutional amendments proposed by the Legislature require a two-thirds affirmative vote of the members of each house, and must be submitted to a direct vote of the people, and adopted and ratified by a majority vote of the qualified voters, before they become a part of our State Constitution.[18]

Prior to its being voted upon by the people, the Legislature may amend or withdraw the proposal.[19]

Although all proposed constitutional amendments are usually submitted to the people at the direct primary or the general election, a special election may be called by the Governor to be held throughout the state for the adoption or rejection of constitutional amendments or other measures.

---

[13] *Constitution,* Article IV, Section 12(d). Appropriations for the public schools may be passed by a majority vote of the membership of each house.

[14] *Constitution,* Article IV, Section 8(a).

[15] This information supplied by the Assembly Budget Committee.

[16] *Constitution,* Article IV, Section 10(e).

[17] Amendments to the United States Constitution must be proposed by a two-thirds vote of both houses of Congress, or, upon application of the legislatures of two-thirds of the several states, Congress must call a convention for proposing amendments. In either case, the amendments become a part of the Constitution only when ratified by the legislatures of three-fourths of the several states, or by conventions in three-fourths thereof, as the one or the other mode of ratification may be proposed by the Congress. *United States Constitution,* Article V.

[18] *Constitution,* Article XVIII, Sections 1, 4. For amendment of the Constitution by the initiative, see Chapter III, *supra,* p. 33.

[19] *Constitution,* Article XVIII, Section 1.

Resolutions

Legislative constitutional amendments are, in fact, resolutions which propose to the people of the State of California amendments to the State Constitution.

There are three other kinds of resolutions used in the Legislature. Two of these, concurrent resolutions and joint resolutions, require consideration and adoption by both houses of the Legislature before they can take effect. House (Assembly) and Senate resolutions are adopted by the house of origin only. All resolutions require a majority vote for passage.

Joint Resolutions

Joint resolutions are those which relate to matters connected with the federal government.[20] These resolutions are used almost exclusively for the purpose of memorializing Congress—that is, expressing approval or disapproval by the California Legislature of legislation pending or proposed in Congress or programs and activities of the federal government. Additionally, the California Legislature utilizes joint resolutions to ratify amendments to the United States Constitution.

Joint resolutions take effect upon their being filed with the Secretary of State.[21]

Concurrent Resolutions

Concurrent resolutions relate to matters to be treated by both houses of the Legislature, and are used for a variety of purposes, such as adopting the Joint Rules, creating joint committees, directing executive departments to make specific reports to the Legislature, and memorializing the death of a Member or a former Member of the Legislature or their immediate families.[22]

Concurrent resolutions take effect upon their being filed with the Secretary of State.[23]

House and Senate Resolutions

House (Assembly) and Senate resolutions are the expression of but one house of the Legislature and take effect upon their adoption. These resolutions are normally used to amend the house rules, to create committees, or to request a committee of the house to study a specific problem.

House resolutions and Senate resolutions are printed as separate documents in the same manner as bills. The previous practice in the Assembly of printing the text of house resolutions in the Journal of the Assembly was discontinued at the beginning of the 1991–92 Regular Session as a cost-saving measure.

---

[20] *Joint Rule 5.*
[21] *Government Code*, Section 9602.
[22] *Joint Rules 5, 34.2.*
[23] *Government Code*, Section 9602.

Introduction of Bills

In the Assembly, the first bills are introduced on the first day of a biennial session. On that day, during the order of business "Introduction and Reference of Bills," the Reading Clerk calls the roll from A to Z and, as each Member's name is called, the Member may introduce one bill or resolution.[24] In the Senate, and in the Assembly following the initial rollcall, Members may introduce bills by presenting them at the Secretary of the Senate or the Chief Clerk's desk in their respective chambers.

Within the meaning of the Rules, the word "bills" includes concurrent and joint resolutions and constitutional amendments, unless joint and concurrent resolutions are specifically exempted by the language of a particular rule.[25]

Before the convening of each session, the respective houses provide the Legislative Counsel with printed covers for use in the preparation of bills for introduction.

The Joint Rules provide that "No bill shall be introduced unless it is contained in a cover attached by the Legislative Counsel and unless it is accompanied by a digest, prepared and attached to the bill by the Legislative Counsel, showing the changes in the existing law which are proposed by the bill." [26] In addition to providing a summary of the changes in the existing law, the digest also contains the number of votes required to pass the bill, and indicates whether or not the bill contains an appropriation or a state-mandated local program.

When the bill is drafted, its text is placed in computer storage and identified by a "request number." A typewritten copy of the bill and three copies of the digest are placed in a bill cover supplied by the house in which the bill is to be introduced. The title of the bill is typed on the cover, and the bill is then delivered to the author for introduction.

When the author wishes to introduce the bill, he or she delivers it to the Chief Clerk or Secretary who gives the bill a number. The Chief Clerk or Secretary notifies the Legislative Counsel that a bill bearing a particular request number has been introduced as Assembly Bill No. ____ or Senate Bill No. ____. The Legislative Counsel then extracts the text, adds the bill number and transmits via computer terminal the text, digest and number to the State Printing Plant.

One copy of the digest is retained by the author, one copy accompanies the bill to the printer, and one copy is retained by the Chief Clerk or the Secretary who provides additional copies for the press.

The Assembly Rules provide that the bill must be signed by the author and coauthors, if any, before it may be accepted for introduction.[27]

If any bill which does not comply with the foregoing requirements is presented to the Secretary of the Senate or Chief Clerk of the Assembly for introduction, the Secretary or Chief Clerk returns it to the member who presented it.

---

[24] *Assembly Rule 47; see also Senate Rule 22.*
[25] *Joint Rule 6. See also Senate Rule 19; Assembly Rules 46, 66, 73.*
[26] *Joint Rule 8.5.*
[27] *Assembly Rule 47.*

After the bill and its accompanying digest is placed across the desk and it has been numbered, the bill is read for the first time and referred to a committee.[28] The bill's number, the date of its introduction and first reading, the committee to which it is referred, the dates it is sent to and received from the printer, as well as any other clerical notations made necessary by a deviation from the ordinary procedure, are shown on the bill cover.

During a regular session, the date of the 31st day after the introduction of the bill is stamped by a clerk on the bill cover. No bill other than the Budget Bill, or a bill introduced in an Extraordinary Session, may be heard by any committee or acted upon by either house until 30 calendar days have elapsed following the date the bill was introduced. This provision, however, may be dispensed with by a vote of three-fourths of the members of the house which is considering the measure.[29] The front section of each Senate and Assembly Daily File charts the 31st day after each bill's introduction, providing the public, staff and clerks with a quick reference as to when the bill may be heard.

Upon introduction Assembly bill covers are white, while those used by the Senate are goldenrod. Covers for concurrent and joint resolutions and constitutional amendments are each of a different and distinctive coloring. The different colored covers provide the clerks with an easy method of identifying the various types of proposed legislation.

A bill shall not contain any indication that it is introduced at the request of any person, state agency, or officer.[30]

Immediately after introduction, a computer "printout" is produced which provides several copies of the title of each bill. These titles are used to produce the legislative journals and histories.

The Assembly bills are sent to print immediately and, upon being returned, are delivered to the Assembly Rules Committee (see example on page 104). These bills are assigned to the appropriate standing committees at the Rules Committee's next meeting. After assignment, the bills are returned to the Chief Clerk who advises the appropriate Assembly committees that bills may be "picked up" at the Assembly Desk. Senate bills are assigned to committees prior to being printed and after printing are delivered to the Senate committees by the Secretary of the Senate. After receiving the necessary information, the State Printing Plant produces 2,500 copies of each bill.[31]

At the same time bills become available in print, they are also available to staff through the Legislature's computer system, the Legislative Inquiry System (LIS). LIS is administered by the Legislative Data Center, which is under the direction of the Legislative Counsel. LIS provides an electronic version of the text of each bill upon introduction and at each stage of the

---

[28] In the Assembly, the Chief Clerk, after notifying the Legislative Counsel of the new bill number assigned to the particular Legislative Counsel request number, sends the bill to be printed. The Rules Committee, at an open public meeting, then formally refers the bill to a policy committee. *Assembly Rule 51.* This introduction procedure is essentially the same in the Senate. *See Senate Rule 22.*

[29] *Constitution,* Article IV, Section 8(a). The bill must also have been in print for 30 days prior to being heard and acted upon. This provision of the Constitution may be dispensed with by a three-fourths vote of the House in which it is being heard (60 votes in the Assembly; 30 votes in the Senate). *See also, Joint Rule 55.*

[30] *Joint Rule 10.7.*

[31] For provisions relative to the manner of printing of bills on their introduction, *see Joint Rules 8.5, 10, 10.7, 12.*

amending process, as well as history actions and vote information. Most of this same information is also available to the public through computer data networks such as the Internet.[32]

For convenience, bills are referred to or designated as AB for Assembly bills and SB for Senate bills. Concurrent resolutions are indicated by ACR or SCR, joint resolutions carry the letters AJR or SJR, and constitutional amendments are identified as ACA or SCA. A single house resolution in the Assembly is designated HR (House Resolution) and SR (Senate Resolution) in the Senate.

Restriction on Bill Introduction

Prior to the adoption of Proposition No. 9 at the 1958 general election, amending Article IV, Section 2, of the Constitution, almost all bills during the general sessions were introduced before the constitutional recess. The Constitution provided that no bills could be offered after the recess without the consent of three-fourths of the elected membership, and in no case could a member offer more than two bills subsequent to the recess. As a result, literally thousands of bills were introduced in the days preceding the recess. In 1957, for instance, more than 6,700 bills were introduced in the Legislature during the 19 days before the recess.

The budget session (even-numbered years), until it was abolished in 1966, was limited to the consideration of the Budget Bill, revenue acts necessary therefor, and the approval or rejection of charters and charter amendments of cities, counties, and cities and counties, and acts necessary to provide for the expenses of the session. There was no limitation on the number of bills that could be introduced in a budget session, as long as they pertained to the above subjects.

With the advent of the regular annual sessions beginning in 1967, there was no limitation on the number or type of bills that could be introduced at each regular session of the Legislature. The only limitation on bill introduction was contained in the Joint Rules. These Rules provided for unlimited bill introduction until March 15, after which date a member was permitted to introduce three additional bills. If the member desired to introduce an additional bill it was necessary to petition the Rules Committee, secure their favorable recommendation, and then offer and have a resolution adopted by a two-thirds vote of the members granting him or her permission to introduce the bill.

The rules in each house presently place a limit on the number of bills that can be introduced in a two-year session. A Senator may introduce a total of 65 and an Assembly Member no more than 30 bills in the regular session.[33] These limits are, in turn, subject to the Joint Rule deadline for bill introduction, after which only committee bills, constitutional amendments,

---

[32] *Government Code*, Section 10248 (added by *Statutes of 1993*, Chapter 1235).

[33] *Assembly Rule 49; Senate Rule 22.5*. House Resolution 4 of the 1993–94 session established the original limit of 50 bills. House Resolution 36, 1995–96 Regular Session, reduced the bill limit per member from 50 to 30. This 30-bill limitation first took effect during the 1997–98 Regular Sesion (House Resolution 1, 1997–98 Regular Session).

Assembly bills approved by the Speaker and Senate bills approved by the Senate Committee on Rules may be introduced.[34]

During extraordinary sessions, the Legislature has no power to legislate on any subjects other than those specified in the Governor's Proclamation which convenes it into extraordinary session, but it may provide for the expenses of the session and other matters incidental thereto.[35] There is no restriction on the number of bills which may be introduced, if they come within the purview of the items in the proclamation.

---

[34] *Joint Rule 54(a), 61.*
[35] *Constitution*, Article IV, Section 3(b). *See also Extraordinary Sessions, supra*, p. 64.

CALIFORNIA LEGISLATURE—1997–98 REGULAR SESSION

ASSEMBLY BILL No. 1216

Introduced by Assembly Member Granlund

February 28, 1997

An act to add Sections 1008.5 and 5090.5 to the Education Code, relating to schools.

LEGISLATIVE COUNSEL'S DIGEST

AB 1216, as introduced, Granlund. School boards: vacancies.

Existing law specifies that vacancies on governing boards of school districts or community college districts are caused by specified events. Existing law provides a procedure for filling a vacancy on the governing board of a school district or community college district, or on a county board of education.

This bill would provide that in the event a person who holds office as a member of the governing board of a school district or community college district, or as a member of a county board of education, is elected or appointed to the governing board of a different school district or community college district, or to a different county board of education, the person's term on the first board is terminated upon taking the oath of office for the second board and the position would be deemed vacated. The bill would provide that the vacated position shall be filled, as specified.

Vote: majority. Appropriation: no. Fiscal committee: no. State-mandated local program: no.

The people of the State of California do enact as follows:

1   SECTION 1. Section 1008.5 is added to the Education
2 Code, to read:
3   1008.5. In the event a person who holds an office as a

Example of a Bill (as introduced)

Bills and Standing Committees

After introduction, bills are referred to the standing committees of the respective houses.

Though the rules of both houses provide that their committees must hold hearings and act upon bills referred to them as soon as practicable after they have been referred to them, certain requirements must first be met.

First, standing committees and their subcommittees are proscribed from taking action on a bill at any hearing held outside of Sacramento or during a joint recess. However, a committee may hear the subject matter of a bill during a period of recess, provided notice is published in the Daily File four days prior to such hearing.[36]

Next, during a regular session, committees must wait for a period of 30 days after a bill has been introduced and in print [37] before they may take action on it. These prohibitions may be dispensed with by an extraordinary vote in the house considering the measure.[38] This waiting period permits proponents and opponents to review the provisions of the bill and to prepare testimony for presentation to the committee.

Finally, a schedule or calendar of bills set for hearing is proposed by each committee. Publication of this list in the Daily File must occur at least four days in advance of a hearing by the first committee and two days in advance by subsequent committees of the same house.[39] For instance, a Senate or Assembly bill first referred to the Assembly Committee on Transportation must be noticed at least four days prior to hearing; if the bill is subsequently rereferred to the Assembly Appropriations Committee, the bill must then be noticed two days prior to hearing in that committee.

Publication of the lists of bills set for hearing gives notice to interested parties, including the general public, of the date and time when they may wish to appear before the committee to offer arguments for or against a bill. Occasionally, when a bill is of statewide importance or of a highly controversial nature, the date for its hearing is set a week or more in advance, to allow ample time for the attendance of those who live a considerable distance from the Capitol.

A bill may be set for hearing in a committee only three times. In order to be counted as one of the three "sets," notice of the hearing on the bill must be placed in the Daily File for at least one day. If the hearing of the bill is postponed at the committee's request, or if "testimony only" is to be taken, the hearing is not counted as one of the three times a bill may be set.[40]

The members of the various committees spend many long and studious hours considering the measures which have been referred to them. It is not unusual for a committee meeting begun during the day to continue well into the night.

---

[36] *Joint Rule 60.*

[37] *Constitution,* Article IV, Section 8(a); *Joint Rule 55.*

[38] The vote required for dispensing with the constitutional provision is three-fourths of the house considering the bill; the joint rule may be dispensed with by a vote of two-thirds of the house, *Constitution,* Article IV, Section 8(a); *Joint Rules 10.8, 55.*

[39] *Joint Rule 62(a).*

[40] *Id.*

Many times, opposition to bills can be overcome by amendments submitted in committee. Amendments proposed by the committees are seldom opposed by the house, since these amendments generally are offered to correct an error in the bill or to remove opposition.

Also, upon request of the author of a bill, the chair of the committee to which it has been referred may, without a committee meeting, cause the bill to be reported to the Assembly with the recommendation that the author's amendments be adopted and the bill be rereferred to the committee.[41] This procedure, known as author's amendments, permits the author to correct any errors in the original bill and to get his or her bill in the exact form he or she wishes it to be before presenting it to the full committee.

It must be noted that the standing committees of the Legislature have only the power to submit, recommend, or propose amendments to legislative measures. Amendments endorsed by a committee must be adopted by the house by a majority of the Members present and voting on second reading before they may become part of the bill. The general practice is that the House ratifies committee recommendations by adopting committee amendments on second reading. The adoption of amendments by the house does not mean that there will be no opposition to the amended bill when it comes up for final passage.

The Joint Rules of the Senate and Assembly are explicit regarding the conduct of the meetings of standing committees. A quorum must be present in order for a bill to be passed out of committee. When a committee takes action on a bill, the vote must be by rollcall. Further, all rollcall votes must be recorded by the committee secretary and transmitted to the Chief Clerk of the Assembly or the Secretary of the Senate for publication as part of the Journals of the respective houses. Committee actions are also published in a manner prescribed by each house.[42] In the event a bill fails to receive the necessary votes to pass it out of committee and reconsideration is not granted within 15 legislative days, it is returned to the Chief Clerk of the Assembly or the Secretary of the Senate, as the case may be, and may not be considered further during the session.[43]

When a bill is reported out of a committee, the committee chairperson submits a report to the house indicating what recommendation the committee makes to the house, such as "do pass," "do pass, as amended," or any other determination made by the committee. The original bill accompanies this report. After the bill has been reported from committee, read the second time, and reported correctly engrossed,[44] the engrossed copy of the printed bill is inserted in a newly created bill cover, and used instead of the original typewritten bill. Engrossed bill covers are green for Assembly bills and yellow for Senate bills unless the measures include an urgency clause where Assembly bill jackets are red and those for Senate bills are orange. Under the

---

[41] *Assembly Rule 68; Senate Rule 27.5.*

[42] *Joint Rule 62(c); Assembly Rule 58.5.* In the Assembly the committee votes are published periodically as an appendix to the Assembly Journal. In the Senate they are printed weekly as part of the Senate Journal.

[43] *Joint Rule 62(a).*

[44] An engrossment is a proofreading and verification in order to be certain that the bill before the house is identical with the original bill as introduced, with all amendments which have been adopted correctly inserted. *Mason's Manual of Legislative Procedure*, Section 735.

direction of the Chief Clerk of the Assembly or Secretary of the Senate, the original bill is filed in the respective Engrossing and Enrolling Unit along with other legislative documents and amendments.

The biennial session is governed by constitutional deadlines for bills to be acted upon. The first occurs on January 31 of the second year of the biennium (1998), at which time those bills introduced in the first year of the biennium (1997) and still in the house of origin may no longer be acted upon by the house, and they are filed with the Chief Clerk or the Secretary of the Senate.[45] No bill may be presented to the Governor after November 15 of the second year of the session (1998). Another deadline occurs at the end of the second year, following adjournment *sine die* [46] (November 30, 1998), when all bills remaining in committee are returned to the Chief Clerk or Secretary.

After final adjournment, the Chief Clerk of the Assembly and the Secretary of the Senate file all the bills of the respective houses in the archives of the Secretary of State's office.

Second Reading and Engrossment of Bills

All bills reported out of committee are placed on the second reading file for the next legislative day. They may not be read a second time except under that order of business, and they must be read the second time in the order of their appearance upon the second reading file.[47]

After a bill has been reported from a committee without amendments, it is read the second time, and then sent to the Engrossing and Enrolling Unit of the Chief Clerk's Office (if it is an Assembly bill), or to the Committee on Rules in the Senate (if it is a Senate bill). There, the printed bill is compared with the original bill and, after comparison, the bill is returned to the Assembly or Senate third reading file.[48]

This comparison of the printed bill with the original bill is called engrossing.[49] Both the Assembly and Senate have an Engrossing and Enrolling Clerk and each house engrosses its own bills. During this engrossment process the Engrossing and Enrolling Clerk is authorized to make technical corrections and changes in the printed bill and may also send "queries" to the Legislative Counsel Bureau when, in his or her professional estimation, there is a drafting error in the text of, or amendments to, a bill.

In the event that the bill has been reported out of committee with amendments, and these committee amendments, or amendments offered from the floor, have been adopted on second reading, it is reprinted, showing such amendments by the use of ~~strikeout type~~ for matter omitted, and *italic type* for the new matter.[50] Thereafter the bill is referred to as of the date of last amendment, e.g., Senate Bill No. 127, as amended in the Assembly

---

[45] *Constitution,* Article IV, Section 10(c); *Joint Rule 56.*

[46] *Constitution,* Article IV, Section 3(a).

[47] *Assembly Rules 63, 66; Senate Rule 29.*

[48] *Assembly Rules 66, 67; Senate Rule 32.*

[49] *Assembly Rule 79; Senate Rules 32, 33.* The engrossing and enrolling process is an ancient one; Blackstone in his *Commentaries,* published in 1765, states that when the house agreed or disagreed with the committee amendments or had added its own amendments the bill was ordered engrossed which literally meant written in a strong *gross* hand. *See* Cooley's Blackstone, *Commentaries on the Laws of England,* Callaghan and Company, 1899 (4th Ed.), Vol. I, p. 166.

[50] *Joint Rule 11.* If the amendments delete the entire contents of the bill, the matter deleted is not reprinted in "strikeout type" in the amended version of the bill. Instead, a brief statement is attached at the end of the bill identifying the previously printed version of the bill containing the deleted material. *Joint Rule 11(b).*

June 23, 1997 (see example on page 111). Each time that the bill is amended it is reprinted; and after each reprinting, if the amendments were adopted in the house of origin, it is reengrossed and a new bill cover and report are prepared to reflect the last amended version of the bill.[51] Any amendments made by the other house are proofread before the bill is enrolled.

In the Assembly, bills amended on second reading, whether by committee amendment or amendment from the floor, shall be ordered reprinted and returned to the second reading file.[52] There is no such requirement in the Senate. In the Senate, a bill that is amended upon its second reading, whether by a committee amendment or an amendment from the floor, is reprinted and is not returned to the second reading file, but is placed upon the third reading file and is eligible for passage the day after the adoption of the amendment.

Third Reading and Passage of Bills

The next step in the progress of the bill is its third reading. On the floor of each respective chamber, immediately after the third reading of the bill, and prior to the final vote, the members present their arguments for and against the measure.

No bill may be considered or acted upon on the floor of the Assembly unless and until a copy of the printed bill as introduced, a printed copy of each amended form of the bill, and an analysis of the bill edited and distributed by the Assembly Floor Analysis Unit of the Chief Clerk's Office, have been placed upon the desks of the members.[53] In addition, both caucuses provide partisan third reading analyses to their respective members.

Bills on third reading may be amended by motion from the floor, and, if the motion to amend carries by a majority vote of those present, the bill is reprinted, engrossed, and returned to its original position on the third reading file. Each house has a waiting period for bills amended on third reading. Assembly Rule 69(d) requires that any bill amended on the third reading file must wait one calendar day after being amended before it is eligible for final passage. This waiting period provides more time to analyze the bill in its newly amended form before being voted on. In the Senate, a bill amended on third reading is returned to second reading pursuant to Senate Rule 29.3, providing a similar waiting period before it returns to third reading for final debate and passage.

The Assembly Rules provide that amendments in excess of 25 words are not in order until a copy of the amendments are placed on the desks of the Members. The Rules also require that the author draft the amendments (except those containing 25 words or less) in Legislative Counsel form. In addition, amendments from the Floor during a bill's third reading, which

---

[51] *Assembly Rules 66, 67, 69, 79; Senate Rule 32.* If the bill is amended in the other house it is not again read and checked until it has been passed by that house and returned to the house of origin, where it is read and checked. This final reading and checking of a bill after its passage by both houses is called enrolling the bill. *Joint Rules 24, 26; Assembly Rule 79; Senate Rule 33. See also Government Code,* Sections 9502–9509.

[52] *Assembly Rule 67.*

[53] *Constitution,* Article IV, Section 8(b); *Assembly Rules 64, 68.6; Senate Rule 29.8.*

would make a substantive change in the bill, shall have an analysis prepared by the committee of origin in conjunction with the Assembly Floor Analyses Unit. A hard copy of the analysis is then distributed to the Members and also made available via the Assembly Floor System.[54]

The Senate requires that the Office of Senate Floor Analysis prepare an has of all bills on third reading. Additionally, any bill amended on the Senate floor is not eligible to be taken up for passage until it has been in print for at least one legislative day.[55]

After any floor amendments have either been taken or rejected and the bill been reprinted to reflect its final form, and after all debate on the bill has been concluded, a vote is taken by rollcall, and the bill is either passed or refused passage. It requires a majority vote of the membership of the Assembly (41 votes) to pass most bills. Certain measures, i.e., urgency bills, bills appropriating money from the General Fund (except money for the public schools), and Constitutional Amendments must receive a two-thirds analysis vote (54 votes).[56] In the Senate, the vote required is proportionately the same—21 affirmative votes are required to pass most bills, and 27 affirmative votes are necessary to pass the others.

The Consent Calendar

During the 1959 Regular Session, the Legislature adopted joint rules permitting the establishment of consent calendars in the respective houses.[57]

A bill must conform to three basic requirements before it may be placed upon the consent calendar. First, the bill cannot be a revenue measure nor a bill upon which the 30-day constitutional waiting period has been dispensed with; second, the bill must receive a "do pass" or a "do pass, as amended" recommendation by a unanimous vote of the committee members present; third, the bill, in its final version as approved by the committee, cannot have had any opposition expressed to it by anyone present at the committee meeting.[58]

Having met these prerequisites, the bill may be reported out of the committee with the recommendation that it be placed on the consent calendar. The bill is then read the second time, the committee amendments, if any, are adopted, and the bill placed upon the consent calendar by the Chief Clerk of the Assembly or the Secretary of the Senate. No consent calendar bill may be considered for adoption until the second legislative day following the day of its placement on the consent calendar.

If any member objects to the placement or retention of any bill on the consent calendar at any time before its final passage, the bill is returned to the third reading file.

Also, if any bill on the consent calendar is amended from the floor, it automatically ceases to be a consent calendar bill, and is returned to the third reading file.[59]

---

[54] *Assembly Rule 69.* The Senate has a similar rule. *See Senate Rule 38.6.*
[55] *Senate Rule 29.3, 29.8.*
[56] *Constitution,* Article IV, Sections 8(d), 12(d), and Article XVIII, Section 1.
[57] *Joint Rules 22.1–22.3.*
[58] *Joint Rule 22.1.* The Assembly has added the additional requirement that the bill must not have received any *"no"* votes in any Assembly standing committee before it is eligible for Assembly Consent Calendar consideration. *See Assembly Rule 71.*
[59] *Joint Rule 22.2.*

Immediately prior to voting on the first bill on the consent calendar, the presiding officer in either house calls to the members' attention that the next rollcall will be on the first bill on the consent calendar. Though consent calendar bills are not debatable, a reasonable time is allowed for questions from the floor.[60]

Following the pause for questions, each bill on the consent calendar is read the third time, and voted upon.

---

[60] *Joint Rule 22.3.*

AMENDED IN ASSEMBLY JUNE 23, 1997

AMENDED IN SENATE FEBRUARY 20, 1997

SENATE BILL   No. 127

Introduced by Senator Ayala

January 8, 1997

An act to amend Section 19533.5 of the Business and Professions Code, relating to horseracing.

LEGISLATIVE COUNSEL'S DIGEST

SB 127, as amended, Ayala.   Horseracing.

Existing law provides, with certain exceptions, that a license granted to an association other than a fair shall be only for one type of horseracing.

This bill would permit an association licensed to conduct quarter horse racing or a fair to conduct races that include paint racing and Appaloosa racing in the same race, with the. *The bill would require the* consent of the organization representing quarter horse horsemen and horsewomen *when paint horses race with quarter horses or when a race that includes paint horses replaces a quarter horse race with more than 7 entries.*

Vote: majority. Appropriation: no. Fiscal committee: no. State-mandated local program: no.

The people of the State of California do enact as follows:

1   SECTION 1. Section 19533.5 of the Business and
2   Professions Code is amended to read:

Example of an Amended Bill

Members Required to Vote

Whenever a rollcall is required by the Constitution or by rule (demanded by three members, or ordered by the Speaker) every member in the Assembly Chamber must record his or her vote openly and without debate, unless the Assembly shall, by a majority vote of the members present, excuse him or her.[61]

The Senate Rules provide that a member answer "Aye" or "No" whenever a rollcall is required by the Constitution or by rule (ordered by the Senate, or demanded by three members).[62]

An electronic rollcall system has been installed in the Assembly Chamber for the recording of votes in the Assembly, but the Senate retains the method of orally calling the roll of Senators in alphabetical order.

The Assembly and Senate Rules both provide that no member shall be permitted to vote or change his or her vote after the announcement of the vote by the presiding officer.[63]

Both the Senate and the Assembly, by rule, have provided for the procedure to be followed in the event that a member refuses to vote.[64]

Absence of Quorum

At any time during the session of either House a member may rise to a point of order that there is an absence of a quorum. It is then the duty of the presiding officer to ascertain whether a quorum is present. A majority of each house shall constitute a quorum to do business, but a smaller number may adjourn from day to day, and may compel the attendance of absent members. A quorum is defined as one-half plus one of the duly elected and qualified members of the house (41 in the Assembly; 21 in the Senate).[65]

Call of the House

The reason for a "call of the house" is different from that for a "quorum call." A call of the house is placed in order to compel the attendance of absent members and to require them to vote upon the matter before the house, even though those members necessary to constitute a quorum are physically present in the house at the time the call of the house is placed. A quorum call, on the other hand, is used to compel the attendance of the minimum number of members required to permit the house to conduct its business, and is not related to a specific matter before the house.

"After the roll has been called, and prior to the announcement of the vote, any member may move a call of the Assembly. The members present may order a call of the Assembly by a majority vote of the members present and voting, and the Speaker shall immediately order the Sergeant at Arms to lock all doors and shall direct the Chief Clerk to prepare a list of absentees as disclosed by the last rollcall. The list of absentees shall be furnished to the

---

[61] *Constitution*, Article IV, Section 7(b); *Assembly Rules 104, 105*.

[62] *Senate Rule 44*.

[63] *Assembly Rules 104, 106; Senate Rule 44*. As a practical matter, Members of the Assembly are routinely allowed to "add on" to, or change their votes on, any rollcall, provided the addition or change doesn't affect the result of the vote as announced by the presiding officer.

[64] *Assembly Rule 104; Senate Rule 45*.

[65] *Constitution*, Article IV, Section 7(a); *Assembly Rule 4; Senate Rules 2, 3;* and, *Mason's Manual of Legislative Procedure*, Section 500(2).

Sergeant at Arms. Thereupon no members shall be permitted to leave the Assembly Chamber except by written permission of the Speaker. No person shall be permitted to enter except members, Senators, or officers, attachés, or employees of the Legislature in the official performance of their duties.

"Those members who are found to be absent, and for whom no leaves of absence have been granted, shall be forthwith taken into custody wherever found by the Sergeant at Arms or his or her assistants or any person designated by the Sergeant at Arms, including members of the California Highway Patrol, and sheriffs or their deputies, and brought to the Assembly Chamber.

"No recess or adjournment shall be taken during a call of the Assembly. Additional business may be conducted and calls placed regardless of the number of calls in effect. A call of the Assembly may be dispensed with at any time upon a majority vote of the members present, such action to become effective upon the completion of the rollcall and the announcement of the vote upon the matter for which the call was ordered . . . ".[66]

The rule governing the call of the Senate, while different in some particulars, has a similar effect as the call of the Assembly, i.e., it compels the attendance of absent members for the purpose of requiring them to vote on the item under call.[67]

Reconsideration of Bills

When a bill has been passed by either house it shall be transmitted promptly to the other house with a message signed by the Secretary of the Senate or by the Chief Clerk of the Assembly, as the case may be, unless a motion to reconsider has been made or it is held pursuant to some rule or order of the house.[68]

In the Assembly, a motion to reconsider on the next legislative day the vote whereby any bill was passed or refused passage, or the vote whereby any motion, amendment, concurrence, Assembly resolution or proposition other than a bill was passed or refused passage, must be made on the same day the vote to be reconsidered was taken.

In the Assembly, no motion to reconsider shall be adopted unless it receives an affirmative recorded vote of 41 members, except that it shall require a vote of 54 members or 60 members, respectively, to reconsider the vote on any matter originally requiring 54 votes or 60 votes, as the case may be. A motion to reconsider may be voted on without a second.

A motion to reconsider a vote must be made by a member voting on the question, and shall take precedence over all motions, except a motion to adjourn.

Upon such motion being made, the matter to be reconsidered is placed upon the unfinished business file, and no further action can be taken prior to the next legislative day. When a motion to reconsider has once been made, it becomes the property of the Assembly, and, with the consent of the house,

---

[66] *Assembly Rule 101.*
[67] *Senate Rule 42.*
[68] *Joint Rule 21; Assembly Rule 100; Senate Rule 43.*

may be continued from day to day. A motion to reconsider which is neither taken-up nor continued lapses. Once a reconsideration motion has lapsed, the question or measure returns to the same position it held prior to the motion being made (e.g., if a motion to reconsider was made on a bill that had already passed, and on a subsequent legislative day the motion was allowed to lapse, the bill would be deemed passed).

Any member voting on any motion, amendment, Assembly resolution or proposition other than a bill or concurrence may move to take up on the same day the motion to reconsider such a question, previously made by another member. The motion to take up the reconsideration on the same day takes precedence over the motion to reconsider, and upon demand of any member, the motion to take up the reconsideration on the same day must be put to an immediate vote. If the motion to take up the reconsideration on the same day is adopted, the motion to reconsider becomes the next order of business before the house.

When reconsideration is granted, the matter to be reconsidered resumes its exact position before the Assembly voted on the question. The author may take it up immediately after reconsideration is granted.[69]

In the Senate, the procedure differs slightly. A motion to reconsider any question may be made by any member on the day on which the vote was taken. The motion may be considered on the day it is made, or on the succeeding legislative day, but may not be further postponed without the concurrence of 30 Senators.[70]

In the Senate, bills may be reconsidered by a majority vote (21) even though the bill required a two-thirds vote (27) for passage. Constitutional amendments that are adopted can be reconsidered by 14 votes, while constitutional amendments that have been defeated require a two-thirds vote (27) for reconsideration.[71]

Amendments by the Other House

After a bill has been passed by the house of origin, transmitted to the other house, and amended in the second house, it is immediately reprinted, as amended, by the house which adopted the amendment or amendments. A copy of the amendments are stapled inside the bill and endorsed as being "adopted." When the bill is passed by the second house, the bill with the amendments attached is returned to the house of origin, where it is placed on the unfinished business file. Every time a bill is amended by the other house it is reprinted in its entirety, unless the amendment affects the bill's title only. Such an amendment must still be concurred-in by the house of origin. [72]

---

[69] *Assembly Rule 100.* There are special provisions governing the motion to reconsider on the last two legislative days preceding the Interim Study Recess, January 31st of the even-numbered year, and the Final Recess. *See Assembly Rule 100(b)(1), (2), (3).*
[70] *Senate Rules 43, 47(2).*
[71] *Senate Rules 47(12), (20), (21), (26).*
[72] *Joint Rule 25.*

Concurrence in Amendments of Other House

When the Senate amends and passes an Assembly bill, or the Assembly amends and passes a Senate bill, the Senate (if it is a Senate bill) or the Assembly (if it is an Assembly bill) must either "concur" or "refuse to concur" in the amendments. If the Senate concurs (if it is a Senate bill), or the Assembly concurs (if it is an Assembly bill), the Secretary or Chief Clerk notifies the house making the amendments and the bill is ordered to enrollment.[73]

If the bill up for a concurrence vote was substantially amended in the other house, there are procedures in the rules in each house for re-referring the bill to the appropriate committee for further review.[74] Absent such a referral, the concurrence vote proceeds and requires the same vote as is required for the passage of the bill. Assembly Rule 77 requires that an Assembly bill returning to the body for concurrence in Senate amendments must wait one calendar day before it is eligible to be taken up on the floor. This waiting period gives the Members, staff, and public ample time to analyze any changes the Senate made to the bill.

If the amendments add an urgency clause to the bill, the house must first adopt the urgency clause section by a two-thirds vote of the elected members, and then concur in the amendments by a two-thirds vote. If the affirmative vote on either of these questions is less than two-thirds, the bill goes to a conference committee.[75]

Conference Committees

If the Senate or the Assembly refuses to concur in the other house's amendments, the Senate Committee on Rules (if it is a Senate bill) or the Speaker of the Assembly (if it is an Assembly bill) appoints a Committee of Three (3) on Conference and the Secretary or the Chief Clerk shall immediately notify the other house of the action taken and request the appointment of a like committee.[76]

Two of the members of such conference committee from each house must have been chosen from those voting with the majority and the other member from each house from the minority, if there is a minority vote, on the question in dispute.

The first Senator named on the conference committee acts as chairperson of the committee from the Senate, and the first Assembly Member named on such committee acts as chairperson of the committee from the Assembly. The chairperson of the committee on conference of the house in which the bill originated (the Assembly chairperson, if it is an Assembly bill, or the Senate chairperson, if it is a Senate bill) arranges for the times and places of the conference meetings, and directs the preparation of the conference committee report.[77]

[73] *Joint Rule 26.*
[74] *Joint Rule 26.5; Senate Rules 28.5, 29.8, 29.10; Assembly Rule 77.2.*
[75] *Joint Rule 27.*
[76] *Joint Rule 28.*
[77] *Joint Rules 28.1, 29.*

The conference committee on the Budget Bill must be open and accessible to the public. All other conference committees must hold open public meetings which are noticed in the Daily File one calendar day prior to the meeting if the conference committee considers amendments that are determined by the Legislative Counsel to be of a substantive nature. If the committee considers only nonsubstantive amendments, their meeting need not be held in public nor noticed.[78]

The committee on conference reports to both the Senate and the Assembly. It requires the affirmative vote of not less than two of the Senate members and two of the Assembly members of the committee to agree upon a report.

The report of the conference committee must be prepared in writing and signed by two Members of the Assembly and two Senators who agree to the report. Provision is also made for a dissenting conference committee member to file a minority report. Two signed copies of the report must go to the house of origin of the bill, and one signed copy must go to the other house. The conference committee's proposed amendments are inserted and the bill is reprinted in the form as proposed by the conference committee.

After the proposal has been in print and noticed in the Daily File for not less than one legislative day, it may be voted upon. The report of the committee on conference is not subject to amendment, and if either house refuses to adopt the report, the conferees are discharged, and new conferees are appointed. However, no member may serve upon more than one conference committee on the same bill, and there can be no more than three conference committees on any one bill.[79] If the third conference committee fails to agree, or if either house fails to adopt its report, the bill is dead.

The vote required for adoption of the conference report is the same as the vote required for passage of the bill. If the amendments in the conference report add an urgency section to the bill, the urgency section must first be put to a vote. If adopted by a two-thirds vote of the elected members, the vote is then taken on the adoption of the conference report, which also requires a two-thirds vote. If the affirmative vote is less than two-thirds of the elected membership of the house, the report is refused adoption.[80] Both houses must agree on the conference report before it becomes effective.

When a conference committee it is unable to agree upon a report (a vote of not less than two of the conferees of each house is required), a letter from the chairperson of the committee indicating that the committee is unable to submit a report is sent to the Chief Clerk of the Assembly and the Secretary of the Senate. Upon such notification, the conferees are discharged and other conferees appointed.[81]

The conference committee on the Budget Bill must report within 15 days after the bill has passed both houses. If they fail to do so, the Chief Clerk and the Secretary are notified and a new conference committee appointed in accordance with the Joint Rules.[82]

---

[78] *Joint Rule 29.5(a). See also Government Code*, Section 9027.
[79] *Joint Rules 29, 30.*
[80] *Joint Rule 30.5.*
[81] *Joint Rule 30.7.*
[82] *Joint Rules 29.5(b), 30.7.*

Enrollment of Bills

After a bill has passed both houses, it is returned to the house of origin. If the bill has not been amended by the other house, it is immediately sent to the Engrossing and Enrolling Unit of the Chief Clerk's office (if it is an Assembly bill), or to the Committee on Rules in the Senate (if it is a Senate bill), to be enrolled. If, however, the other house has amended the bill, such amendments must be concurred in before the bill may be sent to enrollment. If the amendments have not been concurred in, and the bill has gone to conference, the conference committee report must have been adopted by both houses before the bill is enrolled. Each house enrolls its own bills.

The bill is printed in enrolled form, omitting symbols indicating amendments, and compared by the Engrossing and Enrolling Clerk of the house where it originated to determine that it is in the form approved by the houses. The enrolled bill is thereupon signed by the Secretary of the Senate and the Chief Clerk of the Assembly, or their designees, and presented without delay to the Governor. After receipt by the Governor, the Chief Clerk and Senate Rules Committee must report to their respective houses of origin the time of presentation of the bill to the Governor, and the record must be entered in the Journal.

After enrollment and signature by the Secretary of the Senate and the Chief Clerk of the Assembly, or their designees, constitutional amendments, concurrent and joint resolutions are filed without delay in the office of the Secretary of State, the time of filing is reported to the house of origin, and the record is entered in the Journal.[83]

For example, during the 1995–96 Regular Session, there were 1,306 Assembly bills and 1,052 Senate bills enrolled and presented to the Governor, and a total of 189 constitutional amendments, joint and concurrent resolutions enrolled and filed with the Secretary of State, making a total of 2,547 enrolled measures for that session.[84]

Enrollment is the final legislative action taken on a bill before it is presented to the Governor. When the enrolled bill is delivered to the Governor, it shall be endorsed as follows: "This bill was received by the Governor this _____ day of _____, nineteen _____." The endorsement shall be signed by the Private Secretary of the Governor or by some other individual designated by the Governor, whose identity the governor must make known to the Speaker and the President pro Tempore.[85]

Bills Signed by the Governor

The Governor, after receiving a bill from the Senate or Assembly, has 12 days in which to sign or veto it. Should the Governor fail to take any action, the bill becomes law without a signature.

The 12-day "signing" period is applicable to all bills that are presented to the Governor 12 or more days prior to the date the Legislature adjourns for

---

[83] *Government Code*, Sections 9507, 9508; *Joint Rule 24*.
[84] *See, Final Histories of the Assembly and Senate*, 1991–92 Regular Session.
[85] *Government Code*, Section 9509.

a joint recess in the first year of the biennium, and on or before August 20th of the second year of the biennium. The applicable calendar date in the first year is based on the date both houses of the Legislature "consent" to adjourn for the interim recess and is subject to change. For example, in 1995, the Legislature adjourned for the interim recess on September 15th. The Governor had until October 15th to act upon any bill that passed the Legislature on or before September 14th and was presented to him on or after September 4, 1995.

In contrast, the recess date in the second year of the biennium is fixed by the State Constitution. Bills that are passed before September 1st in the second year of the biennium and which are in his or her possession on or after September 1st must be signed or vetoed by September 30th of that year or they become a statute without his or her signature.[86]

Any bill passed by the Legislature at a special session which is in his or her possession on or after the adjournment of the session becomes a statute unless the Governor vetoes the bill within 12 days by depositing the veto with the office of the Secretary of State.[87] Prior to 1973, the Governor could "kill" a bill in his possession after the adjournment of a special session simply by refusing to sign it.[88]

When the Governor approves a bill, he or she signs it, dates it and deposits it with the Secretary of State. This copy is the official record and law of the state. The Secretary of State assigns the bill a number known as the chapter number. The bills are numbered consecutively in the order in which they are received, and the resulting sequence is presumed to be the order in which the bills were approved by the Governor.[89]

There is only one sequence of bill chapter numbers maintained for each year of the regular session of the Legislature. A separate set of chapter numbers is maintained for each extraordinary session.[90]

If a bill presented to the Governor contains one or several items of appropriation, he or she may eliminate or reduce any or all of them while approving the other portions of the bill. When the Governor executes this "item veto," he or she appends to the bill, at the time of signing it, a statement of the items to which he or she objects and his or her reasons therefor. A copy of this statement is then transmitted to the house in which the bill originated. The items then may be separately reconsidered and the vetoes sustained or overridden in the same manner as bills which have been vetoed by the Governor.[91]

---

[86] *Constitution*, Article IV, Section 10(b)(2). *Government Code*, Section 9516.

[87] *Constitution*, Article IV, Section 10(b)(4).

[88] This practice is commonly referred to as the "pocket veto."

[89] *Government Code*, Section 9510. This numerical sequence becomes extremely important, as the bill with a higher chapter number prevails over a bill with a lower number. For example, if the language of Section 400 of the *Government Code* as contained in Chapter 100 conflicts with the language of Section 400 of the *Government Code* as contained in Chapter 99, the language in Chapter 100 will prevail and the conflicting provisions of Chapter 99 are said to be "chaptered out".

[90] *Government Code*, Section 9510.5. Constitutional amendments and joint and concurrent resolutions adopted by both houses and enrolled during the session are designated as Resolution Chapter 1, et seq.

[91] *Constitution*, Article IV, Section 10(e). *Government Code*, Section 9511.

Governor's Veto

When the Governor vetoes a bill, he or she returns it, with his or her objections, to the house of origin. The house may consider the veto immediately or place it on the "unfinished business file."

The Legislature has 60 calendar days, days in joint recess excluded, to act upon the veto.[92] If no action has been taken during this time, the measure is deleted from the file and the veto is effective.

Theoretically, the ability to override the Governor's veto gives the Legislature the ultimate control over exactly what is to become the law.

In 1979, the Legislature overrode the Governor's veto of two bills and eight items in the Budget Bill.[93] Prior to these overrides, the Governor's veto had been overridden on only two occasions since 1973.[94] The Legislature has not overridden a Governor's veto since 1979.

The result of sustaining the Governor's veto or failing to consider it in the time allotted is to "kill" the bill or to reduce or eliminate the appropriation as recommended.

If two-thirds of the elected members of each house disagree with the governor, the bill as passed by the Legislature becomes law notwithstanding his or her objections.[95]

When the Legislature successfully overrides a Governor's veto, the bill, or items are authenticated as having become law by a certificate.

"The certificate shall be endorsed on or attached to the bill, or endorsed on or attached to the copy of the statement of objections. It shall be in the following form: 'This bill having been returned by the Governor with his objections thereto, and, after reconsideration, having passed both houses by the constitutional majority, has become a law this _____ day of _____, _____'; or, 'The following items in the within statement (naming them) having, after reconsideration, passed both houses by the constitutional majority, have become a law this _____ day of _____, _____.' A certificate signed by the President of the Senate and the Speaker of the Assembly is a sufficient authentication thereof." [96]

The bill or statement so authenticated is then delivered to the Governor, and by him or her deposited with the laws in the office of the Secretary of State. Bills so deposited in the office of the Secretary of State are given a chapter number in the same manner as bills approved by the Governor.[97]

---

[92] *Joint Rule 58.5.*

[93] Governor Brown's veto of SB 91 *(1979–80 Regular Session), Journal of the Senate, 1979–80 Regular Session,* p. 5196, *Journal of the Assembly, 1979–80 Regular Session,* p. 7565.   Governor Brown's veto of AB 580 *(1979–80 Regular Session), Journal of the Assembly, 1979–80 Regular Session,* p. 6393, *Journal of the Senate, 1979–80 Regular Session,* p. 5677.
The Legislature also overrode Governor Brown's vetoes of eight items in the Budget Bill, SB 190 *(1979–80 Regular Session), Journal of the Senate, 1979–80 Regular Session,* pp. 6027, 6028, 6029, *Journal of the Assembly, 1979–80 Regular Session,* pp. 8318, 8319, 8333, 8334, 8351.

[94] Governor Reagan's veto of AB 855 *(1973–74 Regular Session). Journal of the Assembly, 1973–74 Regular Session,* p. 9831; *Journal of the Senate, 1973–74 Regular Session,* p. 7722 and Governor Brown's veto of SB 155 (death penalty) *(1977–78 Regular Session). Journal of the Senate, 1977–78 Regular Session,* p. 3895; *Journal of the Assembly, 1977–78 Regular Session,* p. 6553.

[95] *Constitution,* Article IV, Section 10. Prior to the ratification of Proposition No. 4 at the 1972 General Election (Assembly Constitutional Amendment 95), the Legislature recessed for at least 30 days upon concluding their work and then returned for up to five days for the specific purpose of reconsidering the Governor's objections to bills passed during the session. This provision was deleted in 1972.

[96] *Government Code,* Section 9513.

[97] *Government Code,* Section 9514.

When Laws Go Into Effect

With the exception of measures which take effect immediately, bills enacted in the first year of the regular session before the Legislature adjourns for the "interim study recess" shall go into effect on January 1 of the following year.[98] For example, a non-urgency bill passed on September 12, 1997 would take effect on January 1, 1998. A non-urgency measure, however, that is enacted in the second year of the two-year session would go into effect on January 1 following a 90-day period from the date of enactment.[99] For example, a bill that is enacted on or before October 2, 1998 would take effect on January 1, 1999. In contrast, a bill enacted on October 3, 1998 or later would not take effect until January 1, 2000. However, the likelihood of a regular statute (non-urgency, non-tax levy, etc.) being enacted any time after August 31 in the second year is remote. In fact, the only regular (non-urgency, non-tax levy, etc.) legislation that can be enacted after August 31 in the second year would be a "regular" bill that was vetoed and then overridden by the Legislature during Final Recess. In other words, if the Governor vetoed a bill September 28, 1998, and the Legislature were to override the veto November 3, 1998, the bill would go into effect January 1, 2000. This 13-month delay is imposed by operation of the Constitutional requirement that dictates a statute's effective date as occurring on January 1 *next following a 90-day period from enactment.*

By contrast, statutes enacted at a special session do not take effect until the 91st day after the adjournment of the session at which they were passed.[100] The delays in the effective dates of the statutes enacted at regular and special sessions provide a 90-day interval between the enactment and the effective date of the statute as is required by the Constitution in order to permit the circulation and presentation of a referendum petition asking that the statute, or a part of it, be submitted to the electorate.[101]

Any amendment to or revision of the Constitution, proposed by the Legislature, must be submitted to the people for ratification. The amendment or revision is effective the day following its approval by a majority of those voting on the question at the election.[102]

Any measure or constitutional amendment submitted to the electorate through either an initiative or referendum petition, which is approved by a majority of the votes cast on the proposition, takes effect the day after the election, unless the measure itself provides for a different effective date.[103]

---

[98] *Constitution,* Article IV, Sections 8(c)(2), 8(d).
[99] *Constitution,* Article IV, Section 8(c)(1).
[100] *Id.*
[101] *Constitution,* Article II, Section 9(b).
[102] *Constitution,* Article XVIII, Section 4. *See also* p. 18.
[103] *Constitution,* Article II, Section 10(a).

Adjournment

The regular session of the Legislature is adjourned "sine die" [104] by constitutional provision as of midnight on November 30 of the even-numbered year (e.g., 1998).[105]

The Constitution prohibits the Legislature from presenting the Governor with a bill after November 15 of the second year of the biennium. Thereafter, the Legislature will presumably recess, thereby enabling them to return to consider any bill vetoed by the Governor after that date. This would mean that the Governor would have until midnight November 27 to veto the bill, thus providing at least three days for the Legislature to take action before they are adjourned *sine die*.[106]

Prior to 1973, the annual regular sessions were not adjourned *sine die* on a specified date. A concurrent resolution, adopted by both houses, set the adjournment time. At the time appointed the presiding officers of each house announced that the time for final adjournment had arrived and declared the house adjourned *sine die* in accordance with the provisions of the resolution.

At the present time, the Joint Rules provide that the Legislature may recall itself from joint recess and reconvene the regular session. Upon reassembling it may consider any type of legislation, with the exception that when it is recalled on September 1 or after in the even-numbered year, it may consider only Governor's vetoes or urgency bills, bills calling elections, levying taxes or appropriating moneys for the usual and current expenses of the state.[107]

Final Disposition of Legislative Records

The Secretary of State is the custodian of the public archives of the state. The documents required by law to be filed, items ordered filed by the Department of General Services and any material the Secretary deems to have historical value are filed, indexed and preserved in vaults maintained by this office.[108]

These archives contain the original and official records of the State Legislature for all its sessions since 1849.

The Committee System

With the volume of legislation that is introduced and considered, it is impossible for each Member of the Legislature to review in detail all of the changes, additions and deletions that are proposed. In the course of a regular session, the Legislature will consider approximately 7,000 bills in addition to numerous constitutional amendments and other resolutions. To cope with the multitude and the variety of the subject matter contained in these bills, it has been necessary to devise and utilize a system of policy committees.

There are currently 27 policy committees in the Assembly and 24 in the

---

[104] From the Latin meaning "without day" and is commonly used to designate the final adjournment of a legislative body.

[105] *Constitution*, Article IV, Section 3(a).

[106] *Constitution*, Article IV, Section 10(a).

[107] *Constitution*, Article IV, Section 10(a); *Joint Rule 52*. This authority to reconvene the Legislature should not be confused with the Governor's power to call a special session of the Legislature. The authority to reconvene may be exercised by the Speaker and President pro Tempore jointly or by petition of 10 or more Members of the Legislature.

[108] *Government Code*, Sections 12221, 12224, 12227.

Senate.[109] They may best be described as the basic working components of the Legislature. The total number of Standing Committees may fluctuate in a two-year session, but generally averages between 20 and 27 total committees in each respective House. Assembly Committees are created by House Resolution, and the memberships are appointed by the Speaker. Senate Committees are created by Senate resolution, with committee memberships appointed by the Senate Rules Committee.

The committees specialize in specific subject matter areas and are designed to treat the proposed legislation relating to their specialty. By referring the bills to committee it is possible to study, in depth, all the bills which have been introduced.

After the bill has been referred to a committee it is scheduled for hearing. At this point, the private citizen, the lobbyist and any other interested party may testify in favor of or in opposition to the bill. It is at this stage that many of the important policy decisions are made.

As a result of the manner in which the committee is appointed and the house's reliance upon the members' and the staffs' expertise in the area affected, the house usually concurs in the committee's recommendation. It should be borne in mind, however, that the house does have the final word on all legislation, and should it choose to disregard the committee's recommendation, it will do so.

Great care is taken in selecting the chairpersons and members of committees. Certainly, political considerations of the appointing powers are a factor in committee assignments, but another prime criterion of selection is the member's previous experience and training. Therefore, it is not unusual that a majority of the members of the Judiciary Committee are attorneys; many members of the Education Committee are teachers or educators; or that members representing rural constituencies are members of the Committee on Agriculture.

When the committee has completed its deliberations it returns the bill with its recommendation to the house.

In addition to standing committees of each house, the Legislature also employs joint committees. The committees, composed of an equal number of Senators and Assembly Members, study subjects of mutual interest to both houses. These committees are established by statute, concurrent resolution, or the Joint Rules, and the membership and chairpersons are appointed by the Speaker and the Senate Rules Committee, respectively, unless the statute or resolution creating the committee provides for a different manner of selection. The chairperson is selected by the Joint Rules Committee from members recommended by the Speaker and the Senate Rules Committee.[110]

During the joint recess, the standing and joint committees of the Legislature conduct hearings throughout the state.[111] While they are not permitted to act upon bills during this time, they do elicit information and data leading to the eventual formulation of legislation.[112]

[109] *Assembly Rule 11; Senate Rule 12.*
[110] *Joint Rules 36.5, 36.7.*
[111] *Joint Rule 51.* This rule specifies the mandatory joint recesses for each biennium.
[112] *Joint Rule 60(c).*

An Assembly Rules Committee Meeting During 1969 Session

Shown from left to right: Assembly Members Ketchum, Mobley, Gonsalves, Chief Administrative Officer V. G. Neilsen, Chairman Chappie, Secretary Hazel Lombardo, Chief Clerk James D. Driscoll, Assembly Members R. Johnson, Burton, Quimby.

This procedure brings the legislative process to the problem, rather than *vice versa*. It affords the members an opportunity to observe problems at their location and hear from the parties who are directly affected by or involved with the subject at hand.

The Rules Committees

There is in each house of the Legislature a Committee on Rules which acts as the executive committee of the house.[113]

At the beginning of each two-year session the practice is that the "majority party" proposes new House Rules, including the size of the Rules Committee membership. For example, the composition of the Assembly Rules Committee has varied from nine during the 1993–94 Regular Session to 12 during the second year of the 1995–96 Session to 10 upon organization of the 1997–98 Regular Session. The Committee's size and makeup is subject to change by a majority vote in subsequent legislative sessions. In the Assembly, the Speaker appoints the Chair of the Rules Committee under the existing rules. The Speaker also serves on the committee.

Within two days after the November general election in each even-numbered year, the majority and minority caucuses meet for the purpose of electing its members of the Committee on Rules for the upcoming two-year session.[114]

The Senate Committee on Rules consists of the President pro Tempore of the Senate, who is chairperson of the committee, and four other Members of the Senate who are elected by the Senate.[115]

The rules of each house provide that the Rules Committee shall continue in existence during any recess of the Legislature, after final adjournment, and until the convening of the next regular session with the same powers and duties as while the Legislature is in session.[116] A very important function of the Rules Committees is to refer all bills and resolutions to the appropriate standing committees.[117]

The Rules Committees make studies and recommendations designed to promote, improve, and expedite the business and procedure of their respective houses and committees. Amendments to the rules are proposed by the committees when they are deemed necessary.[118]

Some of the important powers and duties the Rules Committees perform for their respective houses are: To authorize the appointment of employees, set their salaries, and adopt rules and regulations limiting the amount, time, and place of expenses and allowances to be paid to committee employees;[119] to approve all claims for expenses incurred by the house's committees, and to approve all proposed expenditures before the expenses are incurred;[120] and to assign the subject matter of bills recommended for study to the appropriate committees.[121]

---

[113] *Assembly Rule 13; Senate Rule 11.*
[114] *Assembly Rule 13.1.*
[115] *Senate Rule 11.*
[116] *Assembly Rule 15; Senate Rule 13.*
[117] *Assembly Rules 14, 45, 51; Senate Rules 12, 22.*
[118] *Assembly Rule 14; Senate Rule 13.*
[119] *Assembly Rules 14, 20; Senate Rules 13, 13.1.*
[120] *Assembly Rule 20; Senate Rule 13.1.*
[121] *Assembly Rule 59.*

AMENDED IN SENATE JUNE 5, 1997

AMENDED IN ASSEMBLY MAY 30, 1997

AMENDED IN ASSEMBLY MAY 28, 1997

ASSEMBLY BILL   No. 107

Introduced by Assembly Member Ducheny

January 9, 1997

An act *making appropriations* for the support of the government of the State of California and for several public purposes in accordance with the provisions of Section 12 of Article IV of the Constitution of the State of California , *and declaring the urgency thereof, to take effect immediately* .

LEGISLATIVE COUNSEL'S DIGEST

AB 107, as amended, Ducheny. 1997–98 Budget.

This bill would ~~contain proposed~~ *make* appropriations for ~~display purposes for~~ support of state government for the 1997–98 fiscal year.

This bill would declare that it is to take effect immediately as an urgency statute.

Vote: ~~majority~~ ⅔ . Appropriation: no. Fiscal committee: yes. State-mandated local program: no.

The people of the State of California do enact as follows:

1   SECTION 1.00.   This act shall be known and may be cited as the
2 "Budget Act of 1997."
3   SEC. 1.50.   (a) In accordance with Section 13338 of the Govern-
4 ment Code, as added by Chapter 1284, Statutes of 1978, and as
5 amended by Chapter 1286, Statutes of 1984, it is the intent of the Leg-
6 islature that this act utilize a coding scheme compatible with the
7 Governor's Budget and the records of the State Controller, and pro-
8 vide for the appropriation of federal funds received by the state and
9 deposited in the State Treasury.

Page one of the 691-page Budget Bill of 1997 (AB 107). Historically, each house conducts hearings and crafts its own version of the budget, subsequently finalizing the budget language in a two-house conference committee.

To incur and pay expenses not otherwise provided for as they deem reasonably necessary, including the repair, alteration, improvement, and equipping of the respective chambers and offices through a process governed by competitive bidding.[122]

To assist the committee with its administrative, fiscal and business affairs, the Assembly Rules Committee employs a staff of secretaries and administrators, headed by the Chief Administrative Officer who is appointed by the Chair of the Rules Committee.[123] The Senate Rules Committee employs a similar staff, supervised by an Executive Officer, to assist it in the performance of its duties.

The Rules Committees, beginning with the biennial session in 1973, were charged with recommending whether or not most of the Joint Rules governing legislative procedure on bills should or should not be suspended by their respective houses. The responsibility of making these recommendations, which are almost always adopted by the house, adds significantly to the powers of the committees, as the nature of their recommendation may well determine the fate of the proposed legislation.

The Senate Rules Committee appoints members to Senate standing committees; the Speaker performs this function in the Assembly. [124]

The Fiscal Committees (Appropriations and Budget Committees)

The Assembly Budget Committee and the Senate Budget and Fiscal Review Committee must, by any standard, be among the hardest working and most powerful committees of the Legislature. They are charged with forging a consensus out of the myriad demands made upon a State Budget which is now in excess of $64.1 billion.

Within the first 10 days of each calendar year,[125] these committees are the recipients of budget bills introduced simultaneously in each house. These identical bills are the result of many months of effort by the executive branch to establish the financial requirements of the state for the forthcoming fiscal year. Initially, then, the priorities reflect the determinations of the Governor. Once introduced, the budget bills immediately come under the scrutiny of the staffs of the fiscal committees of the Legislature and the office of the Legislative Analyst. Opinions are sought regarding every possible service and capital outlay imaginable and are reviewed at numerous hearings by various subcommittees. The entire Legislature necessarily must be attuned to the deliberations of the fiscal committees because every member's constituency will be affected.

A mandatory deadline is placed upon the principal effort of these committees, since the State Budget or alternative financing must be in effect at the beginning of the fiscal year.

So important is the attention to a balanced budget that the Constitution expressly prohibits the Legislature from sending to the Governor "any bill appropriating funds for expenditure during the fiscal year for which the

[122] *Assembly Rule 18; Senate Rule 13.2.*
[123] *Assembly Rule 14(e).*
[124] *Senate Rules 11, 12.5; Assembly Rule 26(a)(6).*
[125] *Constitution*, Article IV, Section 12(a).

budget bill is to be enacted, except emergency bills recommended by the Governor . . .".[126] Thus, every bill appropriating money from the General Fund which is passed by the Legislature prior to the enactment of the Budget Bill must await the Governor's recommendation before being presented to him or her for signature.

Appropriations Committees

Any bill which: appropriates money; imposes new responsibilities or duties on the state; liberalizes any state function, program or responsibility; or results in substantial loss of revenue or reduction of state expenditures, must be heard by the Appropriations Committees in the Assembly and the Senate before it can be voted upon by the respective houses.[127] This means that any bill implicitly or explicitly touching upon one or more of the above criteria must pass through both policy and fiscal committees of both houses. The application of this rule requires these committees to review an estimated 80 percent of all bills considered by the Legislature.

The fiscal committees are generally not thought of as policy committees except for the Budget, although some measures are occasionally referred directly to these committees. The distinction is noted by the Joint Rules which establishes different deadlines for policy committee and fiscal committee action.[128] These staggered deadlines recognize the problem faced by authors of bills which must come under review by the fiscal committee after clearing the policy committee to which they were previously referred.

The Joint Rules Committee

The Joint Rules Committee consists of the Members of the Assembly Committee on Rules, the Assembly Majority and Minority Leaders, the Speaker of the Assembly, and four members of the Senate Committee on Rules. An additional number of Senators may be appointed by the Senate Rules Committee to maintain equality in the number of Assembly Members and Senators on the committee.[129]

The committee has a continuing existence and may meet and conduct business while the Legislature is in recess as well as during the time the Legislature is in session.[130]

The committee ascertains facts and reports its recommendations to the Legislature. Specifically, the committee concerns itself with the relations between the two houses and making recommendations to improve that relationship; changes in the law to cure defects affecting the Legislature; adjustments in legislative procedures governing the processing of proposed legislation; coordination of the work of the Assembly and Senate and their committees by eliminating duplication of effort.

The committee also is empowered to gather data and statistics it deems useful to the houses or the Members. It permits and approves the involvement

---

[126] *Constitution*, Article IV, Section 12(c).
[127] *Joint Rule 10.5. See also, Senate Rule 12(2).*
[128] *Joint Rule 61.*
[129] *Joint Rule 40.*
[130] *Id.*

of the Legislative Counsel in litigation.[131] The committee is also authorized to participate in the work of the National Conference of State Legislative Leaders.[132]

All space in the State Capitol Building Annex, except the first floor of the annex, is allocated from time to time by the Joint Rules Committee in accordance with its determination of the needs of the Senate and Assembly and for facilities and agencies dealing with the Legislature as a whole, including press quarters, bill room, offices for the Legislative Counsel and for committees created by the two houses jointly.

The space thus allocated to the Senate and to the Assembly is allotted from time to time by the Senate Rules Committee and the Assembly Rules Committee, respectively.[133]

The committee appoints and employs the chairpersons and employees of all joint committees except those of the Joint Legislative Budget and the Joint Legislative Audit Committees. It employs its own staff headed by a Chief Administrative Officer.[134]

In summary, the committee's function is to facilitate and promote the joint legislative and committee functions of the two houses and to report to them on matters of mutual concern.

The Joint Legislative Budget Committee

In the 1930's, it became painfully obvious that the Legislature lacked the capacity to adequately analyze and review the fiscal implications and administrative effects of the Governor's proposals. The Chief Executive had at his command a sizable staff to collect data to substantiate and press for his programs. The Legislature found itself unable to initiate a positive program. It was in the position of reacting to the Governor's proposals rather than acting in an independent or affirmative manner by utilizing its own sources of information.

Recognizing the state of affairs, the Legislature, in 1941, passed a bill establishing a Legislative Audit Bureau.[135] This bill was subsequently vetoed by the Governor. Reacting to the Governor's veto, the Legislature promptly amended the Joint Rules creating the Joint Legislative Budget Committee.[136] The committee immediately employed the first Legislative Analyst.

The committee was reconstituted at each successive session by the adoption of the Joint Rules, until 1951, when it was established on a permanent basis by statute.[137]

The committee consists of seven Assembly Members and seven Senators appointed by the Speaker and the Senate Rules Committee, respectively. The chairperson is elected by the committee from its membership.[138]

---

[131] *Id.*

[132] *Government Code,* Section 9111.

[133] *Government Code,* Section 9108.

[134] *Joint Rules 40(i), 40(j).*

[135] *1941 Regular Session,* Assembly Bill 1129.

[136] *Statutes of 1941,* Resolution Chapter 117.

[137] *Government Code,* Sections 9140–9143.

[138] *Government Code,* Section 9141; *Joint Rule 37.*

The rules of the committee require that a quorum consists of at least four members from each house. Its duties are to ascertain facts and to make recommendations to the Legislature and to each of the houses concerning the State Budget, the revenues and expenditures of the state, the organization and functions of the state, its departments, subdivisions, and agencies, and such other matters as may be provided for in the Joint Rules of the Legislature.

The committee may also render services to any other investigating committee of the Legislature pursuant to contract between it and the committee for which the services are to be performed.[139]

The Joint Legislative Audit Committee

California's Legislature established the Joint Legislative Audit Committee by statute in 1955. In establishing the committee, the Legislature recognized the need for a postaudit independent of the audit performed by the executive branch of the state government. Through its own audits and investigations, the Legislature can test the reliability of the financial and operating information that is used in the decisionmaking process.[140]

The Joint Legislative Audit Committee consists of seven Senators and seven Assembly Members. Four Assembly Members and four Senators constitute the quorum necessary to conduct the committee's business.[141] Members of the committee are appointed under the provisions of the Joint Rules of the Senate and Assembly. Senate members of the committee are appointed by the Senate Committee on Rules, and Assembly Members are appointed by the Speaker; the chairperson of the committee is selected by the membership of the committee.[142]

The committee is a factfinding and investigative committee which transmits its reports and recommendations to the Senate and Assembly for further action by the policy committees.

---

[139] *Government Code*, Section 9142; *Joint Rule 37.*
[140] *Government Code*, Sections 10500–10504.1.
[141] *Joint Rule 37.3.*
[142] *Joint Rules 36.5, 37.3.*

Chapter X

Legislative Personnel

At the first session of the California Legislature in 1850, legislative staff consisted of a parliamentarian, a recorder of minutes, a chaplain, a sergeant at arms, and an occasional supernumerary. This level of legislative support remained relatively unchanged for almost 70 years. It was not until the eve of World War I that legislative legal services were formally established. A legislative fiscal service came into being some 30 years later. Following World War II, the legislature faced the multiple pressures of a spiraling population, a technological explosion, federal decentralization and a concomitant demand for increased state services. Vital areas of concern, such as taxes, education, welfare and transportation, became so complex that responsible representation required the support not only of experts, but of coordinators.

The workload is enormous, and lawmaking is now a full-time occupation in California. The staffs of joint and house committees have evolved into year-round positions, while special committees and commissions rely on permanent professional help throughout their existence.

Adequate staff, selected by the Legislature and supported by legislative contingent funds, is the necessary result if the Legislature is to meet its responsibilities and to act as an independent policy and decision making body for the citizens of this state.

Support Staff/Agencies

In certain areas of endeavor, the Legislature has seen fit to create agencies to serve both houses of the Legislature or agencies to support not only the Legislature but other parts of state government as well (e.g., the Governor's Office). These organizations perform functions which would otherwise require a duplication of work and personnel if each house were to employ its own separate sources of legal, fiscal, auditing, and informational services.

The Legislative Counsel

The office of the Legislative Counsel was created by statute in 1913 and serves as the legal counsel to the Legislature and its Members.[1] However, assisted by a staff of over 80 attorneys, the Legislative Counsel provides both to the Legislature and to others a variety of legal services in connection with legislative activities.

The Legislative Counsel is selected by concurrent resolution at the beginning of each regular session of the Legislature, and serves until a successor has been selected and qualified.[2] He or she is chosen without reference to party affiliation and solely on the basis of fitness to perform the duties of the office.[3] In case of a vacancy while the Legislature is not in

---

[1] *Statutes of 1913*, Chapter 322. Mr. Bion M. Gregory has served as Legislative Counsel since 1976.

[2] *Government Code*, Section 10201.

[3] *Government Code*, Section 10203.

session, a committee consisting of the Speaker and Speaker pro Tempore of the Assembly; President pro Tempore of the Senate and the Chairperson of the Senate Committee on Finance selects a person to serve as the Legislative Counsel until the Legislature reconvenes and makes its selection by concurrent resolution.[4]

The Legislative Counsel must be available for the performance of services at all sessions of the Legislature.[5] To this end, a permanent office is maintained in the State Capitol at Sacramento, convenient to the Chambers of the Assembly and Senate. The Legislative Counsel also maintains additional offices nearby.[6]

The Legislative Counsel and his or her staff of deputies maintain an attorney-client relationship with the Legislature and its Members and are prohibited from revealing to any person outside the office the contents or nature of a matter handled by the office which has not become public record.[7] Such material may, however, be revealed with the consent of the person bringing the matter before the Legislative Counsel.

The Legislative Counsel is also authorized to maintain an attorney-client relationship with the Governor in the course of providing him or her legal services concerning, for example, information on bills presented for approval or rejection, or legal opinion as to constitutionality, operation or effect of a bill.[8]

Among the principal duties of this office, the Legislative Counsel assists Members of the Legislature in the drafting of legislative measures;[9] assists the Legislature and its committees in amendment or consideration of measures before them;[10] assists state agencies as to the preparation of legislative measures;[11] advises legislative investigating committees;[12] prepares legislative measures for judges;[13] and, if requested by 25 or more electors proposing an initiative measure, the Legislative Counsel assists in the preparation of the measure if, in his or her judgment, there is a reasonable probability that the measure will be submitted to the state's voters.[14]

A large percentage of the bills, resolutions and amendments considered by the Legislature is drafted by the Legislative Counsel and his or her staff of deputies. Regardless of whether a measure has been actually drafted by the Legislative Counsel or not, it may not be introduced unless it is prepared for introduction by this office in proper bill form, accompanied by a digest of the bill showing the changes proposed in the existing law.[15]

The Legislative Counsel is required to prepare for periodic publication a cumulative Legislative Index of topics of pending legislation, together with tables cross-referencing code section numbers and pending bills which

---

[4] *Government Code*, Section 10202.
[5] *Government Code*, Section 10230.
[6] *Government Code*, Section 10206.
[7] *Government Code*, Sections 10207, 10208.
[8] *Government Code*, Sections 10207 and 10235, as amended by *Statutes of 1993*, Chapter 890.
[9] *Government Code*, Sections 10231, 10233.
[10] *Government Code*, Sections 10231, 10234
[11] *Government Code*, Sections 10231, 10232.
[12] *Government Code*, Sections 10231, 10236.
[13] *Government Code*, Sections 10231, 10237–10241.
[14] *Government Code*, Section 10243.
[15] *Joint Rule 8.5.*

would affect those sections.[16] Also compiled for publication are the text and summary digests of all chaptered bills in a particular year (e.g., the *Statutes of 1997*).[17]

Among other miscellaneous duties, the Legislative Counsel advises the Legislature as to legislation necessary to maintain the accuracy of the codes;[18] with the prior approval of the Joint Rules Committee, he or she participates in litigation involving the Legislature, its committees and members;[19] and he or she may contract with any county or city for the codification, compilation or indexing of any or all of its ordinances or resolutions.[20]

The Legislative Counsel is an ex officio member of the California Law Revision Commission[21] and the California Commission on Uniform State Laws.[22]

The Legislative Analyst

The nonpartisan Legislative Analyst's Office serves as the Legislature's primary source of budgetary and fiscal information. The office is headed by the Legislative Analyst,[23] who is appointed by the Joint Legislative Budget Committee, which also oversees the work of the Legislative Analyst's Office.[24]

The staff of the Legislative Analyst's Office, 36 professional and 13 support personnel, is organized by program area (e.g., education or health and welfare). Each section within the office analyzes budgets and other fiscal and policy issues in its particular area of specialization.

A major function performed by the office is analyzing the Governor's annual proposed budget. As a basis for budget hearings, the analyst's staff prepares two documents, the *Analysis of the Budget Bill* and *Perspectives and Issues*. As a result of a longstanding arrangement under which the Governor's budget staff makes available to the analyst's staff, on a confidential basis, preliminary drafts of the proposed budget as it is being developed, the *Analysis of the Budget Bill* and the *Perspectives and Issues* are available to the Legislature approximately six weeks after the Budget Bill is presented to the Legislature.

As a matter of policy, the recommendations of the Legislative Analyst are presented to the Legislature and its committees without recommendation by the Joint Legislative Budget Committee. In this way, the Legislative Analyst's office presents its own conclusions. The members of the committee are free to accept or oppose these recommendations before other committees and on the floor of their respective houses.

The office provides staff assistance to the Legislature throughout its deliberations on the annual Budget Bill, including testifying on its findings

---

[16] *Joint Rule 13.1.*
[17] *Government Code*, Sections 9764, 9765; *Joint Rules 13.3, 13.5.*
[18] *Government Code*, Section 10242.
[19] *Government Code*, Section 10246.
[20] *Government Code*, Section 10244.
[21] *Government Code*, Section 8281.
[22] *Government Code*, Section 8261.
[23] Elizabeth G. Hill has served as the Legislative Analyst since August 19, 1986.
[24] *Government Code*, Section 9143; *see also Joint Rule 37.*

and recommendations when the Assembly and Senate hear the bill in budget subcommittees as well as in the joint budget conference committee.

The Legislative Analyst's Office also provides reports on subjects of special interest to the Legislature, responds on a confidential basis to individual requests from legislators on fiscal and policy issues, and prepares analyses of statewide initiatives and propositions.

The California Law Revision Commission

The California Law Revision Commission was created in 1953.[25] The commission consists of one Senator and one Member of the Assembly, who constitute a joint investigating committee, and seven members appointed by the Governor with the advice and consent of the Senate. The members appointed by the Governor hold office for a term of four years. The Legislative Counsel is an ex officio member.[26] The members appointed by the Governor receive $100 a day while attending meetings and their actual expenses incurred while in performance of their duties, including travel expenses.[27]

The commission selects one of its members as chairperson,[28] and is authorized to appoint an executive secretary and such other employees as may be necessary.[29] Members of the commission, appointed by the Governor, and all employees of the commission are prohibited from advocating the passage or defeat of any legislation or the approval or veto of any legislation by the Governor in his or her official capacity as a member or employee of the commission.[30]

The State Library, all other state agencies,[31] and the Board of Governors of the State Bar are required to assist the commission in its work.[32]

The commission is required to examine the common law, the statutes of the state and judicial decisions, and to receive and consider suggestions relative thereto, for the purpose of discovering defects and anachronisms in the law and to recommend needed reforms.[33] It is also required to recommend the express repeal of statutes repealed by implication or held unconstitutional.[34] At each regular session of the Legislature, the commission is required to report to the Legislature on its studies and submit a list of topics to be studied. Before any topic is studied by the commission it must be approved by concurrent resolution adopted by the Legislature.[35] Its reports are submitted to the Governor, certain legislative offices, and state agency offices which request them.[36] The reports, exhibits, and proposed legislative measures are printed by the Office of State Printing under the supervision of the commission.

---

[25] *Government Code*, Section 8280.
[26] *Government Code*, Section 8281.
[27] *Government Code*, Section 11564.5.
[28] *Government Code*, Section 8283.
[29] *Government Code*, Sections 8284, 8285.
[30] *Government Code*, Section 8288.
[31] *Government Code*, Section 8286.
[32] *Government Code*, Section 8287.
[33] *Government Code*, Section 8289.
[34] *Government Code*, Section 8290.
[35] *Government Code*, Section 8293.
[36] *Government Code*, Section 8291.

The commission is required to cooperate with legislative committees, and may contract with such committees to render services to them.[37] It is also authorized to cooperate with any bar association or other learned, professional or scientific association,[38] and may, with the approval of the Director of General Services, contract with colleges, universities, schools of law or other research institutions, or with qualified individuals to perform research for the commission.[39]

The Commission on Uniform State Laws

The Commission on Uniform State Laws for California was created in 1927,[40] and consists of one Member of the Assembly, one Senator, six additional members appointed by the Governor, and the Legislative Counsel, who is an ex officio member.[41]

Each appointed member of the commission must be a member of the State Bar in good standing.[42] The term of office is for four years,[43] and they receive no compensation for their services as commissioners,[44] other than travel and actual expenses while conducting the commission's business.[45]

The commissioners must attend the meetings of the National Conference of Commissioners on Uniform State Laws,[46] and they must do all in their power to promote uniformity in state laws upon all subjects where uniformity is deemed desirable and practicable.[47]

The commission must bring about, as far as is feasible, passage of the various uniform acts recommended by the national conference, and must devise and recommend such additional legislation as is deemed necessary to accomplish the purposes of the law creating the commission.[48] It must also report to the Legislature, giving an account of its transactions and its recommendations for legislation.[49]

The legislative members of the commission constitute a joint interim investigating committee on the subject of uniform state laws, and have the same powers and duties as joint investigating committees of the Legislature.[50]

Bureau of State Audits

Examinations and reports of financial statements of state government agencies, and other related assignments including performance audits, are conducted by the Bureau of State Audits. The Bureau operates under the direction of the Milton Marks Commission on California State Government Organization and Economy (known as the Little Hoover Commission), an

---

[37] *Government Code,* Section 8295.
[38] *Government Code,* Section 8296.
[39] *Government Code,* Section 8297.
[40] *Statutes of 1927,* Chapter 498. *See now, Government Code,* Section 8260.
[41] *Government Code,* Section 8261.
[42] *Government Code,* Section 8262.
[43] *Government Code,* Section 8263.
[44] *Government Code,* Section 8266.
[45] *Government Code,* Section 8267.
[46] *Government Code,* Section 8269.
[47] *Government Code,* Section 8270.
[48] *Government Code,* Section 8271.
[49] *Government Code,* Section 8272.
[50] *Government Code,* Section 8261.

independent governmental organization designed to promote economy, efficiency and improved service in state government.[51]

The State Auditor, who is the head of the Bureau of State Audits, is appointed by the Governor from a list of three names submitted by the Joint Legislative Audit Committee, is chosen without reference to party affiliation, and serves a term of four years.[52] To assist in the operation of the Bureau, the State Auditor has authority to employ deputy state auditors as well as professional, technical and clerical assistants.[53]

The purpose of the Bureau of State Audits is to provide periodic audits of state organizations, programs and services. These audits promote sound fiscal and administrative policy for the state government, fulfill the condition for the receipt of billions of dollars in federal grant funds, and provide an independent financial audit report that is relied upon by underwriters, bond-rating companies, and potential investors.[54] To this end, the State Auditor is given legal authority to access and examine any books, accounts, and other records of any agency of the state, as well as city, county, and school or special district, for the purpose of an audit.[55]

The State Auditor is required to annually examine state agency financial statements and to issue an auditor's report which conforms to U.S. Government and American Institute of Certified Public Accountants standards.[56] The State Auditor shall also conduct audits requested by the Joint Legislative Audit Committee to the extent funding is available.[57]

Other significant duties of the State Auditor are examination and audit of any contract involving expenditure of public funds in excess of $10,000,[58] and administration of the Improper Governmental Activities Reporting Act (the Whistle Blower Statute).[59]

Capitol Branch of the State Library

The California Research Bureau (CRB), was established in 1991 to service the research needs of the Legislature and Governor.[60] Although the main offices are located in the Library and Courts Building Annex, a satellite office is maintained in the State Capitol for convenience.

The CRB provides nonpartisan, confidential research to Members of the Legislature and to the Governor's Office. The bureau makes available the vast resources of the California State Library through a wide variety of services, including: specialized legislative library services; seminars; general research; and assistance in preparing legislative proposals.

---

[51] *Government Code,* Sections 8501 and 8543 *et seq.* The Bureau of State Audits was formerly the Auditor General's Office, an organization under the direction of the Joint Legislative Audit Committee. Its current configuration is the result of a reorganization contained in *Statutes of 1993,* Chapter 12, which went into effect May 7, 1993.
[52] *Government Code,* Section 8543.2, 8543.3. The current State Auditor is Kurt R. Sjoberg.
[53] *Government Code,* Section 8544.
[54] *Government Code,* Section 8521.4.
[55] *Government Code,* Section 8545.2.
[56] *Government Code,* Sections 8546.3, 8546.4.
[57] *Government Code,* Section 8546.1.
[58] *Government Code,* Section 8546.7.
[59] *Government Code,* Sections 8547–8547.11.
[60] *Statutes of 1991,* Chapter 118.

Senate and Assembly Staff

The Senate and Assembly are authorized by the Constitution to elect officers,[61] and their Rules Committees are empowered to employ such additional staff for individual members of the Senate and Assembly and their committees as they deem necessary.[62]

The assignment of employees is determined by the Rules Committee of each respective house of the Legislature.[63] They may work for the house, a committee thereof, or for a member. The Rules Committees set the conditions of employment, and pay these employees from the contingent funds of the respective house.

In the absence of its own sources of support and information, it would be extremely difficult for the Legislature to fulfill its role as an equal and independent branch of government as intended and contemplated by the doctrine of the separation of powers between our executive, legislative and judicial branches of government.

Chief Clerk of the Assembly

The Chief Clerk is one of the three nonmember officers that serve the Assembly (the other two are the Sergeant at Arms and the Chaplain),[64] and is elected by a majority vote of the Assembly. The Chief Clerk's primary responsibility is to serve as chief parliamentarian of the Assembly.[65] The present Chief Clerk, E. Dotson Wilson, was first elected in January 1992.

In addition to serving as parliamentarian, the Chief Clerk coordinates the activities of a nonpartisan staff of over 30 individuals. This staff is charged with recording, documenting and assisting the Assembly in processing all legislation at every stage of its development. This information is then made available to the public via publications and the internet.

The Office of the Chief Clerk publishes three important publications for the reference of legislators and the public alike. These publications are the Assembly Daily File, the agenda for committee hearings and floor sessions; the Assembly Daily Journal, the official record of the proceedings of the Assembly which chronicles all official Assembly activities including floor votes; and the Assembly History, published in a daily and weekly format, which reports all actions taken on every Assembly bill being considered.

Other sections of the Office of the Chief Clerk include the Engrossing and Enrolling unit which verifies the printed accuracy of each bill through each amendment and reprinting, and the Floor Analysis unit which coordinates and compiles analyses written by committee consultants on every bill prior to Assembly floor vote.

At each step in the legislative process, from the introduction and three readings of all bills, through the processing of all amendments and tallying of all Assembly floor votes, to the final enrollment of bills and presentation to

---

[61] *Constitution*, Article IV, Section 7(a).
[62] *Assembly Rules 14, 17; Senate Rules 13, 13.6.*
[63] *Assembly Rule 14, Senate Rule 13.*
[64] *Constitution*, Article IV, Section 7(a); *Government Code*, Sections 9171–9173.
[65] For duties of the Chief Clerk, *see generally, Assembly Rule 32.*

the Governor, the members of the Chief Clerk's staff work to ensure the integrity of the most essential functions of the Legislature.

Secretary of the Senate

The Secretary of the Senate is one of the three nonmember officers elected by the membership of the Senate (the other two being the Sergeant at Arms and the Chaplain). The duties of the office of the Secretary of the Senate closely mirror those of the Chief Clerk of the Assembly. The present Secretary of the Senate, Greg Schmidt, was first elected in August 1996.[66]

Sergeant at Arms

The Chief Sergeants at Arms and their Security Officers of each house have the powers and authorities conferred by law upon peace officers, in all parts of the state, and have as their primary duty the maintenance of order and preservation of decorum at the daily sessions of the Legislature, in the committee hearings and in the halls and lobbies.[67] The Chief Sergeant at Arms is elected by a majority vote of the membership of each house.[68] The present Assembly Chief Sergeant at Arms, Ronald E. Pane, was elected in April 1996. The present Senate Chief Sergeant at Arms, Tony Beard, Jr., was elected in December 1979.

The Chief Sergeant at Arms and his or her Security Officers also provide miscellaneous services for the Members of the Legislature and its committees. During the joint recess, for example, the Assembly Security Officers travel with and record the meetings of the Assembly Committees.

While in the performance of their duties, the Chief Sergeant at Arms and his or her Security Officers may exercise their peace officer powers. This authority is most often exercised when the house is placed "under call" and the presiding officer orders the sergeants to compel the absent members to return to the chambers and record their vote on the issue before the house.

The Speaker's Staff

The Speaker of the California Assembly, in effect, is responsible to three separate constituencies. First are the people in the Speaker's Assembly District; second, the people of the entire state as a Speaker is a statewide political figure and leader, and, finally, to the membership of the Assembly who have elected him or her to the position of leadership. In addition, the Speaker is the liaison between the Assembly and the major leaders of the state and the federal administration in Washington.

To fulfill these obligations, it is necessary that the Speaker maintain a staff of wide and varied talents and backgrounds. The staff, with clerical support, consists of consultants with expertise in areas of concern to all Californians, e.g., agriculture, labor, education, health care, etc., who are charged with everything from research to aiding Members of the Legislature in their issue areas. They must brief the Speaker and prepare resource material for the

---

[66] *Journal of the Senate*, 1995–96 Regular Session, p. 6003.
[67] *Government Code*, Sections 9194, 9194.5, and 9195, *Assembly Rule 33, Senate Rule 10.*
[68] *Government Code*, Section 9194.5.

many occasions when he or she addresses various groups and citizens throughout the state. In addition, the Speaker's office has a staff person who acts as a liaison with the media statewide.

The staff itself will, of course, vary in composition and character, depending upon the nature and predilections of a particular Speaker, but it is ultimately their responsibility to keep the Speaker informed on a day-to-day basis about all the major problems confronting the state.

The President pro Tempore's Staff

The President pro Tempore's staff is headed by a Chief of Staff who serves as the liaison between the pro Tempore and Speaker's office, Governor's office, Senate Members, Assembly Members and the administration. This individual directly supervises the pro Tempore's staff and coordinates legislative projects to be completed by professionals in the pro Tempore's office. Among other duties, the chief of staff reviews and approves all speeches and correspondence which requires the pro Tempore's signature, and supervises and coordinates the pro Tempore's schedule.

Senate Office of Research

The Senate Office of Research (SOR) was established in 1969 by the Senate Committee on Rules as the bipartisan research and strategic policy-planning unit for the California Senate. Under the committee's direction, SOR serves the Senate as a whole and is dedicated to developing useful and effective public policy. SOR consultants, specialized in their fields, are available to every member of the Senate to develop problem-solving ideas and options, to organize hearings on policy issues, to draft legislation and to assist in obtaining its enactment. SOR provides objective analysis and recommendations. It analyzes the policy implications of ballot pamphlet propositions prior to each statewide election. SOR also provides questions for the Senate Rules Committee to ask for governor's nominees during their confirmation hearings.[69]

Majority and Minority Caucus Consultants

Each caucus of the State Assembly—Republican and Democratic—receives staff support from either the Minority or Majority Consultants.

These partisan offices are involved in leadership policy development, legislative research, committee monitoring and staffing, and assist with members' public information programs. They maintain records and information systems, work closely with legislators' district offices, and keep abreast of political party structures and issues.

Committee Consultants

The backbone of the Legislature's committee operation is the committee consultant, who is directly responsible to his or her committee chairperson and the members of the committee. Thorough knowledge of his or her subject matter area is a prime requisite for every consultant. A committee consultant's principal duties consist of making preparations for the

---

[69] "The California Senate Office of Research," http://www.sen.ca.gov

committee meetings during the joint recesses and the session, analyzing the bills that are to be heard by his or her committee and providing summaries of their contents for the committee and the public,[70] answering committee correspondence, performing legislative research, providing committee members with technical information, and in some instances presenting a bill before a committee if the author is unable to attend. At least one consultant is assigned to each committee to assist with its legislative workload.

In the Assembly, the committee consultants are charged with the responsibility of writing the floor analyses of the bill reported from their committee to the floor.

Some of the major committees, e.g., Appropriations, Education, and Revenue and Taxation, are provided with additional consulting staff to assist them with their legislative work. Where the committee utilizes additional consultants, one of them, a chief consultant, is usually appointed to supervise their combined activities.

Computer Support Staff

A highly trained technical staff is maintained by the Legislature to provide state-of-the-art computer services. The work of this staff becomes more critical with each passing year as technological innovations are adapted to the unique requirements of the operations of the legislative branch.

The Legislative Data Center was created in 1985, after then-Assembly Speaker Willie L. Brown, Jr. instructed the Legislative Counsel to link the Capitol and Members' district offices with an on-line computer network. This new system was designed to augment the computer system which had been installed in Capitol offices in 1982.

The computer network operated by the Legislative Data Center provides legislators and their staff with easy access to virtually any legislative information through the computer terminals installed in each office. Accessible through this system are bill histories, bill text, daily files, committee analyses, and the complete California Codes. These various categories are updated many times each day, providing the user with up-to-the-minute information.

In 1993, legislation was enacted to provide the general public with the same level of accurate and wide-ranging legislative information available through the Capitol computer network.[71] The new statute directed the Legislative Counsel to establish a connection to link the database maintained by the Legislative Data Center with the Internet, a nonprofit public network. The connection to the Internet, in turn, makes the information available to computer users throughout the state and world.

In addition, the services provided by the Legislative Data Center focus on the practical needs of Members' offices. Word processing, calendars and scheduling, constituent correspondence, electronic messaging, and bill lists for bill tracking are made available through computer connections to offices in the Capitol. These features are also available to Members' district offices.

---

[70] *Assembly Rule 56.5.*
[71] *Statutes of 1993,* Chapter 1235.

Legislative Fellowship Programs

In 1957, the Assembly, the Ford Foundation, and five California institutions of higher learning initiated California's first legislative intern program.[72] Though Congress had previously instituted an intern program, California's program was the pioneering venture on the state government level.

The primary goal of the program is an educational one to provide recent graduates with experience and training in the legislative process and at the same time furnish full-time research and administrative assistance to Members and committees of the Assembly.

While the initial program was jointly funded by the Ford Foundation and the Assembly, the Assembly found the program to be so successful that when the Ford Foundation's funds were depleted the Assembly proceeded to totally finance the program itself under the new title of the Assembly Fellowship Program. In 1987 the program was renamed the Jesse Marvin Unruh Assembly Fellowship in honor of the former Speaker of the Assembly and California State Treasurer.

Each year, 18 fellows are selected by an executive committee consisting of Assembly staff and faculty members from several California colleges and universities.

The fellowship program lasts 11 months. During this time, the fellows work either on the personal staff of a Member of the Assembly or on the staff of an Assembly committee where their activities are directed and supervised by the committee chairperson and the committee consultant. A fellow's duties normally run the gamut of legislative activity: drafting correspondence, answering constituent requests, and research.

Over 300 interns and fellows have served in the Assembly since 1957. The program has provided the Assembly with a high quality research reservoir at a very minimal cost to the taxpayer. The value of the fellowship experience is evidenced by the fact that many former participants have been elected as Members of the Legislature or occupied important consultant and administrative positions in the Assembly. Other postfellowship activities have included the judiciary, teaching, law, journalism, service with state agencies, local government, and graduate study. Beginning in 1973, the Senate funded and initiated an associate program comparable to the fellowship program employed by the Assembly. In 1986 a third fellowship program was created to provide similar opportunities in the executive branch. Each of these programs is administered by the Center for California Studies at CSU Sacramento. The academic qualifications for all three of these programs are similar. The possession of a bachelor's degree is a prerequisite for acceptance in each program.

---

[72] The five institutions were the University of California at Berkeley; the University of California at Los Angeles; Stanford University; the University of Southern California; and, the Claremont Graduate School.

Chief Clerk's Internship Program

In 1989, the Assembly Chief Clerk instituted a paid internship program in cooperation with the University of California, Davis and California State University, Sacramento. Intern applicants are usually screened each October for spring/summer employment. The program gives upper division college students the opportunity to work full-time in the Chief Clerk's office from five to seven months while earning significant college credit. The internships are unique, in that interns are granted floor privileges to encourage total immersion in the intricacies of the legislative process. Jobs performed by the interns include floor amendment tracking, engrossment and enrollment of bills, amending, and liaison duties. Special seminars provide the interns with access to valuable information while interacting with representatives of the legislative, executive, and judicial branches, as well as lobbyists and political journalists. Over 30 students have participated in the program and most students eventually obtain full-time legislative oriented employment.

California's State Capitol, circa 1947

CHAPTER XI

THE CAPITOL

THE SITING OF A CAPITOL

Among the duties of the Constitutional Convention of 1849 was that of proposing a seat of government for the new state. The question was placed before a group of men little affected by historical precedent, for the majority of the delegates had settled in the northern part of the territory for less than a decade, and one-fourth had come west with the gold rush. The few native Californians present might have recalled a territorial capital being moved from Monterey to San Diego, Santa Barbara or Los Angeles at the whim of various Mexican governors. Even Monterey, while playing host to the convention, claimed only the dubious distinction of housing, since 1846, the headquarters of the American military governors.

Thus unencumbered by tradition, the delegates voiced their desire for a location free of the distractions of commerce. Offers of accommodations poured in from communities large and small, all envisioning a substantial return on their investment.

"During the session, two men from the booming little town of Pueblo de San José were sent galloping over the hills to Monterey to offer Washington Square in their town as a capitol site and to assure delegates that a suitable building would await them. After hours of debate the convention accepted the offer and named Pueblo de San José the capital—with the qualification that, by law, it might be moved elsewhere." [1]

---

[1] *California's State Capitol,* Northern California Writers' Program, Works Projects Administration. Office of State Printing, Sacramento, California, 1942, p. 28.
　　"The first session of the Legislature shall be held at the Pueblo de San José, which place shall be the permanent seat of government until removed by law." *Constitution of 1849,* Article XI, Section 1.

San Jose

The First and Second Sessions of the Legislature, which were held in 1850 and 1851, convened at San Jose. Founded in 1777, San Jose was the first incorporated city in the state and the county seat of Santa Clara County.

The Capitol was a two-story adobe hotel, 60 by 40 feet, the upper story being assigned to the Assembly and the lower to the Senate. William Kelly, English author of *A Stroll Through the Diggings of California,* who visited the First Legislature at work, describes the Senate and Assembly Chambers as being ". . . accommodated under the same roof, one downstairs, the other above; but, by a sort of solecism in the arrangement, the Senate, or upper house, occupy the lower apartment, which is a large, ill-lighted, badly-ventilated room, with a low ceiling, and a rough railing a little inside the door, beyond which none but the elect may pass. Each member had a rush-bottomed armchair, and a small desk with stationery, . . . At the farther end, the Speaker was perched in a species of pulpit; the floor was covered with a number of little carpets, of various shapes and patterns, . . . The other apartment (the Assembly Chamber) is of precisely the same size, but has the advantage of greater loftiness, . . . plain common chairs, flat deal tables, and a strip of matting thrown where the feet are erroneously supposed to rest, being the extent of the accommodation . . ." .[2]

Judge Sexton of Oroville said that "no sooner was the Legislature fairly organized than the members began to growl about their accommodations. They didn't like the legislative building and swore terribly between drinks at the accommodations of the town generally. Many of the solons expressed a desire to remove the capital from San Jose immediately." [3]

---

[2] William Kelly, Esq., *A Stroll Through the Diggings of California,* Simms and McIntyre, London, 1852, pp. 190–191.
[3] *California's State Capitol,* p. 31.

During the session of 1850, several proposals to provide suitable lands for state buildings, along with lands, bonds or moneys to establish funding for construction, were presented to the Legislature. General Vallejo's offer was by far the most generous. "The Committee on Public Buildings reported in favor of accepting the Vallejo proposition, and on April 22, an Act was passed and approved directing the Governor to submit to the people at the following general election the various propositions that had been made for the location of the Capital, . . ." .[4] At the general election of October 7, 1850, the proposal of General Vallejo was overwhelmingly favored.

On January 14, 1851, General Vallejo presented a communication to the Senate offering bonds as security for the fulfillment of his proposal. A majority of the Senate Committee on Public Buildings reported a bill recommending removal of the capital to the town of Vallejo which, passing both houses, was approved by the Governor on February 4, 1851.[5]

Vallejo

The Third Session opened at Vallejo on January 5, 1852. The capital was in a state of total chaos. Accommodations of all sorts were in varying stages of construction, with workmen noisily determined upon their completion. The *Sacramento Daily Union* reported: "The furniture, fixtures, etc., are not yet in their places (in the Capitol); many of them have not yet arrived at Vallejo . . . no printing materials in town . . . few or none of the buildings in town finished . . . music of the saw and hammer heard night and day." [6]

[4] "History of the Seat of State Government", *Governmental Roster, 1889: State and County Governments of California*, compiled by W. C. Hendricks, Secretary of State, Office of State Printing, Sacramento, 1889, p. 199.
[5] *Id.*, pp. 199–200.
[6] *Sacramento Daily Union*, January 5, 1852.

Of the State House itself, Bancroft wrote: "The $125,000 capitol so far was a rather insignificant two-story building with a drinking-saloon and a skittle alley in the basement—the third house, as it was ironically called." [7] The site is now marked by a bronze plaque on the corner of York and Sacramento Streets in Vallejo.

The steamer, *Empire,* establishing itself as a floating hotel, berthed some 250 persons, of whom 50 were Members of the Legislature. Anywhere else, wrote the *Daily Union,* should a man become "so prodigal as to purchase the exclusive privileges of a settee or a line of stools, it is perfect destruction on the purse." [8]

The dearth of essentials and the absence of amenities plunged the legislators into a new battle to move the Capitol. The obvious efforts of builders to complete construction and the pledges of townspeople to secure conveniences were countered by charges that General Vallejo had broken his contract to provide a suitable capital. Compromise prevailed, and it was decided that, while the town of Vallejo would remain the permanent capital of the state, the Senate and Assembly would repair to Sacramento to complete the session.

The following year, on January 3rd, the Legislature assembled again in Vallejo for the Fourth Session. Compared with the previous year, conditions were little better, and the weather worse. Transportation and communication, in spite of great effort, fell far short of the needs of the Legislature. Proponents of removal viewed, on the one hand, Sacramento recovering from a flood and, on the other, the town of Benicia offering the free use of its new city hall and a port of call at which all river traffic stopped. Spurred perhaps by the immediate prospect of an uncomfortable session in Vallejo, the Legislature passed a bill on February 4 ordering the seat of government to be moved instantly to the City of Benicia.

Benicia

The newly designated capital promptly welcomed the Legislature as the Fourth Session reconvened on February 11, 1853. Benicia, given the second name of the wife of General Vallejo, had grown with the addition of an ordnance depot and a military post into a major port of call between San Francisco and Sacramento.

The new State Capitol was a roomy, two-story brick building which, besides two large legislative chambers, contained much-demanded rooms for committees. Two Doric pillars and four pilasters presented, for the first time, a suitably grand facade. The lawmakers, with little or no complaint, resumed their labors and adjourned May 19, 1853.

---

[7] Bancroft, Hubert Howe—*History of California, 1848–1859,* The History Co., San Francisco, 1888.
[8] *Sacramento Daily Union,* January 5, 1852.

Yet once more, the capital seemed inadequate to the accommodations required for a legislative session and its entourage of scribes, journalists and advocates. On January 2, 1854, the opening day of the Fifth Session, it is reported that "at least a hundred men had no place to sleep except barrooms of saloons." [9] As with Vallejo, inclement weather heightened the general irritation. The change to Benicia had proved apparently to be a change in the degree of discomfiture.

A handsome proposal from the City of Sacramento arrived at about this time. Free use of the Sacramento County Courthouse as a capitol building, rooms for state officers, fireproof vaults for the records, removal of the Legislature and furnishings from Benicia to Sacramento without charge, and a building site for a permanent capitol—should Sacramento be declared the permanent capital—were included.

Other political considerations were agreed to, and an act was passed repealing all prior legislation which had to do with a state capital and naming Sacramento as the permanent seat of government. On February 25, the bill was signed by Governor Bigler, and the Legislature, bag and baggage, climbed aboard the steamer, *Wilson G. Hunt,* for the voyage to the new capital.

Sacramento—The First State House

A few of the legislators recalled the surroundings of two years before as they reconvened the session of 1854 in Sacramento County's first courthouse. Just prior to its completion in 1851, the wooden two-story building was proudly described in the *Daily Union:* "Sacramento can now boast of the finest and most commodious courthouse in the State . . . The design of the main entrance is very neat and in good taste. Four fluted

---

[9] *California's State Capitol,* p. 37.

columns will support a balcony, surrounding which there will be a handsome iron railing. The building will be ornamented with a neat cupola, in which a bell is to be suspended, and a clock also will show its face and hands to late witnesses and trembling culprits." [10]

The confidence of the city was to be seen everywhere. Sturdy levees braced it against flooding rivers, and the new Capitol looked down upon streets covered with wooden planking, ever-increasing numbers of substantial brick and iron buildings and no less than 55 hotels. Stagecoaches, freight wagons and pack trains combined with frequent steamboat service to make Sacramento one of the most accessible cities in the state. More rapid communications were available by telegraph.

At last, a permanent capital seemed able to offer an abundance of those facilities deemed necessary for the appropriate conduct and comfort of the Legislature. Soon after the conclusion of the session, the stately courthouse, along with a considerable portion of the city, was razed in the disastrous fire of July 13th. Undaunted, the energetic citizenry saw the cornerstone of a more splendid courthouse laid on September 27th.

Sacramento's Second State House

Sacramento's Second County Courthouse was ready for occupancy in less than four months. Completed in January 1855, construction of the new State House neither delayed nor distracted the Legislature.

The facade was graced by eight fluted pillars with Ionic capitals supporting an imposing entablature. The second floor was 80 by 120 feet, granting sufficient space not only for adequate chambers for the Senate and Assembly

---

[10] *Sacramento Daily Union*, December 16, 1851.

but also for nine rooms to be used by officers and clerks of the Legislature. The ground floor provided offices complete with fireproof vaults for the Controller and Treasurer.

The rebuilding of Sacramento caused James G. Read to write: "After four years, in which she had been in turn desolated by flood and pestilence, consumed by fire, and shook [sic] by civil commotion, we will look at her as she stands in her pride of wealth and power. We will look at her extensive levees, her commodious wharves, her noble lines of storehouses, her magnificent post office, her elegant and spacious church, and other public buildings; her fine hotels and her palace-like private residences, and who can forbear astonishment?" [11]

This "pride of wealth and power" embraced the Legislature. In 1854, the public square at 9th and 10th, I and J Streets, was donated by the city as a site for the permanent Capitol. The work, which commenced in December of 1856, was halted by court litigation, and construction was never resumed.[12] The site, which reverted to the city, is now a city park.

Several cities, including San Francisco, Oakland and San Jose, reopened the prospect of change by proposing capitol sites to the Legislature, but Sacramento's gift of four blocks between L and N, 10th and 12th Streets, was finally agreed upon in 1860. The Legislature appropriated $500,000 as a construction fund, and appointed a commission to superintend the building of a capitol.

[11] Quoted in *California's State Capitol*, pp. 39–40.
[12] *California Blue Book*, 1907.

Sojourn in San Francisco

December 9, 1861, found Sacramento completely inundated. Early in January, the *Daily Union*, while describing conditions in the city as normal, reported "a movement, probably having a speculative origin, to attempt to bring about a temporary removal of the Capital of the Legislature to San Francisco, but we do not apprehend that such an attempt will be countenanced by sensible men in either branch." [13]

On January 10th, Sacramento was again awash with flood waters rising 20 inches higher than the crest of the previous month. Governor Leland Stanford reputedly arrived for his inauguration in a rowboat.

The question of removal was not only countenanced, it was pursued to the extent that one legislator feared they would become known as "the changing, mudscow, steamboat moving, forever uncertain legislature of California." On January 24th, the Legislature took up temporary residence in San Francisco.

The business of the state resumed in the Merchants' Exchange Building, which stood on the northeast corner of Battery and Washington Streets. Erected in 1854 for the Hong Kong trading house of Jardine and Matheson, this imposing, three-story structure, capped with a central dome, was done in the palladian style of architecture. Statuary of an allegorical nature embellished the cornice. The site is now occupied in part by the forecourt of the Richard Henry Dana Building.

Any efforts, public or private, to foster another permanent move of the capital must have been rebuffed, for the next session convened in Sacramento.

Sacramento—A House Built for the Legislature

While the Legislature had been away, work proceeded on a magnificent new capitol building designed by M. F. Butler. Ground had been broken on September 24, 1860, and the cornerstone had been laid on May 15, 1861. Details and working drawings were prepared by Reuben Clark, the first of the superintending architects, as problems arose.

Construction of the Capitol covered a period of 14 years, and special taxes had to be levied to sustain the project. "Until the roof was built in 1868, work stopped in the winter, both because wet weather set in and because the year's funds, derived from annual taxes, were exhausted by fall. Supplies contracted for did not always arrive at the stipulated time; during the Civil War many construction items that might previously have been ordered from the East were made in San Francisco, where facilities were limited." [14]

---

[13] *Sacramento Daily Union*, January 6, 1862, p. 2.
[14] *California's State Capitol*, p. 47.

Capitol under construction in Sacramento, circa 1867.

On November 26, 1869, the offices of the Governor and Secretary of State were occupied, and on December 6th of that year the Legislature convened in the new chambers. Work on the Capitol continued until 1874, when it was declared completed.

Five years later, the Constitutional Convention of 1879 incorporated into the Constitution a section declaring Sacramento to be the seat of government of the state.[15] Removal could be obtained only by an extraordinary vote of the Legislature and a majority vote of the people.

On foundations patterned after the ancient Spanish fortress at Panama and cemented by the Constitution, California's Capitol came to rest.

[15] *Constitution*, Article III, Section 2.

The State Capitol, as it appeared in 1879.

THE CAPITOL BUILDING

Known as the "old Capitol" to distinguish it from the more recent addition of an annex, the original structure is of Roman Corinthian design, four stories in height, and surmounted by a magnificent copper covered dome. At the apex of the dome is a cupola or "lantern" with a small domed roof supported by 12 columns. This roof is covered with gold plate and its crowning ornament is a "ball 30 inches in diameter, made of copper, and plated with gold coins with a value of $300." [16] At night, flood lights outline the dome against the sky, making it visible for miles in every direction.

The dome rests on a two-story drum. Around the base of the drum is a colonnade of 24 fluted Corinthian columns supporting a balustered roof, and above that rises a clerestory.

The height of the building, from the street level to the ball surmounting the lantern at the top of the dome, is 219 feet 11½ inches. Its length (greatest dimension) is 320 feet; and its width, 164 feet.[17] The rock quarries of nearby Folsom and Rocklin provided the granite for the construction of the first story of the building, while plaster covered brick was used for the three upper stories.

The "old Capitol" was remodeled from 1906 to 1908, and again in 1928. Until the 1976–1981 restoration, there had been no great structural changes made in the building since its acceptance in 1874, except the addition of the Annex in 1949.

The Annex

Necessitated by the ever-increasing work of the executive and legislative branches of state government, construction of an annex to the State Capitol began on June 3, 1949, and the addition was completed in January 1952. The cost was approximately $7.6 million, the original appropriation being made at the 1946 First Extraordinary Session.[18] Plans and specifications for the building were prepared by the State Division of Architecture, and were made with the approval of an eight-member joint committee of the Legislature.

Prior to commencing the actual construction work, it was necessary to excavate to the base of the old structure. The semicircular wing (apse) on the east side of the Capitol was removed in order to join the new and old sections of the Capitol Building. It was also necessary to perform exploratory work as a basis for planning the wall reconstruction since none of the original drawings of the Capitol could be found and, in fact, it is believed that there never were complete drawings. During the demolition work, it was discovered that a great part of the load of the original structure is supported by heavy box girders and beams of wrought iron bearing the imprint of the Phoenix Iron Works, Philadelphia, 1857.

---

[16] *California Blue Book*, 1907.
[17] Survey of State Department of Architecture.
[18] *Statutes of 1946*, Chapter 145.

A contemporary architectural style distinguishes the Annex while, insofar as is possible, blending with the lines and style of the heavy construction used in the original building. The first two floors are faced in granite, and the remaining stories in concrete stucco. Although the roofline is the same, the new section has two additional floors.

The Annex has six stories and a basement. It is 210 feet long, 269 feet wide and 103½ feet in height from the street level to the top of the sixth floor. Driveways permit vehicle access to the basement garage.

Within the building are numerous stairways, a bank of four public elevators and elevators, located adjacent to each chamber, for the use of the Members of the Legislature. There is also a private elevator for the use of the Governor which operates from his offices, located in the southeast corner of the first floor, to the basement garage.

Legislative committee rooms in the Annex and the restored Capitol are apportioned 10 for the use of the Assembly, and six for the use of the Senate, and include a large committee room for each house with seating capacities of approximately 300 persons. Each committee room has a public address system, and the proceedings may be recorded or televised on statewide cable television[19] if desired. Near each chamber is a small conference room which is used principally by the Rules Committees of the respective houses.

The showplace of the Annex is the first floor. The walls of the corridors are of St. Genevieve rose marble from Tennessee and the flooring is of Adorado marble from Missouri. The main entrance to the Governor's office is outlined in black and gold Montana marble, representing the oil and gold resources of California. The double doors are constructed of native California woods, such as pin oak, redwood burl, orange, and lemon.

Sixty black marble framed glass showcases, with individual displays for each of the 58 counties and two for the state, are placed along the wall of the first floor corridors. These displays give visitors an idea of the vast storehouse of natural resources and the diversity of commerce to be found in the "Golden State."

Restoration of the Old Capitol

Increasing concerns over the seismic safety of the historic Capitol led the Legislature, in 1971, to order a structural study of the building.[20] Responding to this request, the State Architect in 1972 submitted the results of a seismic study of the "old Capitol," declaring it structurally unsafe for continued occupancy without considerable renovation.[21]

---

[19] See Chapter XIII, infra, p. 177.
[20] Statutes of 1971, Resolution Chapter 233.
[21] Seismic Study—West Wing, California State Capitol. Office of Architecture and Construction, Sacramento, California, 1972.

In addition to analyzing the structural strength of the building, the report also focused on Sacramento's numerous experiences with earthquake damage in the past. In particular, a major earthquake in 1892 inflicted significant damage:

> "The Deputy State Librarian reported that the State Capitol rocked wildly. . . large statuary on the top of the building were thrown to the ground with such force that they were buried in the ground . . . All the elegant decorations in the Assembly Chamber are ruined." [22]

Six possible approaches to the problem were explored, two of which were recommended by the State Architect: reconstruction for full use; or strengthening the West wing for use as a museum. Alternative approaches included vacating the building, doing nothing, partial strengthening, or rehabilitation.[23] A subsequent evaluation of the report by a private engineering firm supported the findings and confirmed that any practical effort to preserve the elegant, historic edifice would require the evacuation of the building for a period of three to five years.[24]

Since several proposals were under consideration, $42 million was appropriated in 1973 for the Capitol Improvement Fund. Of this amount, $21 million was to be made available for reconstruction or restoration of the old Capitol, and $21 million for construction of a new legislative building.[25]

Considerable public controversy arose over the proposal to totally reconstruct the historic building. An editorial expressing such concerns read as follows: "If it had been proposed during President Harry Truman's Administration that the White House be torn down instead of strengthened to shore up structural weaknesses, the public outcry would have been deafening."[26] Legislators' emotional attachment to the historic edifice, as well as the public's high regard for their State Capitol, fueled the movement to restore the building to its original grandeur.

To study the whole matter, a subcommittee of the Joint Rules Committee, known as the Subcommittee on Legislative Space and Facilities, was established.[27] Its labors resulted in the presentation, early in 1975, of a massive independent study organized under the direction of a prominent architectural firm.[28] Three alternatives for the construction of a new legislative building were offered together with a recommendation that the old Capitol be preserved by restoration and partial reconstruction.

Shortly thereafter, new legislation was passed which again centered attention on the old Capitol.[29] Moneys earlier appropriated for restoration and for construction of a new legislative building were redirected to the sole purpose of restoration and rehabilitation of the historic old Capitol.

[22] *Id.*, p. 44, quoting *Woodland Daily Democrat,* April 21, 1892.
[23] *Id.*, p. 9–11.
[24] *A report on Evaluation of the State Architect's Study—West Wing, California State Capitol.* VTN Consolidated, Inc., 1973.
[25] *Statutes of 1973,* Chapter 129, Item 332.5.
[26] *Ramifications of Architect to Proceed with Preliminary Plans,* Staff Report, Joint Rules Committee, August 27, 1975.
[27] *Statutes of 1973,* Resolution Chapter 83.
[28] *Restoration and Development of the Capitol for the Joint Committee on Rules—California State Legislature,* Welton Becket and Associates, Architects, and others, February 1975. 2 vols.
[29] *Statutes of 1975,* Chapter 246.

The direction finally taken might have been presaged by earlier expressions of the Legislature. Attachment to the chambers overrode professional exhortations regarding safety when the Assembly rejected a proposal to remove itself from its home of more than 100 years.[30] An informal poll of Senators revealed a like sentiment in the upper house.[31]

Even more than endearment, the "old Capitol" evokes a persistent spirit of pride in California. The pen of an engineer wrote: "Confidence has been defined as one of the prerequisites of civilization. In a very real sense the Capitol represents an expression of the confidence felt by the founders of the State in the continued success of their enterprise . . . ."[32]

In 1976, the "old Capitol" became the object of the most extensive restoration effort in the western hemisphere. After the prime contractor was selected, the dismantling of all decorative elements, both interior and exterior, and the numbering and cataloging of each was immediately commenced.

Gigantic cranes were brought in and positioned to begin the removal of large segments of the interior. As the building slowly became a shell, the outside walls of the Assembly and Senate Chambers were buttressed by huge metal pipes for support during the reinforcement of the original brick walls with thick concrete backing.

When the exterior and interior walls, floors and stairwells were in place, master artisans were brought in to work and to train others in the near-lost crafts of mosaic tiling, ceiling moulding, painting and gilding, and the handcarving of wooden balustrades, stair rails and posts. Lighting fixtures were faithfully copied from old photographs, and more than one original artifact, unearthed in the demolition, was refurbished and replaced. Most imposing of these are the brass facings of the elevator areas which had been plastered over during a prior renovation.

Work was completed in time for the reconvening of the 1981–82 Regular Session on January 4, 1982. Throughout that week, the "Restoration Gala" festivities included a gargantuan cake-cutting ceremony, light shows, symphony and band concerts, parades, tours and theatricals, and concluding with a laser light and fireworks display of imposing proportion, a formal dinner and grand "Occupancy Ball"—a fitting recollection of the first Occupancy Ball held in 1869.

California's Capitol had been returned to the grandeur and dignity of the early 1900's. Completed at a cost of approximately $68 million, the restoration has delighted Californians and has provided the state with one of the truly beautiful and outstanding capitols in the country.[33]

---

[30] *Assembly Concurrent Resolution No. 128, 1973–74 Regular Session. See also Journal of the Assembly, 1973–74 Regular Session,* August 31, 1973, p. 7428.

[31] *"Solons Stand Pat: Senators Decide Not to Leave". The Sacramento Bee,* Sacramento, June 29, 1973.

[32] *Evaluation of the State Architect's Study,* p. 75.

[33] In September 1982 four statuary groups, sculpted by Spero Anargyros, were mounted atop the Capitol. Two of the groups, "Indian Warrior being attacked by a Bear" and "Indian Woman being attacked by a Buffalo" were placed on the west front pediment of the Capitol. The other two groups representing "Union" between the State and Federal Governments and the reuniting of the North and South were set on the Assembly and Senate porticos respectively. The statuary replaced originals created by Pietro Mezzara in 1874.

State Capitol as it appeared during the 1976–81 Restoration.

Temporary Legislative Chambers

During the restoration period, the Legislature maintained offices for the members in the Annex and held its meetings in temporary chambers located on each side of the east entrance to the Capitol.

The temporary chambers were functional and, by comparison with the permanent chambers, spartan. Indirect lighting, acoustical tile and veneered masonite served in place of ornate fixtures, draperies and sculptured native woods. In each chamber, on standards to the left and right of the presiding officer's rostrum, were displayed the American and Bear Flags. A portrait of George Washington occupied a prominent position above the Senate rostrum, while the Assembly's portrait of Abraham Lincoln, lacking suitable space, was placed in storage.

In addition to the chambers these structures each contained a members' lounge; a Sergeant at Arms office; a small committee room; and offices for the Speaker and President pro Tempore, respectively.

The Restored Capitol

In the minds of the planners, function was important, to be sure, but so was the legacy of art and history. While the allocation of space was the principal, practical consideration, great emphasis was given to returning the building to an earlier, more elegant stage. Its history was remembered, not only in its public areas, but also in a number of rooms where the original occupancies were reclaimed and incorporated as museum pieces in an otherwise bustling legislative building. The conjunction of historical rooms with present day offices, committee rooms and legislative chambers, makes this State Capitol truly unique.

The design feature of the basement is the exposure of the original brick walls and foundation. This is especially outstanding in the dining and cafeteria area. Various offices were established in the basement along with an exhibit area showing the various stages of the restoration. A small theater, tour office, bookstore, legislative bill room and public telephones are located on this floor.

The main floor contains a number of rooms for committee hearings and all of the historically recreated offices. The Governor's office is based upon actual photographs of the 1906 office of Governor George Pardee. The Secretary of State's office is a re-creation of that of Secretary of State, C. F. Curry, in 1902. The Treasurer's office is derivative of the era of State Treasurer Truman Reeves, and contains a seven ton safe which was retrieved from Sutter's Fort. The office of the Attorney General reflects the design prevalent during the time of Attorney General, Ulysses Webb. The design of the two remaining museum rooms, the archive exhibit room and the state library exhibit room, are taken from actual designs of an earlier decor. The library exhibit room will keep reference material on the restoration project for the public. In the center of the rotunda is a statue of Columbus asking Queen Isabella to finance his voyage to the "New World".[34]

The Senate and Assembly Chambers are located on the second floor. The only offices on this floor are those reserved for the Speaker of the Assembly and the President pro Tempore of the Senate. From this floor, in the rotunda, the magnificent moulding and painting of the inner dome may be seen at its best.

The third floor offers visitors a view of the Assembly and Senate in session from the galleries of each chamber. In the north wing are two committee hearing rooms and additional office space. The south wing contains the offices of the Senate Majority and Minority leaders.

The fourth floor includes the offices of the Senate Rules Committee, several Assembly committee hearing rooms, some Assembly Members' offices, and various staff offices.

The Restored Legislative Chambers

The Assembly and Senate Chambers are, in a word, opulent. Galleries, extending along both sides and the rear of each chamber, overlook the legislative activity on the floor. Crystal chandeliers are suspended from ornate, heavily moulded ceilings which, in turn, are framed in soft backlighting. The walls are illuminated by crystal wall sconces which compliment the chandeliers. In each chamber is the original presiding officer's rostrum and the original Desk, i.e., the center portion of the large forward area accommodating the staff of the Chief Clerk of the Assembly or the Secretary of the Senate.

Draperies hung between the pillars at the rear of the chambers provide visual and auditory softening effects. The wall covering between pilasters is a kind of fine burlap which screens large areas for further sound absorption. Green is the dominant color of the lower House, and the decor of the Assembly Chamber reflects that everywhere. The traditional red prevails in the Senate's color scheme.[35] Dark shades are reserved for the draperies and carpet while several lighter tones combine with white and gilt to produce a subdued but rich environment.

In both houses, the American and Bear Flags flank the rostrum of the presiding officer. Behind this rostrum are two tiers of pillars which dramatize the height of the chambers. On a projection above the lower pillars are inscribed the mottoes of each house: *"Legislatorum Est Justas Leges Condere"*,[36] the motto of the Assembly, and *"Senatoris Est Civitatis Libertatem Tueri"*,[37] the motto of the Senate. Framed by the motto and the two upper pillars, the portraits of President Lincoln in the Assembly[38] and

---

[34] The statue of Carrara marble is by the American sculptor Larkin Goldsmith Mead. It was presented to the state by Darius Ogden Mills in 1883. The statue was on display in State Office Building 1 during the restoration (1976–1982) and returned to the Capitol on October 6, 1982.

[35] The red and green color scheme for the upper and lower houses can be traced back as far as the British Parliament where the House of Lords chose red and the House of Commons used green.

[36] "It is the duty of Legislators to make just laws."

[37] "It is the duty of a Senator to guard the liberty of the Commonwealth."

[38] The painting is attributed to William Cogswell (1819–1903). Mr. Cogswell also painted some of the Governors' portraits hanging in the first floor corridors of the Capitol. In 1909 the Legislature appropriated $1,700 for the purchase of two portraits, one of President Lincoln which now hangs in the Assembly Chamber and one of President McKinley, the whereabouts of which is unknown. *Statutes of 1909*, Chapter 255.

President Washington[39] in the Senate have been returned to their historical places of prominence. Panels displaying the item of business before the house and the names and manner of voting of each member complete the outstanding features of this wall of the chamber.

In the Assembly, the Speaker is the presiding officer, and, in his or her absence, the Speaker pro Tempore or the Assistant Speaker pro Tempore presides. In the Senate, the Lieutenant Governor is President and presiding officer, and in his or her absence, the President pro Tempore wields the gavel.

Adjacent to the Assembly Chamber are the offices of the Chief Clerk and Sergeant at Arms, and next to the Senate Chamber are the offices of the Secretary and Sergeant at Arms.

The Members' Desks

The seats of the Members of the Legislature in the Assembly and Senate Chambers are assigned by their Committees on Rules.[40]

The desks were originally installed in 1870, shortly after the present chambers were officially opened in 1869. For a number of years, the Assembly attempted to seat its members in a sort of geographical arrangement, that is, with Districts 1 to 40 (those representing northern California) on the north side of the chamber, and Districts 41 to 80 (those representing southern California) on the south side. However, such an arrangement is no longer possible, since recent reapportionments have resulted in a considerable majority of the Members of the Assembly being elected from districts in the southern part of the state. Also, the front row of desks have come to be occupied by such ranking Members of the Assembly as the Majority and Minority Floor Leaders who occupy the two front row center seats and are flanked, respectively, by the Majority and Minority Caucus Chairpersons.

Each desk is equipped with a microphone and voting and page buttons. Some years ago, youths were employed as pages on a temporary basis, but with sessions spanning much of the year, they have been replaced by Special Services employees, under the auspices of the Chief Sergeant at Arms. While the Assembly is in session, an Assistant Sergeant at Arms is stationed in the rear of the Assembly Chamber near an electrical panel showing the location of each Member's seat. When Assembly Members wish to call a sergeant, they press the page button, and their location is immediately visible to the person whose responsibility it is to answer the call.

During floor sessions, there are laptop computers on the Members' desks, which provide instant access to bill and amendment texts, analyses, and desk-to-desk e-mail capabilities.

---

[39] This is one of the many copies of the famous Gilbert Stuart portrait of Washington that were made by Jane Stuart (1812–1888), daughter of the prominent colonial painter. *California's State Capitol* (published by State Department of Finance, 1960), p. 65.
    The painting was saved from the fire of July 1854, which destroyed the Sacramento County Courthouse and a large part of Sacramento's business district. The following excerpt from the *Democratic State Journal* of July 14, 1854, describes the incident: "*Patriotic.*—When the fire threatened the courthouse with destruction, the Governor (Bigler), who was present, and who had been working from the commencement of the fire wherever Sacramento most needed a soldier, asked those present to assist him in saving the furniture. To this many objected, on the ground that private parties, who could not suffer the loss as well as the county, needed their services. A full-length portrait of Washington was standing against the southern wall, and, pointing to it, the Governor said, 'See, there is a portrait of the father of your country; will you permit it to be destroyed?' when a general rush was made for the portrait, and it was saved."

[40] *See, e.g., Assembly Rule 5.*

Media Facilities

Adjacent to each chamber is a press bay for the use of television crews covering legislative floor sessions. Additionally, numerous desks are stationed in the rear of each chamber, reserved for correspondents of leading press associations and California newspapers of large circulation.

Public Address System

Both houses have public address systems to amplify members' voices when speaking before the house. In the Assembly and Senate, there is a stationary microphone on the rostrum for the use of the Speaker and President pro Tempore, one on the desk for the use of the reading clerk, and one at the desk of each member. The system is operated from a station at the side of the chamber.

In the Assembly and the Senate, a sergeant at arms controls the sound system. In both instances, a control panel is in place, showing the diagram of the seating arrangement in the respective chambers. The name and seat number of each Assembly Member and Senator appears below the particular switch which activates the microphone installed at his or her desk.

The members' microphones are attached to a moveable armature at their desks. When a member wishes to be recognized he or she raises his or her microphone. After the presiding officer verbally acknowledges the member, the operator of the console is alerted that the member is to have the floor. The operator then flicks the switch above the member's name, thereby lighting a small red electric light globe on the member's desk, signifying that the system is open and will remain so as long as the member has the floor.

This system reduces the possibility of two members having the use of different microphones at the same time. When one member poses a question to another, both microphones may be opened to permit the answering of the question. The volume of sound transmitted is regulated by the operator of the console.

Portable microphones may, on occasion, be set up at the front of the chamber for the use of those members who desire to speak from the front of the chamber, or for witnesses appearing before the Assembly when it is meeting as a Committee of the Whole.

Floor sessions, committee hearings, and Capitol press conferences may be heard via the numerous in-house radios that are installed in most Capitol offices. This legislative broadcasting system is also located in many committee rooms for the convenience of members attending meetings therein. These useful devices are made available statewide to any person, company, or state agency for a monthly fee.

Electronic Roll Call System

The Assembly uses an electronic system for voting upon most matters, except the election of Assembly officers and certain parliamentary motions. The first electrical machine was installed in 1935; a second replaced it in 1947, and, with the construction of the temporary Assembly Chamber in

1976, an updated electronic device was incorporated. A totally new computerized system was installed in the restored Assembly Chamber in 1981. Subsequent enhancements have been added to the system to keep pace with upgrades in computer software and technology.

The Constitution provides that a rollcall vote shall be taken on a question and entered in the Journal at the request of three members present.[41]

The Assembly Rules further provide that the ayes and noes be recorded by the electronic voting system on the final passage of a bill, when a vote of 41 members or more is required, when demanded by three Members, or when ordered by the Speaker.[42]

On the front wall of the Assembly Chamber, facing the members, are two tall black panels—one to the right, and the other to the left of the Speaker's rostrum. Each panel displays the names of the Members of the Assembly in alphabetical order. Next to each name are two lights, one red and one green. When a member votes "aye," the green light next to his or her name illuminates, and conversely, when voting "no," the red light is activated. If a member is absent or chooses not to vote, neither light will turn on. The total number of ayes and noes are automatically tallied on screens located at the top of each panel. The File item number is also shown on these panels to indicate which measure is being voted on.

A voting unit, consisting of red, green and yellow buttons which can be secured by a key, is located on the desk of each Member and on the Speaker's desk at the rostrum. When the roll is opened for voting, a member may select the red or green button which activates the corresponding light opposite that member's name on the front wall panels, thus displaying the member's vote. The yellow button is used to summon a sergeant at arms. The key is provided so that no person other than the Member can operate the voting unit.

To assist the Speaker in presiding over floor sessions, the rostrum is equipped with a variety of electronic instruments. Included in this array of devices are: microphone control switches; a liquid crystal display counter, showing the number of members in attendance; a digital timer to track the length of speeches (e.g., members are allotted only five minutes for the opening speech on a bill); a small display panel indicating the item number and other pertinent information; and a plate showing the members' seating arrangements and how they are individually voting on each item. Additionally, a computer monitor displays a list of measures that have been placed "on call." Members can also view a list of such measures at either of two kiosks stationed on each side of the Chamber. Laser printers are provided to allow Members to print out vote information should they need it.

At the front of the Chamber, immediately behind and above the Speaker's rostrum, is a large display panel. This panel indicates the File and bill numbers, the author, the bill status, i.e., Second Reading, Third Reading, and any motions pending on the bill, such as amendments, motion to lay on the table, re-refer etc. This large panel also displays the total number of ayes and noes when the roll is closed and the vote electronically tallied. The central

---

[41] *Constitution*, Article IV, Section 7(b).
[42] *Assembly Rule 105*.

display is controlled from the Reading Clerk's console and by a computer terminal located to the Reading Clerk's right. The ability to display any message or information on this board is limited only by the size of the panel.

To begin the voting process, the Speaker orders the clerk to open the roll. The Reading Clerk then manually activates the electronic voting system, which triggers a chime. This chime signals the Members that the system is open and ready for them to vote from their desk units. The Speaker then asks all Members to vote, if they desire to vote, and orders the clerk to close the roll and tally the vote. At this moment, the Reading Clerk closes the voting system, and prints out a ballot at the clerk's desk. Each Member's name is appropriately listed on each ballot under the heading "Ayes," "Noes," or "Not Voting." This information is immediately stored in the computer's memory, and is made available to the membership on their laptop computers or at the Chamber kiosks, should they wish to view a printed ballot. On uncontested matters the rollcall is completed within a few seconds. Once voting has commenced, it may not be interrupted, except that, before the vote is announced, any member may change his or her vote or request that the Speaker direct the clerk to call the roll of absentees.

Prior to announcement of the vote, the Speaker inquires if all members have voted. Any member may move a call of the Assembly after the completion of the roll and before the announcement of the vote. The rules provide that members may change their votes, prior to the adjournment of that legislative day, in the absence of any objection, as long as the outcome of the vote is not changed.[43] A member must announce his or her vote change to the Assembly.

In the Senate, the roll is called orally by the Secretary of the Senate or an assistant. An electronic information panel is located above the dais displaying the item number, author, bill number, and vote tally. The Senate Rules provide that whenever a rollcall is required by the Constitution or rules, or is ordered by the Senate or demanded by three members, every member within the Senate shall without debate answer "Aye" or "No" when his or her name is called. The names of the members are called alphabetically.[44] A call of the Senate may be ordered after the roll has been called, and prior to the announcement of the vote.[45]

The Galleries

There is a gallery across the rear and along the sides of each chamber. From the galleries the public may observe the proceedings of the Senate or the Assembly, for only members, attachés, and other persons who have been granted special permission may go on the floor of the chamber of either house while it is in session.

---

[43] *Assembly Rule 106.*
[44] *Senate Rule 44. See also Senate Rules 45–48.*
[45] *Senate Rule 42.*

Assembly Chamber

Senate Chamber

Capitol Park

California is justly proud of her Capitol Park, for it is widely known as one of the most beautiful in the United States. The well-kept broad green lawns extend over an area of 30.5 acres—from 10th Street east to 15th Street, and from L Street south to N Street in downtown Sacramento.

Beautification of Capitol Park began in 1869, at about the time the Capitol was first occupied. The grounds were graded and the soil enriched with loads of river silt in 1870, and during the winter of 1870–1871, some 800 trees and shrubs from all parts of the world were planted. This original planting consisted of some 200 different kinds of rare plantlife. Today, there are over 40,000 trees, shrubs, and flowers in the park. With more than 800 varieties of flora represented, ranging from subarctic to subtropical in origin, a visitor from virtually any corner of the globe can find some species of plantlife native to their homeland. Capitol Park stands as one of the finest collections of plantlife in the country.

Located on the east side of the park is an extensive grove of camellia trees, where many varieties of this beautiful flower bloom from October through May. The camellia thrives in the capital city climate. A testament to this is the fact that the Sacramento City Council has officially designated Sacramento as the "Camellia City."

The park showcases other special collections, such as the cactus garden, with plantlife representing the California desert, and the rose garden, which contains over 800 roses. Growing individually in Capitol Park, and of special importance to Californians, are the many specimens of the State Tree, the California Redwood, and the State Flower, the Golden Poppy.

The park abounds with squirrels who run wild over the lawns and walks. These squirrels are not native to Sacramento, but were originally imported in 1923 from Fresno and from Golden Gate Park in San Francisco.

Due to security concerns, plans are underway to erect a fence around the Capitol grounds, running along the sidewalks on N Street, 10th and L Streets, and through Capitol Park at 13th Street. The fence is scheduled for completion in 1999. A fence circled the grounds from 1881 until 1949, when it was removed to make room for the Capitol's expansion.

Capitol Park Memorials

Aside from its immense collection of plantlife, Capitol Park is significant for the many memorials which serve to recognize various groups and individuals who have contributed to California's history.

Military tributes are the theme for many of the memorials in the park. On the west side of the Capitol is a memorial to Mexican-American soldiers from California who fought in World War II. "Memorial Grove," on the east side of the Capitol, contains trees which began as saplings on southern battlefields of the Civil War, and were transplanted here in memory of the fallen. Nearby is the bell from the U.S.S. California, the only battleship to be built on the Pacific Coast. As this book went to print, planning was underway for the construction of the California Veterans Memorial. The memorial is to consist of a 28-foot granite obelisk surrounded by a small plaza. It is to be built on the N Street side of Capitol Park between 14th and 15th streets. The memorial will honor the military service of all Californians who have served in military uniform since 1850.[46]

Other monuments in Capitol Park have a different focus. The grove of camellia trees has been designated "Pioneer Camellia Grove," in honor of the early builders of the state. Near this grove is a bronze statue of Father Junípero Serra,[47] the 18th century Franciscan friar who led the movement to establish the missions in California. South of the camellia grove is a memorial to the Native Americans who originally inhabited California. Near the Library and Courts Building is a monument honoring Peace Officers who have died in the line of duty protecting the citizens of the state. In the east end of Capitol Park, there is a bench memorial honoring former Speaker of the Assembly Robert Moretti.[48]

---

[46] *Statutes of 1985*, Chapter 411.

[47] *Government Code*, Section 13082. The statue of Father Serra was dedicated in 1967. The significance of Father Serra's contribution to California is attested to by the fact that his likeness also represents the state in Statuary Hall in the U.S. Capitol.

[48] The memorial is located between 12th and 13th streets, opposite the fishpond, on the south side of the divider. Robert Moretti served as a Member of the Assembly from 1964 until his resignation June 27, 1974. *See also, Statutes of 1994, Resolution Chapter 80* (directing the establishment of a bench memorial in memory of Robert Moretti).

Perhaps the most striking of the memorials is the California Vietnam Veterans Memorial, the end product of a grassroots effort which began with the creation of the Vietnam Veterans Memorial Commission in 1983.[49] Spearheaded by the fundraising efforts of former Army Captain B.T. Collins,[50] who himself had lost an arm and a leg in Vietnam, over $1.6 million was raised from private sources and the memorial was dedicated December 10, 1988.

The circular memorial contains 22 panels of India Black Granite upon which are etched the names of the more than 5,800 Californians who gave their lives in the Vietnam Conflict. The inner walls of the memorial contain bronze panels sculpted from actual photographs of various scenes from the battlefields, the hospitals, and the prisoner-of-war camps.

The California Vietnam Veterans Memorial located in Capitol Park.

---

[49] *Statutes of 1983*, Chapter 1042 (*Military and Veterans Code*, Section 1300).

[50] B.T. Collins also served as a Member of the Assembly from 1991 until his death in office March 19, 1993. *See also, Statutes of 1993*, Resolution Chapter 65 (directing the Department of General Services to establish a bench and plaque near the Vietnam Veterans Memorial in memory of B.T. Collins).

View of the eastern portion of the Capitol and Capitol Park, 1901.
Visible is the semicircular apse, which was removed during the
construction of the Capitol Annex, 1949–52.

Interior view of the apse, circa 1890.
The State Library was located in the apse at this time.

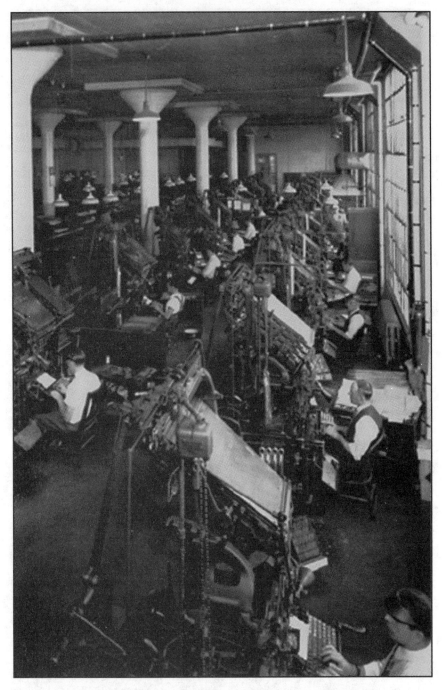

Linotype machines at the Office of State Printing, circa 1940.
These machines have been replaced by computer typesetting methods.

Chapter XII

Legislative Printing

The Office of State Printing

The Office of State Printing (OSP) handles most legislative printing. The Government Code provides that all state printing, and only state printing, shall be done in the Office of State Printing.[1] However, in its 1995–96 performance budgeting, OSP received authorization to print for other public governmental agencies. Furthermore, in its 1996–97 performance budgeting, OSP's services became unmandated. This allows agencies to use private sources if they are more competitive than OSP.

The history of the Office of State Printing dates back to early January of 1850, when the second statute of the First Legislature created the office of State Printer—more than eight months before California was admitted into the Union of States. It was the duty of the State Printer "to execute all of the printing and binding of the two branches of the Legislature." [2]

From 1850 until 1875, the state's printing was handled by private concerns, with the State Printer acting as purchasing agent. In March of 1872, legislation providing for the purchase of a site, equipment, and construction of an Office of State Printing was enacted; but in 1874, the Legislature directed that, instead of constructing a new building, a portion of the old Governor's Mansion in the northeast corner of Capitol Park, at 15th and L Streets, be remodeled to suit the needs of both the Office of State Printing and the State Armory. The mansion, a three-story wooden frame building, was occupied by the printing plant from December of 1875 until the fall of 1923.

Early newspaper accounts reveal that in 1875 the plant had $14,500 invested in machinery and equipment, and employed a force of 21 men at an annual payroll of less than $20,000. The first year's printing amounted to $53,100.10.

A constitutional amendment in 1884 authorized the printing of textbooks for the public schools at the state plant. In 1912, a constitutional amendment was adopted which provided for free distribution of schoolbooks. Textbooks were printed until 1976, when legislation was passed which dramatically expanded the textbook selection procedure for school districts.[3] This allowed for a departure from uniform use of textbooks in districts throughout the state and resulted in individual textbooks being required at such reduced quantities that the printing plant, which by this time no longer provided free distribution of schoolbooks, could not print them at the same level of economy as private publishers.

In 1923, the plant was moved to a new two-story and basement building constructed at a total cost of $245,000 at 11th and O Streets, about two blocks from the State Capitol. The building covered a quarter of a city block in area,

---

[1] *Government Code*, Section 14850. *See also* Sections 14852, 14860.
[2] *Statutes of 1850*, Chapter 2.
[3] *Statutes of 1976*, Chapter 817.

and was equipped with the most up-to-date machinery of its time. In 1932, construction of a $132,000 three-story and basement addition to the building was necessary to accommodate work requirements.

By 1948, the volume of state printing had increased to such an extent that the plant had again outgrown its quarters, and the Legislature appropriated $400,000 for the acquisition of a new site.[4] In 1949, the Legislature approved the purchase of 16 acres of land at North Seventh Street and Richards Boulevard, and appropriated $2,780,000 for the construction and equipment of a modern industrial building.[5] This site is approximately four miles northwest of the State Capitol.

Construction of the building, which covers 6½ acres of floorspace, was started in 1952 and completed in 1954, at an approximate cost of $3,228,000. Its one-story floor plan is so arranged that the work moves from one production section to the next in an orderly flow without backtracking or multiple handling.

At the present time, approximately 500 persons are employed in the printing plant, which operates in three shifts, and produces over $60 million of state printing annually. The plant, which is the largest state printing plant in the United States, is also one of the largest printing establishments on the Pacific Coast.

The Office of State Printing is supervised by the State Printer, who is an appointee of the Governor.

The Department of General Services has the responsibility of supervising the operations of state printing and binding,[6] and decides upon the style and manner of printing all laws and other state documents except those printed for the Legislature.[7]

All printing for state agencies is charged to and paid for from their respective funds or appropriations,[8] and its cost is fixed by the Department of General Services in an amount which will pay for all costs of the printing, including depreciation on plant and equipment.[9]

The Department of General Services has general supervision over the distribution of all public documents and other publications printed for any state agency; and it has custody of all state documents and other publications subject to public distribution, except those printed for the special use of the Legislature, the Governor, or the elective officers of the state.[10] However, the department may accept for distribution or disposal documents and other publications from the Legislature, the Governor, or the elective state officers when requested to do so.[11]

The department fixes the price and disposes of or sells the documents or publications.[12]

[4] *Statutes of 1948*, Chapter 23, Item 167.
[5] *Statutes of 1949*, Chapter 700, Item 372.6b.
[6] *Government Code*, Section 14853.
[7] *Government Code*, Section 14854.
[8] *Government Code*, Section 14865.
[9] *Government Code*, Section 14866.
[10] *Government Code*, Section 14880.
[11] *Government Code*, Section 14881.
[12] *Government Code*, Sections 14880, 14881.

State Printing System

The California Legislature maintains the most complete and sensitive information system of any legislative body in the world. Today's system of formal bill printing, and the many legislative publications that serve to provide complete disclosure of all legislative action, began in 1879.

It was in that year that the State Constitution was changed to require that all bills be printed before action was taken thereon. Previously, the houses had acted on the basis of handwritten copy which was read by the clerk, and it was sometimes noted that the printed statute might not read quite as the legislators thought it did when they passed it.

Over the years the workload of the plant has been increased enormously in the interest of having a better informed public and Legislature. Today's demands include providing, each morning, a record of the previous day's business, and a file of the day's hearings, by 8 a.m.

This volume of material, which on occasion amounts to 3,000 typeset pages in a night, is only possible using the most modern of data-processing and typesetting techniques.

In January of 1972 the Office of State Printing instituted a system of using on-line video data terminals for the input of data to a computerized legislative information system.

Beginning with the 1977–78 Regular Session, the task of inputting bills using this on-line system was transferred to the Office of the Legislative Counsel. The bills and amendments are now composed on video keyboards and stored in a computer system by the Legislative Counsel. When the bill is introduced or amended this text of the bill or amendment is transmitted to the Office of State Printing for publication.

A large general purpose computer is used for the communication and processing of this data. During the session, the data that has been input, using the video keyboards, is accessed in order to rapidly retrieve and amend pending legislation, or update the history of action taken on legislation.

When this information is desired in printed form to meet deadlines of the Legislature, the computer processes magnetic tapes containing all the data required to run a cathode ray tube typesetting device. This method of computerized typesetting allows for completely formatted legislative pages at the rate of 500 per hour ready for platemaking and subsequent printing.

When work has been completed on legislation the same data base is used to produce the printed statutes which become part of California law. The documents that record the activity of a legislative session are compiled in a similar manner.

The Bill Room

The Legislative Bill Room, located in the basement of the restored Capitol, makes available for sale to the general public all books, pamphlets, bills and other publications produced by the Senate and Assembly. The money derived from the sale of these items is returned to the Legislative Printing Fund to help defray the cost of printing.

The Legislative Bill Room is a part of the Office of State Printing in the Department of General Services. The Bill Room acts as the primary liaison between the Legislature and the Office of State Printing to ensure the printed material needs of the Legislature. These activities center mostly around the distribution of the daily file, history and journal prior to each day's session and the overnight return of newly printed copies of amended legislation to the floor of each house in order to meet the print requirement of the California Constitution.[13]

Some of the services provided through the Bill Room can be quite extensive. For example, any organization or individual can purchase a complete Legislative Publication Service, effective for an entire two year session. This service provides the purchaser with copies of all bills introduced by both houses; all subsequent amended copies; all journals, histories and files; and all indexes and digests published by the Legislature.

On a smaller scale, any member of the public may obtain individual copies of bills or resolutions free of charge by either visiting the public counter in the basement of the Capitol or by telephoning the Bill Room. Each request is limited to a single copy of no more than five bills or publications at a time, with an annual maximum of 100 copies per calendar year.[14] Requests in excess of these limits are provided at a nominal charge.

Number of Copies of Legislative Publications

The number of printed copies of bills, constitutional amendments, joint and concurrent resolutions (in the original as well as in the amended form), daily journals, files, and histories for their respective houses is set by the Chief Clerk of the Assembly and the Secretary of the Senate.

Daily Publications

There are three daily publications printed for each house of the Legislature: the journal, the history, and the file. The copy for these publications is compiled by the clerks of the respective houses, under the supervision of the Secretary of the Senate and the Chief Clerk of the Assembly, received by the State Printer after the daily adjournment of the Legislature, and must be printed and available for distribution early the next morning.

The Daily Journal

The State Constitution and the Rules of the Senate and Assembly require each house of the Legislature to publish its proceedings in its journal, and require that upon the request of three Members or when ordered by the Speaker or by the Senate that any vote which is taken on the floor of the Legislature be recorded in the journal.[15] Each House's Minute Clerk compiles and edits the Assembly and Senate Journals, respectively.

---

[13] *Constitution,* Article IV, Section 8(b) (No bill may be passed until the bill with amendments has been printed and distributed to the members). *See also, Assembly Rule 64; Senate Rule 29.5.*
[14] *Joint Rule 13.*
[15] *Constitution,* Article IV, Section 7(b); *Assembly Rule 105; Senate Rule 49.*

The Daily Journal contains an account of the proceedings of each house, the titles of all measures introduced, considered, or acted upon by the house, rollcalls upon all actions requiring a recorded vote, messages from the Governor and the other house, committee reports, motions, acknowledgment of the receipt of all communications, and such other matters as properly come before the respective houses. (See page 274 for example.)

Until the 1985–86 Regular Session, the text of all amendments proposed by committees or by individual members on the floor were printed at the end of each day's journal. Beginning with the 1985–86 Regular Session, both the Senate and Assembly decided to terminate this practice. Currently, all amendments are filed with the respective Minute Clerks where they are available, upon request, for inspection or copying by any interested party. These amendments are ultimately inserted at the end of the appropriate day's journal copy and filed with the State Archives, under the direction of the Secretary of State. This practice has reduced the size of the Daily Journals by approximately 50 percent. It is not unusual, however, for the Daily Journal of either house to contain more than 100 pages.

The Members' speeches are not taken down in shorthand, nor do they appear in the journals. However, an occasional motion is made that certain oratory be printed verbatim in the journal; the Member making the presentation is then requested to reduce it to writing for printing.

In some ways, preparing and printing the Daily Journal may be likened to the publication of a daily metropolitan newspaper. The Minute Clerk records the day's activities in their chronological order, keeping an accurate account of what transpires on the floor while the house is in session, all the while preparing and editing the material for printing without editorial comment. The copy is then rechecked, with special attention given to the true and correct recording of problems of a procedural nature which may have been occasioned by argument or action on the floor. After the Minute Clerk has prepared the copy, it is given to a copyreader, who "marks" it for printing before it is transmitted to the Office of State Printing.

The votes taken in committee on bills, constitutional amendments, joint and concurrent resolutions are published as part of the journals. The committee records are delivered by the secretaries to the Minute Clerks. In the Assembly, these votes are published as a monthly appendix to the journal.[16] The Senate publishes its rollcalls in the body of the journal on a daily basis.[17]

---

[16] *Assembly Rule 58.5.*
[17] *Senate Rule 28.7.*

The Daily File

For each day of the session, a Daily File is printed, which contains the titles of all measures which have been reported out of committee and which are to be considered by the Assembly or the Senate, as well as motions to reconsider, notices of intention to withdraw a bill from committee, and concurrences in amendments of the other house which are pending. The items are grouped according to order of business, numbered consecutively, and considered in this order unless special permission is granted to take up an item out of order, or to pass an item on file.[18] The Daily File shows any vote which has been taken on the bill in a committee or by the other house. By referring to these vote totals, a Member can tell at a glance whether or not another legislator has opposed the bill previously.

When a bill has been amended in the other house and returned to the house of origin, a summary of the changes made in the bill by the other house is printed in the Daily File.[19]

The Daily File also contains a table or listing of all bills and constitutional amendments with their dates of introduction and the 31st day thereafter, in order to facilitate compliance with the provisions of the Constitution; and a list of any bills upon which the 30-day waiting period may have been dispensed with. The Senate and Assembly Files show all bills which have been scheduled for hearing in committees and a listing of the times, places, and bills scheduled for consideration by conference committees in order to provide the public and the members with advance notice of the matters to be heard.[20] (See page 275 for example.)

The Daily Files of the Assembly and Senate are compiled and edited by two Assembly employees and two Senate employees, referred to as the "Daily File Clerks." These staffers work under the direction of the Assembly Chief Clerk and the Secretary of the Senate, respectively. Advanced desktop publishing software is utilized to publish the Files and transmit them to OSP for daily printing.

The History (Daily and Weekly)

The third daily publication issued by each house of the Legislature is the History. This publication, as the name implies, is a history of legislation introduced and considered during the session. The Daily History shows the actions on all measures considered each day, with cumulative actions for each succeeding day until the last session day of the week. The History Clerks of both houses compile and publish this information on a regular basis. (See page 276 for example.)

At the close of each week, a Weekly History is published which contains the titles of all measures introduced during the session, together with all actions taken thereon and showing the dates upon which such actions were taken. The names of the Members of each house, their committee assignments, the measures listed by original author, and much other

---

[18] *Assembly Rule 63; Senate Rule 29.*
[19] *Joint Rule 26.5; Assembly Rule 77.1.*
[20] *Joint Rules 62(a), 29.5.*

information pertinent to the Legislature is contained in these publications.

The Daily and Weekly Histories are produced using computer terminals at the Assembly and Senate Desks. The necessary information is transmitted to the Legislative Counsel's computer system and then relayed to the printing plant. This is another step in the conversion of legislative information to a totally automated system. The automated information (the bills and the histories) can be displayed on PCs in the Capitol, thus providing an additional convenient method of access to supplement the printed volumes.

Bills

All bills, constitutional amendments, and joint and concurrent resolutions must be printed and made available to the members and the public as soon after their introduction or amendment as is possible. Usually the bills are printed and ready for distribution the morning after their introduction.

After printing, the individual bills are arranged in numerical sequence and filed in the Legislative Bill Room, where they are available for distribution to the public.

Complete sets of Assembly and Senate bill books are compiled for any member on request, for the officers of each house, and for the press. The Legislative Bill Room keeps these books up to date with all amendments during the session. Additional sets of up-to-date bill books are maintained in each chamber for ready reference during the daily sessions.

When a bill is amended, the printed amended bills are inserted in the bill books immediately preceding the previous printing of the bill amended. Thus, a complete record of any changes which may have been made in a bill after its introduction is readily available. At the end of the session, the members may retain their sets of bill books if they so desire.

Additional sets of bills are prepared for the Legislative Counsel, other state officers, state agencies, and libraries, as set forth in the Joint Rules.[21] Amended bills and newly introduced bills are forwarded to these agencies and bill service subscribers each day so that they may keep their sets up to date.

Previous to the adoption of the amendment to the Constitution which eliminated the constitutional recess, thousands of bills were introduced in the closing week of the first part of the session. In 1957, for instance, 3,747, or an average of 749 measures a day, were introduced in the Legislature during the last five days of the January session.

The 1957 session, which adjourned *sine die* on June 12, considered 4,183 Assembly bills, 2,680 Senate bills, and 563 other measures (Assembly and Senate constitutional amendments and concurrent and joint resolutions), making a grand total of 7,426 measures. In the history of the California Legislature, this was the greatest number of measures ever introduced during a single year. In addition to this total, there were 352 Assembly house resolutions and 214 Senate resolutions considered by the Legislature during the 120-day session.

---

[21] *Joint Rule 13.*

Not only was an all-time high established in the number of bills introduced, but all records were broken in the number of bills amended and the number of type pages handled by the Office of State Printing. It required 33 feet of library shelving to accommodate a copy of the official publications of the 1957 legislative session.

Until 1959 the number of bills that were introduced at each successive general session (odd-numbered years) increased, as is shown on the following chart. The volume of legislation in some respects was necessitated by the fact that all bills had to be introduced within the first 30 days of the session. Members, therefore, would introduce "spot" or "skeleton" bills ("spot" or "skeleton" bills was the name applied to those bills that made no basic change in the law but were merely introduced as vehicles which might be used in the event that the member was required to take care of an urgent situation), as bill introduction was not permitted after the first 30 days of the session. In addition, the Legislature was not permitted to act on bills except the Budget Bill, revenue acts, amendments to city or county charters and acts necessary to provide for the expenses of the session during the even-numbered years. In 1958 an amendment was adopted to the Constitution which removed the time limitation on the introduction of bills during the general session. The chart indicates the drastic reduction wrought by this constitutional provision. However, the chart also indicates that beginning in 1959 the number of bills introduced and the complexity and type of problems confronting a growing state required more and more legislation.

The year 1967 saw the beginning of annual legislative sessions without a restriction as to the type of legislation that could be introduced each year. The new system, however, simply spread out rather than decreased the legislative volume during the two-year periods. The combined two-year totals, that is, 1967–68, 1969–70, etc., greatly surpassed the previous two-year totals for 1963–64 and 1965–66.

One of the major premises underlying the new two-year session was the belief that its adoption would lead to an overall reduction in the total number of measures introduced during the two-year period, as the new session provided for "carryover bills" thus eliminating the necessity for reintroducing bills that do not become law during the first year of the session. In retrospect, this assumption seemed to have been borne out as a total of 7,848 measures were introduced during the first biennium (1973–74) as opposed to 9,621 for the preceding two annual sessions held in 1971 and 1972. The figures for the 1975–76, 1977–78, and 1979–80 Regular Sessions indicate that this trend continued. However, in the 1981–82 Regular Session a total of 6,494 measures were introduced as opposed to a total of 6,092 for the 1979–80 Regular Session. This upward trend continued through the biennial-session peak of 8,125 measures introduced in the 1987–88 Regular Session, although introductions in the most recent years have receded from these levels.

The number of measures introduced has declined significantly in recent years. For example, in the 1995–96 Regular Session, just 6,074 measures were introduced. This decline is primarily due to the adoption of rules which limit the number of bills that may be introduced. In 1991, the Senate adopted rules which limit the number of bills a Senator may introduce to not more than 65 bills in the regular session.[22] In 1994, the Assembly adopted rules which limited the number of bills an Assembly Member may introduce to not more than 50 bills in the regular session.[23] In 1996, newly adopted rules further reduced the number of bills an Assembly Member may introduce to not more than 30 bills in the regular session.[24]

The following chart gives the reader some idea as to the volume of proposed legislation introduced in the California Legislature over the past several decades:

Measures Introduced—1957–1997 [25]

Year	Total measures introduced
1957	7,426
1959	4,805
1961	5,148
1963	5,109
1965	5,517
1967	4,587
1968	3,808
1969	4,447
1970	4,505
1971	5,337
1972	4,284
1973	4,647
1974	3,201
1975	4,331
1976	3,285
1977	3,719
1978	2,977
1979	3,522
1980	2,570
1981	3,886
1982	2,608
1983	3,847
1984	3,160
1985	4,381
1986	3,210
1987	4,715
1988	3,410
1989	4,625
1990	3,267
1991	3,799
1992	2,607
1993	3,911
1994	2,528
1995	3,573
1996	2,501
1997	3,237

---

[22] *Senate Rule 22.5.*
[23] *Assembly Rule 49,* 1993–94 Regular Session. Served as custom and usage until March 20, 1996.
[24] *Assembly Rule 49,* 1995–96 Regular Session.
[25] "Measures" include Assembly and Senate bills, constitutional amendments, joint and concurrent resolutions. The totals do not include measures introduced in extraordinary sessions of the Legislature.

Other Legislative Publications

In addition to the publications produced by personnel of the Chief Clerk's and Secretary's offices, other legislative documents of significant legal reference and research value to the Members, staff and the public are compiled and printed.

Legislative Index and Table of Sections Affected

During the legislative session, Legislative Counsel prepares periodically and publishes a *Legislative Index* and a *Table of Sections Affected.*[26]

The *Legislative Index* is an alphabetical subject matter arrangement of the legislation introduced while the *Table of Sections Affected* lists alphabetically, by code, all the sections which are to be added, deleted and amended by proposed legislation.

The combination of the two provides a ready "bill locator" and reference for those searching for a particular bill in an instance in which the searching party knows only that a certain subject matter or code section is involved.

Legislative information is also made available to the public via the Internet.

The Summary Digest

Prior to 1973, a *Summary Digest,* including a statutory record of sections affected and subject matter index, was prepared by Legislative Counsel after the adjournment of each regular and extraordinary session.

At present, this publication is printed annually at the end of each year. For example, all the bill and resolution digests for 1993 are printed in one volume and those of 1994 will be printed in another. Together they form the *Summary Digest* for the 1993–94 Regular Session.

The *Digest* consists of a listing, by chapter number, of the digests prepared for and printed on the enrolled bills which provide an abbreviated description of the substance of the bills and resolutions signed by the Governor or filed with the Secretary of State.

This particular document is of great value to attorneys, legislative advocates and an extremely useful source for legal research.

The publication is authorized by and made available to the public at prices set by the Joint Rules Committee.[27]

The Chapters

After a bill has been passed by the Legislature and signed by the Governor it is filed with the Secretary of State. The Secretary of State then assigns the bill a number known as a chapter number. The order in which they are numbered shall be presumed to be the order in which they were signed by the Governor.[28] Constitutional amendments, joint and concurrent resolutions are numbered in the order that they are filed with the Secretary of State by the Senate and Assembly Engrossing and Enrolling Clerks.

---

[26] *Joint Rule 13.1.*
[27] *Joint Rule 13.3.*
[28] "Chaptering out" is discussed in footnote 89, *supra,* p. 118.

A separate series of chapter numbers is assigned annually to bills and resolutions. For example, the first bill and resolution filed in 1997 are designated Bill Chapter No. 1 and Resolution Chapter No. 1 of 1997; in 1998 the number systems revert to Bill and Resolution Chapter No. 1 of 1998.[29] The combined chapters for both years constitute the Statutes of the 1997–98 session.[30]

The chaptered bills and resolutions, still retaining their legislative numbers, are printed and made ready for distribution to the members and the public as soon after their filing date as is practicable.

The following table shows the number of chaptered bills and resolutions of the general sessions in recent years.

Measures Chaptered—1961–1997

Year	Number of bill chapters	Number of resolution chapters
1961	2,282	276
1963	2,169	204
1965	2,070	219
1967	1,725	210
1968	1,474	266
1969	1,619	398
1970	1,628	289
1971	1,821	274
1972	1,442	192
1973	1,218	199
1974	1,545	236
1975	1,280	141
1976	1,487	160
1977	1,261	124
1978	1,432	148
1979	1,207	103
1980	1,381	125
1981	1,186	91
1982	1,644	183
1983	1,327	142
1984	1,760	191
1985	1,607	158
1986	1,521	165
1987	1,504	149
1988	1,647	164
1989	1,467	187
1990	1,707	178
1991	1,231	143
1992	1,374	147
1993	1,307	123
1994	1,299	150
1995	982	104
1996	1,171	86
1997	951	136

---

[29] *Government Code*, Sections 9510, 9510.5.

[30] It has been so often held in this state that it is no longer an open question that the validity of the statute, which had been duly certified, enrolled and approved, and deposited in the office of the Secretary of State, cannot be impeached by a resort to the journals of the Legislature, or by extrinsic evidence of any character. *People v. Camp*, 42 Cal. App. 415. (Enrolled Bill Rule).

The Statutes

The Legislative Counsel prepares the chapters for their final printing as the statutes of the session. The Senate or Assembly bill number and the names of the authors are removed, and the chapter number only is retained. The chapters are then arranged in numerical sequence, the date of approval or adoption of each act and its effective date are prefixed to its text.

The conversion to the two-year session also required the adoption of different methods of printing the statutes of the session. Prior to 1973, the statutes were printed and bound after the *sine die adjournment* of the regular session; now, they are produced in two segments, one for each year of the biennium, i.e., *Statutes of 1997, 1997–98 Regular Session; Statutes of 1998, 1997–98 Regular Session.* The combination of these volumes contain the official text of bills enacted and the resolutions adopted for the 1997–98 biennium.

At the beginning of each volume of the statutes there must be printed: the State Constitution; the names and places of residence of the Governor, the Lieutenant Governor, the other executive officers of the state, Members and presiding officers of the Senate and the Assembly; the certificate of the Secretary of State showing what acts, or sections or parts of acts of the Legislature are delayed from going into effect by a referendum petition; the Secretary of State's certificate showing the result of all elections upon any initiative or referendum measures within the previous year; and the text of all such initiative measures adopted by the electors.[31]

The Legislative Handbook

The Legislative Handbook or Manual is prepared by the Secretary of the Senate and the Chief Clerk of the Assembly. This manual contains compact, comprehensive statistical data; pictures and biographies of the Members of the Legislature; various election results; and other information deemed to be useful by the Secretary and the Chief Clerk.[32]

The handbook is used constantly by the Members and their staff; it is the only legislative publication that contains the complete text of the standing rules of both houses and the Joint Rules.

The Government Code provides that the manual must be uniform in size and style with similar publications of previous sessions, and must include a list of state officers, Members and Officers of the Senate and Assembly, lists of committees, the rules of each house, the Joint Rules, and any other information deemed by the Secretary and the Chief Clerk to be of use to the Members of the Legislature.[33]

The distribution of the manual is provided for by the Government Code. The handbooks remaining after the statutory distribution are sold by the Legislative Bill Room at a price determined by the Joint Rules Committee.

---

[31] *Government Code,* Section 9766.
[32] *Government Code,* Sections 9740, 9741.
[33] *Government Code,* Section 9741.

Such price must be sufficient to cover the cost of printing and binding the manual.[34]

The Constitution

Over the years, the Legislature has maintained a policy of providing citizens, schoolchildren, and students of government with educational material on the government and the Legislature.

Pursuant to this policy, the Senate and the Assembly have made available a limited number of publications on these subjects.

The Senate and Assembly have published and distributed throughout the years a book containing the Constitution of the United States and the Constitution of the State of California. The book also contains the text of the Magna Carta, the Mayflower Compact, the Declaration of Independence and other basic democratic documents.

Each edition incorporates any amendments to the constitutions which have been adopted since the publication of the preceding edition.

Both houses also publish and distribute books, pamphlets, and brochures giving information about the state, the Legislature, the Capitol, and the state emblems.

Postsession Publications

After the final adjournment, the staffs of the Secretary and Chief Clerk check the notations on the bills against the entries made in the journals and the histories before they are printed and filed with the Secretary of State as the official records of the legislative session.

Corrected Journals

After the Daily Journals have been printed, the Minute Clerk checks and makes any necessary corrections before resubmitting them for final printing. When the corrected Assembly Journal copy is returned it is signed by the Chief Clerk; similarly, the Secretary signs the Senate Journal.

After these final or "corrected" journals have been approved, they are deposited in the archives maintained by the office of the Secretary of State as the official record of each day's session.

Final Journals

Copies of the corrected journals of each house are collected and bound to provide a permanent record of the session. In the past, this record was quite large. For example, the Journal of the Assembly for the 1983–84 Regular Session consisted of 11 volumes which contained 21,002 pages. Since the 1985 implementation of the practice of not printing the text of amendments to bills, the size of more recent journals has been reduced dramatically; the Journal of the Assembly for the 1989–90 Regular Session filled only six volumes and totaled 10,954 pages.

---

[34] *Government Code,* Sections 9742, 9744.

The Assembly also publishes, in a separate volume, as an appendix to the journal, all the votes taken on bills in the Assembly committees. The Senate publishes their committee votes in the text of their Daily Journal.

Throughout the session, an alphabetical index of the material contained in the journal and an index of Assembly and Senate measures, with the actions taken thereon, is maintained until the final adjournment. The Minute Clerks then check and send these indices to the printer where they are published and serve as the permanent index for the bound journals.

The Final Histories

The Final Histories contain a complete record of all the proposed legislation introduced and any action taken thereon during the biennium.

Prior to 1973, the Final Histories of both the Senate and Assembly were printed in a single volume designated as the Final Calendar; now, however, the quantity of material reported precludes such a combination. As a result, beginning with the 1973–74 Regular Session, the Final Histories are published in separate Assembly and Senate volumes.

These histories contain the "line actions" (e.g., From committee: "Do pass"); the committee and floor votes taken on the measures; and the final action taken by the house or the Governor up to and including the date of adjournment *sine die*.

The Final Histories contain many useful and informative statistics. Each bill and resolution that has been introduced is listed by author and by the committee to which it was originally referred; summaries of the actions on bills and resolutions that have been passed by both houses and signed by the Governor or filed with the Secretary of State are listed sequentially by chapter and number.

The Final Histories, used in conjunction with the *Summary Digest,* provide a complete record of legislation including: (1) the name of the Member or Members who introduced it; (2) the subject matter; (3) action taken by the Governor and the Legislature; and, (4) its final disposition.

Chapter XIII

Media Coverage of the Legislature

California's importance as a news center has been reflected in the extraordinary attention paid to the activities of the state government, the Legislature and the Governor by the additional newspaper, television, radio and magazine coverage over the past several years.

As the number one state in the nation, not only are the number of reporters from California news media increasing at the Capitol, but more coverage is being given by the national press, television, radio and magazines.

Press associations and wire services, along with the major daily newspapers, maintain bureaus or full-time correspondents at Sacramento to report what happens in and about the Capitol, as well as to relate the activities of the numerous agencies of the state which touch every man's, woman's, and child's life in this rapidly expanding state.

The Associated Press and United Press International, worldwide news-gathering and distributing agencies, long have maintained permanent bureaus at the Capitol. The Associated Press services virtually every daily newspaper and broadcast station in California. In addition, the press corps includes new services which specialize in coverage for various large and small California newspapers, radio and television stations.

At the 1943 session, the accredited correspondents formed the Capitol Correspondents Association and, by action of the Senate and Assembly, officially assumed the task of authenticating credentials of all press representatives. A standing committee of the association examines and passes upon applications for press privileges. The Joint Rules limit full accreditation to those who qualify under the rules, which set forth certain necessary qualifications.[1] Seats and desks in the Senate and Assembly Chambers are allotted only to regular Capitol correspondents of authorized news media.[2] Special press cards for correspondents covering legislative proceedings for a limited period are issued upon proper screening by the standing committee, just as are the press cards for those regularly in attendance at sessions.

Accurate coverage of the Capitol news requires a thorough understanding of governmental functions and a knowledge of public affairs. Many of the press corps members are veterans in the service and have a wide acquaintance with state officials and civil service employees.

News events must be handled speedily and clearly. Press conferences, board and commission meetings, departmental reports, and interviews are a part of the daily routine for those whose beat is the Capitol and the various governmental agencies. Some 20-odd buildings contain state offices. The reporters must cover all of them at some time or other.

---

[1] *Joint Rule 32.*
[2] *Joint Rule 32, Senate Rule 13.*

The main Capitol "beat" includes the Governor's office, other constitutional officers, Department of Finance, Legislative Analyst, and legislators. Such key news sources as the Fair Political Practices Commission, the various major state departments, such as Motor Vehicles, Transportation, Corrections, Health and Welfare, Education, Third District Court of Appeal, and other divisions of government must be covered at various times.

During regular sessions of the Legislature and the occasional special sessions, the job of covering the news becomes more complex. The chief activity, of course, centers on the Senate and the Assembly, the Governor's office, Legislative Analyst, and other agencies allied closely with legislation.

Press conferences are occasionally held by the Governor. Important developments in the Legislature or in the state usually cause special press conferences. A room, especially equipped for newspaper, radio and television, is available for press conferences of the Governor, Members of the Legislature, and newsworthy visitors.

From the day a bill is introduced until it is finally disposed of by either the Legislature or the Governor, the correspondents and photographers for the press associations and services, newspapers, and broadcast media must cover its daily progress because it is of interest to some locality, newspaper, radio or television station. Somebody somewhere is affected by every bill or measure that is introduced in the Legislature.

Though the words were written some time ago, the aims of the Capitol Correspondents Association are, perhaps, best described by a former, longtime Capitol reporter:

> "The press of California . . . is intent upon reporting the business of the Legislature, and the work of its individual members, with the greatest possible degree of thoroughness, accuracy, speed, and fairness. Representing that press, the members of the Capitol Correspondents Association, like the Members of the Legislature, have one primary goal—better service to the districts of the State from which they individually come, and better service to the California public generally." [3]

Televising the Legislature

To bring state government closer to the citizens of California, the legislature has initiated a television production project in each house. Live, unedited, gavel-to-gavel coverage of Assembly floor sessions began in February 1991, and within a year the Senate had also televised their proceedings.

---

[3] Phillips, Herbert, "The Press and the Legislature," *Legislator's Orientation Conference, 1961*, p. 48.

The television signals are made available to any bona fide news or educational organization, and allow Californians to view and participate in the legislative process. The California Channel is a nonprofit cable network which transmits via satellite the unedited footage to 104 cable operators throughout the state. Currently, 4.5 million cable subscribers can view the proceedings of the legislature from the convenience of their homes, schools, or offices.

The Assembly and Senate now televise committee hearings and Capitol press conferences on a regular basis. Live viewer call-in committee hearings have also been produced by each house, enabling citizens to voice their opinions directly to lawmakers.

Each house of the legislature has oversight over its own television production operations. The Assembly Committee on Televising the Assembly and Information Technology coordinates the television coverage of the lower house, while the Senate Rules Committee oversees its television operations. Control rooms are stationed in the Capitol Annex, where technicians operate the remotely controlled cameras that have been installed in each chamber.

GLOSSARY OF
LEGISLATIVE TERMS

GLOSSARY OF LEGISLATIVE TERMS

A

ACROSS THE DESK – The official act of introducing a bill or resolution. The measure is given to the Chief Clerk or his or her representative at the Assembly Desk in the Assembly Chambers or to the Secretary of the Senate or his or her representative in the Senate Chambers. It then receives a number and becomes a public document available in the bill room.

ADJOURNMENT – Motion to end session for that day, with the hour and day of the next meeting being set prior to adjournment or by rule.

ADJOURNMENT SINE DIE – "Adjournment without day." The final termination of a regular or special legislative session.

ADMINISTRATIVE PROCEDURE ACT (APA) – A statute containing required procedures for rule making and administrative hearings. (Chapter 3.5, 4, and 5 (commencing with Section 11340) of Part 1 of Division 3 of Title 2 of the Government Code.)

APA RULEMAKING PROCEDURES – Procedures set forth in the Administrative Procedure Act that generally requires state agencies, when adopting regulations, to give public notice, receive and consider public comments, submit their regulations and supporting RULEMAKING files to the Office of Administrative Law for review, and have the regulations published in the CALIFORNIA CODE OF REGULATIONS, the recognized source of California administrative law.

ADOPTION – The approval or acceptance of motions, amendments or resolutions.

AMENDMENT – Any alteration made, or proposed to be made, in a bill, motion, resolution or clause, by adding, changing, substituting or omitting language.

> **AUTHOR'S AMENDMENTS** – Amendments submitted by the author of a bill and signed by the chair of the committee to which the bill has been referred. Permits the adoption of amendments by the house without the benefit of a committee hearing and recommendation.

> **HOSTILE AMENDMENT** – An amendment that is proposed by a member or committee that is not supported by the bill's author.

ANALYSIS OF THE BUDGET BILL – The Legislative Analyst's comprehensive examination of the Governor's budget available to legislators and the public about six weeks after the budget is submitted to the Legislature.

APPEAL – A parliamentary procedure for challenging the decision of a presiding officer.

APPROPRIATION – The amount of money set aside for a specific purpose and designated from a specific source, such as, the General Fund, Environmental License Plate Fund, etc.

APPROPRIATIONS LIMIT – Established by Prop. 4 (Article XIII B, California Constitution). Passed by voters in 1979, this is the maximum amount of tax proceeds that state and local government may appropriate in a fiscal year. The limit is adjusted annually but based on 1986-87 appropriation limits.

APPROVED BY GOVERNOR – The signature of the Governor on a bill passed by the Legislature.

B

BUDGET CHANGE PROPOSAL (BCP) – A document prepared by a state agency and submitted to an agency secretary and the Department of Finance to propose and document budget changes to maintain the existing level of service or to change the level of service; and is used in preparing the Governor's Budget.

BILL – A draft of a proposed law introduced by a member of the Legislature (Assembly Bill 4000 = AB 4000, Senate Bill 1 = SB 1)

> **PREPRINT BILL** – A prototype, or first draft, of a bill used primarily to present a bill idea before the measure has been officially drafted. It is used primarily during interim hearings to test bill ideas.

BILL ANALYSIS – A brief summary of the purpose, content and effect of a proposed measure or amendment for committee and floor proceedings.

BILL DIGEST – The legal synopsis of measures prepared by Legislative Counsel.

BLUE PENCIL – The California Constitution grants the Governor "line item veto" authority to reduce or eliminate any item of appropriation from any bill including the budget bill.

BOND BILL – A bill authorizing the sale of state general obligation bonds to finance specified projects or activities, which must subsequently be approved by the voters.

BUDGET ACT – The budget bill after it has been signed into law by the Governor.

BUDGET BILL – The spending proposal for the next fiscal year prepared by the Department of Finance and submitted to the Legislature by the Governor.

BUDGET YEAR – The next, rather than the current fiscal year, beginning July 1 and ending June 30.

C

CALIFORNIA CODE OF REGULATIONS – The official compilation of regulations legally adopted by state agencies and filed with the Secretary of State, the recognized source of California administrative law.

CALL OF THE HOUSE – The procedure used to compel attendance of members and to require those in attendance to remain in the Chamber.

CAL-SPAN – The cable television channel which televises Assembly and Senate proceedings.

CAPITAL OUTLAY – Funds to be spent acquiring or constructing fixed assets.

CAPITOL PRESS CORP – Those members of the press who are responsible for covering events in the Capitol.

CAUCUS – A group of legislators who formally meet because of their interest in particular issues (e.g. Democratic Caucus, Republican Caucus, Rural Caucus, Women's Caucus, etc.).

CAUCUS CHAIR – A member that is selected and required to perform the duties prescribed by their respective party caucus.

CAUCUS SECRETARY – An officer of the party caucus whose duties are prescribed by the caucus.

CHAMBER – The Assembly or Senate chamber where floor sessions are held.

CHAPTER – After a bill has been signed by the Governor, the Secretary of State assigns the bill a "Chapter Number" such as "Chapter 123, Statutes of 1992," which is subsequently used to refer to the measure rather than the bill number.

CHAPTERING OUT – When the provisions of one chaptered bill amends the same code section as another chaptered bill. Chaptering out can be avoided with the adoption of **"double joining"** amendments. (Absent "double joining" language, the code section as amended by the bill with the higher chapter number takes effect and "chapters out" the code section as amended by the bill with the lower chapter number.

CHECK-IN SESSION – On non-floor session days, Members come to the Assembly floor throughout the day to be added to the roll for attendance purposes. A quorum must be recorded in order for legislative business to be transacted.

CHIEF ADMINISTRATIVE OFFICER – The chief Assembly staff person responsible for Assembly administrative, fiscal and business affairs.

CHIEF CLERK – A non-partisan, non-member officer of the Assembly elected by the majority of the membership each session as its legislative officer and parliamentarian.

COAUTHOR – Any member of either house, with the agreement of the author of a bill, may add his or her name on that member's bill as a coauthor, usually indicating support for the proposal.

CODES – Bound volumes of law organized by subject matter. The code to be changed by a bill is referred to in the title at the top of the bill.

COLA – Cost-of-living adjustment.

COMMITTEE OF THE WHOLE – The entire Assembly or Senate sitting as a committee to consider any matter properly presented to it.

COMPANION BILL – An identical bill introduced in the other house. This is far more common in Congress than in the California Legislature.

CONCURRENCE – Approval by the house of origin to changes made to one of its bills while it was in the other house. (e.g., Assembly approval of Senate amendments.)

CONCURRENT RESOLUTION – A measure that can be introduced in either house, but must be approved by both houses and filed with the Secretary of State to take effect. These measures usually involve the business of the Legislature. (e.g., adoption of the Joint Rules.)

CONDITIONAL (OR CONTINGENT) EFFECT – Effectiveness of a bill, or portion thereof, is made dependent upon the occurrence of some event (for example, passage of another measure, securing a federal waiver, receipt of revenues, and so forth).

CONFEREES – Official designated members of a conference committee.

CONFERENCE COMMITTEE – A joint committee composed of three legislators from each house who meet in public session to reconcile differences in the Assembly and Senate versions of a measure. Assembly conferees are chosen by the Speaker; Senate conferees are chosen by the Senate Rules Committee.

CONFERENCE REPORT – A draft of a bill proposed by the conference committee that reconciles the differences in the Assembly and Senate versions of a measure. The report must be approved by both the Assembly and Senate.

CONFIRM – The process of approving gubernatorial appointments to executive departments and many boards and commissions.

CONSENT CALENDAR – A group of noncontroversial bills passed by a committee or the full Assembly or Senate on one vote without debate.

CONSULTANT – A committee professional staff person.

CONTINGENCY FUND – Monies appropriated by the respective houses for operational expenses.

CURRENT YEAR – The current fiscal year that began on July 1 and ends next June 30.

D

DAILY FILE – A booklet published by each house, showing bills eligible for floor action. The official agenda of each house, including a schedule of committee hearings.

DAILY JOURNAL – A publication that is produced for each legislative day that contains the minutes of the session, vote information, motions, parliamentary inquiries, and letters of legislative intent.

DEADLINES – The dates by which bills must be introduced, heard and enacted.

DELEGATED AUTHORITY – Power granted by the Legislature to a state agency to implement and/or enforce a statute, including the power to adopt regulations.

DESK – The desk at the front of the chamber where much of the clerical work of the body is conducted. Also, a generic term for the staff and offices of the Chief Clerk of the Assembly and the Secretary of the Senate.

DESK IS CLEAR – A statement by the presiding officer, prior to the motion to adjourn, meaning there is no further business.

DISTRICT BILL – Legislation introduced specifically on behalf of a Legislator's district, generally affecting only that district.

DOUBLE JOINING – Technical amendments that will prevent the amended bill from "CHAPTERING OUT" the provisions of another bill.

DOUBLE REFER – Legislation recommended for referral to two policy committees rather than one for hearing. The first committee is not bound by the recommended second referral. Both committees must approve the measure to keep it moving in the process. This is typically used for sensitive issue areas that transcend the jurisdiction of one policy committee. Bill referrals are made by the Assembly and Senate Rules Committees for their respective houses.

E

EFFECTIVE DATE – The date, specified by the constitution, when a law becomes binding.

ENGROSSED BILL – Whenever a bill is amended, the printed form of the bill is proofread to make sure all amendments are inserted properly. After being proofread, the bill is "correctly engrossed" and is therefore in proper form.

ENGROSSING AND ENROLLING – A non-partisan unit in each house, responsible for proofreading amended measures. The unit also prepares and delivers bills to the Governor for consideration.

ENROLLED BILL – Whenever a bill passes both houses of the Legislature, it is ordered enrolled. In enrollment, the bill is again proofread for accuracy and then delivered to the Governor. The "enrolled bill" contains the complete text of the bill with the dates of passage certified by the Chief Clerk of the Assembly and the Secretary of the Senate.

EXECUTIVE SESSION – A committee meeting restricted to only committee members and specifically invited guests.

"EXEMPT FROM REVIEW BY THE OFFICE OF ADMINIS-TRATIVE LAW" – A statutory provision exempts a state agency only from the requirement in The Administrative Procedure Act to submit proposed regulations and supporting RULEMAKING file to the Office of Administrative Law for review. Other APA requirements apply.

"EXEMPT FROM THE APA" – A statutory provision exempting a state agency or its regulations from compliance with all standards and procedures set forth in the Administrative Procedure Act.

EXPUNGE – A motion to delete from the record any reference to a specific action. The motion must be made on the day the vote is taken.

EXTRAORDINARY SESSION – A special legislative session called by the Governor to address only those issues specified in the proclamation. Measures introduced in these sessions are numbered chronologically with a lower case "x" after the number (e.g., AB 28x); they take effect generally the 91st day after adjournment of the special session.

F

FILE NOTICE – Bills that are scheduled for a committee hearing must be listed in the Daily File for not less than four days prior to the hearing. Two days notice is required if a bill is subsequently heard by another committee.

FILE NUMBER – The number assigned to a measure in the Assembly or Senate Daily File. The file number changes each day as bills move on or off the Daily File. These include measures on second and third reading and unfinished business. Legislation is taken up on the Assembly or Senate Floor in chronological order according to file number. Items considered on the floor are frequently referred to by file number.

FINANCE LETTER – Revisions to the budget bill and the Governor's budget for the current year proposed by the Department of Finance and addressed to appropriate committee chairs in the Assembly and Senate.

FIRST READING – The initial introduction of a bill. The clerk assigns it a number and reads its title. The bill is usually referred to committee for future hearing.

FISCAL BILL – Any measure that contains an appropriation of funds or requires a state agency to spend money for any purpose or results in a substantial loss of revenue to the state. Legislative Counsel determines which bills are fiscal bills. The designation appears at the end of the Legislative Counsel's Digest found on the first page of each bill. Fiscal bills must be heard by the Assembly Appropriations Committee and the Senate Appropriations Committee in addition to the appropriate policy committee in each house.

FISCAL COMMITTEE – The Appropriations Committee in the Assembly and the Appropriations Committee in the Senate are the fiscal committees to which all fiscal bills are referred if they are approved by policy committees. If the fiscal committee approves a bill, it then moves to the floor.

FISCAL DEADLINE – The date on the legislative calendar by which all bills with fiscal implications must have been taken up in a policy committee and referred to a fiscal committee. Any fiscal bill missing the deadline is considered "dead" unless it receives a rule waiver allowing further consideration.

FISCAL YEAR – The twelve-month period on which the budget is planned. The State fiscal year begins July 1 and ends June 30 of the following year. The federal fiscal year begins October 1 and ends September 30 of the following year.

FLOOR – That portion of the Assembly or Senate Chamber reserved for members and officers of the Assembly or Senate and other persons granted the privilege of the floor.

FLOOR ANALYSIS UNIT – A nonpartisan unit in the Chief Clerk's office which is responsible for editing the bill analyses that are prepared by committee staff. This "packet" of analyses are then made available to Members during floor sessions for reference purposes.

FLOOR JOCKEY OR MANAGER – The legislator responsible for taking up a measure on the floor. This is always the bill's author in the house of origin and a member of the other house designated by the author when the bill is considered by the other house. The name of the floor jockey in the other house appears in parenthesis after the author's name in the second or third reading section of the Daily File.

FLOOR PASS – No visitor may observe the Assembly or Senate from the rear of the chambers without a pass. Assembly passes are issued by the Speaker's office; Senate passes are issued by the President pro Tempore's office. Passes are not required for the viewing area in the gallery above the chambers.

FOUR DAY FILE NOTICE – The announcement which must appear in the Daily File four days prior to consideration of a bill or constitutional amendment at the original meeting of a policy committee. The second committee of reference, usually a fiscal committee, requires only a two day notice. The File notice requirement may be waived by permission of the house.

G

GALLERY – The balconies of the chamber from which visitors may view proceedings of the Legislature.

GERMANE – This question refers to whether an amendment is relevant to the subject matter already being considered in a bill. Legislative Counsel may opine on germaneness, but the determination of germaneness is decided by the presiding officer, subject to an appeal by the membership.

GOVERNOR'S BUDGET – The spending plan submitted by the Governor in January.

GOVERNOR'S PROCLAMATION – A means by which the Governor may call an extraordinary or special session.

GRANDFATHERING – Specific situations that are allowed to continue while a law would make changes henceforth.

H

HANDBOOK – The 3″ x 5-3/4″ hardbound edition of California Legislature published for each two-year legislative session. It contains indexed versions of the Assembly, Senate, and Joint Rules; biographies of members; and other useful information. The handbook is published by the Assembly Chief Clerk and Secretary of the Senate for their respective houses.

HEARING – A committee meeting convened for the purpose of gathering information on a specific subject or considering specific legislative measures.

HELP DESK – The place to call with questions about the hardware or software of the legislative computer network. (Assembly 322-9931; Senate 445-1991)

HIJACK – An action to delete the contents of a bill and insert entirely new provisions.

HISTORY – A publication that gives a comprehensive list of all actions taken on every bill. It is published in volumes, daily and weekly, by each house.

HOST – The communal file cabinet of the mainframe computer allowing access by all legislative employees in Sacramento and district offices. The Host is maintained by the Legislative Data Center under the direction of Legislative Counsel. It contains information such as bill analyses, bill status, bill text, votes, and other useful information for bill tracking.

HOUSE RESOLUTION – A document that is the expression of one house. House resolutions are generally used to amend house rules or to create committees.

I

INACTIVE FILE – The portion of the Daily File containing legislation that is ready for floor consideration, but, for a variety of reasons, is dormant or dead. An author may move a bill to the inactive file if they wish not to take it up until a later date. Once a bill is on the inactive file, it requires one day's public notice to place the bill back on the daily agenda.

INITIATIVE – A method of legislating that requires a vote of the people instead of a vote of the Legislature for a measure to become law. To qualify for a statewide ballot, statutory initiatives must receive signatures of voters equal to 5% of the votes cast for all candidates for Governor at the last gubernatorial election and constitutional amendment initiatives must receive 8%.

INQUIRY SYSTEM – The computer information system maintained by Legislative Data Center which contains all bill text, File information, analyses, codes, etc.

INTERIM – The period of time between the end of the legislative year and the beginning of the next legislative year. The legislative year ends on August 31 in even-numbered years and mid-September in odd-numbered years.

J

JOINT COMMITTEE – Membership composed of equal numbers of Assembly members and Senators.

JOINT RESOLUTION – Expresses an opinion about an issue pertaining to the federal government; forwarded to Congress for its information. Joint resolutions require the approval of both the Assembly and Senate but does not require the signature of the Governor to take effect.

JOINT SESSION – The Assembly and Senate meeting together, usually in the Assembly chambers. The purpose is to receive special information such as the Governor's State of the State Address.

L

LAY ON THE TABLE – A motion to set aside a matter (e.g., amendments) before the house which may not be taken up again during session. The motion is not debatable.

LEGISLATIVE ADVOCATE – A person engaged to present views of a group or organization to legislators. Commonly called lobbyists.

LEGISLATIVE ANALYST – Staff director of the joint budget committee. The Legislative Analyst provides thorough, nonpartisan analysis on the fiscal impact of legislation.

LEGISLATIVE COUNSEL – The attorney for the Legislature, elected jointly by both houses. The Legislative Counsel and his or her legal staff is responsible for drafting all bills and amendments, preparing a digest (summary) of each bill, providing legal opinions, and generally representing the Legislature in legal proceedings.

LEGISLATIVE COUNSEL'S DIGEST – The digest is a brief summary of changes the proposed bill would make to current law. The digest is found on the front of each printed bill.

LOBBYIST – An individual who seeks to influence the outcome of legislation or administrative decisions. The law requires formal registration as a lobbyist if an individual's activity exceeds 25 contacts with decision makers in a two month period.

LOBBYIST BOOK – The *Directory of Lobbyists, Lobbying Firms,* and *Lobbyist Employers* published every session by the Secretary of State; available to the public for $12.00 from the Legislative Bill Room at the State Capitol or the Secretary of State's office. Photos and addresses of lobbyists are included with a list of the clients they represent. Employers of lobbyists are also listed alphabetically.

M

MAJORITY FLOOR LEADER – Elected by the majority caucus. Represents the Speaker on the floor, expedites Assembly Floor proceedings through parliamentary procedures such as motions and points of order and promotes harmony among the membership.

MAJORITY HOUSE – Quorum requirement of one more than half of the qualified members sitting at that time. For example, if there are four vacancies in the Assembly, 39 members would make a majority of the house.

MAJORITY OF THOSE PRESENT AND VOTING – A vote threshold that is determined by the number of members voting at that time. For example, if 40 members are voting on the adoption of amendments, a minimum of 21 "aye" votes would be necessary to adopt the amendments.

MAJORITY VOTE – A vote of more than half of the legislative body considering a measure. The full Assembly requires a majority vote of 41 and the full Senate requires 21, based on their membership of 80 and 40 respectively.

MASON'S MANUAL – The definitive reference manual for parliamentary procedure unless specifically covered by the Legislature's own written rules. Most parliamentary situations are covered by the State Constitution, Joint Rules or Assembly Rules.

MAY REVISION – Occurring in early May, the updated estimate of revenues and expenditures that replaces the estimates contained in the Governor's budget submitted in January.

MINORITY FLOOR LEADER – Elected by the caucus having the second largest house membership. Generally responsible for making motions, points of order and to represent the minority caucus on the floor.

MESSAGE FROM THE GOVERNOR – An official communication from the Governor which is read into the official record.

MOTION – A formal request for action made by a legislator during a committee hearing or Floor Session.

MOTION TO RECONSIDER – A parliamentary procedure which, if adopted, places the question in the same status it had been prior to the vote on the question.

MOVE A CALL – A parliamentary procedure that delays the announcement of the vote on a measure. This action gives a member additional time to gain more support for his or her bill, or to build opposition. A call must be "lifted" before the Houses adjourn that day.

MOVE THE PREVIOUS QUESTION – A motion made to end debate on a measure.

N

NONFISCAL BILL – A measure having no financial impact on the state and, therefore, not required to be heard in an Assembly or Senate fiscal committee as it moves through the legislative process. Nonfiscal bills are subject to somewhat different legislative calendar deadlines than fiscal bills.

O

OATH OF OFFICE – An oath that is taken by members-elect prior to being seated and embarking upon official duties.

OFFICE OF ADMINISTRATIVE LAW (OAL) – The independent executive branch agency charged with reviewing state agency RULE MAKING and regulations for compliance with procedures and standards set forth in the RULE MAKING portion of the Administrative Procedure Act (APA).

OUT OF ORDER – A parliamentary ruling by the presiding officer of a committee or the house that an action is not properly before the body or relevant to its discussion and, therefore, cannot be discussed at that moment.

OVERRIDE – An effort to reverse a Governor's veto by a vote of two-thirds of the members of each house. This requires 54 votes in the Assembly and 27 votes in the Senate.

P

PARLIAMENTARY INQUIRY – A question posed by a legislator during a committee hearing or Floor Session. A member must be recognized for this purpose and the question is then answered by the committee chair or presiding officer.

PASS AND RETAIN – If a member wishes to wait an additional day before taking up a bill, the member may ask the House for unanimous consent to "pass" his or her bill on File until the next legislative day without penalty.

PASS ON FILE – When the House refuses to "Pass and Retain" a measure on the agenda, it is "Passed on File." Although the bill remains on the agenda for the next day, if it is not taken-up the second time, it will automatically be placed on the inactive file.

PASS TEMPORARILY – A measure temporarily skipped on the agenda. If the bill's author does not take-up the measure by the end of the day, it may be penalized or retain is place on File by unanimous consent. (See Pass on File)

PER DIEM – Literally means "per day." It is the daily expense money rendered to legislators.

POINT OF ORDER – A parliamentary procedure used by a member to bring attention to a possible violation of the rules. The presiding officer then makes a ruling on the validity of the point of order.

PRESIDENT OF THE SENATE – The State Constitution designates the Lieutenant Governor as President of the Senate, allowing him or her to preside over the Senate and cast a vote only in the event of a 20–20 tie.

PRESIDING OFFICER – The member who presides over a legislative Floor Session. In the Assembly, the presiding officer is usually the Speaker or Speaker pro Tempore.

PRESS CONFERENCE – A presentation of information to a group of reporters. Press conferences are frequently held in Room 1190 of the Capitol, the Governor's press room, available to members on a reservation basis.

PRINCIPAL COAUTHOR – A legislator singled out to share credit along with the author of a bill or resolution.

PUT OVER – An action delayed on a legislative measure until a future date without jeopardy to the measure.

Q

QUASI-LEGISLATIVE – The term applied to the action or discretion of public administrative officers or agencies to make law, primarily through RULE MAKING.

QUORUM – The minimum number of legislators needed to begin conducting official business in committee or on the floor. The absence of a quorum is grounds for immediate adjournment of a committee hearing or Floor Session.

QUORUM CALL – Transmitting the message that members are needed to establish a quorum so proceedings can begin.

R

RECESS – (1) An official pause of any length in a committee hearing or Floor Session that halts the proceedings for a period of time but does not have finality of adjournment; (2) A break of more than four days in the regular session schedule such as for "Easter recess," etc.

RECONSIDERATION – A motion that, if carried, allows a measure that failed to be heard again in committee or on the floor.

REFERENDUM – A method by which a measure adopted by the Legislature may be submitted to popular vote of the electorate.

REGULATION – "Every rule, regulation, order, or standard of general application . . . adopted by any state agency to implement, interpret, or make specific the law enforced or administered by it, or to govern its procedure." (Government Code, Section 11342.) A legally adopted regulation has the force of law.

RESOLUTION – An opinion expressed by one or both houses which does not have the force of law. Concurrent and joint resolutions are voted on by both houses but do not require the Governor's signature.

ROLL CALL – A vote of a committee or the full Assembly or Senate. Committee roll calls are conducted by the committee secretary who calls each member's name in alphabetical order with the Chair's name last. Assembly roll calls are conducted electronically with each Member pushing a button from their assigned seat. The green button designates "aye" and the red button designates "no". Senate roll calls are conducted by the Reading Clerk who reads each Senator's name in alphabetical order.

RULE MAKING – The exercise of power granted by the Legislature to a state agency to adopt regulations to implement, interpret, or make specific the law enforced or administered by it, or to govern its procedure.

RULE WAIVER – A specific exemption to the Assembly, Senate, or Joint Rules; formal permission must be sought to receive.

S

SECOND READING – The first order of business on the Daily File. The house approves or denies committee recommendations at this stage. This is usually accomplished without debate or vote.

SECRETARY OF THE SENATE – The principal parliamentarian and record keeper for the Senate, elected by Senators at the beginning of each two-year session. The Senate Secretary and his or her staff are responsible for publishing the Senate daily and weekly publications.

SERGEANT-AT-ARMS – Staff responsible for maintaining order and providing security for legislators. The Chief Sergeant-at-Arms in each house is elected by a majority of the Members of that house at the beginning of every legislative session.

SHORT COMMITTEE – Lacking sufficient members of the committee; less than a quorum.

SPEAKER – The leading officer of the Assembly; elected by the Assembly members at the beginning of each two-year legislative session. This member presides over floor sessions.

SPEAKER PRO TEMPORE – An officer who presides over floor sessions in the absence of the Speaker.

SPECIAL ORDER OF BUSINESS – Occasionally a bill is of such importance that advanced notice is given before it will be considered in the full Assembly or Senate. A request is made during a Floor Session by requesting unanimous consent to set the bill as a special order of business on a specific date and time. This assures adequate time for debate and allows all Members the opportunity to be present.

SPONSOR – The legislator, private individual, or group who developed a piece of legislation and advocates its passage.

SPOT BILL – A bill that amends a code section in such an innocuous way as to be totally nonsubstantive. The bill has been introduced to assure that a germane vehicle will be available at a later date after the deadline had passed to introduce bills. At that future date, the bill can be amended to incorporate more substantive provisions.

STATE MANDATE – Chapter 1406, Statutes of 1972, first established the requirement for the state to reimburse units of local government for all costs mandated on them by the state resulting from either legislative acts or administrative regulations which impose a new program or demand an increased level of service in an existing program. Proposition 4 of 1979 (Gann Initiative) incorporated this requirement into Section 6 of Article XIIIB of the State Constitution.

SUBCOMMITTEE – A subgroup of a full committee, composed of committee members from both parties.

SUMMARY DIGEST – Brief summaries of each piece of legislation passed in the two-year session; prepared by Legislative Counsel. Measures are listed in the order they were signed into law.

T

TAX LEVY – Any bill that imposes, repeals, or materially alters a state tax. Legislative Counsel determines whether a bill is a tax levy.

THIRD READING – The stage at which bills are eligible for floor debate and final vote.

THIRD READING ANALYSIS – A summary of a measure ready for floor consideration. It contains most recent amendments and information regarding how Members voted on the measure when it was heard in committees.

THIRD READING FILE – The portion of the Daily File that lists the bills that are ready to be taken up for final passage.

THIRD SET – The third date scheduled by a committee for hearing a bill after two prior settings as requested by the author. Date changes made by the committee chairperson do not count as "sets."

THIRTY-DAY PROVISION – The thirty-day waiting period following a bill's introduction before a bill may be heard or acted upon by the Legislature. The waiting period is required by the State Constitution and the Joint Rules and can be waived by a three-fourths vote (60 in the Assembly; 30 in the Senate).

TOMBSTONE – Specification in a bill that the act it creates will be named for a state legislator; i.e., "The (last name of individual) Act."

U

UNANIMOUS CONSENT – The consent (permission) of those members present, absent any objection, debate, or vote. (i.e., Unanimous consent was granted to suspend the four day File notice requirement to hear a bill in committee.)

UNDERGROUND REGULATION – An agency regulation that should have been, but was not, adopted following procedures set forth in the RULE MAKING portion of the Administrative Procedure Act (commencing with Government Code Section 11340) and, consequently, invalid.

UNFINISHED BUSINESS – The section of the Daily File containing bills vetoed by the Governor, concurrence items, conference reports, and certain motions to be voted on.

V

VETO – The formal action of the Governor in disapproving a bill. A two-thirds vote of each house is necessary to override the veto and make the bill become law.

VOICE VOTE – A vote that requires only an oral "aye" or "no" with no official count taken. The presiding officer determines whether the "ayes" or "noes" carry.

W

WHIP – A party officer charged with monitoring floor activity of caucus members.

WITHDRAW FROM COMMITTEE – A floor vote to compel the discharge of a bill from committee.

Appendices

APPENDIX A

SESSIONS OF THE CALIFORNIA LEGISLATURE—1849–1998

The first two sessions were held in San Jose; the Third Session met at Vallejo and later removed to Sacramento; the Fourth Session met at Vallejo and later removed to Benicia; the Fifth Session met at Benicia and later removed to Sacramento. Beginning with the Sixth Session all Legislatures have met in Sacramento, except the Thirteenth which convened at Sacramento but later removed to San Francisco; the 1958 session met at Benicia for one day.

Session	Convened	Adjourned	Legislative days † Assembly	Senate	Length *
1	Dec. 15, 1849	April 22, 1850	103	103	129
2	Jan. 6, 1851	May 1, 1851	98	98	116
3	Jan. 5, 1852	May 4, 1852	96	96	120
4	Jan. 3, 1853	May 19, 1853	108	109	137
5	Jan. 2, 1854	May 15, 1854	110	108	134
6	Jan. 1, 1855	May 7, 1855	103	102	127
7	Jan. 7, 1856	April 21, 1856	87	85	106
8	Jan. 5, 1857	April 30, 1857	99	100	116
9	Jan. 4, 1858	April 26, 1858	93	96	113
10	Jan. 3, 1859	April 19, 1859	89	88	107
11	Jan. 2, 1860	April 30, 1860	100	96	120
12	Jan. 7, 1861	May 20, 1861	108	106	134
13	Jan. 6, 1862	May 15, 1862	101	106	130
14	Jan. 5, 1863	April 27, 1863	93	94	113
15	Dec. 7, 1863	April 4, 1864	88	89	120
16	Dec. 4, 1865	April 2, 1866	87	85	120
17	Dec. 2, 1867	Mar. 30, 1868	85	82	120
18	Dec. 6, 1869	April 4, 1870	88	86	120
19	Dec. 4, 1871	April 1, 1872	86	85	120
20	Dec. 1, 1873	Mar. 30, 1874	88	89	120
21	Dec. 6, 1875	April 3, 1876	90	86	120
22	Dec. 3, 1877	April 1, 1878	84	84	120
23	Jan. 5, 1880	April 16, 1880	87	84	103
24	Jan. 3, 1881	Mar. 4, 1881	49	51	61
24, 1st ex.	April 4, 1881	May 13, 1881	34	35	40
25	Jan. 8, 1883	Mar. 13, 1883	53	52	65
25, 1st ex.	Mar. 24, 1884	May 13, 1884	40	38	51
26	Jan. 5, 1885	Mar. 11, 1885	52	51	66
26, 1st ex.	July 20, 1886	Aug. 20, 1886 (Proclamation) ‡			
	(Reconvened) Sept. 7, 1886	Sept. 11, 1886	25	26	54
27	Jan. 3, 1887	Mar. 12, 1887	55	53	69
28	Jan. 7, 1889	Mar. 16, 1889	55	54	69
29	Jan. 5, 1891	Mar. 25, 1891	63	64	80
30	Jan. 2, 1893	Mar. 14, 1893	58	57	72
31	Jan. 7, 1895	Mar. 16, 1895	55	54	69
32	Jan. 4, 1897	Mar. 20, 1897	61	61	76
33	Jan. 2, 1899	Mar. 19, 1899	66	67	77
33, 1st ex.	Jan. 29, 1900	Feb. 10, 1900	12	12	13
34	Jan. 7, 1901	Mar. 16, 1901	55	52	69
35	Jan. 5, 1903	Mar. 14, 1903	57	52	69
36	Jan. 2, 1905	Mar. 10, 1905	52	50	68
36, 1st ex.	June 2, 1906	June 12, 1906	11	10	11
37	Jan. 7, 1907	Mar. 12, 1907	55	52	65
37, 1st ex.	Nov. 19, 1907	Nov. 23, 1907	5	5	5
2d ex.	Nov. 23, 1907 (1 p.m.)	Nov. 23, 1907 (2:30 p.m.)	1	1	1
38	Jan. 4, 1909	Mar. 24, 1909	66	60	80
38, 1st ex.	Sept. 6, 1910	Sept. 9, 1910	4	4	4
2d ex.	Oct. 3, 1910	Oct. 5, 1910	3	3	3
39	Jan. 2, 1911	Mar. 27, 1911	69	68	85
39, 1st ex.	Nov. 27, 1911	Dec. 24, 1911	27	24	28
2d ex.	Dec. 24, 1911 (12:05 p.m.)	Dec. 24, 1911 (3:30 p.m.)	1	1	1
40, 1st part	Jan. 6, 1913	Feb. 4, 1913 ⎤	79	79	94
2d part	Mar. 10, 1913	May 12, 1913 ⎦			
41, 1st part	Jan. 4, 1915	Jan. 30, 1915 ⎤	72	69	90
2d part	Mar. 8, 1915	May 9, 1915 ⎦			
1st ex.	Jan. 5, 1916	Jan. 11, 1916	6	7	7

* The length of session is by calendar days, excluding constitutional recesses during the sessions of 1913 through 1957.
† Actual days in session.
‡ Governor Stoneman adjourned the extraordinary session by proclamation from August 20 to September 7, 1886.

Appendix A—Sessions of the California Legislature—1849–1998—Continued

Session	Convened	Adjourned	Legislative days † Assembly	Senate	Length *
42, 1st part	Jan. 8, 1917	Jan. 26, 1917 ⎫	66	61	80
2d part	Feb. 26, 1917	April 27, 1917 ⎭			
43, 1st part	Jan. 6, 1919	Jan. 24, 1919 ⎫	63	59	77
2d part	Feb. 24, 1919	April 22, 1919 ⎭			
43, 1st ex.	Nov. 1, 1919 (2 p.m.)	Nov. 1, 1919 (6 p.m.)	1	1	1
44, 1st part	Jan. 3, 1921	Jan. 24, 1921 ⎫	71	66	87
2d part	Feb. 24, 1921	April 29, 1921 ⎭			
45, 1st part	Jan. 8, 1923	Feb. 2, 1923 ⎫	78	74	101
2d part	Mar. 5, 1923	May 18, 1923 ⎭			
46, 1st part	Jan. 5, 1925	Jan. 24, 1925 ⎫	63	60	80
2d part	Feb. 24, 1925	April 24, 1925 ⎭			
46, 1st ex.	Oct. 22, 1926 (10 a.m.)	Oct. 22, 1926 (2 p.m.)	1	1	1
47, 1st part	Jan. 3, 1927	Jan. 21, 1927 ⎫	63	63	85
2d part	Feb. 23, 1927	April 29, 1927 ⎭			
47, 1st ex.	Sept. 4, 1928	Sept. 5, 1928	2	2	2
48, 1st part	Jan. 7, 1929	Jan. 18, 1929 ⎫	72	73	99
2d part	Feb. 18, 1929	May 15, 1929 ⎭			
49, 1st part	Jan. 5, 1931	Jan. 23, 1931 ⎫	74	74	100
2d part	Feb. 24, 1931	May 15, 1931 ⎭			
50, 1st part	Jan. 2, 1933	Jan. 28, 1933 ⎫	88	88	111
2d part	Feb. 28, 1933	May 12, 1933 ⎬			
3d part	July 17, 1933	July 26, 1933 ⎭			
50, 1st ex.	Sept. 12, 1934	Sept. 15, 1934	4	4	4
51, 1st part	Jan. 7, 1935	Jan. 26, 1935 ⎫	98	95	125
2d part	Mar. 4, 1935	June 16, 1935 ⎭			
51, 1st ex.	May 25, 1936	May 26, 1936	2	2	2
52, 1st part	Jan. 4, 1937	Jan. 22, 1937 ⎫	82	81	108
2d part	Mar. 1, 1937	May 28, 1937 ⎭			
52, 1st ex.	Mar. 7, 1938	Mar. 12, 1938	6	6	6
53, 1st part	Jan. 2, 1939	Jan. 25, 1939 ⎫	99	97	131
2d part	Mar. 6, 1939	June 20, 1939 ⎭			
53, 1st ex.	Jan. 29, 1940 May 13, 1940 Sept. 21, 1940 Dec. 2, 1940	Feb. 25, 1940 ⎫ May 24, 1940 ⎪ Sept. 22, 1940 ⎬ Dec. 5, 1940 ⎭	40	40	312
2d ex.	May 13, 1940	May 24, 1940	10	10	12
3d ex.	Sept. 13, 1940 (2 p.m.)	Sept. 13, 1940 (9 p.m.)	1	1	1
4th ex.	Sept. 21, 1940 Dec. 2, 1940	Sept. 22, 1940 ⎫ Dec. 5, 1940 ⎭	6	6	76
5th ex.	Dec. 2, 1940	Dec. 5, 1940	4	4	4
54, 1st part	Jan. 6, 1941	Jan. 25, 1941 ⎫	94	93	124
2d part	Mar. 3, 1941	June 14, 1941 ⎭			
54, 1st ex.	Dec. 19, 1941 Jan. 12, 1942	Dec. 22, 1941 ⎫ Jan. 22, 1942 ⎭	15	15	35
2d ex.	Jan. 17, 1942	Jan. 18, 1942	2	2	2
55, 1st part	Jan. 4, 1943	Jan. 31, 1943 ⎫	71	71	87
2d part	Mar. 8, 1943	May 5, 1943 ⎭			
55, 1st ex.	Jan. 28, 1943	Jan. 30, 1943	3	3	3
2d ex.	Mar. 20, 1943	Mar. 25, 1943	5	5	6
3d ex.	Jan. 27, 1944	Jan. 31, 1944	5	5	5
4th ex.	June 5, 1944	June 13, 1944	8	8	9
56, 1st part	Jan. 8, 1945	Jan. 27, 1945 ⎫	97	97	124
2d part	Mar. 5, 1945	June 16, 1945 ⎭			
56, 1st ex.	Jan. 7, 1946	Feb. 19, 1946	33	33	44
2d ex.	July 22, 1946	July 25, 1946	4	4	4
57, 1st part	Jan. 6, 1947	Feb. 5, 1947 ⎫	94	92	127
2d part	Mar. 17, 1947	June 20, 1947 ⎭			
57, 1st ex.	Jan. 13, 1947	Feb. 5, 1947 ⎫	84	63	138
1st ex., 2d part	Mar. 3, 1947	June 24, 1947 ⎭			
1948	Mar. 1, 1948	Mar. 27, 1948	20	20	27
1949, 1st part	Jan. 3, 1949	Jan. 29, 1949 ⎫	106	108	145
2d part	Mar. 7, 1949	July 2, 1949 ⎭			
1st ex.	Dec. 12, 1949	Dec. 21, 1949	8	9	10
1950	Mar. 6, 1950	April 4, 1950	20	21	30
1st ex.	Mar. 6, 1950	April 15, 1950	28	26	41
2d ex.	Mar. 6, 1950 (12:15 p.m.)	Mar. 6, 1950 (6 p.m.)	1	1	1
3d ex.	Sept. 20, 1950	Sept. 26, 1950	6	6	7
1951, 1st part	Jan. 8, 1951	Jan. 23, 1951 ⎫	88	88	120
2d part	Mar. 12, 1951	June 23, 1951 ⎭			

* The length of session is by calendar days, excluding constitutional recesses during the sessions of 1913 through 1957.
† Actual days in session.

Appendix A—Sessions of the California Legislature—1849–1998—Continued

Session	Convened	Adjourned	Legislative days † Assembly	Senate	Length *
1952	Mar. 3, 1952	April 1, 1952	20	21	30
1st ex.	Mar. 3, 1952	April 2, 1952	21	22	31
2d ex.	Aug. 4, 1952	Aug. 13, 1952	9	9	10
1953, 1st part	Jan. 5, 1953	Jan. 17, 1953 ⎫	91	91	120
2d part	Feb. 24, 1953	June 10, 1953 ⎭			
1954	Mar. 1, 1954	Mar. 30, 1954	21	21	30
1st ex.	Mar. 1, 1954	April 1, 1954	22	23	32
1955, 1st part	Jan. 3, 1955	Jan. 21, 1955 ⎫	93	89	120
2d part	Feb. 28, 1955	June 8, 1955 ⎭			
1956	Mar. 5, 1956	April 3, 1956	21	21	30
1st ex.	Mar. 5, 1956	April 5, 1956	23	23	32
1957, 1st part	Jan. 7, 1957	Jan. 25, 1957 ⎫	97	91	120
2d part	Mar. 4, 1957	June 12, 1957 ⎭			
1958, 1st part	Feb. 3, 1958	Feb. 4, 1958 ⎫	24	24	30
2d part	Mar. 3, 1958	Mar. 30, 1958 ⎭			
1st ex.	Mar. 4, 1958	April 23, 1958	36	35	51
2d ex.	Mar. 31, 1958	April 24, 1958	17	17	25
1959	Jan. 5, 1959	June 19, 1959	113	112	166
1960	Feb. 1, 1960	Mar. 26, 1960	22	21	30
1st ex.	Feb. 1, 1960	April 7, 1960	31	30	67
2d ex.	Mar. 2, 1960	Mar. 10, 1960	6	4	9
1961	Jan. 2, 1961	June 16, 1961	114	116	166
1962	Feb. 5, 1962	April 3, 1962	22	20	30
1st ex.	Mar. 7, 1962	April 13, 1962	25	24	38
2d ex.	April 9, 1962	April 13, 1962	5	4	5
3d ex.	June 26, 1962	June 28, 1962	3	3	3
1963	Jan. 7, 1963	June 21, 1963	109	109	166
1st ex.	July 8, 1963	Aug. 1, 1963	16	16	25
1964	Feb. 3, 1964	Mar. 26, 1964	18	17	30
1st ex.	Feb. 3, 1964	May 23, 1964	56	55	111
2d ex.	Mar. 30, 1964	May 23, 1964	34	24	55
1965	Jan. 4, 1965	June 18, 1965	106	107	166
1st ex.	June 25, 1965	July 6, 1965	8	8	12
2d ex.	Sept. 20, 1965	Nov. 4, 1965	28	27	46
1966	Feb. 7, 1966	April 4, 1966	18	19	30
1st ex.	Feb. 10, 1966	July 7, 1966	81	81	148
2d ex.	April 5, 1966	July 8, 1966	52	36	95
1967	Jan. 2, 1967	Sept. 8, 1967	142	143	250
1st ex.	Sept. 5, 1967	Sept. 7, 1967	3	3	3
2d ex.	Nov. 6, 1967	Dec. 8, 1967	21	21	33
1968	Jan. 8, 1968	Aug. 3, 1968 (Proclamation)‡			
	(Reconvened) Sept. 9, 1968	Sept. 13, 1968	131	137	250
1st ex.	Sept. 9, 1968	Sept. 20, 1968	10	10	12
1969	Jan. 6, 1969	Sept. 10, 1969	140	136	248
1970	Jan. 5, 1970	Sept. 23, 1970	141	150	262
1971	Jan. 4, 1971	Jan. 3, 1972	193	199	365
1st ex.	Dec. 6, 1971	Mar. 1, 1972	29	36	87
1972	Jan. 3, 1972	Jan. 5, 1973	139	148	369
1973–74	Jan. 8, 1973	Nov. 30, 1974	239	254	692
1st ex.	Dec. 4, 1973 (12 noon)	Dec. 4, 1973 (1 p.m.)	1	1	1
2d ex.	Sept. 25, 1974	Oct. 2, 1974	4	4	8
1975–76	Dec. 2, 1974	Nov. 30, 1976	256	255	730
1st ex.	Feb. 17, 1975	June 27, 1975	76	46	131
2d ex.	May 19, 1975	Sept. 12, 1975	56	44	117
3d ex.	May 20, 1975	May 29, 1975	7	5	10
1977–78	Dec. 6, 1976	Nov. 30, 1978	256	260	725
1st ex.	Jan. 5, 1978	April 24, 1978	58	59	110
1979–80	Dec. 4, 1978	Nov. 30, 1980	251	262	728
1981–82	Dec. 1, 1980	Nov. 30, 1982	248	257	729
1st ex.	Nov. 9, 1981	Feb. 25, 1982	29	23	109
1983–84	Dec. 6, 1982	Nov. 30, 1984	262	266	726
1st ex.	Dec. 6, 1982	July 19, 1983	68	72	226
2d ex.	Jan. 19, 1984	Feb. 17, 1984	5	3	30
1985–86	Dec. 3, 1984	Nov. 30, 1986	251	254	728
1st ex.	Sept. 8, 1986	Nov. 30, 1986	68	66	84

* The length of session is by calendar days, excluding constitutional recesses during the sessions of 1913 through 1957.
† Actual days in session.
‡ Acting Governor Hugh Burns adjourned the regular session by proclamation from August 3, 1968 to September 9, 1968.

Appendix A—Sessions of the California Legislature—1849–1998—Continued

Session	Convened	Adjourned	Legislative days †		Length *
			Assembly	Senate	
1987–88	Dec. 1, 1986	Nov. 30, 1988	246	253	731
1st ex.	Nov. 9, 1987	Nov. 10, 1987	2	2	2
1989–90	Dec. 5, 1988	Nov. 30, 1990	264	269	726
1st ex.	Nov. 2, 1989	Sept. 1, 1990	44	66	304
1991–92	Dec. 3, 1990	Nov. 30, 1992	292	284	728
1st ex.	Dec. 3, 1990	Nov. 30, 1992	141	127	728
2d ex.	Oct. 8, 1992	Nov. 30, 1992	2	2	54
1993–94	Dec. 7, 1992	Nov. 30, 1994	245	255	724
1st ex.	Jan. 4, 1993	Aug. 31, 1994	124	142	605
1995–96	Dec. 5, 1994	Nov. 30, 1996	264	265	637
1st ex.	Jan. 19, 1995	Sept. 1, 1996	79	98	592
2nd ex.	Feb. 17, 1995	Sept. 1, 1996	65	87	563
3rd ex.	Jan. 4, 1996	Mar. 15, 1996	19	15	71
4th ex.	Feb. 13, 1996	Mar. 18, 1996	16	9	45
1997–98	Dec. 2, 1996	—	—	—	—
1st ex.	Jan. 13, 1997‡	—	—	—	—

* The length of session is by calendar days, excluding constitutional recesses during the sessions of 1913 through 1957.
† Actual days in session.
‡ Assembly convened the 1997–98 1st. Ex. Session on January 14, 1997.

APPENDIX B

GOVERNORS, LIEUTENANT GOVERNORS, AND SPEAKERS OF THE ASSEMBLY—1849–1998

(See footnotes on pages 219–220 for oaths of office, deaths in office, resignations, and succession information)

Governors

Name	Party Affiliation	Date of Inauguration
Peter H. Burnett [1]	ID	Dec. 20, 1849
John McDougall [2]	ID	Jan. 9, 1851
John Bigler	D	Jan. 8, 1852
John Bigler	D	Jan. 7, 1854
J. Neeley Johnson	Am	Jan. 9, 1856
John B. Weller	D	Jan. 8, 1858
Milton S. Latham [6]	LD	Jan. 9, 1860
John G. Downey	LD	Jan. 14, 1860
Leland Stanford	R	Jan. 10, 1862
Frederick F. Low	Un	Dec. 10, 1863
Henry H. Haight	D	Dec. 5, 1867
Newton Booth [10]	R	Dec. 8, 1871
Romualdo Pacheco [11]	R	Feb. 27, 1875
William Irwin	D	Dec. 9, 1875
George C. Perkins	R	Jan. 8, 1880
George Stoneman	D	Jan. 10, 1883
Washington Bartlett [13]	D	Jan. 8, 1887
Robert W. Waterman [14]	R	Sept. 13, 1887
Henry H. Markham	R	Jan. 8, 1891
James H. Budd	D	Jan. 11, 1895
Henry T. Gage	R	Jan. 3, 1899

Lieutenant Governors

Name	Party Affiliation	Date of Inauguration
John McDougall [2]	ID	Dec. 20, 1849
David C. Broderick (Acting) [3]	D	Jan. 9, 1851
Samuel Purdy	D	Jan. 8, 1852
Samuel Purdy	D	Jan. 7, 1854
Robert M. Anderson	Am	Jan. 9, 1856
John Walkup	D	Jan. 8, 1858
John G. Downey [7]	LD	Jan. 9, 1860
Isaac N. Quinn (Acting) [8]	D	Jan. 20, 1860
Pablo de la Guerra (Acting) [9]	D	Jan. 7, 1861
John F. Chellis	R	Jan. 10, 1862
T. N. Machin	Un	Dec. 10, 1863
William Holden	D	Dec. 5, 1867
Romualdo Pacheco [11]	R	Dec. 8, 1871
William Irwin (Acting) [12]	D	Feb. 27, 1875
James A. Johnson	D	Dec. 9, 1875
John Mansfield	R	Jan. 8, 1880
John Daggett	D	Jan. 10, 1883
Robert W. Waterman [14]	R	Jan. 8, 1887
Stephen M. White (Acting) [15]	D	Sept. 13, 1887
John B. Reddick	R	Jan. 8, 1891
Spencer G. Millard [16]	R	Jan. 11, 1895
William T. Jeter [17]	D	Oct. 25, 1895
Jacob H. Neff	R	Jan. 3, 1899

Speakers of the Assembly

Name	Party Affiliation	Session No.	Date Session Convened
Thomas J. White [4]	*	1	Dec. 15, 1849
John Bigler [5]	D		
John Bigler	D	2	Jan. 6, 1851
Richard P. Hammond	D	3	Jan. 5, 1852
Isaac B. Wall	D	4	Jan. 3, 1853
Charles S. Fairfax	D	5	Jan. 2, 1854
William W. Stow	W	6	Jan. 1, 1855
Jas. T. Farley	Am	7	Jan. 7, 1856
Elwood T. Beatty	D	8	Jan. 5, 1857
N. E. Whiteside	D	9	Jan. 4, 1858
William C. Stratton	D	10	Jan. 3, 1859
Philip Moore	D	11	Jan. 2, 1860
R. Burnell	DD	12	Jan. 7, 1861
George Barstow	D	13	Jan. 6, 1862
Tim N. Machin	Un	14	Jan. 5, 1863
William H. Sears	Un	15	Dec. 7, 1863
John Yule	D	16	Dec. 4, 1865
Caius T. Ryland	D	17	Dec. 2, 1867
George H. Rogers	R	18	Dec. 6, 1869
Thos. B. Shannon	Ind	19	Dec. 4, 1871
Morris M. Estee	D	20	Dec. 1, 1873
G. J. Carpenter	D	21	Dec. 6, 1875
Campbell P. Berry	R	22	Dec. 3, 1877
Jabez F. Cowdery	R	23	Jan. 5, 1880
William H. Parks	R	24	Jan. 3, 1881
Hugh M. LaRue	D	1st Ex.	April 4, 1881
William H. Parks	R	25	Jan. 8, 1883
William H. Jordan	R	1st Ex.	Mar. 24, 1884
Robert Howe	D	26	Jan. 5, 1885
Frank L. Coombs	R	1st Ex.	July 20, 1886
F. H. Gould	D	27	Jan. 3, 1887
John C. Lynch	R	28	Jan. 7, 1889
Frank L. Coombs [18]	D	29	Jan. 5, 1891
Howard E. Wright [18]	R	30	Jan. 2, 1893
Alden Anderson	R	1st Ex.	Jan. 29, 1900
Cornelius W. Pendleton	R	34	Jan. 7, 1901

APPENDIX B—GOVERNORS, LIEUTENANT GOVERNORS, AND SPEAKERS OF THE ASSEMBLY—1849-1998—Continued

Governors			Lieutenant Governors			Speakers of the Assembly			
Name	Party Affiliation	Date of Inauguration	Name	Party Affiliation	Date of Inauguration	Name	Party Affiliation	Session No.	Date Session Convened
George C. Pardee	R	Jan. 6, 1903	Alden Anderson	R	Jan. 6, 1903	Arthur G. Fisk	R	35	Jan. 5, 1903
						Frank C. Prescott	R	36	Jan. 2, 1905
								1st Ex.	June 2, 1906
James N. Gillett	R	Jan. 8, 1907	Warren R. Porter	R	Jan. 8, 1907	R. L. Beardslee	R	37	Jan. 7, 1907
								1st Ex.	Nov. 19, 1907
								2d Ex.	Nov. 23, 1907
						P. A. Stanton	R	38	Jan. 4, 1909
								1st Ex.	Sept. 6, 1910
								2d Ex.	Oct. 3, 1911
Hiram W. Johnson	R	Jan. 3, 1911	A. J. Wallace	R	Jan. 3, 1911	A. H. Hewitt	R	39	Jan. 2, 1911
								1st Ex.	Nov. 27, 1911
								2d Ex.	Dec. 24, 1911
						C. C. Young	R	40	Jan. 6, 1913
Hiram W. Johnson [20]	R	Jan. 5, 1915	John M. Eshleman [21]	Prog	Jan. 5, 1915	C. C. Young	Prog	41	Jan. 4, 1915
			William D. Stephens [22]	R	July 22, 1916			1st Ex.	Jan. 5, 1916
William D. Stephens [22]	R	Mar. 15, 1917	Vacancy			C. C. Young	R	42	Jan. 8, 1917
William D. Stephens	R	Jan. 7, 1919	C. C. Young	R	Jan. 7, 1919	Henry W. Wright	R	43	Jan. 6, 1919
								1st Ex.	Nov. 1, 1919
						Frank F. Merriam	R	44	Jan. 3, 1921
Friend Wm. Richardson	R	Jan. 9, 1923	C. C. Young	R	Jan. 9, 1923	Frank F. Merriam	R	45	Jan. 8, 1923
								1st Ex.	Oct. 5, 1923
						Edgar C. Levey	R	46	Jan. 5, 1925
								1st Ex.	Jan. 22, 1926
C. C. Young	R	Jan. 4, 1927	Buron Fitts [23]	R	Jan. 4, 1927	Edgar C. Levey	R	47	Jan. 3, 1927
			H. L. Carnahan [24]	R	Dec. 4, 1928			1st Ex.	Sept. 4, 1928
						Walter J. Little	R	48	Jan. 7, 1929
James Rolph, Jr. [25]	R	Jan. 6, 1931	Frank F. Merriam [26]	R	Jan. 6, 1931			49	Jan. 5, 1931
						F. C. Clowdsley	D	50	Jan. 5, 1933
Frank F. Merriam [26]	R	June 7, 1934	Vacancy		June 7, 1934			1st Ex.	Sept. 12, 1934
Frank F. Merriam	R	Jan. 8, 1935	George F. Hatfield	R	Jan. 8, 1935	Edward Craig	R	51	Jan. 7, 1935
								1st Ex.	May 25, 1935
						Wm. Moseley Jones	D	52	Jan. 4, 1937
								1st Ex.	Mar. 7, 1938
Culbert L. Olson	D	Jan. 2, 1939	Ellis E. Patterson	D	Jan. 2, 1939	Paul Peek	D	53	Jan. 2, 1939
						Gordon H. Garland	D	1st Ex.	
								2d Ex.	May 13, 1940
								3d Ex.	Sept. 21, 1940
								4th Ex.	Dec. 2, 1940
								5th Ex.	
						Gordon H. Garland	D	54	Jan. 6, 1941
								1st Ex.	Jan. 19, 1941
								2d Ex.	Jan. 17, 1942

Session	Convened		Governor		Lieutenant Governor		Speaker of the Assembly	
55	Jan. 4, 1943	R	Earl Warren	Jan. 4, 1943	Frederick F. Houser	Jan. 4, 1943	Charles W. Lyon	R
1st Ex.	Jan. 28, 1943							
2d Ex.	Mar. 20, 1943							
3d Ex.	Mar. 27, 1944							
4th Ex.	June 5, 1944							
56	Jan. 8, 1945							R
1st Ex.	Jan. 7, 1946						Charles W. Lyon	
2d Ex.	July 22, 1946							
57	Jan. 6, 1947	R	Earl Warren	Jan. 6, 1947	Goodwin J. Knight	Jan. 6, 1947	Sam L. Collins	R
1st Ex.	Jan. 13, 1947							
1948	Mar. 1, 1948						Sam L. Collins	R
1949	Jan. 3, 1949						Sam L. Collins	R
1st Ex.	Dec. 12, 1949							
1950	Mar. 6, 1950						Sam L. Collins	R
1st Ex.	Mar. 6, 1950							
2d Ex.	Mar. 6, 1950							
3d Ex.	Sept. 20, 1950							
1951	Jan. 8, 1951	R	Earl Warren [27]	Jan. 8, 1951	Goodwin J. Knight [28]	Jan. 8, 1951	Sam L. Collins	R
1952	Mar. 3, 1952						Sam L. Collins	R
1st Ex.	Mar. 3, 1952							
2d Ex.	Aug. 4, 1952							
1953	Jan. 1, 1953	R	Goodwin J. Knight [28]	Oct. 5, 1953	Harold J. Powers [29]	Oct. 5, 1953	James W. Silliman	R
1954	Mar. 5, 1954						James W. Silliman	R
1st Ex.	Mar. 1, 1954							
1955	Jan. 3, 1955	R	Goodwin J. Knight	Jan. 3, 1955	Harold J. Powers	Jan. 3, 1955	L. H. Lincoln	R
1956	Mar. 5, 1956						L. H. Lincoln	R
1st Ex.	Mar. 7, 1957							
1957	Jan. 7, 1957						L. H. Lincoln	R
1958	Feb. 3, 1958						L. H. Lincoln	R
1st Ex.	Mar. 4, 1958							
2d Ex.	Mar. 31, 1958							
1959	Jan. 5, 1959	D	Edmund G. Brown	Jan. 5, 1959	Glenn M. Anderson	Jan. 5, 1959	Ralph M. Brown	D
1960	Feb. 1, 1960						Ralph M. Brown	D
1st Ex.	Feb. 2, 1960							
1961	Jan. 2, 1961						Ralph M. Brown [30]	D
							Jesse M. Unruh	D
1962	Feb. 5, 1962						Jesse M. Unruh	D
1st Ex.	Mar. 7, 1962							
2d Ex.	April 9, 1962							
3d Ex.	June 26, 1962							
1963	Jan. 8, 1963	D	Edmund G. Brown	Jan. 7, 1963	Glenn M. Anderson	Jan. 7, 1963	Jesse M. Unruh	D
1964	July 3, 1964						Jesse M. Unruh	D
1st Ex.	Feb. 3, 1964							
2d Ex.	Mar. 30, 1964							
1965	Jan. 25, 1965						Jesse M. Unruh	D
1st Ex.	June 20, 1965							
2d Ex.	Sept. 7, 1966							
1966	Feb. 10, 1966						Jesse M. Unruh	D
1st Ex.	Feb. 10, 1966							
2d Ex.	April 5, 1966							

APPENDIX B—GOVERNORS, LIEUTENANT GOVERNORS, AND SPEAKERS OF THE ASSEMBLY—1849–1998—Continued

Governors			Lieutenant Governors			Speakers of the Assembly			
Name	Party Affiliation	Date of Inauguration	Name	Party Affiliation	Date of Inauguration	Name	Party Affiliation	Session No.	Date Session Convened
Ronald Reagan	R	Jan. 2, 1967	Robert H. Finch [31]	R	Jan. 2, 1967	Jesse M. Unruh	D	1967	Jan. 2, 1967
								1st Ex.	Sept. 5, 1967
								2d Ex.	Nov. 6, 1967
						Jesse M. Unruh		1968	Jan. 8, 1968
								1st Ex.	Sept. 9, 1968
			Ed Reinecke [32]	R	Jan. 21, 1969	Bob Monagan	R	1969	Jan. 6, 1969
						Bob Monagan	R	1970	Jan. 5, 1970
Ronald Reagan	R	Jan. 4, 1971	Ed Reinecke [35]	R	Jan. 4, 1971	Bob Moretti	D	1971	Jan. 4, 1971
						Bob Moretti	D	1st Ex.	Dec. 6, 1971
						Bob Moretti	D	1972	Jan. 3, 1972
						Bob Moretti [33]	D	1973-74	Jan. 4, 1973
						Bob Moretti [33]	D	1st Ex.	Dec. 6, 1973
			John L. Harmer [36]	R	Oct. 4, 1974	Leo T. McCarthy [34]	D	1973-74	June 27, 1974
						Leo T. McCarthy		2d Ex.	Sept. 25, 1974
Edmund G. Brown, Jr.	D	Jan. 6, 1975	Mervyn M. Dymally	D	Jan. 6, 1975	Leo T. McCarthy	D	1975-76	Dec. 2, 1974
								1st Ex.	Feb. 17, 1975
								2d Ex.	May 19, 1975
								3d Ex.	May 20, 1975
								1977-78	Dec. 6, 1976
								1st Ex.	Jan. 4, 1978
Edmund G. Brown, Jr.	D	Jan. 8, 1979	Mike Curb	R	Jan. 8, 1979	Leo T. McCarthy	R	1979-80	Dec. 1, 1980
						Willie L. Brown, Jr.		1981-82	Dec. 6, 1982
George Deukmejian	R	Jan. 3, 1983	Leo T. McCarthy	D	Jan. 3, 1983	Willie L. Brown, Jr.	D	1983-84	Jan. 19, 1984
								1st Ex.	Dec. 3, 1984
								2d Ex.	Sept. 8, 1986
								1985-86	Dec. 1, 1986
								1st Ex.	Nov. 5, 1987
George Deukmejian	R	Jan. 5, 1987	Leo T. McCarthy	D	Jan. 5, 1987	Willie L. Brown, Jr.	D	1987-88	Dec. 5, 1988
								1st Ex.	Nov. 2, 1989
								1989-90	Dec. 3, 1990
								1st Ex.	Dec. 3, 1990
Pete Wilson	R	Jan. 7, 1991	Leo T. McCarthy	D	Jan. 7, 1991	Willie L. Brown, Jr.	D	1991-92	Oct. 8, 1992
								1st Ex.	Dec. 7, 1992
								2d Ex.	Jan. 4, 1993
								1993-94	Dec. 7, 1992
								1st Ex.	Jan. 4, 1993

Pete Wilson .... R Jan. 2, 1995

Gray Davis .... D Jan. 2, 1995

Session	Date	
1995–96	Dec.	5, 1994
1st Ex.	Jan.	19, 1995
2nd Ex.	Feb.	17, 1995
3rd Ex.	Jan.	4, 1996
4th Ex.	Feb.	13, 1996
1997–98	Dec.	2, 1996
1st Ex.	Jan.	13, 1997

Name	Party
Willie L. Brown, Jr. [37]	D
Doris Allen [38] [39]	R
Brian Setencich [40]	R
Curt Pringle [41]	D
Willie L. Brown, Jr. [42]	R
Doris Allen [43]	R
Brian Setencich [43]	R
Curt Pringle [44]	D
Willie L. Brown, Jr. [46]	R
Doris Allen [47]	R
Brian Setencich [48]	R
Curt Pringle	R
Curt Pringle	D
Cruz M. Bustamante [49]	D
Antonio R. Villaraigosa [50]	D
Antonio R. Villaraigosa	D

PARTY DESIGNATIONS

Am—American
D—Democrat
DD—Douglas Democrat

Ind—Independent
ID—Independent Democrat
LD—Lecompton Democrat
Prog—Progressive

R—Republican
Un—Union
W—WHIG

* First Legislature was nonpartisan.
1 Peter H. Burnett resigned as Governor on January 8, 1851.
2 John McDougall became Governor on January 9, 1851, succeeding Peter H. Burnett.
3 David C. Broderick was elected President of the Senate on January 9, 1851, becoming Acting Lieutenant Governor on the same day. Succeeded John McDougall, who resigned to become Governor.
4 Thomas J. White resigned as Speaker of the Assembly on February 6, 1850.
5 John Bigler was elected Speaker of the Assembly on February 6, 1850, vice Thomas J. White, resigned.
6 Milton S. Latham resigned as Governor on January 14, 1860.
7 John G. Downey became Governor on January 14, 1860, succeeding Milton S. Latham, resigned.
8 Isaac N. Quinn was elected President of the Senate on January 20, 1860, becoming Acting Lieutenant Governor on the same day. Succeeded John G. Downey, who resigned to become Governor.
9 Pablo de la Guerra was elected President of the Senate on January 7, 1861, becoming Acting Lieutenant Governor on the same day. Succeeded Isaac N. Quinn, who was President of the Senate at the preceding session of 1860.
10 Newton Booth resigned as Governor on February 27, 1875.
11 Romualdo Pacheco became Governor on February 27, 1875, succeeding Newton Booth, resigned.
12 William Irwin, President of the Senate, became Acting Lieutenant Governor on February 27, 1875, succeeding Romualdo Pacheco, who resigned to become Governor.
13 Washington Bartlett died in office on September 12, 1887.
14 Robert W. Waterman became Governor on September 13, 1887, succeeding Washington Bartlett, who died in office.
15 Stephen N. White elected President pro Tempore of the Senate on January 5, 1887, became Acting Lieutenant Governor on September 13, 1887. Succeeded Robert W. Waterman, who resigned to become Governor.
16 Spencer G. Millard died in office on October 24, 1895.
17 William T. Jeter was appointed Lieutenant Governor by Governor James H. Budd on October 25, 1895, succeeding Spencer G. Millard, who died in office.
18 Howard E. Wright resigned as Speaker of the Assembly on January 31, 1899.
19 Alden Anderson was elected Speaker of the Assembly on January 31, 1899, vice Howard E. Wright, resigned.
20 Hiram W. Johnson resigned as Governor on March 15, 1917.
21 John M. Eshleman died in office on February 28, 1916.
22 William D. Stephens was appointed Lieutenant Governor on July 22, 1916, by Governor Hiram W. Johnson, succeeding John M. Eshleman, who died in office. On March 15, 1917, he became Governor, succeeding Hiram W. Johnson, who resigned to become United States Senator.

23 Buron Fitts resigned as Lieutenant Governor on November 30, 1928.

24 H. L. Carnahan was appointed Lieutenant Governor by Governor C. C. Young on December 4, 1928, succeeding Buron Fitts, resigned.

25 James Rolph, Jr., died in office on June 2, 1934.

26 Frank F. Merriam became Governor on June 7, 1934, succeeding James Rolph, Jr., who died in office.

27 Earl Warren was appointed Chief Justice of the United States Supreme Court by President Eisenhower. Resigned October 4, 1953.

28 Goodwin J. Knight resigned as Lieutenant Governor on October 4, 1953. On October 5, 1953, he became Governor, succeeding Earl Warren, resigned.

29 Harold J. Powers became Lieutenant Governor on October 5, 1953, succeeding Goodwin J. Knight, who resigned to become Governor.

30 Jesse M. Unruh was elected Speaker at an Assembly caucus held on September 30, 1961, succeeding Ralph M. Brown, who resigned from the Assembly September 19, 1961.

31 Robert H. Finch resigned as Lieutenant Governor on January 20, 1969. Appointed Secretary of the U.S. Department of Health, Education, and Welfare.

32 Ed Reinecke appointed Lieutenant Governor by Governor Ronald Reagan on January 21, 1969; succeeding Robert H. Finch, resigned.

33 Bob Moretti resigned as Speaker of the Assembly on June 27, 1974.

34 Leo T. McCarthy elected Speaker of the Assembly on June 27, 1974, succeeding Bob Moretti, resigned.

35 Ed Reinecke resigned as Lieutenant Governor on October 2, 1974.

36 John L. Harmer appointed Lieutenant Governor by Governor Ronald Reagan on October 4, 1974, succeeding Ed Reinecke, resigned.

37 1995–96 Regular Session, Willie L. Brown, Jr. served as Speaker of the Assembly January 23, 1995–June 5, 1995

38 1995–96 Regular Session, Doris Allen served as Speaker of the Assembly June 5, 1995–September 14, 1995

39 1995–96 Regular Session, Brian Setencich served as Speaker of the Assembly September 14, 1995–January 4, 1996

40 1995–96 Regular Session, Curt Pringle served as Speaker of the Assembly January 4, 1996–November 30, 1996

41 1995–96 1st Ex Session, Willie L. Brown, Jr. served as Speaker of the Assembly February 23, 1995–June 5, 1995

42 1995–96 1st Ex Session, Doris Allen served as Speaker of the Assembly June 5, 1995–September 14, 1995

43 1995–96 1st Ex Session, Brian Setencich served as Speaker of the Assembly September 15, 1995–June 24, 1995

44 1995–96 1st Ex Session, Curt Pringle served as Speaker of the Assembly June 24, 1996–September 1, 1996

45 1995–96 2nd Ex Session, Willie L. Brown, Jr. served as Speaker of the Assembly February 23, 1995–July 14, 1995

46 1995–96 2nd Ex Session, Doris Allen served as Speaker of the Assembly July 14, 1995–September 13, 1995

47 1995–96 2nd Ex Session, Brian Setencich served as Speaker of the Assembly September 15, 1995–June 24, 1995

48 1995–96 2nd Ex Session, Curt Pringle served as Speaker of the Assembly June 24, 1995–September 1, 1996

49 1997–98 Regular Session, Antonio Villaraigosa elected Speaker on January 26, 1998, but took oath on February 26, 1998

APPENDIX C

California's Statewide Elective Officers

GOVERNORS OF CALIFORNIA—1849–1998

Name	Party	Date of Inauguration	Notes
Burnett, Peter H.	Ind. D.	Dec. 20, 1849	Resigned January 8, 1851.
McDougall, John	Ind. D.	Jan. 9, 1851	Lieutenant Governor, succeeded Burnett.
Bigler, John	D.	Jan. 8, 1852	Assemblyman, 1849–1851.
Bigler, John	D.	Jan. 7, 1854	Re-elected Sept. 7, 1853.
Johnson, J. Neeley	Amer.	Jan. 9, 1856	Assemblyman, 1853.
Weller, John B.	D.	Jan. 8, 1858	U.S. Senator, 1851–1857.
Latham, Milton S.	Lecomp. D.	Jan. 9, 1860	Resigned Jan. 14, 1860. U.S. Senator, 1860–1863.
Downey, John G.	Lecomp. D.	Jan. 14, 1860	Lieutenant Governor, succeeded Latham.
Stanford, Leland	R.	Jan. 10, 1862	U.S. Senator, 1885–1897.
Low, Frederick F.	Union	Dec. 10, 1863	Representative in Congress, 1861–1863.
Haight, Henry H.	D.	Dec. 5, 1867	Member of Second Constitutional Convention.
Booth, Newton	R.	Dec. 8, 1871	Resigned Feb. 27, 1875. U.S. Senator, 1875–1881.
Pacheco, Romualdo	R.	Feb. 27, 1875	Lieutenant Governor, succeeded Booth.
Irwin, William	D.	Dec. 9, 1875	Harbor Commission, 1883–1886.
Perkins, George C.	R.	Jan. 8, 1880	U.S. Senator, 1893–1903.
Stoneman, George	D.	Jan. 10, 1883	Transportation Commissioner.
Bartlett, Washington	D.	Jan. 8, 1887	Railroad Commissioner.
Waterman, Robert W.	R.	Sept. 13, 1887	Lieutenant Governor, succeeded Bartlett.
Markham, Henry H.	R.	Jan. 8, 1891	Representative in Congress, 1885–1887.
Budd, James H.	D.	Jan. 11, 1895	Representative in Congress, 1883–1885.
Gage, Henry T.	R.	Jan. 4, 1899	Minister to Portugal, December 21, 1909.
Pardee, George C.	R.	Jan. 6, 1903	Regent of University of California, 1899.
Gillett, James N.	R.	Jan. 8, 1907	Representative in Congress, 1903–1906.
Johnson, Hiram W.	R.	Jan. 3, 1911	
Johnson, Hiram W.	R.	Jan. 8, 1915	Elected U.S. Senator, Nov. 7, 1916. Resigned as Governor, March 15, 1917.
Stephens, Wm. D.	R.	Mar. 15, 1917	Member of Congress, 10th Dist., 1910–1916. Appointed Lieutenant Governor, July 19, 1916.
Stephens, Wm. D.	R.	Jan. 7, 1919	Elected 1918.
Richardson, Friend Wm.	R.	Jan. 9, 1923	State Treasurer, 1915–1922.
Young, C. C.	R.	Jan. 4, 1927	Lieutenant Governor, 1919–1927.
Rolph, James, Jr.	R.	Jan. 6, 1931	Mayor of San Francisco, 1911–1930. Deceased, June 2, 1934.
Merriam, Frank F.	R.	June 7, 1934	Lieutenant Governor, succeeded Rolph.
Merriam, Frank F.	R.	Jan. 8, 1935	Lieutenant Governor, 1931–1934.
Olson, Culbert L.	D.	Jan. 2, 1939	State Senator, 1935–1938.
Warren, Earl	R.	Jan. 4, 1943	Attorney General, 1939–1942.
Warren, Earl	R.	Jan. 6, 1947	Re-elected Nov. 5, 1946.
Warren, Earl	R.	Jan. 8, 1951	Re-elected Nov. 7, 1950. Became Chief Justice, U.S. Supreme Court, Oct. 5, 1953.
Knight, Goodwin J.	R.	Oct. 5, 1953	Lieutenant Governor, succeeded Warren.
Knight, Goodwin J.	R.	Jan. 3, 1955	
Brown, Edmund G.	D.	Jan. 5, 1959	Attorney General, 1951–1958.
Brown, Edmund G.	D.	Jan. 7, 1963	Re-elected Nov. 6, 1962.
Reagan, Ronald	R.	Jan. 2, 1967	
Reagan, Ronald	R.	Jan. 4, 1971	Re-elected Nov. 3, 1970.
Brown, Edmund G., Jr.	D.	Jan. 6, 1975	Secretary of State, 1971–1974.
Brown, Edmund G., Jr.	D.	Jan. 8, 1979	
Deukmejian, George	R.	Jan. 3, 1983	Attorney General, 1979–1982.
Deukmejian, George	R.	Jan. 5, 1987	Re-elected Nov. 4, 1986
Wilson, Pete	R.	Jan. 7, 1991	U.S. Senator, 1982–1990
Wilson, Pete	R.	Jan. 2, 1995	Re-elected Nov. 1, 1994.

LIEUTENANT GOVERNORS OF CALIFORNIA—1849–1998

Name	Party	Date of Inauguration	Notes
McDougall, John	Ind. D.	Dec. 20, 1849	Became Governor January 9, 1851, succeeding Governor Burnett, resigned.
Broderick, David C. (Acting)	D.	Jan. 9, 1851	Elected President of Senate January 9, 1851, thereby becoming Acting Lieutenant Governor, vice John McDougall, resigned.
Purdy, Samuel	D.	Jan. 8, 1852	
Purdy, Samuel	D.	Jan. 7, 1854	
Anderson, Robert M.	Amer.	Jan. 9, 1856	
Walkup, John	D.	Jan. 8, 1858	
Downey, John G.	Lecomp. D.	Jan. 9, 1860	Became Governor January 14, 1860, succeeding Governor Latham, resigned.
Quinn, Isaac N. (Acting)	D.	Jan. 20, 1860	Elected President of Senate January 20, 1860, thereby becoming Acting Lieutenant Governor, vice John G. Downey, resigned.
de la Guerra, Pablo (Acting)	D.	Jan. 7, 1861	Elected President of Senate January 7, 1861, thereby becoming Acting Lieutenant Governor, vice Isaac N. Quinn, resigned.
Chellis, John F.	R.	Jan. 10, 1862	
Machin, T. N.	Union	Dec. 10, 1863	
Holden, William	D.	Dec. 5, 1867	
Pacheco, Romualdo	R.	Dec. 8, 1871	Became Governor February 27, 1875, succeeding Governor Booth, resigned.
Irwin, William (Acting)	D.	Feb. 27, 1875	Became Acting Lieutenant Governor February 27, 1875; vice Romualdo Pacheco, resigned.
Johnson, James A.	D.	Dec. 9, 1875	
Mansfield, John	R.	Jan. 8, 1880	
Daggett, John	D.	Jan. 10, 1883	
Waterman, Robert W.	R.	Jan. 8, 1887	Became Governor September 13, 1887, succeeding Governor Bartlett, who died in office.
White, Stephen M. (Acting)	D.	Sept. 13, 1887	Elected President pro Tempore of Senate January 5, 1887, thereby becoming Acting Lieutenant Governor, vice Robert W. Waterman, resigned.
Reddick, John B.	R.	Jan. 8, 1891	
Millard, Spencer G.	R.	Jan. 11, 1895	Died in office October 24, 1895.
Jeter, William T.	D.	Oct. 25, 1896	Appointed October 25, 1895, by Governor Budd, vice Spencer G. Millard, deceased.
Neff, Jacob H.	R.	Jan. 3, 1899	
Anderson, Alden	R.	Jan. 6, 1903	
Porter, Warren R.	R.	Jan. 8, 1907	
Wallace, A. J.	R.	Jan. 3, 1911	
Eshleman, John M.	Prog.	Jan. 5, 1915	Died in office February 28, 1916.
Stephens, William D.	R.	July 22, 1916	Appointed July 22, 1916, by Governor Johnson, vice John M. Eshleman, deceased. Became Governor March 15, 1917, vice Hiram W. Johnson, resigned.
Vacancy from Mar. 15, 1917, to Jan. 7, 1919			
Young, C. C.	R.	Jan. 7, 1919	
Young, C. C.	R.	Jan. 9, 1923	Elected Governor November 2, 1926.
Fitts, Buron	R.	Jan. 4, 1927	Resigned November 30, 1928.
Carnahan, H. L.	R.		Appointed December 4, 1928, by Governor Young, vice Buron Fitts, resigned.
Merriam, Frank F.	R.	Jan. 6, 1931	Became Governor June 7, 1934, succeeding Governor Rolph who died in office.
Vacancy from June 7, 1934, to Jan. 8, 1935			
Hatfield, George J.	R.	Jan. 8, 1935	
Patterson, Ellis E.	D.	Jan. 2, 1939	
Houser, Frederick F.	R.	Jan. 4, 1943	
Knight, Goodwin J.	R.	Jan. 6, 1947	
Knight, Goodwin J.	R.	Jan. 8, 1951	Became Governor October 5, 1953, succeeding Governor Warren, resigned.
Powers, Harold J.	R.	Oct. 5, 1953	Served as President pro Tempore of Senate from 1947 until October 5, 1953, when he became Lieutenant Governor, vice Goodwin J. Knight, resigned.
Powers, Harold J.	R.	Jan. 3, 1955	
Anderson, Glenn M.	D.	Jan. 5, 1959	
Anderson, Glenn M.	D.	Jan. 7, 1963	
Finch, Robert H.	R.	Jan. 2, 1967	Resigned January 20, 1969, to become Secretary, U.S. Department of Health, Education, and Welfare.
Reinecke, Ed	R.	Jan. 21, 1969	Appointed January 21, 1969, by Governor Reagan, vice Robert H. Finch, resigned.
Reinecke, Ed	R.	Jan. 4, 1971	Resigned October 2, 1974.
Harmer, John L.	R.	Oct. 4, 1974	Appointed October 4, 1974, by Governor Reagan, vice Ed Reinecke, resigned.
Dymally, Mervyn M.	D.	Jan. 6, 1975	
Curb, Mike	R.	Jan. 8, 1979	
McCarthy, Leo T.	D.	Jan. 3, 1983	Speaker of the Assembly, June 28, 1974–1980
McCarthy, Leo T.	D.	Jan. 5, 1987	
McCarthy, Leo T.	D.	Jan. 7, 1991	
Davis, Gray	D.	Jan. 2, 1995	Former State Assembly Member and State Controller.

CALIFORNIA SECRETARIES OF STATE—1849–1998

Name	Party	Date Assumed Office	Notes
Van Voorhies, William	D.	Dec. 21, 1849	Appointed by Governor Burnett. Confirmed by Senate December 21, 1849.
Van Voorhies, William	D.	Jan. 9, 1852	Reappointed by Governor Bigler. Confirmed by Senate January 9, 1852. Resigned February 19, 1853.
Denver, James W.	D.	Feb. 19, 1853	Appointed by Governor Bigler. Confirmed by Senate March 3, 1853.
Denver, James W.	D.	Jan. 9, 1854	Reappointed by Governor Bigler. Confirmed by Senate January 10, 1854. Resigned November 1, 1855.
Hempstead, Charles H.	D.	Nov. 5, 1855	Appointed by Governor Bigler, vice Denver, resigned.
Douglass, David F.	Amer.	Jan. 10, 1856	Appointed by Governor Johnson. Confirmed by Senate January 10, 1856.
Forman, Ferris	D.	Jan. 11, 1858	Appointed by Governor Weller. Confirmed by Senate January 9, 1858.
Price, Johnson	Lecomp. D.	Jan. 10, 1860	Appointed by Governor Latham. Confirmed by Senate January 10, 1860.
Weeks, William H.	R.	Jan. 11, 1862	Appointed by Governor Stanford. Confirmed by Senate January 14, 1862. Died in office August 16, 1863.
Tuttle, A. A. H.	R.	Aug. 17, 1863	Appointed by Governor Stanford, vice Weeks, deceased.
Redding, Benjamin B.	Union	Dec. 7, 1863	First Secretary of State to be elected.
Nichols, H. L.	D.	Dec. 2, 1867	
Melone, Drury	R.	Dec. 4, 1871	
Beck, Thomas	D.	Dec. 6, 1875	
Burns, Daniel M.	R.	Jan. 5, 1880	
Thompson, Thomas L.	D.	Jan. 8, 1883	
Hendricks, William C.	D.	Jan. 3, 1887	
Waite, Edwin G.	R.	Jan. 5, 1891	Died in office October 30, 1894.
Hart, Albert	R.	Nov. 1, 1894	Appointed by Governor Markham, vice Waite, deceased.
Brown, Lewis H.	R.	Jan. 7, 1895	
Curry, C. F.	R.	Jan. 2, 1899	
Curry, C. F.	R.	Jan. 5, 1903	
Curry, C. F.	R.	Jan. 7, 1907	
Jordan, Frank C.	R.	Jan. 2, 1911	
Jordan, Frank C.	R.	Jan. 4, 1915	
Jordan, Frank C.	R.	Jan. 6, 1919	
Jordan, Frank C.	R.	Jan. 8, 1923	
Jordan, Frank C.	R.	Jan. 3, 1927	
Jordan, Frank C.	R.	Jan. 5, 1931	
Jordan, Frank C.	R.	Jan. 7, 1935	
Jordan, Frank C.	R.	Jan. 18, 1939	Died in office January 18, 1940.
Peek, Paul	D.	Mar. 1, 1940	Appointed by Governor Olson, vice F. C. Jordan, deceased. Resigned December 22, 1942.
Jordan, Frank M.	R.	Jan. 4, 1943	
Jordan, Frank M.	R.	Jan. 6, 1947	
Jordan, Frank M.	R.	Jan. 8, 1951	
Jordan, Frank M.	R.	Jan. 3, 1955	
Jordan, Frank M.	R.	Jan. 5, 1959	
Jordan, Frank M.	R.	Jan. 7, 1963	
Jordan, Frank M.	R.	Jan. 2, 1967	Died in office March 29, 1970.
Sullivan, H. P.	R.	Apr. 3, 1970	Appointed by Governor Reagan, vice F. M. Jordan, deceased.
Brown, Edmund G., Jr.	D.	Jan. 4, 1971	Elected Governor November 5, 1974.
Fong Eu, March	D.	Jan. 6, 1975	
Fong Eu, March	D.	Jan. 8, 1979	
Fong Eu, March	D.	Jan. 3, 1983	
Fong Eu, March	D.	Jan. 5, 1987	
Fong Eu, March	D.	Jan. 7, 1991	Resigned February 17, 1994.
Miller, Tony (Acting)	D.	Feb. 17, 1994	
Jones, Bill	R.	Jan. 2, 1995	Former State Assembly Member.

ATTORNEYS GENERAL OF CALIFORNIA—1849–1998

Name	Party	Date Assumed Office	Notes
Kewan, Edward J. C.	D.	Dec. 22, 1849	Elected by the Legislature. Resigned August 9, 1850.
McDougall, James A.	D.	Oct. 8, 1850	Resigned December 30, 1851.
Hastings, S. Clinton	D.	Jan. 5, 1852	
McConnell, John R.	D.	Jan. 2, 1854	
Stewart, William M.	D.	June 7, 1854	Appointed by Governor John Bigler to fill office during temporary absence of John R. McConnell from the state by legislative consent.
Wallace, William T.	Amer.	Jan. 7, 1856	
Williams, Thomas H.	D.	Jan. 4, 1858	
Williams, Thomas H.	D.	Jan. 2, 1860	
Pixley, Frank M.	R.	Jan. 6, 1862	
McCullough, John G.	Union	Dec. 7, 1863	
Hamilton, Jo	D.	Dec. 2, 1867	
Love, John Lord	R.	Dec. 4, 1871	
Hamilton, Jo	D.	Dec. 6, 1875	
Hart, Augustus L.	R.	Jan. 5, 1880	
Marshall, Edward C.	D.	Jan. 8, 1883	
Johnson, George A.	D.	Jan. 3, 1887	
Hart, William H. H.	R.	Jan. 5, 1891	
Fitzgerald, William F.	R.	Jan. 7, 1895	
Ford, Tirey L.	R.	Jan. 2, 1899	Resigned September 15, 1902.
Webb, Ulysses S.	R.	Sept. 15, 1902	Appointed by Governor Henry T. Gage, vice Tirey L. Ford, resigned.
Webb, Ulysses S.	R.	Jan. 5, 1903	
Webb, Ulysses S.	R.	Jan. 7, 1907	
Webb, Ulysses S.	R.	Jan. 2, 1911	
Webb, Ulysses S.	R.	Jan. 4, 1915	
Webb, Ulysses S.	R.	Jan. 6, 1919	
Webb, Ulysses S.	R.	Jan. 8, 1923	
Webb, Ulysses S.	R.	Jan. 3, 1927	
Webb, Ulysses S.	R.	Jan. 5, 1931	
Webb, Ulysses S.	R.	Jan. 7, 1935	
Warren, Earl	R.	Jan. 2, 1939	
Kenny, Robert W.	D.	Jan. 4, 1943	
Howser, Fred N.	R.	Jan. 6, 1947	
Brown, Edmund G.	D.	Jan. 8, 1951	
Brown, Edmund G.	D.	Jan. 3, 1955	
Mosk, Stanley	D.	Jan. 5, 1959	
Mosk, Stanley	D.	Jan. 7, 1963	Appointed to State Supreme Court, September 1, 1964, by Governor Edmund G. Brown.
Lynch, Thomas C.	D.	Aug. 31, 1964	Appointed by Governor Edmund G. Brown, vice Stanley Mosk, resigned.
Lynch, Thomas C.	D.	Jan. 2, 1967	
Younger, Evelle J.	R.	Jan. 4, 1971	
Younger, Evelle J.	R.	Jan. 6, 1975	
Deukmejian, George	R.	Jan. 8, 1979	Elected Governor November 2, 1982.
Van de Kamp, John	D.	Jan. 3, 1983	
Van de Kamp, John	D.	Jan. 5, 1987	
Lungren, Dan	R	Jan. 7, 1991	
Lungren, Dan	R.	Jan. 2, 1995	Former Member of Congress.

STATE TREASURERS OF CALIFORNIA—1849–1998

Name	Party	Date Assumed Office		Notes
Roman, Richard	D.	Dec.	22, 1849	Elected by the Legislature.
Roman, Richard	D.	Jan.	5, 1852	
McMeans, Selden A.	D.	Jan.	2, 1854	
Bates, Henry	Amer.	Jan.	7, 1856	Resigned February 11, 1857.
English, James L.	Amer.	Feb.	13, 1857	Appointed by Governor J. Neeley Johnson, vice Henry Bates, resigned.
Findley, Thomas	D.	Jan.	4, 1858	
Findley, Thomas	D.	Jan.	2, 1860	
Ashley, Delos R.	R.	Jan.	6, 1862	Resigned October 5, 1863.
Pacheco, Romualdo	R.	Oct.	10, 1863	Appointed by Governor Leland Stanford, vice Delos R. Ashley, resigned.
Pacheco, Romualdo	R.	Dec.	7, 1863	
Coronel, Antonio F.	D.	Dec.	7, 1867	
Baehr, Ferdinand	R.	Dec.	2, 1871	
Estudillo, Jose G..........................	D.	Dec.	4, 1875	
Weil, John	R.	Jan.	5, 1880	
January, William A.	D.	Jan.	1, 1883	Resigned December 24, 1884.
Oullahan, D. J.	D.	Dec.	24, 1884	Appointed by Governor George Stoneman, vice William A. January, resigned.
Herold, Adam	D.	Jan.	3, 1887	
McDonald, J. R.	R.	Jan.	5, 1891	
Rackliffe, Levi	R.	Jan.	7, 1895	Died in office, April 21, 1898.
Green, Will S.	D.	Apr.	22, 1898	Appointed by Governor James H. Budd, vice Levi Rackliffe, deceased.
Reeves, Truman	R.	Jan.	2, 1899	
Reeves, Truman	R.	Jan.	5, 1903	
Williams, William R.	R.	Jan.	7, 1907	
Williams, William R.	R.	Jan.	2, 1911	Resigned February 20, 1911.
Roberts, E. D.	R.	Feb.	20, 1911	Appointed by Governor Hiram W. Johnson, vice William R. Williams, resigned.
Richardson, Friend William	Prog.	Jan.	4, 1915	
Richardson, Friend William	Prog.	Jan.	6, 1919	
Johnson, Charles G.	R.	Jan.	8, 1923	
Johnson, Charles G.	R.	Jan.	3, 1927	
Johnson, Charles G.	R.	Jan.	5, 1931	
Johnson, Charles G.	R.	Jan.	7, 1935	
Johnson, Charles G.	R.	Jan.	2, 1939	
Johnson, Charles G.	R.	Jan.	4, 1943	
Johnson, Charles G.	R.	Jan.	6, 1947	
Johnson, Charles G.	R.	Jan.	8, 1951	
Johnson, Charles G.	R.	Jan.	3, 1955	Resigned, October 31, 1956.
Button, A. Ronald	R.	Nov.	1, 1956	Appointed by Governor Goodwin J. Knight, vice Charles G. Johnson, resigned.
Betts, Bert A.	D.	Jan.	5, 1959	
Betts, Bert A.	D.	Jan.	7, 1963	
Priest, Ivy Baker	R.	Jan.	2, 1967	
Priest, Ivy Baker	R.	Jan.	4, 1971	
Unruh, Jesse M............................	D.	Jan.	6, 1975	Speaker of the Assembly, September 30, 1961–1968.
Unruh, Jesse M............................	D.	Jan.	8, 1979	
Unruh, Jesse M............................	D.	Jan.	3, 1983	
Unruh, Jesse M............................	D.	Jan.	5, 1987	Died in office, August 4, 1987.
Whitney, Elizabeth (Acting)	D.	Aug.	4, 1987	
Hayes, Thomas	R.	Jan.	6, 1989	Appointed by Governor George Deukmejian, vice Jesse M. Unruh, deceased.
Brown, Kathleen	D.	Jan.	7, 1991	
Fong, Matt	R.	Jan.	2, 1995	Former Member, Board of Equalization.

STATE CONTROLLERS OF CALIFORNIA—1849-1998

Name	Party	Date Assumed Office	Notes
Houston, John S.	D.	Dec. 22, 1849	Elected by the Legislature.
Pierce, Winslow S.	D.	Jan. 5, 1852	
Bell, Samuel	D.	Jan. 2, 1854	
Whitman, George W.	Amer.	Jan. 7, 1856	Did not serve as Controller from February 25 to April 21, 1857 during impeachment proceedings. Subsequently acquitted.
Burton, Edward F.	Amer.	Feb. 25, 1857	Appointed as custodial Controller by Governor J. Neeley Johnson during impeachment proceedings of Controller George W. Whitman.
Whitman, George W.	Amer.	Apr. 21, 1857	Resumed office after acquittal in impeachment proceedings.
Mandeville, James W.	D.		Elected September 2, 1857, but did not take office, having been appointed U.S. Surveyor General for California.
Melony, Aaron R.	Lecomp. D.	Apr. 27, 1858	Appointed by Governor John B. Weller to fill unexpired term of James W. Mandeville.
Brooks, Samuel H.	Lecomp. D.		Elected September 7, 1859, but did not take office until Supreme Court settled litigation during its January 1860 term. His predecessor, Aaron R. Melony, had refused to relinquish the office on technical grounds. Resigned from office November 20, 1861.
Gillan, James S.		Nov. 23, 1861	Appointed Controller by Governor John G. Downey, vice Samuel H. Brooks, resigned.
Warren, Gilbert R.	R.	Jan. 6, 1862	
Oulton, George R.	Union	Dec. 9, 1863	First Controller to serve four-year term.
Watt, Robert	D.	Dec. 7, 1867	
Green, James J.	R.	Dec. 2, 1871	
Mandeville, James W.	D.	Dec. 4, 1875	Died in office, February 4, 1876.
Brown, William B. C.	D.	Feb. 8, 1876	Appointed by Governor William Irwin, vice James W. Mandeville, deceased.
Kenfield, Daniel M.	R.	Jan. 15, 1877	
Kenfield, Daniel M.	R.	Jan. 5, 1880	
Dunn, John P.	D.	Jan. 1, 1883	
Dunn, John P.	D.	Jan. 3, 1887	
Colgan, Edward P.	R.	Jan. 5, 1891	
Colgan, Edward P.	R.	Jan. 7, 1895	
Colgan, Edward P.	R.	Jan. 2, 1899	
Colgan, Edward P.	R.	Jan. 5, 1903	Re-elected November 6, 1906; died in office November 20, 1906.
Nye, A. B.	R.	Nov. 24, 1906	Appointed by Governor George C. Pardee, vice Edward P. Colgan, deceased.
Nye, A. B.	R.	Jan. 7, 1907	
Nye, A. B.	R.	Jan. 2, 1911	Died in office, August 19, 1913.
Chambers, John S.	R.	Aug. 28, 1913	Appointed by Governor Hiram W. Johnson, vice A. B. Nye, deceased.
Chambers, John S.	R.	Jan. 4, 1915	
Chambers, John S.	R.	Jan. 6, 1919	Resigned July 15, 1920.
Riley, Ray L.	R.	July 16, 1921	Appointed by Governor William D. Stephens, vice John S. Chambers, resigned.
Riley, Ray L.	R.	Jan. 8, 1923	
Riley, Ray L.	R.	Jan. 3, 1927	
Riley, Ray L.	R.	Jan. 5, 1931	
Riley, Ray L.	R.	Jan. 7, 1935	Appointed to State Railroad Commission.
Riley, Harry B.	R.	Jan. 9, 1937	Appointed by Governor Frank F. Merriam, vice Ray L. Riley, resigned.
Riley, Harry B.	R.	Jan. 2, 1939	
Riley, Harry B.	R.	Jan. 4, 1943	Died in office, February 4, 1946.
Kuchel, Thomas	R.	Feb. 11, 1946	Appointed by Governor Earl Warren, vice Harry B. Riley, deceased.
Kuchel, Thomas	R.-D.	Jan. 6, 1947	
Kuchel, Thomas	R.-D.	Jan. 8, 1951	Appointed United States Senator by Governor Earl Warren, December 22, 1952.
Kirkwood, Robert C.	R.	Jan. 6, 1953	Appointed by Governor Earl Warren, vice Thomas Kuchel, resigned.
Kirkwood, Robert C.	R.	Jan. 3, 1955	
Cranston, Alan	D.	Jan. 5, 1959	
Cranston, Alan	D.	Jan. 7, 1963	
Flournoy, Houston I.	R.	Jan. 2, 1967	
Flournoy, Houston I.	R.	Jan. 4, 1971	
Cory, J. Kenneth	D.	Jan. 6, 1975	
Cory, J. Kenneth	D.	Jan. 8, 1979	
Cory, J. Kenneth	D.	Jan. 3, 1983	
Davis, Gray	D.	Jan. 5, 1987	
Davis, Gray	D.	Jan. 7, 1991	
Connell, Kathleen	D.	Jan. 2, 1995	

SUPERINTENDENTS OF PUBLIC INSTRUCTION—1851–1998

Name	Party	Date Assumed Office	Notes
Marvin, John G.	D.	Jan. 1, 1851	
Hubbs, Paul K.	D.	Jan. 1, 1854	
Moulder, Andrew J.	D.	Jan. 1, 1857	
Moulder, Andrew J.	D.	Jan. 1, 1860	
Swett, John	Union	Jan. 2, 1863	
Swett, John	Union	Dec. 7, 1863	
Fitzgerald, O. P.	D.	Dec. 2, 1867	
Bolander, Henry N.	R.	Dec. 4, 1871	
Carr, Ezra S.	R.	Dec. 6, 1875	
Campbell, Frederick M.	R.	Jan. 5, 1880	
Welcker, William T.	D.	Jan. 8, 1883	
Hoit, Ira G.	R.	Jan. 3, 1887	
Anderson, J. W.	R.	Jan. 5, 1891	
Black, Samuel T.	R.	Jan. 7, 1895	Resigned from office September 24, 1898.
Meredith, C. T.	D.	Sept. 24, 1898	Appointed by Governor James H. Budd, vice Samuel T. Black, resigned.
Kirk, Thomas J.	R.	Jan. 2, 1899	
Kirk, Thomas J.	R.	Jan. 5, 1903	
Hyatt, Edward	R.	Jan. 7, 1907	
Hyatt, Edward	R.	Jan. 2, 1911	
Hyatt, Edward	Nonpartisan	Jan. 4, 1915	
Wood, Will C.	Nonpartisan	Jan. 6, 1919	
Wood, Will C.	Nonpartisan	Jan. 8, 1923	
Wood, Will C.	Nonpartisan	Jan. 3, 1927	Resigned from office January 20, 1927.
Cooper, William John	Nonpartisan	Jan. 20, 1927	Appointed by Governor C. C. Young January 20, 1927, vice Will C. Wood, resigned. Resigned from office, February 11, 1929.
Kersey, Vierling	Nonpartisan	Feb. 11, 1929	Appointed by Governor C. C. Young February 11, 1929, vice William John Cooper, resigned.
Kersey, Vierling	Nonpartisan	Jan. 5, 1931	
Kersey, Vierling	Nonpartisan	Jan. 5, 1935	Resigned from office February 1, 1937.
Dexter, Walter F.	Nonpartisan	Feb. 1, 1937	Appointed by Governor Frank F. Merriam February 1, 1937, vice Vierling Kersey, resigned.
Dexter, Walter F.	Nonpartisan	Jan. 2, 1939	
Dexter, Walter F.	Nonpartisan	Jan. 4, 1943	Died in office October 21, 1945.
Simpson, Roy E.	Nonpartisan	Nov. 13, 1945	Appointed by Governor Earl Warren November 6, 1945, vice Walter F. Dexter, deceased.
Simpson, Roy E.	Nonpartisan	Jan. 6, 1947	
Simpson, Roy E.	Nonpartisan	Jan. 8, 1951	
Simpson, Roy E.	Nonpartisan	Jan. 3, 1955	
Simpson, Roy E.	Nonpartisan	Jan. 5, 1959	
Rafferty, Maxwell L., Jr.	Nonpartisan	Jan. 7, 1963	
Rafferty, Maxwell L., Jr.	Nonpartisan	Jan. 2, 1968	
Riles, Wilson C.	Nonpartisan	Jan. 4, 1971	
Riles, Wilson C.	Nonpartisan	Jan. 6, 1975	
Riles, Wilson C.	Nonpartisan	Jan. 8, 1979	
Honig, William	Nonpartisan	Jan. 3, 1983	
Honig, William	Nonpartisan	Jan. 5, 1987	
Honig, William	Nonpartisan	Jan. 7, 1991	Removed from office February 22, 1993, pursuant to *Government Code*, Section 1770.2.
Dawson, William D. (Acting)	Nonpartisan	Feb. 24, 1993	
Eastin, Delaine	Nonpartisan	Jan. 2, 1995	Former State Assembly Member.

INSURANCE COMMISSIONERS—1991–1998

Name	Party	Date Assumed Office	Notes
Garamendi, John [1]	D.	Jan. 7, 1991	Former State Senator and Assembly Member.
Quackenbush, Charles	R.	Jan. 2, 1995	Former State Assembly Member.

[1] John Garamendi was the first person to become Insurance Commisioner in a statewide election following the passage of Proposition 103, which changed the office of Insurance Commissioner from being one appointed by the Governor. *See Insurance Code,* Section 12900. (Roxani M. Gillespie served as Insurance Commissioner from 1986–1990, a position to which she was appointed by Governor George Deukmejian.)

APPENDIX D

California's Supreme Court

CHIEF JUSTICES—1849-1998

Name	Date Assumed Office		Served Until	
S. Clinton Hastings	Dec.	22, 1849	Jan.	1, 1852
Soloman Heydenfeldt	Jan.	1, 1852	Jan.	6, 1857
Peter H. Burnett	Jan.	13, 1857	Oct.	12, 1857
Stephen J. Field	Oct.	13, 1857	May	20, 1863
Edwin B. Crocker	May	21, 1863	Jan.	2, 1864
Silas W. Sanderson	Jan.	2, 1864	Jan.	4, 1870
Jackson Temple	Jan.	10, 1870	Jan.	1, 1872
Addison C. Niles	Jan.	1, 1872	Jan.	5, 1880
Robert F. Morrison	Jan.	5, 1880	Mar.	2, 1887
Niles Searls	Apr.	20, 1887	Nov.	6, 1888
William H. Beatty	Nov.	6, 1888	Aug.	4, 1914
Matt I. Sullivan	Aug.	22, 1914	Jan.	4, 1915
Frank M. Angellotti	Jan.	4, 1915	Nov.	1921
Lucien Shaw	Nov.	14, 1921	Jan.	1923
Curtis D. Wilber	Jan.	13, 1923	Mar.	19, 1924
Louis W. Myers	Apr.	10, 1924	Jan.	1, 1926
William H. Waste	Jan.	1, 1926	June	6, 1940
Phil S. Gibson	June	17, 1940	Aug.	30, 1964
Roger J. Traynor	Sept.	1, 1964	Jan.	31, 1970
Donald R. Wright	Apr.	17, 1970	Feb.	1, 1977
Rose Elizabeth Bird	Mar.	26, 1977	Jan.	5, 1987 *
Malcolm Lucas	Feb.	5, 1987	May	1, 1996
Ronald M. George	May	1, 1996	Present	

* Not elected to a new term, Nov. 4, 1986 general election.

JUSTICES OF THE SUPREME COURT—1849–1998

Name	Date Assumed Office		Served Until	
S. Clinton Hastings *	Dec.	22, 1849	Jan.	1, 1852
Nathaniel Bennett	Dec.	26, 1849	Oct.	3, 1851
Henry A. Lyons	Dec.	26, 1849	Mar.	31, 1852
Hugh C. Murray	Oct.	11, 1851	Sept.	18, 1857
Soloman Heydenfeldt *	Jan.	20, 1852	Jan.	6, 1857
Alexander Anderson	Apr.	6, 1852	Nov.	2, 1852
Alexander Wells	Jan.	3, 1853	Oct.	31, 1854
Chas. H. Bryan	Nov.	24, 1854	Nov.	15, 1855
David S. Terry	Nov.	15, 1855	Sept.	12, 1859
Peter H. Burnett *	Jan.	13, 1857	Oct.	12, 1857
Stephen J. Field *	Oct.	13, 1857	May	20, 1863
Joseph G. Baldwin	Oct.	2, 1858	Jan.	2, 1864
W. W. Cope	Sept.	20, 1859	Jan.	2, 1864
Edward Norton	Dec.	18, 1861	Jan.	2, 1864
Edwin B. Crocker *	May	21, 1863	Jan.	2, 1864
John Currey	Jan.	2, 1864	Jan.	6, 1868
A. L. Rhodes	Jan.	2, 1864	Jan.	5, 1880
Silas W. Sanderson *	Jan.	2, 1864	Jan.	4, 1870
Lorenzo Sawyer	Jan.	2, 1864	Jan.	10, 1870
O. L. Shafter	Jan.	2, 1864	Dec.	11, 1867
Joseph B. Crockett	Dec.	1867	Jan.	5, 1880
Royal T. Sprague	Jan.	6, 1868	Feb.	24, 1872
William T. Wallace	Jan.	10, 1870	Jan.	5, 1880
Jackson Temple *	Jan.	10, 1870	Jan.	1872
	Dec.	13, 1886	June	25, 1889
	Jan.	7, 1895	Dec.	25, 1902
Addison C. Niles *	Jan.	1, 1872	Jan.	5, 1880
Isaac S. Belcher	Mar.	4, 1872	Jan.	5, 1880
Elisha W. McKinstry	Dec.	29, 1873	Oct.	1, 1888
Robert F. Morrison *	Jan.	5, 1880	Mar.	2, 1887
Samuel B. McKee	Jan.	5, 1880	Jan.	3, 1887
W. H. Myrick	Jan.	5, 1880	Jan.	3, 1887
Erskine M. Ross	Jan.	5, 1880	Oct.	1, 1886
John R. Sharpstein	Jan.	5, 1880	Dec.	28, 1892
James D. Thornton	Jan.	5, 1880	Jan.	5, 1891
A. Van R. Patterson	Dec.	22, 1886	May	3, 1894
Thomas B. McFarland	Dec.	28, 1886	May	3, 1894
Niles Searls *	Apr.	20, 1887	Nov.	6, 1888
John D. Works	Oct.	2, 1888	Jan.	5, 1891
William H. Beatty *	Nov.	6, 1888	Aug.	4, 1914
Charles N. Fox	June	25, 1889	Jan.	7, 1895
John J. DeHaven	Dec.	18, 1890	Jan.	7, 1895
C. H. Garoute	Dec.	19, 1890	Jan.	5, 1903
Ralph C. Harrison	Dec.	20, 1890	Jan.	5, 1903
William F. Fitzgerald	Feb.	2, 1893	Jan.	7, 1895
W. C. Van Fleet	May	7, 1894	Jan.	3, 1899
Frederick W. Henshaw	Dec.	29, 1894	Jan.	1919
Walter Van Dyke	Dec.	22, 1898	Dec.	25, 1905
Frank M. Angellotti *	Dec.	11, 1902	Nov.	1921
Lucien Shaw *	Dec.	11, 1902	Jan.	1923
William G. Lorigan	Jan.	7, 1903	Jan.	1919
M. C. Sloss	Dec.	19, 1906	Mar.	1, 1919
Henry A. Melvin	Sept.	28, 1908	Dec.	1920
Matt I. Sullivan *	Aug.	22, 1914	Jan.	4, 1915
William P. Lawlor	Dec.	22, 1914	July	25, 1926
Curtis D. Wilbur *	Jan.	1, 1918	Mar.	19, 1924
Thomas J. Lennon	Dec.	20, 1918	Aug.	14, 1926
Warren Olney, Jr.	Mar.	1, 1919	July	1921
W. A. Sloane	Dec.	15, 1920	Jan.	1923
Charles A. Shurtleff	July	2, 1921	Dec.	1922
William H. Waste *	Nov.	25, 1921	June	6, 1940
Terry W. Ward	Dec.	19, 1922	Jan.	8, 1923
Frank H. Kerrigan	Jan.	8, 1923	Feb.	11, 1924
Emmett Seawell	Jan.	8, 1923	July	7, 1939
Louis W. Myers *	Jan.	15, 1923	Jan.	1, 1926
John E. Richards	Feb.	11, 1924	Dec.	1932
John W. Shenk	Apr.	14, 1924	Aug.	3, 1959

* Chief Justice.

JUSTICES OF THE SUPREME COURT—1849–1998—Continued

Name	Date Assumed Office		Served Until	
Jesse W. Curtis	Jan.	1, 1926	Jan.	1, 1945
Frank G. Finlayson	Oct.	4, 1926	Dec.	1926
Jeremiah F. Sullivan	Nov.	22, 1926	Dec.	1926
John W. Preston	Dec.	27, 1926	Sept.	1935
William H. Langdon	Jan.	4, 1927	Aug.	1939
Ira F. Thompson	Dec.	31, 1932	Jan.	1, 1947
Nathaniel P. Conrey	Oct.	1, 1935	Nov.	1936
Douglas L. Edmonds	Nov.	23, 1936	Dec.	31, 1955
Frederick W. Houser	Oct.	1, 1937	Oct.	12, 1942
Jesse W. Carter	Sept.	12, 1939	Mar.	15, 1950
Phil S. Gibson *	Oct.	2, 1939	Aug.	30, 1964
Roger J. Traynor *	Aug.	13, 1940	Jan.	31, 1970
B. Rey Schauer	Dec.	18, 1942	Sept.	15, 1965
Homer Spence	Jan.	2, 1945	June	1, 1964
Marshal F. McComb	Jan.	3, 1956	May	3, 1977
Raymond E. Peters	Mar.	25, 1959	Jan.	2, 1973
Thomas P. White	Aug.	25, 1959	Oct.	31, 1962
Maurice T. Dooling, Jr.	June	30, 1960	June	30, 1962
Mathew O. Tobriner	July	2, 1962	Jan.	20, 1981
Paul Peek	Dec.	2, 1962	Dec.	16, 1966
Stanley Mosk	Sept.	1, 1964	Present	
Louis H. Burke	Nov.	20, 1964	Nov.	30, 1974
Raymond L. Sullivan	Dec.	20, 1966	Jan.	19, 1977
Donald R. Wright *	Apr.	17, 1970	Feb.	1, 1977
William P. Clark	Mar.	23, 1973	Mar.	24, 1981
Frank K. Richardson	Dec.	2, 1974	Dec.	2, 1983
Wiley W. Manuel	Mar.	24, 1977	Jan.	5, 1981
Rose Elizabeth Bird *	Mar.	26, 1977	Jan.	5, 1987 **
Frank C. Newman	July	16, 1977	Dec.	13, 1982
Otto Kaus	July	21, 1981	Oct.	16, 1985
Allen Broussard	July	22, 1981	Aug.	31, 1991
Cruz Reynoso	Feb.	11, 1982	Jan.	5, 1987 **
Joseph Grodin	Dec.	27, 1982	Jan.	5, 1987 **
Malcolm Lucas *	Apr.	6, 1984	May	1, 1996
Edward Panelli	Dec.	24, 1985	May	3, 1994
John Arguelles	Mar.	18, 1987	Mar.	1, 1989
David Eagleson	Mar.	18, 1987	Jan.	6, 1991
Marcus Kaufman	Mar.	18, 1987	Jan.	31, 1990
Joyce Kennard	Apr.	5, 1989	Present	
Armand Arabian	Mar.	1, 1990	Mar.	1, 1996
Marvin Baxter	Jan.	7, 1991	Present	
Ronald M. George *	Sept.	3, 1991	Present	
Kathryn M. Werdegar	May	3, 1994	Present	
Janice Rogers Brown	May	2, 1996	Present	
Ming W. Chin	Mar.	1, 1996	Present	

* Chief Justice.
** Not elected to a new term, Nov. 4, 1986 general election.

APPENDIX E

California's Legislature
Elected Officers

OFFICERS OF THE ASSEMBLY—1849–1998

Session	Speaker	Speaker pro Tem.	Chief Clerk	Sergeant at Arms
1849	Thomas J. White [1] .... John Bigler [4]	George B. Tingley [2]	E. H. Tharp [3] .... John Nugent [5]	Samuel N. Houston
1851	John Bigler (D)........................		George O. McMullin...	William W. Gift
1852	Richard P. Hammond (D)		Blanton McAlpin.........	C. C. Hornsby
1853	Isaac B. Wall (D)...................	Patrick Canney (D) [6]	Blanton McAlpin [7] .... J. G. Stebbins [8].............	G. W. Coffey
1854	Charles S. Fairfax (D)	Jas. W. Mandeville (D) [9]	Blanton McAlpin.........	George H. Blake
1855	William W. Stow (Whig)......		J. M. Anderson............	Blanton McAlpin
1856	James T. Farley (Am.)............		J. M. Anderson............	E. Gates
1857	Elwood T. Beatty (D)...........	James O'Neil (D) [10]	William Campbell.........	Silas Brown
1858	N. E. Whiteside (D)		Joseph W. Scoby.........	James F. Quinn
1859	William C. Stratton (D)		Caleb Gilman..............	James H. Moore
1860	Philip Moore (D)	E. A. Stevenson (D) [11]	J. M. Anderson............	Charles S. Tozer
1861	R. Burnell (Doug. D)............	D. Showalter (Breck. D) [12]..	J. M. Anderson............	M. Gray
1862	George Barstow (R)		John Sedgwick.............	H. J. Clayton
1863	Tim N. Machin (Union).......	James Collins (D)...............	H. G. Worthington	Thomas Eager
1864	William H. Sears (Union)	J. J. Owen (Union)...............	Osgood C. Wheeler.....	W. M. Rider
1866	John Yule (Union).................	John W. Wilcox (Union) ...	Marcus D. Boruck.......	Benjamin Dore
1868	Caius T. Ryland (D).............	J. J. O'Malley (D)	John A. Eagon.............	John K. Luttrell
1870	George H. Rogers (D)..........	Charles Gildea (D)	Robert Ferral................	W. Dana Perkins
1872	Thomas B. Shannon (R)	Peter J. Hopper (R)	Marcus D. Boruck.........	A. J. Rhodes
1874	Morris M. Estee (Ind.).........	Robert Howe (D).................	D. L. Loafborrow	Wm. M. Crutcher
1876	G. J. Carpenter (D)...............	James E. Murphy (D)	Robert Ferral................	W. Dana Perkins
1878	Campbell P. Berry (D)..........	James E. Murphy (D)	Robert C. Page	J. M. Farrelly
1880	Jabez F. Cowdery (R)...........	Thomas Fraser (R)...............	C. E. Gunn..................	Robert W. Parker
1881	William H. Parks (R)...........	Thomas Fraser (R)...............	George E. McStay	E. Walters
1883	Hugh M. LaRue (D)	John T. Campbell (D)........	M. C. Haley	J. M. Farrelly
1885	William H. Parks (R)...........	J. H. G. Weaver (R)	Frank D. Ryan.............	Jerome Porter
1887	William H. Jordan (R)	John R. Brierly (R)	Frank D. Ryan.............	P. R. Klein
1889	Robert Howe (D)...................	T. W. H. Shanahan (D)	Edward E. Leake...........	J. J. Driscoll
1891	Frank L. Coombs (R)............	Nestor A. Young (R)	H. A. Mason................	H. J. McKusick
1893	F. H. Gould (D)	William P. Mathews (D).....	George W. Peckham ...	Thomas E. Healy
1895	John C. Lynch (R).................	E. V. Spencer (R)...............	S. J. Duckworth..........	George C. Parkinson
1897	Frank L. Coombs (R)............	Brewster C. Kenyon (R).......	S. J. Duckworth..........	William O. Banks
1899	Howard E. Wright (R) [13] ..... Alden Anderson (R) [14].......	Alden Anderson (R)............ F. E. Dunlap (R)	C. W. Kyle	William O. Banks
1901	Cornelius W. Pendleton (R)..	William C. Ralston (R)	Clio Lloyd	William O. Banks
1903	Arthur G. Fisk (R)................	Henry E. Carter (R)	Clio Lloyd	John T. Stafford
1905	Frank C. Prescott (R)............	T. E. Atkinson (R) [16].........	Clio Lloyd	John T. Stafford
1907	R. L. Beardslee (R)...............	J. P. Transue (R)	Clio Lloyd	John T. Stafford
1909	P. A. Stanton (R)	George M. Perine (R)	Clio Lloyd	John T. Stafford
1911	A. H. Hewitt (R)	H. G. Cattell (R)	L. B. Mallory...............	E. H. Whyte
1913	C. C. Young (R)...................	W. A. Johnstone (R)...........	L. B. Mallory...............	Ed E. Reese
1915	C. C. Young (Prog)..............	Howard J. Fish (R)	L. B. Mallory...............	H. B. Miller
1917	C. C. Young (R)	James J. Ryan (R)..............	B. O. Boothby.............	W. J. Leflar
1919	Henry W. Wright (R)...........	Clarence W. Morris (R).......	B. O. Boothby.............	W. J. Leflar
1921	Henry W. Wright (R)...........	Albert A. Rosenshine (R).....	J. B. Kavanaugh...........	W. J. Leflar
1923	Frank F. Merriam (R)	Frank W. Anderson (R).......	Arthur A. Ohnimus.....	W. J. Leflar
1925	Frank F. Merriam (R)	Homer R. Spence (R)	Arthur A. Ohnimus.....	Charles H. Wilkinson
1927	Edgar C. Levey (R)	William M. Byrne (R)	Arthur A. Ohnimus.....	William J. McQuillan
1929	Edgar C. Levey (R)..............	William M. Byrne (R)	Arthur A. Ohnimus.....	Arthur Ferguson
1931	Edgar C. Levey (R)..............	Chester M. Kline (R).........	Arthur A. Ohnimus.....	Arthur Ferguson
1933	Walter J. Little (R)...............	F. C. Clowdsley (D)	Arthur A. Ohnimus.....	Michael Connolly
1934 (Ex.)	F. C. Clowdsley (D).............	Harry B. Riley (R)	Arthur A. Ohnimus.....	Michael Connolly
1935	Edward Craig (R).................	John H. O'Donnell (D).......	Arthur A. Ohnimus.....	Joseph Moloney
1937	Wm. Moseley Jones (D)	Henry P. Meehan (D)	James G. Smyth	Delwin W. Smith
1939	Paul Peek (D).......................	Hugh P. Donnelly (D)	Jack Carl Greenburg....	David V. Gill
1940 (Ex.)	Gordon H. Garland (D) [17] ..	Gardiner Johnson (R) [18]......		Wilkie Ogg [19]
1941	Gordon H. Garland (D)	Earl D. Desmond (D).........	Arthur A. Ohnimus.....	Wilkie Ogg
1943	Charles W. Lyon (R)	Thomas A. Maloney (R)......	Arthur A. Ohnimus.....	Wilkie Ogg
1945	Charles W. Lyon (R)	Thomas A. Maloney (R)......	Arthur A. Ohnimus.....	Wilkie Ogg
1947	Sam L. Collins (R)	Thomas A. Maloney (R)......	Arthur A. Ohnimus.....	Wilkie Ogg
1948	Sam L. Collins (R)	Thomas A. Maloney (R)......	Arthur A. Ohnimus.....	Wilkie Ogg
1949	Sam L. Collins (R)	Thomas A. Maloney (R)......	Arthur A. Ohnimus.....	Wilkie Ogg
1950	Sam L. Collins (R)	Thomas A. Maloney (R)......	Arthur A. Ohnimus.....	Wilkie Ogg
1951	Sam L. Collins (R)	Thomas A. Maloney (R)......	Arthur A. Ohnimus.....	Wilkie Ogg

OFFICERS OF THE ASSEMBLY—1849–1998—Continued

Session	Speaker	Speaker pro Tem.	Chief Clerk	Sergeant at Arms
1952	Sam L. Collins (R)	Thomas A. Maloney (R)......	Arthur A. Ohnimus......	Wilkie Ogg
1953	James W. Silliman (R)	Thomas A. Maloney (R)......	Arthur A. Ohnimus......	Wilkie Ogg
1954	James W. Silliman (R)	Thomas A. Maloney (R)......	Arthur A. Ohnimus......	Wilkie Ogg
1955	L. H. Lincoln (R)...................	Thomas A. Maloney (R)......	Arthur A. Ohnimus......	Wilkie Ogg [20]
1956	L. H. Lincoln (R)...................	Thomas A. Maloney (R)......	Arthur A. Ohnimus......	Tony Beard
1957	L. H. Lincoln (R)...................	Charles J. Conrad (R)........	Arthur A. Ohnimus......	Tony Beard
1958	L. H. Lincoln (R)...................	Charles J. Conrad (R)........	Arthur A. Ohnimus......	Tony Beard
1959	Ralph M. Brown (D).............	Carlos Bee (D).....................	Arthur A. Ohnimus......	Tony Beard
1960	Ralph M. Brown (D).............	Carlos Bee (D)	Arthur A. Ohnimus......	Tony Beard
1961	Ralph M. Brown (D) [21] Jesse M. Unruh (D) [22]	Carlos Bee (D)	Arthur A. Ohnimus......	Tony Beard
1962	Jesse M. Unruh (D)..............	Carlos Bee (D)	Arthur A. Ohnimus......	Tony Beard
1963	Jesse M. Unruh (D)..............	Carlos Bee (D)	Arthur A. Ohnimus [23] .. James D. Driscoll [24]......	Tony Beard
1964	Jesse M. Unruh (D)..............	Carlos Bee (D).....................	James D. Driscoll.........	Tony Beard
1965	Jesse M. Unruh (D)..............	Carlos Bee (D)	James D. Driscoll.........	Tony Beard
1966	Jesse M. Unruh (D)..............	Carlos Bee (D)	James D. Driscoll.........	Tony Beard
1967	Jesse M. Unruh (D)..............	Carlos Bee (D)	James D. Driscoll.........	Tony Beard
1968	Jesse M. Unruh (D)..............	Carlos Bee (D)	James D. Driscoll.........	Tony Beard
1969	Bob Monagan (R)..................	Charles J. Conrad (R)........	James D. Driscoll.........	Tony Beard
1970	Bob Monagan (R)..................	Charles J. Conrad (R)........	James D. Driscoll.........	Tony Beard
1971	Bob Moretti (D)	Carlos Bee (D).....................	James D. Driscoll.........	Tony Beard
1972	Bob Moretti (D)	Carlos Bee (D).....................	James D. Driscoll.........	Tony Beard
1973–74	Bob Moretti (D) [25] .... Leo T. McCarthy (D) [26]........	Carlos Bee (D) [27]	James D. Driscoll.........	Tony Beard
1975–76	Leo T. McCarthy (D)............	Louis J. Papan (D) [28] .... John T. Knox (D) [29]	James D. Driscoll.........	Tony Beard
1977–78	Leo T. McCarthy (D)............	John T. Knox (D)	James D. Driscoll.........	Tony Beard [30] Charles E. Greene [31]
1979–80	Leo T. McCarthy (D)............	John T. Knox (D)	James D. Driscoll.........	Charles E. Greene
1981–82	Willie L. Brown, Jr. (D)	Leo T. McCarthy (D)	James D. Driscoll [32]	Charles E. Greene [33]
1983–84	Willie L. Brown, Jr. (D)	Frank Vicencia (D)	James D. Driscoll [34]....	Charles E. Greene [35] Charles E. Bell [36]
1985–86	Willie L. Brown, Jr. (D)	Frank Vicencia (D)	James D. Driscoll.........	Charles E. Bell
1987–88	Willie L. Brown, Jr. (D)	Mike Roos (D).....................	James D. Driscoll [37]...... R. Brian Kidney [38]	Charles E. Bell
1989–90	Willie L. Brown, Jr. (D)	Mike Roos (D).....................	R. Brian Kidney	Charles E. Bell
1991–92	Willie L. Brown, Jr. (D)	Mike Roos (D) [39] .... Jack O'Connell (D) [41]	R. Brian Kidney [40] .... Lawrence A. Murman [42] E. Dotson Wilson [43]	Charles E. Bell
1993–94	Willie L. Brown, Jr. (D)	Jack O'Connell (D)	E. Dotson Wilson........	Charles E. Bell
1995–96	Willie L. Brown, Jr. (D) [44] .... Doris Allen (R) [47]................ Brian Setencich (R) [50]	Joe Baca (D) [45] .... Brian Setencich (R)............ (Majority) [48] Joe Baca (D) (Minority) [49] Doris Allen (R) (Majority) [51] Joe Baca (D) (Minority).......... Fred Aguiar (R) (Majority) [52]..........	E. Dotson Wilson........	Charles E. Bell [46]
	Curt Pringle (R) [53]	Fred Aguiar (R) [54].........		Ronald E. Pane [55]
1997–98	Cruz M. Bustamante (D) Antonio R. Villaraigosa (D) [56]	Sheila James Kuehl (D)	E. Dotson Wilson	Ronald E. Pane

1 Resigned February 6, 1850.
2 Elected March 25, 1850.
3 Resigned February 21, 1850.
4 Elected February 6, 1850.
5 Elected February 21, 1850.
6 Elected April 2, 1853.
7 Resigned February 15, 1853.
8 Elected February 15, 1853.
9 Elected January 11, 1854.
10 Elected January 9, 1857.
11 Elected February 13, 1860.
12 Elected April 12, 1861.
13 Resigned January 31, 1899.
14 Elected January 31, 1899.
15 Elected January 31, 1899.
16 Assumed duties of the Speakership for the 1906 1st Extraordinary Session when Frank C. Prescott resigned January 1, 1906.
17 Elected January 29, 1940.
18 Elected January 29, 1940.
19 Elected January 29, 1940.
20 Died in office November 23, 1955.
21 Resigned September 19, 1961.
22 Elected by Assembly Caucus September 30, 1961.
23 Resigned October 4, 1963.
24 Appointed by the Rules Committee October 5, 1963.

[25] Resigned June 27, 1974.

[26] Elected June 28, 1974.

[27] Died in office November 29, 1974.

[28] Elected December 2, 1974 (convening of 1975–76 Regular Session). Resigned January 19, 1976.

[29] Elected January 19, 1976.

[30] Resigned January 15, 1977.

[31] Elected January 3, 1978.

[32] Continued as Chief Clerk without election until February 1, 1982, *Government Code,* Section 9150. Elected February 1, 1982.

[33] Continued as Sergeant at Arms without election until February 1, 1982, *Government Code,* Section 9150. Elected February 1, 1982.

[34] Continued as Chief Clerk without election until July 19, 1983, *Government Code,* Section 9150. Elected July 19, 1983.

[35] Resigned March 31, 1983.

[36] Elected July 19, 1983.

[37] Resigned December 30, 1986.

[38] Assumed duties of Chief Clerk for the 1987–88 Regular Session on January 1, 1987. Elected Chief Clerk January 4, 1988.

[39] Resigned March 20, 1991.

[40] Resigned January 31, 1991.

[41] Elected March 18, 1991.

[42] Assumed duties as Acting Chief Clerk, February 1, 1991 to January 6, 1992.

[43] Elected January 6, 1992. Re-elected January 4, 1996 and Dec. 2, 1996.

[44] Served January 23, 1995–June 5, 1995

[45] Elected Speaker pro Tempore February 23, 1995. *See also, footnote 49.*

[46] Replaced January 4, 1996

[47] Served June 5, 1995–September 14, 1995

[48] Appointed Majority Speaker pro Tempore June 21, 1995. Served until September 14, 1995. *(Pursuant to the Isenberg Substitute Rules, Assembly Rule 6, 1995–96 Regular Session, adopted June 5, 1995, there were two Speakers pro Tempore appointed, a Majority and a Minority. See Assembly Daily Journal, page 2000)*

[49] Appointed Minority Speaker pro Tempore June 26, 1995. Served until January 4, 1996.

[50] Served September 14, 1995–January 4, 1996

[51] Appointed Majority Speaker pro Tempore September 14, 1995 but did not take oath of office

[52] Appointed Majority Speaker pro Tempore December 7, 1995, succeeding Doris Allen, recalled

[53] Served January 4, 1996–November 30, 1996

[54] Appointed Speaker pro Tempore January 4, 1996. Served until November 30, 1996. *(Pursuant to the Motion by Assembly Member Richter, relative to Legislative Powers and Duties, adopted January 3, 1996, there was one Speaker pro Tempore appointed. See Assembly Daily Journal, pages 4252 and 4264)*

[55] Appointed Acting Chief Sergeant at Arms January 4, 1996. Elected Chief Sergeant at Arms April 22, 1996 and re-elected Dec. 2, 1996.

[56] Elected Speaker on Jan. 26, 1998; took oath of office on Feb. 26, 1998.

OFFICERS OF THE SENATE—1849–1998

Session	President pro Tempore	Secretary	Sergeant at Arms
1849	E. Kirby Chamberlain	James F. Howe	Thomas J. Austin
1851	Elcan Heydenfeldt (W) [1]	James F. Howe	Clark Burnham
1852	Benj. F. Keene (D)	A. C. Bradford	Clark Burnham
1853	Benj. F. Keene (D)	A. C. Bradford	G. W. Tenbrook
1854	Benj. F. Keene (D) [2]	John Y. Lind	W. H. Harvey
1855	Royal T. Sprague (D)	Wm. A. Cornwall [3]	John T. Knox
1856	Delos R. Ashley (Am.)	William Bausman	J. W. Ross
1857	Samuel H. Dosh (D)	George S. Evans	Alex Hunter
1858	Samuel A. Merritt (D)	Thomas N. Cazneau	James W. Hawkins
1859	W. B. Dickinson (D)	Edwin C. Palmer	James W. Hawkins
1860	Isaac N. Quinn (D) [4]	Joseph R. Beard	W. H. Bell
1861	Richard Irwin (Doug. D) [5]	C. W. Tozer	William F. Williamson
1862	James McM. Shafter (Rep.)	Thomas Hill	Archibald G. Turner
1863	A. M. Crane (Union)	John White	George I. Lytl
1864	R. Burnell (Union)	Charles Westmoreland	John Helmsley
1866	S. P. Wright (Union)	John White	John H. Morgan
1868	Lansing B. Mizner (Union)	John White	F. S. Lardner
1870	Edward J. Lewis (D)	Joseph Roberts, Jr.	Nat Boyce
1872	James T. Farley (D)	Robert Ferral	James W. Hawkins
1874	William Irwin (D)	T. J. Shackelford	James W. Hawkins
1876	Benj. F. Tuttle (D)	T. J. Shackelford	James W. Hawkins
1878	Edward J. Lewis (D)	Rufus Shoemaker	William H. Bell
1880	George F. Baker (R)	Marcus D. Boruck	Andrew Wasson
1881	William Johnston (R)	Marcus D. Boruck	Andrew Wasson
1883	R. F. Del Valle (D)	Edwin F. Smith	I. G. Messec
1885	Benj. Knight, Jr. (D)	Edwin F. Smith	I. G. Messec
1887	Stephen M. White (D)	Edward H. Hamilton	John W. Wilcox
1889	Stephen M. White (D)	George W. Peckham	George W. Taylor
1891	Thomas Fraser (R)	Frank J. Brandon	Thomas Rogers
1893	R. B. Carpenter (R)	Frank J. Brandon	Thomas Rogers
1895	Thomas Flint, Jr. (R)	Frank J. Brandon	L. B. Blackburn
1897	Thomas Flint, Jr. (R)	Frank J. Brandon	L. B. Blackburn
1899	Thomas Flint, Jr. (R)	Frank J. Brandon	J. Louis Martin
1901	Thomas Flint, Jr. (R)	Frank J. Brandon	J. Louis Martin
1903	Thomas Flint, Jr. (R)	Frank J. Brandon	J. Louis Martin
1905	Edward I. Wolfe (R)	Lewis A. Hilborn	J. Louis Martin
1907	Edward I. Wolfe (R)	Lewis A. Hilborn	J. Louis Martin
1909	Edward I. Wolfe (R)	Lewis A. Hilborn	J. Louis Martin
1911	A. E. Boynton (R)	Walter N. Parrish	Joseph L. Coughlin
1913	A. E. Boynton (R)	Walter N. Parrish	Joseph L. Coughlin
1915	N. W. Thompson (R)	Edwin F. Smith	Thomas A. Brown
1917	Arthur H. Breed (R)	Clifton E. Brooks	Thomas A. Brown
1919	Arthur H. Breed (R)	Joseph A. Beek	Thomas A. Brown
1921	Arthur H. Breed (R)	Grace S. Stoermer	Thomas A. Brown
1923	Arthur H. Breed (R)	Joseph A. Beek	Joseph F. Nolan
1925	Arthur H. Breed (R)	Joseph A. Beek	Joseph F. Nolan
1927	Arthur H. Breed (R)	Joseph A. Beek	Joseph F. Nolan
1929	Arthur H. Breed (R)	Joseph A. Beek	Joseph F. Nolan
1931	Arthur H. Breed (R)	Joseph A. Beek	Joseph F. Nolan
1933	Arthur H. Breed (R)	Joseph A. Beek	Joseph F. Nolan
1935	William P. Rich (R)	Joseph A. Beek	Joseph F. Nolan
1937	William P. Rich (R)	Joseph A. Beek	Joseph F. Nolan
1939	Jerrold L. Seawell (R)	Joseph A. Beek	Joseph F. Nolan
1941	William P. Rich (R)	Joseph A. Beek	Joseph F. Nolan
1943	Jerrold L. Seawell (R)	Joseph A. Beek	Joseph F. Nolan
1945	Jerrold L. Seawell (R)	Joseph A. Beek	Joseph F. Nolan
1947	Harold J. Powers (R)	Joseph A. Beek	Joseph F. Nolan
1948	Harold J. Powers (R)	Joseph A. Beek	Joseph F. Nolan
1949	Harold J. Powers (R)	Joseph A. Beek	Joseph F. Nolan
1950	Harold J. Powers (R)	Joseph A. Beek	Joseph F. Nolan
1951	Harold J. Powers (R)	Joseph A. Beek	Joseph F. Nolan
1952	Harold J. Powers (R)	Joseph A. Beek	Joseph F. Nolan
1953	Harold J. Powers (R) [6]	Joseph A. Beek	Joseph F. Nolan
1954	Clarence C. Ward (R)	Joseph A. Beek	Joseph F. Nolan
1955	Clarence C. Ward (R) [7]	Joseph A. Beek	Joseph F. Nolan
	Ben Hulse (R)		
1956	Ben Hulse (R)	Joseph A. Beek	Joseph F. Nolan
1957	Hugh M. Burns (D)	Joseph A. Beek	Joseph F. Nolan
1958	Hugh M. Burns (D)	Joseph A. Beek	Joseph F. Nolan
1959	Hugh M. Burns (D)	Joseph A. Beek	Joseph F. Nolan
1960	Hugh M. Burns (D)	Joseph A. Beek	Joseph F. Nolan
1961	Hugh M. Burns (D)	Joseph A. Beek	Joseph F. Nolan
1962	Hugh M. Burns (D)	Joseph A. Beek	Joseph F. Nolan

OFFICERS OF THE SENATE—1849–1998—Continued

Session	President pro Tempore	Secretary	Sergeant at Arms
1963	Hugh M. Burns (D)..........................	Joseph A. Beek.................................	P. H. Kenealy
1964	Hugh M. Burns (D)..........................	Joseph A. Beek.................................	P. H. Kenealy
1965	Hugh M. Burns (D)..........................	Joseph A. Beek.................................	P. H. Kenealy
1966	Hugh M. Burns (D)..........................	Joseph A. Beek.................................	P. H. Kenealy
1967	Hugh M. Burns (D)..........................	Joseph A. Beek.................................	P. H. Kenealy
1968	Hugh M. Burns (D)..........................	Joseph A. Beek [8]	P. H. Kenealy
1969	Hugh M. Burns (D).......................... Howard Way (R) [9]........................	C. D. Alexander..............................	P. H. Kenealy
1970	Howard Way (R)............................ Jack Schrade (R) [10]	Darryl R. White	P. H. Kenealy
1971	James R. Mills (D)............................	Darryl R. White	P. H. Kenealy
1972	James R. Mills (D)..........................	Darryl R. White	P. H. Kenealy
1973–74	James R. Mills (D)..........................	Darryl R. White	P. H. Kenealy
1975–76	James R. Mills (D)..........................	Darryl R. White	Frank Thomas
1977–78	James R. Mills (D)..........................	Darryl R. White	Frank Thomas
1979–80	James R. Mills (D)	Darryl R. White	Frank Thomas [11] Tony Beard, Jr. [12]
1981–82	David A. Roberti (D)......................	Darryl R. White	Tony Beard, Jr.[13]
1983–84	David A. Roberti (D)......................	Darryl R. White	Tony Beard, Jr.
1985–86	David A. Roberti (D)......................	Darryl R. White	Tony Beard, Jr.
1987–88	David A. Roberti (D)......................	Darryl R. White	Tony Beard, Jr.
1989–90	David A. Roberti (D)......................	Darryl R. White	Tony Beard, Jr.
1991–92	David A. Roberti (D)......................	Darryl R. White [14] .... John W. Rovane [15] .... Rick Rollens [16].............................	Tony Beard, Jr.
1993–94	David A. Roberti (D)...................... Bill Lockyer (D) [17]........................	Rick Rollens..................................	Tony Beard, Jr.
1995–96	Bill Lockyer (D).............................	Rick Rollens [18]............................. John W. Rovane [19]....................... Gregory Schmidt [20]......................	Tony Beard, Jr.
1997–98	Bill Lockyer (D)............................. John Burton (D) [21]	Gregory Schmidt............................	Tony Beard, Jr.

[1] David C. Broderick was elected President of the Senate January 9, 1851, when McDougall was inaugurated Governor; and on the 24th, Heydenfeldt was elected President pro Tempore.

[2] Elected January 10, 1853.

[3] Removed March 22, 1855, and Charles Dickinson elected Secretary.

[4] Became acting Lieutenant Governor on the resignation of Governor Latham, having been elected President of the Senate January 20, 1860, and Charles J. Lansing was elected President pro Tempore.

[5] Pablo de la Guerra was elected President of the Senate and acting Lieutenant Governor, and Richard Irwin was elected President pro Tempore.

[6] Harold J. Powers became Lieutenant Governor on October 5, 1953, when Goodwin J. Knight resigned to become Governor.

[7] Clarence C. Ward died in office on May 9, 1955, and Ben Hulse was elected President pro Tempore on June 6, 1955.

[8] Joseph A. Beek died in office October 20, 1968.

[9] Howard Way elected President pro Tempore May 14, 1969.

[10] Jack Schrade elected President pro Tempore February 10, 1970.

[11] Resigned October 31, 1980.

[12] Tony Beard, Jr. appointed Sergeant at Arms November 1, 1980.

[13] Continued as Sergeant at Arms without election until January 14, 1982. *Government Code*, Section 9150. Elected January 14, 1982.

[14] Resigned January 31, 1991.

[15] Assumed duties as Acting Secretary, February 1, 1991.

[16] Elected February 15, 1991.

[17] Bill Lockyer elected President pro Tempore January 31, 1994.

[18] Resigned December 31, 1995.

[19] Assumed duties as Acting Secretary, January 1, 1996.

[20] Elected August 31, 1996.

[21] Elected February 5, 1998.

CHAPLAINS OF THE SENATE AND ASSEMBLY
1851–1998

	Assembly Chaplain	Senate Chaplain
1851		
1852		Rev. Mr. Woodbridge
1853		Rev. Mr. Woodbridge
1854		Rev. Mr. Woodbridge
1855		Rev. Mr. Pratt/Rev. Mr. Crouch
1856	Rev. Mr. Crouch	Rev. Mr. Pratt
1857		
1858		
1859		
1860		
1861		
1862		
1863		
1864	Rev. M.C. Briggs	
1866	Rev. M.C. Briggs	Rev. J.E. Dwinelle
1868	Rev. T.H.B. Anderson	Rev. J.S. McDonald
1870	Rev. J.G. Johnson	Rev. W.R. Grober
1872		Rev. J.H.C. Bonte
1874	George Charles Shelling	Rev. J.H.C. Bonte
1876	Rev. Richard Pratt	
1878	Rev. O.P. Fitzgerald	
1880	Rev. Mr. Bentley	
1881	Rev. Dr. Deal	
1883	Rev. E.B. Ware	
1885	Rev. Carrol M. Davis	Rev. J.F. Trefren
1887	Rev. E.R. Dille	Rev. H.C. Christian
1889	Rev. E.N. Early	Rev. A.C. Bane
1891	Rev. A.C. Herrick	Rev. J.A. Bruner
1893	Rev. H.W. Conry	Rev. W.S. Hoskinson
1895	Rev. O. Summers	Rev. G.A. Ottmann
1897	Rev. Charles F. Oehler	Rev. C.L. Miel
1899	Rev. B.W. Perry	Rev. A.J. Sturtevant
1901	Rev. C.P. Wilson	Rev. W.C. Evans
1903	Rev. J.B. Stevenson	Rev. C.L. Miel
1905	Rev. G.C. King	Rev. W.S. Hoskinson
1907	Rev. P.H. Willis	Rev. C.H. Darling
1909	Rev. S.N. Marsh	Rev. H.H. Wyman
1910 (ex)	Rev. W.C. Sherman	
1911	Rev. Frank K. Baker	Rev. H.H. Wyman
1913	Rev. Frank K. Baker	Rev. B. Dent Naylor
1915	Rev. James Whittaker	Rev. Henry I. Stark
1917	Rev. W.S. Hoskinson	Rev. Isaac Dawson
1919	Rev. Robert L. McArthur	Rev. S. Fraser Langford
1921	Rev. William E. Harrison	Rev. Bryant Wilson
1923	Bishop William H. Moreland	Rev. William E. Harrison
1925	Dr. Rudolph I. Coffee	Rev. William E. Harrison
1927	Rev. A. Watson Brown	Rev. Bryant Wilson
1929	Rev. William H. Hermitage	Rev. Bryant Wilson
1931	Rev. Lawrence Wilson	Rev. Sherman L. Divine
1933	Rabbi Norman A. Goldberg	Rev. William F. Ehmann
1934 (ex)	Rabbi Norman A. Goldberg	Rev. William F. Ehmann
1935	Rev. John E. Tumulty	Rev. Newton W. Moats
1937	Rev. William F. Ehmann	Rev. Clarence A. Kircher
1939	Rev. Raymond Lull Bailey	Rev. A. Raymond Grant
1940 (ex)	Rev. Raymond Lull Bailey	Rev. A. Raymond Grant
1941	Rev. Thomas H. Markham	Rev. H.W. Opperman
1943	Rev. Clarence A. Kircher	Rev. Richard C. Dwyer
1945	Dr. Torrance Phelps	Rev. Nelson E. Hinman
1947	Rev. Raymond Renwald	Rev. William C. Pearson
1948	Rev. Raymond Renwald	Rev. William C. Pearson
1949	Dr. Torrance Phelps	Rev. Nelson E. Hinman
1950	Dr. Torrance Phelps	Rev. Nelson E. Hinman
1951	Rev. Clarence A. Kircher	Rev. John G. Terwilliger
1952	Rabbi Irving I. Hausman	Rev. John G. Terwilliger
1953	Fr. James D. Poole	Rabbi Irving I. Hausman
1954	Fr. James D. Poole	Rabbi Irving I. Hausman
1955	Rev. William C. Pearson	Rev. Torrance Phelps
1956	Rev. William C. Pearson	Fr. Luke Powleson
1957	Rev. Robert S. Romeis	Fr. Luke Powleson
1958	Rev. Robert S. Romeis	Fr. Luke Powleson
1959	Rev. R. Wilbur Simmons	Rev. I.E. Metcalf

CHAPLAINS OF THE SENATE AND ASSEMBLY — Continued
1851–1998

	Assembly Chaplain	Senate Chaplain
1960	Rev. R. Wilbur Simmons	Rev. I.E. Metcalf
1961	Rev. Richard C. Dwyer	Rev. Edwin Peet
1962	Rev. Richard C. Dwyer	Rev. John W. Pressly, Jr.
1963	Rev. Robert R. Ferguson	Fr. Keith Kenny
1964	Rev. Robert R. Ferguson	Fr. Keith Kenny
1965	Rev. Robert R. Ferguson	Fr. John W. Pressly, Jr.
1966	Rev. Robert R. Ferguson	Very Rev. J. Ogden Hoffman
1967	Rev. Robert R. Ferguson	Rev. Wilbur W.Y. Choy
1968	Fr. Leo McAllister	Fr. Constantine Raptis
1969	Fr. Leo McAllister	Rev. Robert L. Carlson
1970	Fr. Leo McAllister	Rev. Robert S. Romeis
1971	Fr. Leo McAllister	Rabbi Amiel Wohl
1972	Fr. Leo McAllister	Rev. Wilbur C. Christians
1973–74	Fr. Leo McAllister	Rev. A. Paul Jones
1975–76	Fr. Leo McAllister	Rev. Shoko Masunaga
1977–78	Richard F. Barram	Rabbi Lester A. Frazin
1979–80	Rev. Walter R. Link	Rev. Robert F. Clazie
1981–82	Rev. Walter R. Link	Rev. Wilbur A. Korfhage
1983–84	Rabbi Michael Bourne	Rev. Wilbur A. Korfhage
1985–86	Rev. Hamilton T. Boswell	Rev. Wilbur A. Korfhage
1987–88	Rev. Hamilton T. Boswell	Fr. Leo McAllister
1989–90	Rev. Hamilton T. Boswell	Fr. Leo McAllister
1991–92	Rev. Hamilton T. Boswell	Rev. Winnie Gaines
1993–94	Rev. Hamilton T. Boswell	Rev. Deacon Walter J. Little
1995–96	Fr. Constantine C. "Dino" Pappademos	Rev. Deacon Walter J. Little
1997–98	Fr. Constantine C. "Dino" Pappademos [1]	Rev. Deacon Walter J. Little

[1] Acting Chaplain.

APPENDIX F

LEGISLATIVE COUNSELS OF CALIFORNIA
1914–1998

Legislative Counsel	Tenure	Notes
Arthur Will [1]	1914–1920	Selected by a board consisting of Governor Hiram W. Johnson and two Members of each House of the Legislature.
George Bush [2]	1921	Appointed by Governor William D. Stephens
John McGilvray	1923	Appointed by Governor Friend William Richardson
Thomas Gannon	1925	Appointed by Governor Friend William Richardson
Fred B. Wood [3]	1927–1950	Selected by adoption of a concurrent resolution
Ralph N. Kleps	1950–1961	
Angus C. Morrisson	1961–1964	
George H. Murphy	1964–1976	
Bion M. Gregory	1976–Present	

[1] The first Legislative Counsel was selected by a board consisting of the Governor and two Members of each House of the Legislature.

[2] In 1917, the Legislative Counsel position was made appointive at the pleasure of the Governor.

[3] The law was changed in 1927 to the present procedure for the selection of the Legislative Counsel by the Legislature—the adoption of a concurrent resolution at the beginning of each session.

APPENDIX G

CALIFORNIA BUDGET BILLS
1968–1997

Year	Bill No.	Date Passed Assembly (& Vote)	Date Passed Senate (& Vote)	Date Signed	Chapter Number
1968	SB 240	June 28 (55–20)	June 27 (33–4)	June 29	430
1969	SB 255	July 3 (58–19)	July 3 (31–5)	July 3	355
1970	AB 525	July 2 (62–15)	July 4 (27–9)	July 4	303
1971	SB 207	July 2 (54–26)	July 2 (36–2)	July 3	266
1972	SB 50	June 15 (72–4)	June 15 (31–2)	June 22	156
1973	AB 110	June 28 (69–3)	June 28 (34–6)	June 30	129
1974	SB 1525	June 28 (67–7)	June 28 (27–4)	June 30	375
1975	SB 199	June 26 (67–11)	June 17 (32–5)	July 1	176
1976	SB 1410	July 1 (60–16)	June 24 (27–8)	July 2	320
1977	AB 184	June 24 (60–17)	June 24 (30–9)	June 30	219
1978	AB 2190	July 5 (70–10)	July 5 (27–10)	July 6	359
1979	SB 190†	July 12 (56–23)	July 11 (27–12)	July 13	259
1980	AB 2020	July 10 (55–24)	July 16 (27–13)	July 16	510
1981	SB 110	June 15 (54–26)	June 15 (35–4)	June 28	99
1982	AB 21	June 25 (54–24)	June 25 (28–8)	June 30	326
1983	SB 123	July 19 (65–10)	July 19 (35–2)	July 21	324
1984	AB 2313	June 14 (55–24)	June 15 (33–6)	June 27	258
1985	SB 150	June 13 (54–26)	June 13 (33–6)	June 28	111
1986	AB 3217	June 12 (57–20)	June 12 (36–3)	June 25	186
1987	SB 152	July 1 (68–10)	June 23 (29–8)	July 7	135
1988	AB 224	June 30 (58–20)	June 30 (34–2)	July 8	313
1989	SB 165	June 28 (75–4)	June 29 (34–3)	July 7	93
1990	SB 899	July 27 (55–14)	July 28 (28–9)	July 31	467
1991	AB 222 ‡	June 20 (54–22)	June 15 (27–8)	July 16	118
1992	AB 979	Aug. 29 (54–24)	Aug. 29 (33–5)	Sept. 2	587
1993	SB 80	June 21 (54–24)	June 22 (27–11)	June 30	55
1994	SB 2120	July 2 (56–21)	July 4 (27–11)	July 8	139
1995	AB 903	Aug. 2 (56–19)	July 29 (31–9)	Aug. 3	303
1996	SB 1393	July 8 (61–17)	July 7 (32–5)	July 15	162
1997	AB 107	Aug. 11 (63–15)	Aug. 11 (30–6)	Aug. 18	282

† Item vetoes overridden by Assembly 7-20-79, 2-4-80.
Item vetoes overridden by Senate 7-19-79, 8-30-79, and 9-5-79.
‡ Withdrawn from Governor 7-3-91. Returned to enrollment and to Governor 7-4-91.

APPENDIX H

State Emblems, Insignia, Song, and Poet Laureate

The State Emblems

In the enactment of the laws designating a State Flag, Animal, Bird, Tree, Flower, Fish, Rock, Mineral, Colors, Nickname, and Song, etc., California's Legislature has proved that sentiment may be included in prosaic law. The Bear Flag is emblematic of California's romantic past; the valley quail and the golden trout represent her abundance of wild game and fish; while the redwood and golden poppy are in recognition of the beauty of her trees and flowers; serpentine and gold suggest the richness and variety of her natural resources. The State Colors of blue and gold depict the azure skies and precious California metal; the song "I Love You, California" portrays the regard Californians hold for their native state.

State Animal

Until it became extinct in 1922, the California grizzly bear (*Ursus californicus*) played an important part in the early period of the state. Avidly hunted and at the same time mightily respected by the early rancheros, it became the most arresting symbol on the flag raised in independence at Sonoma in 1846. The Native Sons of the Golden West used the bear as an emblem as early as 1875.

Long identified with the University of California, the California grizzly bear was officially designated the State Animal in 1953.[1]

State Bird

Widely distributed throughout the state, the California valley quail (*Lophortyx californica*) is a fine game bird especially noted for its hardihood and adaptability.

A plump, gray-colored bird, it is somewhat smaller than a pigeon. Outstanding features include a black plume on top of the head, curving downward, and a black bib with a white stripe under the beak. The birds flock together in numbers ranging from a few to 60 or more in the fall and winter months, but in the spring break up into pairs. They nest in hollows scratched in the ground and concealed by foliage, and their eggs, 6 to 28 in number, are creamy white and thickly spotted with golden brown.

A large number of societies and clubs voted to determine the selection of an official bird, and the California valley quail was found to be the popular choice. Official recognition followed when the Legislature named it the State Bird and avifaunal emblem in 1931.[2]

---

[1] *Government Code*, Section 425.
[2] *Government Code*, Section 423.

State Colors

In 1951, the Legislature adopted the combination of blue and gold (Yale blue and golden yellow) as the official State Colors.[3] These colors frequently appear on formal resolutions of the Legislature and official documents of the Secretary of State. They are also the colors of the University of California.

State Dance

The official state dance is the West Coast Swing Dance, also known as the Swing, Whip, or Jitterbug, designated in 1988.[4] The West Coast Dance originated in California in the 1930's responding to the new musical forms of the time. The official dance has since been nurtured and kept alive in California.

State Folk Dance

The Square Dance, which has been danced in California since 'Gold Rush Days', was adopted as the state folk dance in 1988.[5] It shares a long and proud history as an art form that is truly an original of our country. The dance is alive and thiriving today with more than 200,000 residents square dancing weekly.

State Fish

The golden trout (*Salmo agua-bonita*) is sparsely distributed in the lakes and streams of the High Sierra. Originally it was isolated in a few small tributaries of upper Little Kern and South Fork of the Kern River, including a rocky stream south of Sequoia National Park once called Volcano Creek but now renamed Golden Trout Creek. The first transplant of the golden trout occurred in 1876 from the coffeepot of sheepherders at Cottonwood Creek, Inyo County. Stock originating from this transplanted source is now used by the Department of Fish and Game for producing fingerling fish used in stocking other high streams and lakes. Some fish were transplanted to other states until 1939 when the California Legislature passed a law prohibiting transportation of eggs and fry out of the state.

For most of the year, the golden trout lives beneath ice as spring arrives late high in the mountains and their summer is brief. The growing season being very short, the golden trout rarely exceeds one foot in length, particularly in streams.

The golden trout, native only to California, is considered to be the most beautiful of freshwater fish with its profusion of vivid colors.

The *Salmo agua-bonita* was designated the official State Fish by the Legislature of 1947.[6]

---

[3] *Government Code*, Section 424.
[4] *Government Code*, Section 421.5(a).
[5] *Government Code*, Section 421.5(b).
[6] *Statutes of 1947*, Resolution Chapter 90.

State Flag

It is generally accepted that the "Bear Flag" was raised over Sonoma on June 14, 1846. This banner was carried by a small number of disgruntled Americans living in the north central part of California, who marched on that town and, in friendly fashion, made a prisoner of Mariano G. Vallejo, the Mexican commandant. A member of the group, William B. Ide, issued what became known as Ide's Proclamation, which declared California to be a Republic independent of Mexico.

The color of the flag—white—symbolizes purity, and the red in the star and bar, courage. The grizzly bear, regarded as the possessor of great strength, signifies this quality. The star denotes sovereignty, emulating the Lone Star of Texas.

William L. Todd, credited with the actual making of the original flag, wrote that a piece of new unbleached cotton domestic with four-inch stripes of red flannel attached to its lower side was used, that a star was placed in the upper left-hand corner of the flag, and a grizzly bear passant was placed in the center. Beneath the bear were the words "California Republic."

The original Bear Flag was preserved for many years in the offices of the Society of California Pioneers at San Francisco, but was destroyed in the earthquake and fire of 1906.

In 1911, the Legislature adopted the Bear Flag as the State Flag of California.[7]

---

[7] *Statutes of 1911*, Chapter 9. *See Government Code*, Section 420. "This bill sets forth in the statutes a legal description of the Bear Flag of the State of California. There never has been legislative determination of the specifications for the Bear Flag. Each manufacturer uses his own idea as to how the Flag should look. As a result, there are State Flags with bears that sometimes look like hogs, sometimes like wolves and sometimes like a combination of both. This bill will prescribe specifically how the bear shall be portrayed and also the specific colors of the Flag which shall be included in Flags manufactured hereafter.

"The bill also establishes the California grizzly bear (*Ursus californicus*) as the State Animal. The bill also sets forth the botanical names of the two species of redwoods (*Sequoia sempervirens, Sequoia gigantea*) which shall be considered the official State Tree."—*Statement by Mr. Charles Edward Chapel relative to Senate Bill No. 1014, Journal of the Assembly*, June 2, 1953, p. 4990.

State Flower

The golden poppy, also known as the flame flower, *la amapola,* and *copa de oro* (cup of gold) is said to be found blooming somewhere in California throughout the year.

The botanical name, *Eschscholtzia californica,* was given to this beautiful wildflower by Adelbert von Chamisso, a naturalist and member of the Royal Prussian Academy of Sciences. Chamisso was a member of a three-year scientific expedition under the patronage of Count Romanzoff, ex-Chancellor of the Russian Empire. He chose *Eschscholtzia* to honor Johann Friedrich Eschscholtz, his good friend and entomologist and surgeon of the expedition, and *californica* for the place of origin. The expedition dropped anchor in the harbor of San Francisco in 1816, surrounded by hills of the golden flowers.

In early days the golden poppy grew in great profusion the length and breadth of California, and it is said that some of the rolling foothills, aglow with their golden bloom, served as beacons to ships far out at sea. This spectacle so fired the imaginations of the sailors on the ships that they nicknamed the country "La Tierra del Fuego" or "Land of Fire."[8]

The golden poppy was officially adopted as the State Flower by the Legislature in 1903.[9]

State Marine Fish

The Garibaldi *(Hypsypops rubicundus)* was adopted by the Legislature in 1995 as the official State Marine Fish.[10] The Garibaldi is a resident of Pacific kelp beds from Monterey Bay, California to Baja California, Mexico. The adult Garibaldi is a uniform golden-orange color; young Garibaldi are reddish-orange with bright blue spots. They can reach 14 inches in length and have a lifespan of 17 years or more. Southern California's most conspicuous shore fish, Garibaldi utilize their bright orange color and a loud clicking sound to indicate their territory. They are very aggressive and will even nip or threaten divers. This bold territorial behavior makes them vulnerable to spearfisherman. However, they are protected by California Law.[11]

State Motto and Official Nickname

The official state motto, "Eureka", appears at the top of the Great Seal of the State.[12] It is from the Greek word meaning "I have found it."

California has always been synonymous with gold. *Las Sergas de Esplandian,* de Montalvo's 16th century novel, describes an island, "California", on which there was no metal but gold. In 1846, John C. Fremont named the entrance to San Francisco Bay *Chrysopylae* [13] (Golden Gate) after the manner of Byzantium's *Chrysoceras* (Golden Horn). Gold, irst discovered in southern California in 1841, brought renown to the state with the famous discovery by James Wilson Marshall at Coloma in 1848.

---

[8] *California Blue Book 1958,* p. 25.
[9] *Government Code,* Section 421.
[10] *Statutes of 1995,* Chapter 948.
[11] *Statutes of 1995,* Chapter 948; "Garibaldi," http://aqua.ucsd.edu.
[12] *Government Code,* Section 420.5.
[13] Fremont, J. C., *Geographical Memoir Upon Upper California in Illustration of His Map of Oregon and California,* Washington, 1848, U.S. Senate, 30th Congress, 1st Session, Misc. No. 148.

California's official nickname is *"The Golden State"*.[14] This appellation has long been a popular designation, especially appreciated in the spring when the fields are covered with a profusion of golden poppies.

State Prehistoric Artifact

The Chipped Stone Bear (bear-shaped eccentric) is the official state prehistoric artifact adopted by the Legislature in 1991.[15] Discovered during an excavation in southern California, this artifact successfully combines California's historic, natural and cultural heritage in one symbolic object. During an archaeological investigation lead by Dr. Henry Koerper with Cypress college students in 1985, the artifact was removed from an ancient site on the edge of a lagoon in northern San Diego County. The 2½ inch shaped bear is one of the earliest artifacts of its kind ever found in the western United States, and the oldest such object found in California. It is estimated to be more than 7,000 years old.

State Song

California's official State Song is "I Love You, California", written by F. B. Silverwood, a Los Angeles merchant. The music was composed by A. F. Frankenstein, also of Los Angeles. The song was publicly introduced by Mary Garden in 1913. It was the official song of the San Francisco and San Diego Expositions of 1915, and it was played aboard the first ship to go through the Panama Canal.

It was not given official recognition by the state, however, until 1951, when a resolution designating it as California's State Song was adopted by both houses of the Legislature.[16] All royalties from the song have been given to various charitable agencies.

State Tree

Common in the geologic past throughout much of the northern hemisphere, the California redwood has now reached its last stand on the Pacific Coast, where many of the finest groves are protected in state and national parks and forests. Except for a small area in Oregon, forests of these giant trees exist nowhere outside California.

There are two species: The Sierra Redwood (*Sequoia gigantea*) is to be found in the Sierra Nevada mountain region, and the Coast Redwood (*Sequoia sempervirens*) grows in the mountains and valleys along the central and northern coast of California and the southern coastal edge of Oregon.

The maximum recorded height of the redwood is 364 feet; circumference, 101 feet; diameter, 36½ feet. The General Sherman Redwood in Sequoia National Park, with an estimated age of between 3,000 and 4,000 years, is

---

[14] *Government Code*, Section 420.75.
[15] *Government Code*, Section 425.8.
[16] *Statutes of 1951*, Resolution Chapter 87. The words and music of the song were printed in the *Journal of the Assembly*, April 24, 1951, pp. 3404–3407.

272 feet tall. The General Grant Tree, with a base diameter of 35 feet and a height of 267 feet, is known as "The Nation's Christmas Tree."

Both species of the California redwood were designated as the State Tree by the Legislature in 1937.[17]

Other Emblems

In recent years, numerous proposals have been made to identify, publicize and protect California's prominent natural endowments. Those which have achieved official rank are listed below in line of recognition by the Legislature.

State Mineral

Gold was designated as the State Mineral by legislation in 1965.[18] More has been produced by this state than any other in the Union. Native gold is widely distributed in California, having been found in every county, occurring as free flakes or nuggets in sand and gravel, or in quartz veins. It is often found in association with copper and lead deposits. The largest nugget found to date in California was in 1854 at Carson Hill.

State Rock

Serpentine, designated officially in 1965,[19] is found in great abundance in the Coast Range from Del Norte County to San Diego County, and on the western slope of the Sierra Nevadas. It ranges in color from light green to greenish black and has a waxy feeling and appearance. A basic substance in the asbestos industry, it is found in greater quantity in California than in any other state.

State Gemstone

Benitoite is designated as the official gemstone. Sometimes called the "blue diamond," it was first discovered at the headwaters of the San Benito River, deriving its name therefrom. The gem is extremely rare and ranges in coloration from a light transparent blue to dark, vivid sapphire blue, and occasionally it is found in a violet shade.[20]

State Reptile

The Desert Tortoise (*Gopherus agassizii*) is indigenous to the southeastern desert areas of California. The color of the tortoise ranges from a yellowish brown to dark brown; they are of a robust build and have a high, arched upper shell. The average adult attains a shell size of about 10 to 12 inches in length.

---

[17] *Government Code*, Section 422.
[18] *Government Code*, Section 425.1.
[19] *Government Code*, Section 425.2.
[20] *Government Code*, Section 425.3.

There are no records of the longevity of the desert tortoise but turtles generally live longer than any other vertebrate, including humans. Tortoises are not plentiful and are gradually disappearing. In California they are now protected; it is illegal to remove them from their native area. In 1972, the California Legislature adopted the desert tortoise as the official State Reptile.[21]

State Insect

The California Dog-face Butterfly (*Zerene eurydice*) officially designated as the State Insect in 1972, is strictly a native California butterfly. It inhabits the lower mountain area from the Mexican border north to the San Francisco Bay region. It is particularly common in the San Bernardino Mountains. The male is orange and black in color with a striking design on the upper wing; the female is yellow-orange in color with a small black dot on the upper wing.[22]

State Fossil

The Sabre-tooth Cat was adopted by the Legislature in 1973 as the official State Fossil.[23] Fossil bones of this large cat have been found in abundance preserved in the tar pits of Rancho La Brea in Los Angeles.

A muscular, short-limbed cat with a stubby tail, *Smilodon californicus* was more massive than the modern lion. It had immense upper canine teeth up to 20 cm. long which were probably used for slashing, stabbing attacks on its prey.

The cat became extinct during the Pleistocene epoch at about the same time that the mastodon disappeared.

State Marine Mammal

The California Gray Whale (*Eschrichtius robustus*) was adopted by the Legislature as the State Marine Mammal in 1975.[24] Measuring 35 to 50 feet in length and around 20 to 40 tons in weight, it is identified by its mottled gray color and low hump in place of a dorsal fin.

The Gray Whale feeds mainly on small crustaceans along the ocean bottom in the western Bering Sea where they spend the summer. From December through February, the California Gray Whale can be seen traveling southward in small groups along the California coast on their way to the bays and lagoons of Baja California where mating occurs and the females calve. In March and April, they once again travel north following the shoreline. The whales cover approximately 6,000 to 7,000 miles each way. It is believed that memory and vision aid them on their long migration.

---

[21] *Government Code*, Section 422.5.
[22] *Government Code*, Section 424.5.
[23] *Government Code*, Section 425.7.
[24] *Government Code*, Section 425.5.

State Soil

San Joaquin Soil was designated as the official State Soil in 1997.[25] This designation was made in order to promote awareness of, and to acknowledge the importance of, soil and the many benefits derived from it in everyday life.

Poet Laureate

The honorary title of Poet Laureate was apparently first used in England during the Middle Ages. However, there does not appear to be any authentic record of the origin of the office.

The degree of Poet Laureate was awarded to those who were skilled in verse, and, in later times, the custom arose of crowning distinguished men of letters with the title.

In the history of California, there have been but five persons upon whom the Legislature has conferred the honorary title of Poet Laureate of California.

Ina Coolbrith, California's first Poet Laureate, was named "The Loved Laurel Crowned Poet of California" by the Legislature of 1919,[26] and held the title until her death in 1928.

Henry Meade Bland, named "The Laurel Crowned Poet of California" by the 1929 Legislature,[27] held the title until his death in 1931, just two years later.

In 1933, the Legislature designated John Steven McGroarty as "Poet Laureate of California,"[28] which title he held until his death in 1944.

Gordon W. Norris was appointed by the Legislature in 1953 [29] and served until his death on December 18, 1961.

The present Poet Laureate, the Honorable Charles Garrigus, was appointed by the Legislature in March 1966.[30] Mr. Garrigus' appointment is unique, as he is the first Poet Laureate ever appointed who has also served as a Member of the State Legislature.

---

[25] *Statutes of 1997*, Chapter 331.
[26] *Statutes of 1919*, Resolution Chapter 51.
[27] *Statutes of 1929*, Resolution Chapter 23.
[28] *Statutes of 1933*, Resolution Chapter 105.
[29] *Statutes of 1953*, Resolution Chapter 210.
[30] *Statutes of 1966*, Resolution Chapter 8.

Official Seals

State—Executive—Legislative—Judicial

The origin of the use of a seal as a manner of authenticating and attesting various documents is lost in antiquity. It is enough to state their use can be traced to the beginnings of all official written communication between government and the governed.

Seals affixed to, or impressed upon wax or paper have been used by the various jurisdictions in our government since its inception. The seals shown and described below are those used by the Governor, the Legislature and the Supreme Court of California.[1]

The Great Seal

The Constitutional Convention of 1849 adopted a "Great Seal of the State of California."[2] The seal was designed by Major Robert Selden Garnett of the United States Army, and presented to the convention by Caleb Lyon, one of the clerks of the convention. The explanation accompanying the seal, as read to the convention on October 2, 1849, is as follows:[3]

Explanation

"Around the bevel of the ring are represented thirty-one stars being the number of states of which the union will consist upon the admission of California.

"The foreground figure represents the Goddess Minerva having sprung full grown from the brain of Jupiter.[4] She is introduced as a type of the political birth of the State of California without having gone through the probation of a Territory. At her feet crouches a grizzly bear feeding upon clusters from a grape vine emblematic of the peculiar characteristics of the country. A miner is engaged with a rocker and bowl at his side, illustrating the golden wealth of the Sacramento upon whose waters are seen shipping typical of commercial greatness and the Snow-clad peaks of the Sierra Nevada make up the background while above [is] the Greek motto 'Eureka' (I have found it) applying either to the principle involved in the admission of the State, or the success of the miner at work."[5]

An amendment adding the words, "The Great Seal of the State of California," to the design was adopted on October 11, 1849.[6]

[1] The lower courts and most of the counties in this state have their own distinctive seals. *See Government Code*, Sections 25004, 68075–68080; Thomas, Martin E., *"County Seals of California"*, California State Library, 1971, pp. 1–12.
[2] *Constitution of 1849*, Article V, Section 14; *Government Code*, Section 399(a).
[3] *Journal of the Convention, Assembled to Frame a Constitution, for the State of California, Sept. 1st, 1849*, pp. 95–96 (October 2, 1849). This is the only legal definition and explanation of the Seal.
[4] In the original document, "Jupiter" is spelled "Jupitor," and "grizzly" is spelled "grisley."
[5] *Journal of the Convention, Assembled to Frame a Constitution, for the State of California, Sept. 1st, 1849*, p. 158 (October 11, 1849).
[6] *Government Code*, Sections 399, 400.

This seal, as designed and submitted to the convention, with some slight changes, has been made the official State Seal by statute [7] and is called "The Great Seal of the State of California."

The design of the Great Seal of the State shall correspond substantially with the following representation:[8]

The Great Seal is located in the office of the Secretary of State, where its impression is affixed to official state documents.[9]

Any person who maliciously or for commercial purposes uses or allows to be used any reproduction or facsimile of the Great Seal of the State in any manner whatsoever is guilty of a misdemeanor.[10]

Governor's Seal

In 1957 a law was enacted providing an official seal for the use of the Governor.[11]

[7] *Government Code*, Section 400, *Government Code*, Section 405, prescribes the exact colors to be used when the Great Seal is prepared in color.
[8] *Id.*
[9] *Government Code*, Section 12160.
[10] *Government Code*, Section 402.
[11] *Government Code*, Sections 426, 427.

The seal is basically a combination of other state insignia. Its center is dominated by a state flag; the most of which is anchored in a poppy plant, the official state flower. On the upper edge of the inner circle are 31 stars, emblematic of the state being the 31st to join the Union. The sun atop the flag presumably represents its setting in the west at day's end off the coast of California.

The seal is individualized to a certain extent by changing the Roman numerals at the bottom of the outer ring after the inauguration of each successive governor. The seal above contains the number XXXVI, as the present Governor, the Honorable Pete Wilson, is the 36th Governor of the State of California.

The Seal of the Assembly

At the 1967 Regular Session, the Assembly adopted a seal designed to convey the spirit and tradition of that body it represents.

The border bears the phrase "California State Assembly." In the center is a design featuring a quartered shield; in the upper left quarter is a gavel, symbolizing the legislature, in the lower right quarter is the top of a Corinthian column; in the upper right quarter are mountain peaks rising over a forest and in the lower left quarter is the top of a palm. On top of the shield is a California Grizzly and on either side are poppies. The motto of the Assembly is lettered on a banner on the lower portion and is interwoven with the shield and the poppies.[12]

Any person who maliciously for commercial purposes uses the seal is guilty of a misdemeanor.[13]

---

[12] *House Resolution 410, 1967 Regular Session; Government Code,* Sections 445, 446.
[13] *Government Code,* Section 447; *Assembly Rule 121.*

The Seal of the Senate

The Senate Seal is circular in shape, and the border bears the phrase "Seal of the Senate of the State of California." The center features a quill pen placed diagonally across an open scroll. On the top of the scroll is inscribed "LEGIS" (law) and the Roman numerals MDCCCL, designating 1850, the year California was admitted to the Union. Surrounding the pen and scroll is a cluster of California live oak leaves and acorns.[14]

Any person who maliciously or for commercial purposes uses the seal is guilty of a misdemeanor.[15]

The Senate adopted the seal in 1967.

Seal of the Supreme Court

---

[14] *Senate Resolution 204, 1967 Regular Session; Government Code*, Sections 440, 441.
[15] *Government Code*, Section 442.

The Secretary of State provided the first official seals for state agencies. Accordingly, a Seal of the Supreme Court was engraved by Mr. Albert Kuner in 1850.[16] The design showed a Roman nobleman standing beside a Masonic altar. This seal was used until 1866 when a new seal, believed to have been engraved by Mr. Edmund L. Barber of San Francisco, was adopted. This seal, with minor variations is presently used in the court.[17]

The current seal depicts the goddess of justice (Roman *Justitia*) clasping a sword in her right hand; in her left hand she holds the scales of justice.

---

[16] Kuner also engraved the *"Great Seal of the State of California"*.

[17] For a discussion of the origin and history of the seal, *see* Bowman, J. N., "The Seal of the California Supreme Court", *California Historical Quarterly,* Vol. XXXIII, March 1954, pp. 73–75.

The center panel from a three mural set, painted by Depression–era artist
Lucile Lloyd on the theme of "California's Name." The murals, dedicated
in 1937 in the California State Building in Los Angeles, currently reside
in the "California Room" of the State Capitol.

APPENDIX J

Origin and
Meaning of the Name California

Numerous theories exist as to the origin and meaning of the word "California." All that is known for certain is that someone, presumably a Spanish navigator, applied the name to the territory that now comprises the State of California sometime before the year 1541. It is probable that either Ortuno Ximenez (1533) or Hernando Cortés (1535) christened California, and that the name was perpetuated by word of mouth until it was definitely established as a geographical location on a map in 1541.

The etymology of the word California is also uncertain.[1] Some writers have attributed the name to a combination of the Latin words *calida* and *fornax,* "a hot furnace." General Mariano G. Vallejo and his nephew, Juan B. Alvarado, one of the Governors when California was a territory of Mexico, maintained that the word evolved from the Lower California Native American term *kali forno,* meaning "high hill" or "native land."

The most acceptable theory, however, is the one presented by the Rev. Edward Everett Hale, who, in 1862, discovered the name "California" in a romantic novel *Las Sergas de Esplandian* (The Deeds of Esplandian) by Garcia Ordonez de Montalvo. This novel was first published early in the 16th century. Hale points out that it is likely that the Spanish adventurers were familiar with the then popular novel. The name first appears in the following passage:

> "* * * Know, then, that, on the right hand of the Indies, there is an island called California, very close to the side of the Terrestrial Paradise, and it was peopled by black women, without any man among them, * * * Their island was the strongest in all the world, with its steep cliffs and rocky shores. Their arms were all of gold, * * * For, in the whole island there was no metal but gold." [2]

At the time of the explorations of Ximenez and Cortés, it was believed that California was an island; and, sailing up the west side of Mexico, these explorers thought they were at the exact site of de Montalvo's California, "on the right hand of the Indies."

Although Mr. Hale could not furnish the etymology for the word, in recent years P. Boissonade, a French investigator, has shed some light upon its origin.[3] Boissonade points out that a city, Califerne, is mentioned in the

---

[1] For further discussion of the origin and meaning of the name of California, *see* Erwin G. Gudde, *California Place Names,* pp. 50–51, and *California Blue Book,* 1958, p. 651, where Gudde states that, in 1849, George Ticknor found the name California in the Spanish romance *Las Sergas de Esplandian.*

[2] Edward Everett Hale, *The Queen of California,* p. 15. In this work Mr. Hale discusses other theories concerning the origin and meaning of the word California, and furnishes a translation of those passages from Montalvo's work which relate to the mythical California.

[3] For a discussion of Boissonade's work, *see* Rockwell D. Hunt and Nellie Van De Grift Sanchez, *A Short History of California,* pp. 35–38.

Chanson de Roland (Song of Roland), a French epic poem of the 11th century. This, he believes is the source of de Montalvo's more Spanish version "California." He points out that Califerne was the capital of Barbary in North Africa, a city so ancient that even in the 11th century its origin was attributed to giants. He suggests that Califerne stems from two Berber-Arabic words *kalaa,* a fortified city, and *iferne* or *ifrene,* its principal citizens, hence a capital city.

APPENDIX K

Origin and Meaning of the Names of the Counties of California With County Seats and Dates Counties Were Created [1]

ALAMEDA COUNTY. County seat, Oakland. Created March 25, 1853. The word Alameda is derived from *alamo*, the Spanish name for cottonwood or poplar tree, and means a "grove of poplar trees." The name was applied both to the southern portion of the county (*La Alameda*), and to the stream running through it (*Río de la Alameda*) as early as 1795.

ALPINE COUNTY. County seat, Markleeville. Created March 16, 1864. This county derived its name from the English word *Alpine*, meaning "of, pertaining to, or connected with, the Alps." Its geographical position, lying as it does on the crest of the Sierra Nevada Mountains, makes it particularly an alpine county, and hence its name.

AMADOR COUNTY. County seat, Jackson. Created May 11, 1854. The county is named for José María Amador, soldier, rancher, and miner, who was born in San Francisco on December 18, 1794, the son of Sergeant Pedro Amador, a Spanish soldier who settled in California in 1771. In 1848, José María Amador, with several Native Americans, established a successful gold mining camp near the present town of Amador. In Spanish, the word *amador* means "lover of inanimate objects."

BUTTE COUNTY. County seat, Oroville. Created February 18, 1850. One of the original 27 counties of the State of California. Its name is derived from the Marysville or Sutter Buttes, which lay within the boundaries of the county when it was created. The word *butte* is derived from the Teutonic word meaning "a blunt extension or elevation." In the French language, it signifies "a small hill or mound of earth detached from any mountain range."

CALAVERAS COUNTY. County seat, San Andreas. Created February 18, 1850. Also one of the original 27 counties of California. The meaning of the word *Calaveras* is "skulls." This county "takes its name from the Calaveras River, which was reportedly so designated by an early explorer, when he found, on the banks of the stream, many skulls of Indians who had either died of famine or had been killed in tribal conflicts over hunting and fishing grounds."

[1] The following sources were used in the preparation of the section relating to the origin and meaning of the names of California counties: *The Names of the Counties of California* by Erwin G. Gudde; *Origin and Meaning of the Names of the Counties of California* by Prentiss Maslin; *Economic Survey of California and its Counties* by the Research Department of the California State Chamber of Commerce; *Report of General Mariano G. Vallejo to the First Legislative Session*, April 16, 1850; *Historical Background of Los Angeles County* by J. F. Moroney; *California Blue Books* for 1946, 1950, 1958; *Statutes of 1850*, Chapters 15, 61.

COLUSA COUNTY. County seat, Colusa. Created February 18, 1850. One of the original 27 counties of the state. Named after two Mexican land grants: *Coluses* (1844) and *Colus* (1845). The name of this county in the original act of 1850 was spelled *Colusi,* and oftentimes in newspapers was spelled *Coluse.* The word is derived from the name of a Native American tribe living on the west side of the Sacramento River.

CONTRA COSTA COUNTY. County seat, Martinez. Created February 18, 1850. One of the original 27 counties of the state. This name signifies "opposite coast," and the county is so called from its situation opposite San Francisco, in an easterly direction, on San Francisco Bay. In 1853, Alameda County was formed from territory originally included in this county.

DEL NORTE COUNTY. County seat, Crescent City. Created March 2, 1857, from territory formerly included in Klamath County. The name of this county signifies "the north," and the county being situated in the extreme northwest corner of the state, derived its name from its geographical position.

EL DORADO COUNTY. County seat, Placerville. Created February 18, 1850. Also one of the original 27 counties of the state. *"El Dorado*—the far-famed fabulous region of genial clime and never-fading verdure, where gold and precious stones are as common as rocks and pebbles, where wines gently flow from fountains, where wheat spontaneously grows overtopped with tiny loaves of bread, and pigeons fly about already roasted. . . . Francis Orellana, a companion of Pizarro, first spread the account of the supposed existence of this province in South America.

"The name, meaning 'the gilded one,' appears at the beginning of the Sixteenth Century as that of a mythical Indian chief . . . who was said to have been covered with gold dust during the performance of religious rites. This chief was eagerly sought by the Spanish and German conquerors of northern South America until his abode was assertedly found in 1537."

When the discovery of gold by James W. Marshall at Coloma in January, 1848, became known to the world, California, and particularly that section where gold was discovered, was called "El Dorado." From this fact the county received its name.

FRESNO COUNTY. County seat, Fresno. Created April 19, 1856. Named after Fresno Creek. *Fresno* in Spanish signifies "ash tree," and it was because of the abundance of mountain ash in Fresno County's mountains that the county received its name.

GLENN COUNTY. County seat, Willows. Created March 11, 1891. This county was created out of the northern portion of Colusa County, and was named for Dr. Hugh J. Glenn, who, during his lifetime, was the largest wheat farmer in the state, and a man of great prominence in political and commercial life in California.

HUMBOLDT COUNTY. County seat, Eureka. Created May 12, 1853. This county derived its name from Humboldt Bay. Humboldt Bay was entered by a sea otter party in 1806, but was not rediscovered until 1849. In 1850, Douglas Ottinger and Hans Buhne entered the bay, naming it *Humboldt* in honor of the great naturalist and world explorer, Baron Alexander von Humboldt.

IMPERIAL COUNTY. County seat, El Centro. Created August 15, 1907. It derived its name from the Imperial Valley, situated therein, and is the "youngest" of California's counties. The valley had been named for the Imperial Land Company, a subsidiary of the California Development Company, which, at the turn of the century, had reclaimed the south portion of the Colorado desert for agriculture.

INYO COUNTY. County seat, Independence. Created March 22, 1866. This county derived its name from the Native American name for the mountains in its area. The meaning of the word *Inyo* is "dwelling place of a great spirit."

KERN COUNTY. County seat, Bakersfield. Created April 2, 1866. This county derived its name from the Kern River, which was named for Edward Kern, topographer of General John C. Frémont's 1845 expedition.

KINGS COUNTY. County seat, Hanford. Created March 22, 1893. This county was created out of a part of Tulare County in 1893. Some 100 square miles of territory from Fresno County was added to the county in 1908. It derived its name from the Kings River, which, according to Padre Muñoz' diary of the Morago Expedition of 1806, was discovered in 1805 by an exploring expedition and named *Río de los Santos Reyes* (River of the Holy Kings).

LAKE COUNTY. County seat, Lakeport. Created May 20, 1861, from territory formerly included in Napa County. This county derived its name because of the many charming lakes that are within its boundaries.

LASSEN COUNTY. County seat, Susanville. Created April 1, 1864. The name of this county was derived from Mount Lassen, which was named for Peter Lassen, one of General Frémont's guides and a famous trapper and frontiersman, who was killed by the Paiutes at the base of the mountain in 1859.

LOS ANGELES COUNTY. County seat, Los Angeles. Created February 18, 1850. This county was one of the original 27 counties of the state, and, when created in 1850, "occupied a comparatively small area along the coast line between Santa Barbara and San Diego with Mariposa County forming its northern boundary. . . . In the following year, however, the Legislature revised the boundaries of these counties. Mariposa and San Diego Counties, which had originally been the two largest in the State, were considerably reduced, and Los Angeles County was greatly enlarged forming a broad, sprawling empire of some 35,000 square miles, extending from San Diego to Santa Barbara and from the Pacific Ocean to the Colorado River and the eastern boundary of the State." There have been three major changes in the boundaries of Los Angeles County: in 1853, 1866, and 1889, leaving the county with a total area of 4,083.21 square miles.

The words *Los Angeles* literally means "the angels," and are a contraction of the original name *Pueblo del Río de Nuestra Señora la Reina de Los Angeles de Porciúncula* (The Town of the River of Our Lady, Queen of the Angels). In 1781, Governor Felipe de Neve issued orders for the establishment of this pueblo on El Río Nuestra Señora de Los Angeles. The pueblo in time became known as the *Ciudad de Los Angeles* or the "City of the Angels," and it is from this contraction that the present name is derived.

MADERA COUNTY. County seat, Madera. Created March 11, 1893, from a portion of Fresno County lying north of the San Joaquin River. *Madera* in Spanish signifies "timber." The county derived its name from the Town of Madera, so named when the California Lumber Company built a flume to carry lumber to the railroad there in 1876.

MARIN COUNTY. County seat, San Rafael. Created February 18, 1850. One of the original 27 counties of the state. The origin of its name is not clear. One version is that the county was named for Chief Marin, of the Licatiut tribe of Native Americans who inhabited that section and waged fierce battle against the early Spanish military explorers. Chief Marin afterwards was Christianized and baptized under the name of *Marinero*, "The Mariner," because of his intimate knowledge of the Bay of San Francisco, where he often served as ferryman for the whites. The other version is that the bay between San Pedro and San Quentin points was named *Bahía de Nuestra Señora del Rosario la Marinera* by Ayala in 1775, and it is quite possible that *Marin* is simply an abbreviation of this name.

MARIPOSA COUNTY. County seat, Mariposa. Created February 18, 1850. One of the original 27 counties. This county took its name from Mariposa Creek. The meaning of *Mariposa* in Spanish is "butterfly" or "moth." Gudde states that the name for the stream originated September 27, 1806, when the Moraga Expedition camped there, and called the place "of the Mariposas" because of the great number of butterflies and moths. Maslin gives two versions, one of which is that the first explorers in the mountains of that region beheld for the first time a beautiful lily growing everywhere, gay-colored, spotted, and in some respects resembling the wings of a butterfly. In their admiration, they gave to this dainty flower the name of *Mariposa* (butterfly) lily.

MENDOCINO COUNTY. County seat, Ukiah. Created February 18, 1850. One of the original 27 counties of the State of California. This county derived its name from Cape Mendocino, which was probably named in honor of either Antonio de Mendoza, Viceroy of New Spain, 1535–1542 (who sent the Juan Cabrillo Expedition to this coast in 1542), or Lorenzo Suárez de Mendoza, Viceroy from 1580 to 1583. "Mendocino is an adjective form of the family name of Mendoza, which was rarely used as a geographical term. Hence the name might have been chosen without reference to either of the two viceroys."

MERCED COUNTY. County seat, Merced. Created April 19, 1855, from a part of Mariposa County. The county derived its name from the Merced River, or *El Río de Nuestra Señora de la Merced* (River of Our Lady of Mercy), so named by an expedition headed by Gabriel Moraga when they came upon it on September 29, 1806, at the end of a hot dusty ride.

MODOC COUNTY. County seat, Alturas. Created February 17, 1874, from the easterly section of Siskiyou County. This county derived its name from a tribe of Native Americans who lived at the headwaters of the Pit River. Maslin suggests that the word *Modoc* means "the head of the river." Gudde states that the word is derived from the Klamath word *Moatokni*, meaning "southerners," i.e., the people living south of the Klamath tribe.

MONO COUNTY.   County seat, Bridgeport. Created April 24, 1861. The county is named after Mono Lake, which, in 1852, was named for a Native American tribe which inhabited the Sierra Nevada from north of Mono Lake to Owens Lake. Their western neighbors, the *Yokuts,* called them *monachie,* meaning "fly people" because the pupae of a fly (*Ephyda hyans*) was their chief food staple and trading article.

MONTEREY COUNTY.   County seat, Salinas. Created February 18, 1850. This county is one of the original 27 counties of the State of California. It derived its name from the Bay of Monterey. The word itself is composed of the Spanish words *monte* and *rey,* and literally means "king of the forest." The bay was named by Sebastión Vizcaíno on December 16, 1602, in honor of the Conde de Monterey, then Viceroy of New Spain.

NAPA COUNTY.   County seat, Napa. Created February 18, 1850. One of the original 27 counties of the State of California. Named after Napa Valley. The word *Napa* is of Native American derivation, and has been variously translated as "grizzly bear," "house," "motherland," or "fish." "Of the many explanations of the origin of the name, the most plausible seems to be that it is derived from the Patwin word *napo* meaning 'house.' "

NEVADA COUNTY.   County seat, Nevada City. Created April 25, 1851. Named after the mining town of Nevada City, which had been named from the second element of the term "Sierra Nevada." The word *Nevada* in Spanish means "snowy" or "snowcovered."

ORANGE COUNTY.   County seat, Santa Ana. Created March 11, 1889. This county was given the name of "Orange" because of its extensive orange groves for which it is justly famous.

PLACER COUNTY.   County seat, Auburn. Created April 25, 1851. *Placer* is probably a contraction of the words *plaza de oro,* the place of gold, and means in Spanish "a place near a river where gold is found." The county derived its name from the numerous places therein where the method of extracting the gold from the earth, called placer mining, was practiced.

PLUMAS COUNTY.   County seat, Quincy. Created March 18, 1854. The Spanish originally called one of the tributaries of the Sacramento River *El Río de las Plumas,* or the "River of the Feathers." The Legislature, in creating this county, gave it the name of *Plumas,* because of the fact that all of the numerous branches of the Feather River have their origin in its mountains.

RIVERSIDE COUNTY.   County seat, Riverside. Created March 11, 1893. This county was created from portions of San Diego and San Bernardino Counties, and derived its name from the City of Riverside, so christened when the upper canal of the Santa Ana River reached it in 1871.

SACRAMENTO COUNTY. County seat, Sacramento. Created February 18, 1850. This county is one of the original 27 counties of the State of California and was named after the Sacramento River. The word *Sacramento* signifies "Sacrament" or "Lord's Supper." "The streams known as Feather and Sacramento Rivers were first respectively named by Captain Moraga 'Sacramento' and 'Jesus Maria'; but the latter now assumes the name of Sacramento, whilst the former is called Feather."

SAN BENITO COUNTY. County seat, Hollister. Created February 12, 1874. Named after San Benito Valley. Crespi, in his expedition in 1772, named a small river in honor of *San Benedicto* (Saint Benedict), the patron saint of the married, and it is from the contraction of this name that the county took its name.

SAN BERNARDINO COUNTY. County seat, San Bernardino. Created April 26, 1853. Saint Bernard is the patron saint of mountain passes. The name *Bernardino* means "bold as a bear." The Spanish gave to the snow-capped peak in southern California the name of *San Bernardino* in honor of the saint, and from this the county derived its name. Gudde states that the county was named after the City of San Bernardino which was founded as a Mormon colony in 1850, and that the name was first applied by Padre Dumetz to a temporary chapel on May 20, 1810.

SAN DIEGO COUNTY. County seat, San Diego. Created February 18, 1850. One of the original 27 counties of the State of California. Named after San Diego Bay, which had been rechristened by Vizcaíno on November 12, 1602, in honor of the Franciscan, San Diego de Alcalá de Henares, whose name was borne by his flagship. The Bay of San Diego was first discovered in 1542 by Juan Rodríguez Cabrillo who named it San Miguel.

SAN FRANCISCO COUNTY. County seat, San Francisco. Created February 18, 1850. This county is one of the original 27 counties of the State of California. The sixth mission in California was established here by Padre Junípero Serra on October 9, 1776, and was named *Misión San Francisco de Asís a la Laguna de los Dolores* (Saint Francis of Assisi at the Lagoon of Sorrows). The mission is now known as "Mission Dolores." The name *San Francisco* appears on maps since 1590, but it was not identified with this bay until a detachment of the Portolá Expedition discovered it in 1769. Establishment of the presidio and mission in 1776 definitely fixed the name on the peninsula.

SAN JOAQUIN COUNTY. County seat, Stockton. Created February 18, 1850. This is one of the original 27 counties of the State of California, and takes its name from the San Joaquin River. In the early 1800's, Lieutenant Moraga, commanding an expedition in the lower great Central Valley of California, gave to a small rivulet, which springs from the Sierra Nevada Mountains and empties into Buena Vista Lake, the name of *San Joaquín* (meaning Saint Joachim) and it is from this that the present river derived its name.

SAN LUIS OBISPO COUNTY. County seat, San Luis Obispo. Created February 18, 1850. One of the original 27 counties of the State of California. On September 1, 1772, the Mission San Luis Obispo was established here by Padre Junípero Serra, and named for Saint Louis, the Bishop of Toulouse. The county derived its name from the mission.

SAN MATEO COUNTY. County seat, Redwood City. Created April 19, 1856, from territory originally a part of San Francisco County. The county was reorganized and enlarged in 1868 by adding territory from Santa Cruz County. This county bears the Spanish name for Saint Matthew. As a place name, *St. Matthew* appears as early as 1776 in Anza's diary; and the arroyo, the point, and the settlement at the unofficial San Mateo Mission are all so designated on the early maps. Until about 1850, the name appeared as *San Matheo*.

SANTA BARBARA COUNTY. County seat, Santa Barbara. Created February 18, 1850. This is another of the original 27 counties of the state. The Santa Barbara channel received its name from Sebastián Vizcaíno, when he sailed over the channel waters on December 4, 1602. In 1782, Father Junípero Serra dedicated a site near the channel for a presidio, and on December 4, 1786, he founded the nearby Mission Santa Barbara (Saint Barbara). The county derives its name from the mission.

SANTA CLARA COUNTY. County seat, San Jose. Created February 18, 1850. One of the original 27 counties of the State of California. The county is named after Mission Santa Clara, which was established on January 18, 1777, and named for Saint Clara of Assisi, Italy. The name *Clara* means "clear" or "bright."

SANTA CRUZ COUNTY. County seat, Santa Cruz. Created February 18, 1850, one of the original 27 counties of the state. In the original act passed February 18, 1850, the county was given the name of *Branciforte* after the Spanish pueblo founded there in 1797. However, less than two months later, on April 5, 1850, the name was changed to *Santa Cruz*. The Santa Cruz Mission, established in 1791, and completed in 1794, was destroyed by earthquake in 1857, but a smaller-scaled replica was erected in 1931. *Santa* is the Spanish feminine of "saint" or "holy"; *Cruz* is the Spanish for "cross," and *Santa Cruz* signifies "holy cross."

SHASTA COUNTY. County seat, Redding. Created February 18, 1850. This county is another of the original 27, and was named after Mount Shasta. The name *Shasta* is derived from the English equivalent for the name of a Native American tribe that once lived in the area. The name of this tribe was spelled in various ways until the present version was used when the county was established.

SIERRA COUNTY. County seat, Downieville. Created April 16, 1852. *Sierra* is the Spanish word for "saw," and *Sierra Nevada* or "snow saw" was applied to the Sierra Nevada chain of mountains because of the jagged, serrated or saw-tooth peaks which form their skyline. The county was so called because of these jagged peaks within its borders. Gudde states that *Sierra* means "mountain range"; and that, in Spanish times, any two or more peaks in a row formed a *sierra*.

SISKIYOU COUNTY. County seat, Yreka. Created March 22, 1852, and named after the mountain range. The origin of the word *Siskiyou* is not known. One version is that it is the Chinook word for "bobtailed horse," such an animal belonging to a Hudson's Bay Company trapper having been lost in these mountains in 1828. Another version, given in an argument delivered by Senator Jacob R. Snyder of San Francisco before the State Senate on April 14, 1852, is that the French name *Six Callieux,* meaning "six-stone," was given to a ford on the Umpqua River by Michel La Frambeau and a party of Hudson's Bay Company trappers in 1832 because six large stones or rocks lay in the river where they crossed. Gudde suggests that the Canadian French word *six-cailloux* was used in this version.

SOLANO COUNTY. County seat, Fairfield. Created February 18, 1850. One of the original 27 counties of the state. The county derives its name indirectly from that of the Franciscan missionary, Father Francisco Solano, whose name was given in baptism to the chief of one of the important Native American tribes of the region when he accepted Christianity. At the request of General Mariano Vallejo, the county was named for Chief Solano, who at one time ruled over most of the land and tribes between the Petaluma Creek and the Sacramento River. Before receiving the name of *Solano,* this chief was called *Sem-yeto,* which signifies "brave or fierce hand." In 1934, a bronze statue of Chief Solano was erected in Fairfield.

SONOMA COUNTY. County seat, Santa Rosa. Created February 18, 1850. This county is also one of the original 27 counties of the state. *Sonoma* is a Native American name, translated by some as "Valley of the Moon," and by others as "land or tribe of Chief Nose." It is also the name of a Native American tribe once occupying the area.

STANISLAUS COUNTY. County seat, Modesto. Created April 1, 1854. The word *Stanislaus* is a corruption of *Estanislao,* the baptismal name of a mission-educated Native American chief who led a band of Native Americans in a series of battles against Mexican troops. He was finally defeated by General Mariano G. Vallejo in 1826. The county is named for the Stanislaus River, first discovered by Gabriel Moraga in 1806, and christened *Río de Nuestra Señora de Guadalupe.* The river was later renamed *Rio Estanislao* for the Native American chief.

SUTTER COUNTY. County seat, Yuba City. Created February 18, 1850. This is one of the original 27 counties of the State of California. Sutter County was named after General John Augustus Sutter, a native of Switzerland, who obtained a large grant from the Mexican government, and called his first settlement New Helvetia, now the City of Sacramento. In 1841, the general established a great stock ranch in this area, to which he retired in 1850 when gold seekers deprived him of most of his holdings at Sacramento.

TEHAMA COUNTY. County seat, Red Bluff. Created April 9, 1856. The county is named for the City of Tehama, which, until 1857, was the county seat. Gudde states that it is not certain whether or not the name is of Native American origin, although a tribe of Native Americans by this name is mentioned in reports of the early 1850's. Suggested possible roots are the Arabic word *tehama,* "hot lowlands" or the Mexican word *tejamanil,* "shingle."

TRINITY COUNTY. County seat, Weaverville. Created February 18, 1850. This is one of the original 27 counties of the State of California. It takes its name from the Trinity River, first so called in 1845 by Major Pearson B. Reading who was under the mistaken impression that the stream emptied into Trinidad Bay. Trinity is the English version of Trinidad.

TULARE COUNTY. County seat, Visalia. Created April 20, 1852. Commandant Fages, while hunting for deserters in 1772, discovered a great lake surrounded by marshes and filled with rushes, which he named *Los Tules,* "the tules." It is from this lake that the county derives its name. "The root of the name [Tulare] is found in the Mexican word *tullin,* designating cattail or similar reeds." The geographical term *Los Tulares* was used as early as 1776.

TUOLUMNE COUNTY. County seat, Sonora. Created February 18, 1850. This county is one of the original 27 counties. "The name *Tuolumne* is of Indian origin and has been given different meanings, such as 'Many Stone Houses,' 'The Land of Mountain Lions,' and 'Straight Up Steep,' the latter an interpretation of William Fuller, a native Indian chief." Vallejo, in his Report to the First Legislature in 1850, said that the word is "a corruption of the Indian word *talmalamne,* which signifies 'cluster of stone wigwams.' " Gudde states that the county is named after the river, which, in turn, was named for a Native American tribe "mentioned as *Taulamne* in 1806, and as *Taualames* in 1810. The name may mean 'people who dwell in stone houses,' i.e., in caves. The suffix *umne* means 'people'."

VENTURA COUNTY. County seat, Ventura. Created March 22, 1872. On March 31, 1782, the Mission San Buenaventura was founded at San Buenaventura (now known as Ventura). *Buenaventura* is composed of two Spanish words, *buena,* meaning "good," and *ventura,* meaning "fortune"; hence the name signifies "good fortune." The county derives its name from the latter word, *Ventura.*

YOLO COUNTY. County seat, Woodland. Created February 18, 1850. This is one of the original 27 counties of the State of California, and in the original act of 1850, the name was spelled "Yola." *Yolo* is a Native American name variously believed to be a corruption of a Native American tribal name *Yo-loy,* meaning "a place abounding in rushes," or of the name of a Native American chief, *Yodo,* or of the Native American village of *Yodoi.*

YUBA COUNTY. County seat, Marysville. Created February 18, 1850. This is another of the original 27 counties of the state, and was named after the Yuba River, so named by Captain John A. Sutter for the Native American village *Yubu, Yupu,* or *Jubu,* near the confluence of the Yuba and Feather Rivers. Vallejo, in his Report to the First Legislature in 1850, stated that the river was named *Uba* by an exploring expedition in 1834, because of the quantities of wild grapes (*uvas silvestres* in Spanish) which they found growing upon its banks.

Governor's Mansion and Flag

The Mansion

At present, there is no official residence for the Governor. The most recent Governor's mansion was sold without ever being occupied by a Governor of the state.

First Mansion

First Mansion

The original mansion was a two-story, Italian style villa erected in 1871. However, when the Legislature failed to provide the funds necessary to complete it, Governor Newton Booth refused to move in. The building was later converted into quarters for the first State Printing Plant without ever having been occupied by a Governor of California. The site of this ill-fated mansion is now part of the Capitol Park.[1]

Second Mansion

[1] *Government Code*, Section 8170.

Second Mansion

The second mansion was designed by Nathaniel D. Goodell and built in 1877–78 by U. M. Reese. Its original owner was Albert Gallatin, a prosperous Sacramento hardware merchant.

In 1877, the house was sold to Joseph Steffens, father of the noted journalist and newspaper correspondent, Lincoln Steffens.

The mansion was purchased by the state in 1903 for $32,500 and housed 13 successive governors. It was first occupied by Governor George C. Pardee, and then in order by Governors James N. Gillett; Hiram W. Johnson; William D. Stephens; Friend William Richardson; C. C. Young; James Rolph, Jr.; Frank F. Merriam; Culbert L. Olson; Earl Warren; Goodwin J. Knight; Edmund G. Brown, Sr.; and Ronald Reagan.

The mansion, of Victorian Gothic lines, consists of three stories and an attic surmounted by a cupola, and contains 15 rooms and five bathrooms. The well-kept grounds are enclosed by an elaborate wrought-iron fence.

In 1941, the mansion was determined to be unsuitable for occupancy although five governors occupied it until Governor Reagan moved out during the first part of 1967.

The second Governor's Mansion is now operated and maintained by the State Department of Parks and Recreation and is open for public tours.

Unoccupied Mansion

In 1967, a citizens group raised $200,000 and acquired property in Carmichael as a prospective site for a new Governor's Mansion. This property was conveyed to the state by grant deed in 1969. The following year, the Legislature designated the donated property as the site of the mansion.[2] In 1972, an appropriation provided $150,000 for preliminary plans and working drawings.[3]

Subsequently, the Legislature provided additional funds ($1.3 million) for the actual construction.[4]

Prior to the bids being opened, attempts were made to halt the construction of the mansion. Controversies arose over the question of whether or not to permit an archaeological dig on the site which was alleged to have been formerly occupied by an ancient Maidu Native American village and burial ground and over the adequacy of the "Environmental Impact Report" required by state law. The court ruled in favor of the defendants, i.e., the state,[5] and the contract was awarded.

Finally, in 1975, the mansion was completed.

---

[2] *Government Code*, Section 8170.
[3] *Statutes of 1972*, Chapter 156, Item 300.3.
[4] *Statutes of 1973*, Chapter 129, Item 339.
[5] *Friends of Carmichael v. State of California*, Superior Court for the County of Sacramento, Case No. 249677, August 19, 1974.

Unoccupied Mansion

In style, the proposed gubernatorial residence, with its tiled roof, resembles a Spanish hacienda and the architecture may best be described as "early California." The structure contains 12,000 square feet and consists of a family area including four bedrooms, a master bedroom, three baths, a recreation area and a study area. The remaining space is devoted to a library, living room, dining room, guest bedroom and bath, a kitchen, a pantry and two additional bedrooms.

Its completion did not signal the end of controversy. Edmund G. Brown, Jr., the incumbent governor at the time, chose not to take up residence for the remainder of his term, and further refinements on the site were suspended. At that point, the cost of maintaining an unoccupied mansion became the subject of much debate, which concluded with the decision to sell.

The mansion was on the verge of being sold when George Deukmejian became Governor in January 1983, but, because he indicated an interest in living in the facility, it was withdrawn from sale. However, later that year, the mansion was sold to a private citizen.

The Governor's Flag

In 1957, the Legislature adopted a flag to be used by the Governor at official state occasions.[6]

In its center is a representation similar to the Great Seal of the State of California. A close comparison of the two shows considerable deviation. A cornucopia rests next to the grizzly at the Goddess' feet and the sun is shown setting in the Pacific; neither of these symbols are part of the Great Seal. In addition, the topography in the background is considerably altered and the miner's "rocker" and some of the ships in the harbor are missing.

The general design and details of the flag, excluding colors, shall be as follows:

[6] *Government Code,* Section 428, 429.

APPENDIX M

Flags That Have Flown Over California

Ten different flags have flown over California since 1542. Prior to the restoration of the Capitol, replicas of these flags were mounted on the rotunda railing on the second floor. A brief description of these flags follows:

The Spanish Empire Flag, 1542–1785. This is the royal standard of Carlos V which appeared at the head of every band of Spanish explorers, as Spain had no national flag at the time. The field is white and bears the arms of Castile and Leon, with the royal crown at the top of the shield and around it the collar of the Order of the Golden Fleece.

The Flag of England, 1579. Planted by Sir Francis Drake at Drake's Bay in 1579, it flew over California for only 37 days. The flag is white with the red cross of St. George.

The Spanish National Ensign, 1785–1822. The flag of the Spanish Empire was replaced by the newly adopted Spanish national flag in 1785. The flag is red with a broad center stripe of yellow which bears the shield and crown with the arms of Castile and Leon.

The Flag of Russia, 1812–1841. Russian trading posts were established along the northern coast of California at Fort Ross, and remained until Captain John Sutter bought out their properties in 1841. The flag is white with the blue diagonal cross of St. Andrew. With it flew the flag of the Russian American Company which was the same as the then Russian merchant flag, except that it bore the double eagle in the white portion.

The Buenos Aires Flag, 1818. Raised at Monterey by the pirate Hypolite Bouchard when he raided and captured the city, the flag was flown for only 16 days in November of 1818. It consists of three bars of equal width, the outer two of blue, and the middle one of white with a yellow sun to the left of its center.

The Mexican Flag, 1822–1846. Raised over California when Mexico secured her independence from Spain, and flown until it was replaced by the American Flag. The Mexican flag has three broad stripes, one each of green, white, and red, with an eagle perched on a cactus in the center of the white stripe.

The Fremont Flag, 1842–1846. Special American Flag assigned to Captain John Charles Fremont, who carried it on his explorations from 1842 to 1846. There are 26 stars representing the 26 states then in the Union. The eagle carried a pipe of peace instead of the usual 13 arrows in order to reassure the Native Americans that Fremont's mission was one of peace.

The First Bear Flag, 1846.   Raised at Sonoma on June 14, 1846, by a small band of Americans in revolt against Mexican authority. Replaced by the Stars and Stripes on July 9, 1846, when news of the seizure of California by Commodore Sloat reached the pueblo. The field is white with a red stripe at its lower edge, a brown star in the upper left-hand corner, and a brown bear in the center field of white with the words "California Republic" in black below it.

The Stars and Stripes, 1846.   Raised by Commodore Sloat at Monterey on July 7, 1846. It has 28 stars arranged in four rows of seven stars each, and was modified as new states entered the Union. The 31st star, for California when she entered the Union, was added on July 4, 1850.

The Flag of the United States.   The Flag of the United States contained 48 stars with the admission of New Mexico and Arizona in 1912. The admissions were on January 6th and February 14th, respectively, and the new stars were added on July 4, 1912. Alaska was admitted as the 49th state on January 3, 1959, and the 49th star was added July 4, 1959. Hawaii became the 50th state on August 21, 1959, and the 50th star was added to the National Flag on July 4, 1960.

APPENDIX N

Samples of Legislative Publications

Sept. 11, 1997　　　　ASSEMBLY JOURNAL　　　　4507

PARLIAMENTARY INQUIRY

Assembly Member House arose to the following parliamentary inquiry:

Has it not been the established practice of the Presiding Officer to recognize Members to debate in the order their microphones are raised?

Reply by Speaker pro Tempore Kuehl

The Speaker pro Tempore replied in the affirmative.

Point of Order

Assembly Member House arose to the following point of order:

The Presiding Officer has been recognizing a Member for the purpose of closing debate.

Ruling by Speaker pro Tempore Kuehl

The Speaker pro Tempore ruled the point of order not well-taken; that debate is closed upon determination of the House and not by the Presiding Officer.

CONSIDERATION OF SENATE CONCURRENT RESOLUTION NO. 50
BY UNANIMOUS CONSENT

Assembly Member Morrissey was granted unanimous consent to take up Senate Concurrent Resolution No. 50, out of order.

SENATE CONCURRENT RESOLUTION NO. 50 (Johannessen)—Relative to the 50th Anniversary of the United States Air Force.

Resolution read, and presented by Assembly Member Morrissey.

Members Made Coauthors of
Senate Concurrent Resolution No. 50

Assembly Member Morrissey was granted unanimous consent to open the roll for the purpose of permitting Members to add as coauthors of Senate Concurrent Resolution No. 50.

Roll Call

The following Assembly Members indicated a desire to become coauthors:

Aroner, Battin, Baugh, Brown, Bustamante, Campbell, Cardenas, Cardoza, Davis, Ducheny, Escutia, Figueroa, Firestone, Frusetta, Gallegos, Goldsmith, Granlund, Hertzberg, Honda, Kaloogian, Keeley, Kuehl, Kuykendall, Lempert, Machado, Martinez, Mazzoni, Migden, Murray, Napolitano, Oller, Ortiz, Pacheco, Papan, Perata, Prenter, Pringle, Richter, Shelley, Sweeney, Takasugi, Thompson, Torlakson, Villaraigosa, Vincent, Washington, Wildman, and Wright.

Sample of a Daily Journal

136   ASSEMBLY DAILY FILE

                    COMMITTEE HEARINGS—Continued

TUESDAY, AUGUST 19, 1997

CONSUMER PROTECTION, GOVERNMENTAL EFFICIENCY, AND ECONOMIC DEVELOPMENT

DAVIS, Chair
9 a.m.—Room 447

Measure:	*Author:*	*Summary:*
S.B. No. 937	Polanco.	Modifies the state procurement process for acquisition of goods and information technology.
S.B. No. 1086	Schiff.	Self–storage facilities: regulation of transportation and storage of individual containers.

SELECT COMMITTEE ON AEROSPACE

FIGUEROA, Chair
1:30 p.m.—Room 127

INFORMATIONAL HEARING

SUBJECT: Understanding California's Aerospace Industry

WEDNESDAY, AUGUST 20, 1997

JOINT HEARING
ASSEMBLY AND SENATE JUDICIARY COMMITTEES

ESCUTIA and BURTON, Chairs
1 p.m.—Room 2040

HEARING CANCELED

TUESDAY, AUGUST 26, 1997

SELECT COMMITTEE ON DEFENSE CONVERSION

BACA, Chair
8–9 a.m.—Room 444

BASE RETENTION AND CONVERSION

Sample of a Daily File

FRIDAY, SEPTEMBER 12, 1997   241

A.B. No. 335—Wayne and Cunneen.

An act to add Section 25184.1 to the Health and Safety Code, relating to hazardous waste and substances.

1997

Feb. 18—Read first time. To print.
Feb. 19—From printer. May be heard in committee March 21.
Mar. 6—Referred to Com. on E.S. & T.M.
April 2—From committee: Do pass, and re-refer to Com. on APPR. Re-referred. (Ayes 7. Noes 0.) (April 1).
April 9—From committee: Do pass. To Consent Calendar. (April 9).
April 10—Read second time. To Consent Calendar.
April 17—Read third time, passed, and to Senate. (Ayes 76. Noes 0. Page 1118.)
April 17—In Senate. Read first time. To Com. on RLS. for assignment.
April 21—Referred to Com. on ENV. QUAL.
May 6—From committee chair, with author's amendments: Amend, and re-refer to committee. Read second time, amended, and re-referred to Com. on ENV. QUAL.
June 16—In committee: Hearing postponed by committee.
July 8—From committee: Do pass, and re-refer to Com. on APPR. with recommendation: To Consent Calendar. Re-referred. (Ayes 9. Noes 0.).
July 18—From committee: Be placed on second reading file pursuant to Senate Rule 28.8.
July 21—Read second time. To third reading.
Aug. 4—Read third time, passed, and to Assembly. (Ayes 38. Noes 0. Page 2460.)
Aug. 4—In Assembly. Concurrence in Senate amendments pending. May be considered on August 6 pursuant to Assembly Rule 77. Ordered to Special Consent Calendar.
Aug. 7—Senate amendments concurred in. To enrollment. (Ayes 74. Noes 0. Page 3541.)
Aug. 14—Enrolled and to the Governor at 11:30 a.m.
Aug. 26—Approved by the Governor.
Aug. 26—Chaptered by Secretary of State - Chapter 363, Statutes of 1997.

A.B. No. 336—Miller (Coauthors: Ackerman, Alby, Baldwin, Battin, Bordonaro, Bowler, Brewer, Cunneen, Frusetta, Goldsmith, Granlund, Havice, House, Leach, Leonard, Machado, Margett, McClintock, Morrissey, Olberg, Oller, Papan, Prenter, Runner, Scott, Takasugi, and Washington) (Senators Alpert, Costa, Dills, Hayden, Karnette, Leslie, McPherson, Mountjoy, Rainey, and Watson, coauthors).

An act to add and repeal Section 17053.25 of the Revenue and Taxation Code, relating to taxation, to take effect immediately, tax levy.

1997

Feb. 18—Read first time. To print.
Feb. 19—From printer. May be heard in committee March 21.
Mar. 3—Referred to Com. on REV. & TAX.
April 8—In committee: Set, first hearing. Held under submission.
April 21—From committee chair, with author's amendments: Amend, and re-refer to Com. on REV. & TAX. Read second time and amended.
April 28—Re-referred to Com. on REV. & TAX.
May 13—From committee: Do pass, and re-refer to Com. on APPR. Re-referred. (Ayes 7. Noes 1.) (May 12).
May 28—In committee: Set, first hearing. Referred to APPR. suspense file.
May 30—In committee: Set, second hearing. Held under submission.
June 2—Notice of motion to withdraw from committee given by Assembly Member Miller.
June 5—Motion to withdraw bill from committee failed (Ayes 38. Noes 28. Page 2534.)

Sample of a Daily History

Index

Photoelectronic composition by
CALIFORNIA OFFICE OF STATE PUBLISHING